The Mind's I

THE MIND'S I

Fantasies and
Reflections
on Self and Soul

COMPOSED AND ARRANGED BY

Douglas R. Hofstadter

AND

Daniel C. Dennett

BANTAM BOOKS
TORONTO • NEW YORK • LONDON • SYDNEY • AUCKLAND

THE MIND'S I

A Bantam Book / published by arrangement with
Basic Books Inc., Publishers

PRINTING HISTORY

Basic Books edition published November 1981
3 printings through February 1982
A Selection of Book-of-the-Month/Science, Macmillan Book
Clubs, and Readers' Subscription, January 1982
Serialized in Book Digest, *March 1982*
Bantam edition / November 1982

COVER ILLUSTRATION: Magritte, Rene, The False Mirror.
(1928). Oil on Canvas, 21¼ × 31⅞". Collection, The Museum
of Modern Art, New York. Purchase.

Library of Congress Cataloging in Publication Data
Hofstadter, Douglas R., 1945–
The mind's I.
Includes selected writings of Jorge Luis Borges and others
with reflections by the authors.
Bibliography: p. 465
Includes index.
1. Self (Philosophy)—Addresses, essays, lectures. 2. Self
(Philosophy)—Literary collections. 3. Intellect—Addresses, essays,
lectures. 4. Intellect—Literary collections. 5. Consciousness—
Addresses, essays, lectures. 6. Consciousness—Literary collections.
7. Soul—Addresses, essays, lectures. 8. Soul—Literary collections.
I. Dennett, Daniel C. II. Title.
B29.H58   126   81-66099

ISBN 0-553-01412-9

Published simultaneously in the United States and Canada

PRINTED IN THE UNITED STATES OF AMERICA

0 9 8 7 6

Contents

III. From Hardware to Software

IV. Mind as Program

V. Created Selves and Free Will

Contents

VI. The Inner Eye

Preface

What is the mind? Who am I? Can mere matter think or feel? Where is the soul? Anyone who confronts these questions runs headlong into perplexities. We conceived this book as an attempt to reveal those perplexities and make them vivid. Our purpose is not so much to answer the big questions directly as to jolt everyone: people who are committed to a hard-nosed, no-nonsense, scientific world view, as well as people who have a religious or spiritualistic vision of the human soul. We believe there are at present no easy answers to the big questions, and it will take radical rethinking of the issues before people can be expected to reach a consensus about the meaning of the word "I." This book, then, is designed to provoke, disturb, and befuddle its readers, to make the obvious strange and, perhaps, to make the strange obvious.

We would like to thank all the contributors and the many people who have advised and inspired us: Kathy Antrim, Paul Benacerraf, Maureen Bischoff, Larry Breed, Scott Buresh, Don Byrd, Pat and Paul Churchland, Francisco Claro, Gray Clossman, Paul Csonka, Susan Dennett, Mike Dunn, Dennis Flanagan, Bill Gosper, Bernie Greenberg, John Haugeland, Pat Hayes, Robert and Nancy Hofstadter, Martin Kessler, Scott Kim, Henry Lieberman, John McCarthy, Debra Manette, Marsha Meredith, Marvin Minsky, Fanya Montalvo, Bob Moore, David Moser, Zenon Pylyshyn, Randy Read, Julie Rochlin, Ed Shulz, Paul Smolensky, Ann Trail, Rufus Wanning, Sue Wintsch, and John Woodcock.

This book grew out of conversations in 1980 at the Center for Advanced Study in the Behavioral Sciences, in Palo Alto, where Dennett was a Fellow engaged in research on artificial intelligence and philosophy, sponsored by NSF Grant (BNS 78–24671) and the Alfred P. Sloan Foundation. It was completed while Hofstadter was a John Simon Guggenheim Fellow engaged in research in artificial intelligence at Stanford University. We want to thank these foundations for supporting our research, and for providing settings in which our discussions could lead to collaboration.

Douglas R. Hofstadter
Daniel C. Dennett
Chicago
April 1981

The Mind's I

Introduction

You see the moon rise in the east. You see the moon rise in the west. You watch two moons moving toward each other across the cold black sky, one soon to pass behind the other as they continue on their way. You are on Mars, millions of miles from home, protected from the killing, frostless cold of the red Martian desert by fragile membranes of terrestrial technology. Protected but stranded, for your spaceship has broken down beyond repair. You will never ever return to Earth, to the friends and family and places you left behind.

But perhaps there is hope. In the communication compartment of the disabled craft you find a Teleclone Mark IV teleporter and instructions for its use. If you turn the teleporter on, tune its beam to the Teleclone receiver on Earth, and then step into the sending chamber, the teleporter will swiftly and painlessly dismantle your body, producing a molecule-by-molecule blueprint to be beamed to Earth, where the receiver, its reservoirs well stocked with the requisite atoms, will almost instantaneously produce, from the beamed instructions—you! Whisked back to Earth at the speed of light, into the arms of your loved ones, who will soon be listening with rapt attention to your tales of adventures on Mars.

One last survey of the damaged spaceship convinces you that the Teleclone is your only hope. With nothing to lose, you set the transmitter up, flip the right switches, and step into the chamber. 5, 4, 3, 2, 1, FLASH! You open the door in front of you and step out of the Teleclone receiver chamber into the sunny, familiar atmosphere of Earth. You've come home, none the worse for wear after your long-distance Teleclone fall from Mars. Your narrow escape from a terrible fate on the red planet calls for a celebration, and as your family and friends gather around, you notice how everyone has changed since last you saw them. It has been almost three years, after all, and you've all grown older. Look at Sarah, your daughter, who must now be eight and a half. You find yourself thinking, "Can this be the little girl who used to sit on my lap?" Of course it is, you reflect, even though you must admit that you do not so much recognize her as extrapolate from memory and deduce her identity. She is so much taller, looks so much older, and knows so much more. In fact, most of the cells now in her body were not there when last you cast eyes on her. But in spite of growth and change, in spite of replacement of cells, she's the same little person you kissed good-bye three years ago.

Then it hits you: "Am *I,* really, the same person who kissed this little girl good-bye three years ago? Am I this eight-year-old child's mother or am I actually a brand-new human being, only several hours old, in spite of my memories—or apparent memories—of days and years before that? Did this child's mother recently die on Mars, dismantled and destroyed in the chamber of a Teleclone Mark IV?

"Did I die on Mars? No, certainly *I* did not die on Mars, since I am alive on Earth. Perhaps, though, *someone* died on Mars—Sarah's mother. Then I am not Sarah's mother. But I must be! The whole point of getting into the Teleclone was to return home to my family! But I keep forgetting; maybe *I* never got into that Teleclone on Mars. Maybe that was someone else—if it ever happened at all. Is that infernal machine a tele-*porter*—a mode of transportation—or, as the brand name suggests, a sort of murdering twinmaker? Did Sarah's mother survive the experience with the Teleclone or not? She thought she was going to. She entered the chamber with hope and anticipation, not suicidal resignation. Her act was altruistic, to be sure—she was taking steps to provide Sarah with a loved one to protect her—but also selfish—she was getting herself out of a jam into something pleasant. Or so it seemed. How do *I* know that's how it seemed? Because I was *there;* I *was* Sarah's mother thinking those thoughts; I *am* Sarah's mother. Or so it seems."

In the days that follow, your spirits soar and plummet, the moments of relief and joy balanced by gnawing doubts and soul searching. *Soul searching.* Perhaps, you think, it isn't right to go along with Sarah's joyous assumption that her mother's come home. You feel a little bit like an impostor and wonder what Sarah will think when some day she figures out what really happened on Mars. Remember when she figured out about Santa Claus and seemed so confused and hurt? How could her own mother have deceived her all those years?

So now it's with more than idle intellectual curiosity that you pick up this copy of *The Mind's I* and begin to read it, for it promises to lead you on a voyage of discovery of the self and the soul. You will learn, it says, something about what and who you are.

You think to yourself:

Here I am reading page 5 of this book. I'm alive; I'm awake; I see the words on the page with my eyes; I see my hands holding this book. I have hands. How do I know they're *my* hands? Silly question. They're fastened to my arms, to my body. How do I know this is *my* body? I control it. Do I own it? In a sense I do. It's mine to do with as I like, so long as I don't harm others. It's even a sort of legal possession, for while I may not legally sell it to anyone so long as I'm alive, I can legally transfer ownership of my body to, say, a medical school once it is dead.

If I *have* this body, then I guess I'm something other than this body. When I say "I own my body" I don't mean "This body owns itself"— probably a meaningless claim. Or does everything that no one else owns own itself? Does the moon belong to everyone, to no one, or to itself? What can be an owner of anything? I can, and my body is just one of the things I own. In any case, I and my body seem both intimately connected and yet distinct. I am the controller; it is the controlled. Most of the time.

Then *The Mind's I* asks you if in that case you might exchange your body for another, a stronger or more beautiful or more controllable body.

You think that this is impossible.

But, the book insists, it is perfectly imaginable and hence possible in principle.

You wonder whether the book has in mind reincarnation or the transmigration of souls, but, anticipating the wonder, the book acknowledges that while reincarnation is one interesting idea, the details of how this might happen are always left in the dark, and there are other more interesting ways it might happen. What if your brain were to be transplanted into a new body, which it could then control? Wouldn't you think of that as switching bodies? There would be vast technical problems, of course, but, given our purposes, we can ignore them.

It does seem then (doesn't it?) that if your brain were transplanted into another body, *you* would go with it. But *are* you a brain? Try on two sentences, and see which one sounds more like the truth to you:

I have a brain.
I am a brain.

Sometimes we talk about smart people being brains, but we don't mean it literally. We mean they have good brains. You have a good brain, but who or what, then, is the *you* that has the brain? Once again, if you have a brain, could you trade it in for another? How could anyone detach you from your brain in a brain switch, if you always *go with* your brain in a body switch? Impossible? Maybe not, as we shall see. After all, if *you* have recently returned from Mars, you left your old brain behind, didn't you?

So suppose we agree that you *have* a brain. Have you ever stopped to ask yourself how you know you have a brain? You've never seen it, have you? You can't see it, even in a mirror, and you can't feel it. But of course you do know you have a brain. You know it because you know that you're a human being and all human beings have brains. You've read it in books and been told it by people you trust. All people have livers too, and strangely enough what you know about your own brain is rather like what you know about your own liver. You trust what you've read in books. For many centuries people didn't know what their livers were for. It took science to discover the answer. People haven't always known what their brains were for either. Aristotle is said to have thought that the brain was an organ for cooling the blood—and of course it does cool your blood quite efficiently in the course of its operations. Suppose our livers had been in our skulls and our brains were snuggled into our ribcages. As we looked out at the world and listened, do you think we might have found it plausible that we *thought with our livers*? Your thinking seems to happen behind your eyes and between your ears—but is that because that's where your brain is, or is that because you locate yourself, roughly, *at the place you see from*? Isn't it in fact just as mind-boggling to try to imagine how we could think with our brains—those soft grayish cauliflower-shaped things—as to imagine how we could think with our livers—those soft reddish-brown liver-shaped things?

The idea that *what you are* is not simply a living body (or a living brain) but also a soul or spirit seems to many people to be unscientific, in spite of its ancient tradition. "Souls," they might want to say, "have no place in science and could never fit into the scientific world view. Science teaches us that there are no such things as souls. We don't believe in leprechauns and ghosts any more, thanks to science, and the suspect idea of a soul inhabiting a body—the 'ghost in the machine'—will itself soon give up the ghost." But not all versions of the idea that you are something distinct from your purely physical body are so vulnerable to ridicule and refutation. Some versions, as we shall see, actually flourish in the garden of science.

Our world is filled with things that are neither mysterious and ghostly nor simply constructed out of the building blocks of physics. Do you believe in voices? How about haircuts? Are there such things? What are they? What, in the language of the physicist, is a hole—not an exotic black hole, but just a hole in a piece of cheese, for instance? Is it a physical thing? What is a symphony? Where in space and time does "The Star

Spangled Banner" exist? Is it nothing but some ink trails on some paper in the Library of Congress? Destroy that paper and the anthem would still exist. Latin still *exists,* but it is no longer a living language. The language of the cavepeople of France no longer exists at all. The game of bridge is less than a hundred years old. What sort of a thing is it? It is not animal, vegetable, or mineral.

These things are not physical objects with mass, or a chemical composition, but they are not purely abstract objects either—objects like the number π, which is immutable and cannot be located in space and time. These things have birthplaces and histories. They can change, and things can happen to them. They can move about—much the way a species, a disease, or an epidemic can. We must not suppose that science teaches us that every *thing* anyone would ever want to take seriously is identifiable as a collection of particles moving about in space and time. Some people may think it is just common sense (or just good scientific thinking) to suppose *you* are nothing but a particular living, physical organism—a moving mound of atoms—but in fact this idea exhibits a lack of scientific imagination, not hard-headed sophistication. One doesn't have to believe in ghosts to believe in *selves* that have an identity that transcends any particular living body.

You are Sarah's mother, after all. But is Sarah's mother you? Did she die on Mars, or was she moved back to Earth? It seems to you she returned to Earth—and of course it seemed to *her* before she stepped into the teleporter that she would return to Earth. Was she right? Maybe, but what would you say about the results of using the new, improved Tele-clone Mark V? Thanks to the miracles of noninvasive CAT-scanning techniques, it obtains its blueprint *without destroying the original.* Sarah's mother might still decide to push the button and step into the chamber —for Sarah's sake, and in order to get the full story of her tragedy back to Earth in the words of an eloquent spokeswoman—but she would also expect to step out of the chamber and find herself still on Mars. Could someone—some *one*—literally be two places at once? Not for long, in any case, for soon the two would accumulate different memories, and different lives. They would be as distinct as any two people could be.

Private Lives

What makes you you, and what are your boundaries? Part of the answer seems obvious—*you* are a center of consciousness. But what in the world is consciousness? Consciousness is both the most obvious and the most mysterious feature of our minds. On the one hand, what could be more certain or manifest to each of us than that he or she is a subject of experience, an enjoyer of perceptions and sensations, a sufferer of pain, an entertainer of ideas, and a conscious deliberator? On the other hand, what in the world can consciousness be? How can living physical bodies in the physical world produce such a phenomenon? Science has revealed the secrets of many initially mysterious natural phenomena—magnetism, photosynthesis, digestion, even reproduction—but consciousness seems utterly unlike these. For one thing, particular cases of magnetism or photosynthesis or digestion are in principle equally accessible to any observer with the right apparatus, but any particular case of consciousness seems to have a favored or privileged observer, whose access to the phenomenon is entirely unlike, and better than, the access of any others—no matter what apparatus they may have. For this reason and others, so far there is no good theory of consciousness. There is not even agreement about what a theory of consciousness would be like. Some have gone so far as to deny that there is any real thing for the term "consciousness" to name.

The mere fact that such a familiar feature of our lives has resisted for so long all attempts to characterize it suggests that our conception of it is at fault. What is needed is not just more evidence, more experimental and clinical data, but a careful rethinking of the assumptions that lead us to suppose there is a single and familiar phenomenon, consciousness, answering to all the descriptions licensed by our everyday sense of the term. Consider the baffling questions that are inevitably raised whenever one turns one's attention to consciousness. Are other animals conscious? Are they conscious in the same way we are? Could a computer or robot be conscious? Can a person have unconscious thoughts? Unconscious pains or sensations or perceptions? Is a baby conscious at or before birth? Are we conscious when we dream? Might a human being harbor more than one conscious subject or ego or agent within one brain? Good answers to these questions certainly will depend heavily on empirical discoveries about the behavioral capacities and internal circumstances of the various problematic candidates for consciousness, but about every such empirical finding we can ask: what is its bearing on the question of consciousness and why? These are not directly empirical questions but rather conceptual ones, which we may be able to answer with the help of thought experiments.

Our ordinary concept of consciousness seems to be anchored to two separable sets of considerations that can be captured roughly by the phrases "from the inside" and "from the outside." *From the inside,* our own consciousness seems obvious and pervasive: we know that much goes on around us and even inside our own bodies of which we are entirely unaware or unconscious, but nothing could be more intimately known to us than those things of which we are, individually, conscious. Those things of which I am conscious, and the ways in which I am conscious of them, determine *what it is like to be me.* I know in a way no other could know what it is like to be me. From the inside, consciousness seems to be an all-or-nothing phenomenon—an inner light that is either on or off. We grant that we are sometimes drowsy or inattentive, or asleep, and on occasion we even enjoy abnormally heightened consciousness, but when we are conscious, *that* we are conscious is not a fact that admits of degrees. There is a perspective, then, from which consciousness seems to be a feature that sunders the universe into two strikingly different kinds of things: those that have it and those that do not. Those that have it are *subjects,* beings *to whom* things can be one way or another, beings it is like something to be. It is not like anything at all to be a brick or a pocket calculator or an apple. These things have insides, but not the right sort of insides—no *inner life,* no point of view. It is certainly like something to be me (something *I* know "from the inside") and almost certainly like something to be you (for you have told me, most convincingly, that it is the same with you), and probably like something to be a dog or a dolphin (if only they could tell us!), and maybe even like something to be a spider.

Other Minds

When one considers these others (other folk and other creatures), one considers them perforce *from the outside,* and then various of their observable features strike us as relevant to the question of their consciousness. Creatures react appropriately to events within the scope of their senses; they recognize things, avoid painful circumstances, learn, plan, and solve problems. They exhibit intelligence. But putting matters this way might be held to prejudge the issue. Talking of their "senses" or of "painful" circumstances, for instance, suggests that we have already settled the issue of consciousness—for note that had we described a robot in those terms, the polemical intent of the choice of words would have been obvious (and resisted by many). How do creatures differ from robots, real or imagined? By being organically and biologically similar to us—and we are the paradigmatic conscious creatures. This similarity admits of degrees, of course, and one's intuitions about which sorts of similarity count are probably untrustworthy. Dolphins' fishiness subtracts from our conviction that they are conscious like us, but no doubt should not. Were chimpanzees as dull as seaslugs, their facial similarity to us would no doubt nevertheless favor their inclusion in the charmed circle. If houseflies were about our size, or warmblooded, we'd be much more confident that when we plucked off their wings they felt pain (*our* sort of pain, the kind that matters). What makes us think that some such considerations ought to count and not others?

The obvious answer is that the various "outside" indicators are more or less reliable signs or symptoms of the presence of that whatever-it-is each conscious subject knows from the inside. But how could this be confirmed? This is the notorious "problem of other minds." In one's own case, it seems, one can directly observe the coincidence of one's inner life with one's outwardly observable behavior. But if each of us is to advance rigorously beyond solipsism, we must be able to do something apparently impossible: confirm the coincidence of inner and outer in others. Their telling us of the coincidence in their own cases will not do, officially, for that gives us just more coincidence of outer with outer: the demonstrable capacities for perception and intelligent action normally go hand in hand with the capacity to talk, and particularly to make "introspective" reports. If a cleverly designed robot could (seem to) tell us of its inner life (could utter all the appropriate noises in the appropriate contexts), would we be right to admit it to the charmed circle? We might be, but how could we ever tell we were not being fooled? Here the question seems to be: is that special inner light really turned on, or is there nothing but darkness inside? And this question looks unanswerable. So perhaps we have taken a misstep already.

My use of "we" and "our" in the last few paragraphs, and your unworried acceptance of it, reveals that *we* don't take the problem of other minds seriously—at least for ourselves and the human beings with whom we normally associate. It is tempting to conclude that insofar as there is a serious question yet to be answered about the imagined robot (or about some problematic creature), it must turn out to be answerable by straightforward observation. Some theorists think that once we have better theories of the organization of our brains and their role in controlling our behavior, we will be able to use those theories to distinguish conscious entities from nonconscious entities. This is to suppose that somehow or other the facts we get individually "from the inside" reduce to facts publicly obtainable from the outside. Enough of the right sort of outside facts will settle the question of whether or not some creature is conscious. For instance, consider neurophysiologist E. R. John's* recent attempt to define consciousness in objective terms:

> . . . a process in which information about multiple individual modalities of sensation and perception is combined into a unified multidimensional representation of the state of the system and its environment, and integrated with information about memories and the needs of the organism, generating emotional reactions and programs of behavior to adjust the organism to its environment.

Determining that this hypothesized internal process occurs in a particular organism is *presumably* a difficult but empirical task in the province of a new science of neural information processing. Suppose that with regard to some creature it were completed successfully: the creature is, by this account, conscious. If we have understood the proposal correctly, we will not find any room to wonder further. Reserving judgment here would be like being shown in detail the operations of an automobile engine and then asking, "But is it *really* an internal combustion engine? *Might* we not be deluded in thinking it was?"

Any proper scientific account of the phenomenon of consciousness must inevitably take this somewhat doctrinaire step of demanding that the phenomenon be viewed as objectively accessible, but one may still wonder if, once the step is taken, the truly mysterious phenomenon will be left behind. Before dismissing this skeptical hunch as the fancy of romantics, it would be wise to consider a striking revolution in the recent history of thinking about the mind, a revolution with unsettling consequences.

Freud's Crutch

For John Locke and many subsequent thinkers, nothing was more essential to the mind than consciousness, and more particularly self-consciousness. The mind in all its activities and processes was viewed as transparent to itself; nothing was hidden from its inner view. To discern what went on in one's mind one just "looked"—one "introspected"—and the limits of what one thereby found were the very boundaries of the mind. The notion of unconscious thinking or perceiving was not entertained, or if it was, it was dismissed as incoherent, self-contradictory nonsense.

*For additional information on the authors and the works cited in the text, consult "Further Reading" beginning on p. 465.

For Locke, indeed, there was a serious problem of how to describe all one's memories as being continuously in one's mind when yet they were not continuously "present to consciousness." The influence of this view has been so great that when Freud initially hypothesized the existence of *un*conscious mental processes, his proposal met widely with stark denial and incomprehension. It was not just an outrage to common sense, it was even self-contradictory to assert that there could be unconscious beliefs and desires, unconscious feelings of hatred, unconscious schemes of self-defense and retaliation. But Freud won converts. This "conceptual impossibility" became respectably thinkable by theorists once they saw that it permitted them to explain otherwise inexplicable patterns of psychopathology.

The new way of thinking was supported by a crutch: one could cling to at least a pale version of the Lockean creed by imagining that these "unconscious" thoughts, desires, and schemes *belonged to other selves* within the psyche. Just as I can keep my schemes secret from you, my id can keep secrets from my ego. By splitting the subject into many subjects, one could preserve the axiom that *every mental state must be someone's conscious mental state* and explain the inaccessibility of some of these states to their putative owners by postulating other interior owners for them. This move was usefully obscured in the mists of jargon so that the weird question of whether it was like anything to be a superego, for instance, could be kept at bay.

Freud's expansion of the bounds of the thinkable revolutionized clinical psychology. It also paved the way for the more recent development of "cognitive" experimental psychology. We have come to accept without the slightest twinge of incomprehension a host of claims to the effect that sophisticated hypothesis testing, memory searching, inference —in short, information processing—occurs within us though it is entirely inaccessible to introspection. It is not repressed unconscious activity of the sort Freud uncovered, activity driven out of the "sight" of consciousness, but just mental activity that is somehow beneath or beyond the ken of consciousness altogether. Freud claimed that his theories and clinical observations gave him the authority to overrule the sincere denials of his patients about what was going on in their minds. Similarly the cognitive psychologist marshalls experimental evidence, models, and theories to show that people are engaged in surprisingly sophisticated reasoning processes of which they can give no introspective account at all. Not only are minds accessible to outsiders, some mental activities are more accessible to outsiders than to the very "owners" of those minds!

In the new theorizing, however, the crutch has been thrown away.

Although the new theories abound with deliberately fanciful homunculus metaphors—subsystems like little people in the brain sending messages back and forth, asking for help, obeying and volunteering—the actual subsystems are deemed to be unproblematic *non*conscious bits of organic machinery, as utterly lacking in a point of view or inner life as a kidney or kneecap. (Certainly the advent of "mindless" but "intelligent" computers played a major role in this further dissolution of the Lockean view.)

But now Locke's extremism has been turned on its head; if before the very idea of *un*conscious mentality seemed incomprehensible, now we are losing our grip on the very idea of *conscious* mentality. What is consciousness for, if perfectly unconscious, indeed subjectless, information processing is in principle capable of achieving all the ends for which conscious minds were supposed to exist? If theories of cognitive psychology can be true of us, they could also be true of zombies, or robots, and the theories seem to have no way of distinguishing us. How could *any amount* of mere subjectless information processing (of the sort we have recently discovered to go on in us) add up to that special feature with which it is so vividly contrasted? For the contrast has not disappeared. The psychologist Karl Lashley once suggested provocatively that "no activity of the mind is ever conscious," by which he meant to draw our attention to the inaccessibility of the processing that we know must go on when we think. He gave an example: if asked to think a thought in dactylic hexameter, those who know which rhythm that is can readily oblige. For instance: *How* in the *world* did this *case* of dac*tyl*ic hex*am*eter *come* to me? How we do it, what goes on in us to produce such a thought, is something quite inaccessible to us. Lashley's remark might seem at first to herald the demise of consciousness as a phenomenon for psychological study, but its true effect is just the opposite. It draws our attention unmistakably to the *difference* between all the unconscious information processing—without which, no doubt, there could be no conscious experience—and the conscious thought itself, which is somehow directly accessible. Accessible to what or to whom? To say that it is accessible to some subsystem of the brain is not yet to distinguish it from the unconscious activities and events, which are also accessible to various subsystems of the brain. If some particular and special subsystem is so constituted that its traffic with the rest of the system somehow makes it the case that there is one more *self* in the world, one more "thing it is like something to be," this is far from obvious.

Strangely enough, this problem is the old chestnut, the problem of other minds, resurrected as a serious problem now that cognitive science has begun to analyze the human mind into its functional components. This comes out most graphically in the famous split-brain cases. (See "Further Reading" for details and references.) There is nothing very problematic in granting that the people who have undergone severing of the *corpus callosum* have two somewhat independent minds, one associated with the dominant brain hemisphere, and another associated with the non-dominant brain hemisphere. This is not problematic, for we have grown used to thinking of a person's mind as an organization of communicating subminds. Here the lines of communication have simply been cut, revealing the independent character of each part particularly vividly. But what remains problematic is whether both subminds "have an inner life." One view is that there is no reason to grant consciousness to the non-dominant hemisphere, since all that has been shown is that that hemisphere, like many other unconscious cognitive subsystems, can process a lot of information and intelligently control some behavior. But then we may ask what reason there is to grant consciousness to the dominant hemisphere, or even to the whole, intact system in a normal person. We had thought this question frivolous and not worth discussing, but this avenue forces us to take it seriously again. If on the other hand we grant full "inner life" consciousness to the non-dominant hemisphere (or more properly to the newly discovered *person* whose brain is the non-dominant hemisphere), what will be said about all the other information-processing subsystems posited by current theory? Is the Freudian crutch to be taken up again at the expense of populating our heads, quite literally, with hosts of subjects of experience?

Consider, for example, the striking discovery by the psycholinguists James Lackner and Merrill Garrett (see "Further Reading") of what might be called an unconscious channel of sentence comprehension. In dichotic listening tests subjects listen through earphones to two different channels and are instructed to attend to just one channel. Typically they can paraphrase or report with accuracy what they have heard through the attended channel, but usually they can say little about what was going on concomitantly in the unattended channel. Thus, if the unattended channel carries a spoken sentence, the subjects typically can report they heard a voice, or even a male or female voice. Perhaps they even have a conviction about whether the voice was speaking in their native tongue, but they cannot report *what was said.* In Lackner and Garrett's experiments subjects heard ambiguous sentences in the attended channel, such as "He put out the lantern to signal the attack." Simultaneously, in the unattended channel one group of subjects received a sentence that suggested one interpretation of the sentence in the attended channel (e.g., "He extinguished the lantern"), while another group had a neutral or irrelevant sentence as input. The former group *could not report* what was presented through the unattended channel, but they favored the suggested reading of the ambiguous sentences significantly more than the control group did. The influence of the unattended channel on the interpretation of the attended signal can be explained only by the hypothesis that the unattended signal is processed all the way to a semantic level—that is, the unattended signal is *comprehended*—but this is apparently unconscious sentence comprehension! Or should we say it is evidence of the presence in the subjects of at least two different and only partially communicating consciousnesses? If we ask the subjects what it was like to comprehend the unattended channel, they will reply, sincerely, that it was not like anything *to them*—they were quite unaware of that sentence. But perhaps, as is often suggested about the split-brain patients, there is in effect someone else to whom our question ought to be addressed—the subject who consciously comprehended the sentence and relayed a hint of its meaning to the subject who answers our questions.

Which should we say, and why? We seem to be back to our unanswerable question, which suggests we should find different ways of looking at the situation. A view of consciousness that does justice to the variety of complications will almost certainly demand a revolution in our habits of thought. Breaking bad habits is not that easy. The fantasies and thought experiments collected here are games and exercises designed to help.

In Part I the exploration begins with some swift forays into the territory, noting a few striking landmarks but mounting no campaigns. In Part II our target, the mind's I, is surveyed from the outside. What is it that reveals the presence of *other* minds, other souls, to the searcher? Part III examines the physical foundation—in biology—of the mind, and then from this foundation moves up several levels of complexity to the level of internal representations. The mind begins to emerge as a self-designing system of representations, physically embodied in the brain. Here we encounter our first roadblock—"The Story of a Brain." We suggest some paths around it, and in Part IV we explore the implications of the emerging view of the mind as software or program—as an abstract sort of thing whose identity is independent of any particular physical embodiment. This opens up delightful prospects, such as various technologies for the transmigration of souls, and Fountains of Youth, but it also opens a Pandora's box of traditional metaphysical problems in untraditional costumes, which are confronted in Part V. Reality itself is challenged by various rivals: dreams, fictions, simulations, illusions. Free will, something no self-respecting mind would be caught without, is put under an unusual spotlight. In "Minds, Brains, and Programs" we encounter our second roadblock, but learn from it how to press on, in Part VI, past our third roadblock, "What Is It Like to Be a Bat?" into the inner sanctum, where our mind's-eye view affords us the most intimate perspectives on our target, and allows us to relocate our selves in the metaphysical and physical world. A guide to further expeditions is provided in the last section.

D.C.D.

I

A Sense of Self

1

JORGE LUIS BORGES

Borges and I

The other one, the one called Borges, is the one things happen to. I walk through the streets of Buenos Aires and stop for a moment, perhaps mechanically now, to look at the arch of an entrance hall and the grillwork on the gate; I know of Borges from the mail and see his name on a list of professors or in a biographical dictionary. I like hourglasses, maps, eighteenth-century typography, the taste of coffee and the prose of Stevenson; he shares these preferences, but in a vain way that turns them into the attributes of an actor. It would be an exaggeration to say that ours is a hostile relationship; I live, let myself go on living, so that Borges may contrive his literature, and this literature justifies me. It is no effort for me to confess that he has achieved some valid pages, but those pages cannot save me, perhaps because what is good belongs to no one, not even to him, but rather to the language and to tradition. Besides, I am destined to perish, definitively, and only some instant of myself can survive in him. Little by little, I am giving over everything to him, though I am quite aware of his perverse custom of falsifying and magnifying things. Spinoza knew that all things long to persist in their being; the stone eternally wants to be a stone and the tiger a tiger. I shall remain in Borges, not in myself (if it is true that I am someone), but I recognize myself less in his books than in many others or in the laborious strumming of a guitar. Years ago I tried to free myself from him and went from the mythologies of the suburbs to the games with time and infinity, but those games belong to Borges now and I shall have to imagine other things. Thus my life is a flight and I lose everything and everything belongs to oblivion, or to him.

I do not know which of us has written this page.

Reflections

Jorge Luis Borges, the great Argentinian writer, has a deserved international reputation, which creates a curious effect. Borges seems to himself to be two people, the public personage and the private person. His fame magnifies the effect, but we all can share the feeling, as he knows. You read your name on a list, or see a candid photograph of yourself, or overhear others talking about someone and suddenly realize it is *you.* Your mind must leap from a third-person perspective—"he" or "she"— to a first-person perspective—"I." Comedians have long known how to exaggerate this leap: the classic "double-take" in which, say, Bob Hope reads in the morning newspaper that Bob Hope is wanted by the police, casually comments on this fact, and then jumps up in alarm: "That's me!"

While Robert Burns may be right that it is a gift to see ourselves as others see us, it is not a condition to which we could or should aspire at all times. In fact, several philosophers have recently presented brilliant arguments to show that there are two fundamentally and irreducibly different ways of thinking of ourselves. (See "Further Reading" for the details.) The arguments are quite technical, but the issues are fascinating and can be vividly illustrated.

Pete is waiting in line to pay for an item in a department store, and he notices that there is a closed-circuit television monitor over the counter—one of the store's measures against shoplifters. As he watches the jostling crowd of people on the monitor, he realizes that the person over on the left side of the screen in the overcoat carrying the large paper bag is having his pocket picked by the person behind him. Then, as he raises his hand to his mouth in astonishment, he notices that the victim's hand is moving to his mouth in just the same way. Pete suddenly realizes that *he* is the person whose pocket is being picked! This dramatic shift is a discovery; Pete comes to know something he didn't know a moment before, and of course it is important. Without the capacity to entertain the sorts of thoughts that now galvanize him into defensive action, he would hardly be capable of action at all. But before the shift, he wasn't entirely ignorant, of course; he was thinking about "the person in the overcoat" and seeing that that person was being robbed, and since the person in the overcoat is himself, he was thinking *about himself.* But he wasn't thinking about himself *as himself;* he wasn't thinking about himself "in the right way."

For another example, imagine someone reading a book in which a descriptive noun phrase of, say, three dozen words in the first sentence of a paragraph portrays an unnamed person of initially indeterminate sex who is performing an everyday activity. The reader of that book, on reading the given phrase, obediently manufactures in his or her mind's eye a simple, rather vague mental image of a person involved in some mundane activity. In the next few sentences, as more detail is added to the description, the reader's mental image of the whole scenario comes into a little sharper focus. Then at a certain moment, after the description has gotten quite specific, something suddenly "clicks," and the reader gets an eerie sense that he or she is the very person being described! "How stupid of me not to recognize earlier that I was reading about *myself!*" the reader muses, feeling a little sheepish, but also quite tickled. You can probably imagine such a thing happening, but to help you imagine it more clearly, just suppose that the book involved was *The Mind's I.* There now—doesn't your mental image of the whole scenario come into a little sharper focus? Doesn't it all suddenly "click"? What page did you imagine the reader as reading? What paragraph? What thoughts might have crossed the reader's mind? If the reader were a real person, what might he or she be doing *right now?*

It is not easy to describe something capable of such special *self-representation.* Suppose a computer is programmed to control the locomotion and behavior of a robot to which it is attached by radio links. (The famous "Shakey" at SRI International in California was so controlled.) The computer contains a representation of the robot and its environment, and as the robot moves around, the representation changes accordingly. This permits the computer program to control the robot's activities with the aid of up-to-date information about the robot's "body" and the environment it finds itself in. Now suppose the computer represents the robot as located in the middle of an empty room, and suppose you are asked to "translate into English" the computer's internal representation. Should it be *"It* (or *he* or *Shakey*) is in the center of an empty room" or *"I* am in the center of an empty room"? This question resurfaces in a different guise in Part IV of this book.

D.C.D.
D.R.H.

2

D. E. HARDING

On Having No Head

The best day of my life—my rebirthday, so to speak—was when I found I had no head. This is not a literary gambit, a witticism designed to arouse interest at any cost. I mean it in all seriousness: *I have no head.*

It was eighteen years ago, when I was thirty-three, that I made the discovery. Though it certainly came out of the blue, it did so in response to an urgent enquiry; I had for several months been absorbed in the question: what am I? The fact that I happened to be walking in the Himalayas at the time probably had little to do with it; though in that country unusual states of mind are said to come more easily. However that may be, a very still clear day, and a view from the ridge where I stood, over misty blue valleys to the highest mountain range in the world, with Kangchenjunga and Everest unprominent among its snow-peaks, made a setting worthy of the grandest vision.

What actually happened was something absurdly simple and unspectacular: I stopped thinking. A peculiar quiet, an odd kind of alert limpness or numbness, came over me. Reason and imagination and all mental chatter died down. For once, words really failed me. Past and future dropped away. I forgot who and what I was, my name, manhood, animalhood, all that could be called mine. It was as if I had been born that instant, brand new, mindless, innocent of all memories. There existed only the Now, that present moment and what was clearly given in it. To look was enough. And what I found was khaki trouserlegs terminating

Selections from *On Having No Head*, by D. E. Harding, Perennial Library, Harper & Row. Published by arrangement with the Buddhist Society, 1972. Reprinted by permission.

downwards in a pair of brown shoes, khaki sleeves terminating sideways in a pair of pink hands, and a khaki shirtfront terminating upwards in—absolutely nothing whatever! Certainly not in a head.

It took me no time at all to notice that this nothing, this hole where a head should have been, was no ordinary vacancy, no mere nothing. On the contrary, it was very much occupied. It was a vast emptiness vastly filled, a nothing that found room for everything—room for grass, trees, shadowy distant hills, and far above them snow-peaks like a row of angular clouds riding the blue sky. I had lost a head and gained a world.

It was all, quite literally, breathtaking. I seemed to stop breathing altogether, absorbed in the Given. Here it was, this superb scene, brightly shining in the clear air, alone and unsupported, mysteriously suspended in the void, and (and *this* was the real miracle, the wonder and delight) utterly free of "me," unstained by any observer. Its total presence was my total absence, body and soul. Lighter than air, clearer than glass, altogether released from myself, I was nowhere around.

Yet in spite of the magical and uncanny quality of this vision, it was no dream, no esoteric revelation. Quite the reverse: it felt like a sudden waking from the sleep of ordinary life, an end to dreaming. It was self-luminous reality for once swept clean of all obscuring mind. It was the revelation, at long last, of the perfectly obvious. It was a lucid moment in a confused life-history. It was a ceasing to ignore something which (since early childhood at any rate) I had always been too busy or too clever to see. It was naked, uncritical attention to what had all along been staring me in the face—my utter facelessness. In short, it was all perfectly simple and plain and straightforward, beyond argument, thought, and words. There arose no questions, no reference beyond the experience itself, but only peace and a quiet joy, and the sensation of having dropped an intolerable burden.

*   *   *

As the first wonder of my Himalayan discovery began to wear off, I started describing it to myself in some such words as the following.

Somehow or other I had vaguely thought of myself as inhabiting this house which is my body, and looking out through its two round windows at the world. Now I find it isn't like that at all. As I gaze into the distance, what is there at this moment to tell me how many eyes I have here—two, or three, or hundreds, or none? In fact, only one window appears on this side of my facade, and that one is wide open and frameless, with nobody looking out of it. It is always the other fellow who has eyes and a face to frame them; never this one.

There exist, then, two sorts—two widely different species—of man. The first, of which I note countless specimens, evidently carries a head on its shoulders (and by "head" I mean a hairy eight-inch ball with various holes in it) while the second, of which I note only one specimen, evidently carries no such thing on its shoulders. And till now I had overlooked this considerable difference! Victim of a prolonged fit of madness, of a lifelong hallucination (and by "hallucination" I mean what my dictionary says: *apparent perception of an object not actually present*), I had invariably seen myself as pretty much like other men, and certainly never as a decapitated but still living biped. I had been blind to the one thing that is always present, and without which I am blind indeed—to this marvellous substitute-for-a-head, this unbounded clarity, this luminous and absolutely pure void, which nevertheless is—rather than contains—all things. For, however carefully I attend, I fail to find here even so much as a blank screen on which these mountains and sun and sky are projected, or a clear mirror in which they are reflected, or a transparent lens or aperture through which they are viewed—still less a soul or a mind to which they are presented, or a viewer (however shadowy) who is distinguishable from the view. Nothing whatever intervenes, not even that baffling and elusive obstacle called "distance": the huge blue sky, the pink-edged whiteness of the snows, the sparkling green of the grass—how can these be remote, when there's nothing to be remote from? The headless void here refuses all definition and location: it is not round, or small, or big, or even here as distinct from there. (And even if there *were* a head here to measure outwards from, the measuring-rod stretching from it to the peak of Everest would, when read end-on—and there's no other way for me to read it—reduce to a point, to nothing.) In fact, these colored shapes present themselves in all simplicity, without any such complications as near or far, this or that, mine or not mine, seen-by-me or merely given. All twoness—all duality of subject and object—has vanished: it is no longer read into a situation which has no room for it.

Such were the thoughts which followed the vision. To try to set down the first-hand, immediate experience in these or any other terms, however, is to misrepresent it by complicating what is quite simple: indeed the longer the postmortem examination drags on the further it gets from the living original. At best, these descriptions can remind one of the vision (without the bright awareness) or invite a recurrence of it; but they can no more convey its essential quality, or ensure a recurrence, than the most appetizing menu can taste like the dinner, or the best book about humour enable one to see a joke. On the other hand, it is impossible to stop thinking for long, and some attempt to relate the lucid intervals of one's life to the confused background is inevitable. It could also encourage, indirectly, the recurrence of lucidity.

In any case, there are several commonsense objections which refuse to be put off any longer, questions which insist on reasoned answers, however inconclusive. It becomes necessary to "justify" one's vision, even to oneself; also one's friends may need reassuring. In a sense this attempt at domestication is absurd, because no argument can add to or take from an experience which is as plain and incontrovertible as hearing middle-C or tasting strawberry jam. In another sense, however, the attempt has to be made, if one's life is not to disintegrate into two quite alien, idea-tight compartments.

*   *   *

My first objection was: my head may be missing, but not its nose. Here it is, visibly preceding me wherever I go. And my answer was: if this fuzzy, pinkish, yet perfectly transparent cloud suspended on my right, and this other similar cloud suspended on my left, are noses, then I count two of them and not one; and the perfectly opaque single protuberance which I observe so clearly in the middle of your face is *not* a nose: only a hopelessly dishonest or confused observer would deliberately use the same name for such utterly different things. I prefer to go by my dictionary and common usage, which oblige me to say that, whereas nearly all other men have a nose apiece, I have none.

All the same, if some misguided skeptic, overanxious to make his point, were to strike out in this direction, aiming midway between these two pink clouds, the result would surely be as unpleasant as if I owned the most solid and punchable of noses. Again, what about this complex of subtle tensions, movements, pressures, itches, tickles, aches, warmths, and throbbings, never entirely absent from this central region? Above all, what about these touch-feelings which arise when I explore here with my hand? Surely these findings add up to massive evidence for the existence of my head right here and now, after all?

They do nothing of the sort. No doubt a great variety of sensations are plainly given here and cannot be ignored, but they don't amount to a head, or anything like one. The only way to make a head out of them would be to throw in all sorts of ingredients that are plainly missing here —in particular, all manner of coloured shapes in three dimensions. What sort of head is it that, though containing innumerable sensations, is observed to lack eyes, ears, mouth, hair, and indeed all the bodily equipment which other heads are observed to contain? The plain fact is that this place must be kept clear of all such obstructions, of the slightest mistiness or colouring which could cloud my universe.

In any case, when I start groping round for my lost head, instead of finding it here I only lose my exploring hand as well: it, too, is swallowed up in the abyss at the centre of my being. Apparently this yawning cavern, this unoccupied base of all my operations, this magical locality where I thought I kept my head, is in fact more like a beacon-fire so fierce that all things approaching it are instantly and utterly consumed, in order that its world-illuminating brilliance and clarity shall never for a moment be obscured. As for these lurking aches and tickles and so on, they can no more quench or shade that central brightness than these mountains and clouds and sky can do so. Quite the contrary: they all exist in its shining, and through them it is seen to shine. Present experience, whatever sense is employed, occurs only in an empty and absent head. For here and now my world and my head are incompatibles: they won't mix. There is no room for both at once on these shoulders, and fortunately it is my head with all its anatomy that has to go. This is not a matter of argument, or of philosophical acumen, or of working oneself up into a state, but of simple sight—of LOOK-WHO'S-HERE instead of THINK-WHO'S-HERE. If I fail to see what I am (and especially what I am not) it is because I am too busily imaginative, too "spiritual," too adult and knowing, to accept the situation exactly as I find it at this moment. A kind of alert idiocy is what I need. It takes an innocent eye and an empty head to see their own perfect emptiness.

*   *   *

Probably there is only one way of converting the skeptic who still says I have a head here, and that is to invite him to come here and take a look for himself; only he must be an honest reporter, describing what he observes and nothing else.

Starting off on the far side of the room, he sees me as a full-length man-with-a-head. But as he approaches he finds half a man, then a head, then a blurred cheek or eye or nose, then a mere blur, and finally (at the point of contact) nothing at all. Alternatively, if he happens to be equipped with the necessary scientific instruments, he reports that the blur resolves itself into tissues, then cell-groups, then a single cell, a cell-nucleus, giant molecules . . . and so on, till he comes to a place where nothing is to be seen, to space which is empty of all solid or material objects. In either case, the observer who comes here to see what it's really like finds what I find here—vacancy. And if, having discovered and shared my nonentity here, he were to turn round (looking out with me instead of in at me) he would again find what I find—that this vacancy is filled to capacity with everything imaginable. He, too, would find this central Point exploding into an Infinite Volume, this Nothing into the All, this Here into Everywhere.

And if my skeptical observer still doubts his senses, he may try his camera instead—a device which, lacking memory and anticipation, can register only what is contained in the place where it happens to be. It records the same picture of me. Over there, it takes a man; midway, bits and pieces of a man; here, no man and nothing—or else, when pointed the other way round, the universe.

*   *   *

So this head is not a head, but a wrong-headed idea. If I can still find it here, I am "seeing things," and ought to hurry off to the doctor. It makes little difference whether I find a human head, or an ass's head, a fried egg, or a beautiful bunch of flowers: to have any topknot at all is to suffer from delusions.

During my lucid intervals, however, I am clearly headless here. Over there, on the other hand, I am clearly far from headless: indeed, I have more heads that I know what to do with. Concealed in my human observers and in cameras, on display in picture frames, pulling faces behind shaving mirrors, peering out of door knobs and spoons and coffeepots and anything which will take a high polish, my heads are always turning up—though more-or-less shrunken and distorted, twisted back-to-front, often the wrong way up, and multiplied to infinity.

But there is one place where no head of mine can ever turn up, and that is here "on my shoulders," where it would blot out this Central Void which is my very life-source: fortunately nothing is able to do that. In fact, these loose heads can never amount to more than impermanent and unprivileged accidents of that "outer" or phenomenal world which, though altogether one with the central essence, fails to affect it in the slightest degree. So unprivileged, indeed, is my head in the mirror, that I don't necessarily take it to be mine: as a very young child I didn't recognize myself in the glass, and neither do I now, when for a moment I regain my lost innocence. In my saner moments I see the man over there, the too-familiar fellow who lives in that other room behind the looking-glass and seemingly spends all his time staring into this room—that small, dull, circumscribed, particularized, ageing, and oh-so-vulnerable gazer—as the opposite in every way of my real Self here. I have never been anything but this ageless, adamantine, measureless, lucid, and altogether immaculate Void: it is unthinkable that I could ever have confused that staring wraith over there with what I plainly perceive myself to be here and now and forever!

*   *   *

Film directors . . . are practical people, much more interested in the telling re-creation of experience than in discerning the nature of the experiencer; but in fact the one involves some of the other. Certainly these experts are well aware (for example) how feeble my reaction is to a film of a vehicle obviously driven by someone else, compared with my reaction to a film of a vehicle apparently driven by myself. In the first instance I am a spectator on the pavement, observing two similar cars swiftly approaching, colliding, killing the drivers, bursting into flames—and I am mildly interested. In the second, I am the driver—headless, of course, like all first-person drivers, and my car (what little there is of it) is stationary. Here are my swaying knees, my foot hard down on the accelerator, my hands struggling with the steering wheel, the long bonnet sloping away in front, telegraph poles whizzing by, the road snaking this way and that, the other car, tiny at first, but looming larger and larger, coming straight at me, and then the crash, a great flash of light, and an empty silence. . . . I sink back onto my seat and get my breath back. I have been taken for a ride.

How are they filmed, these first-person sequences? Two ways are possible: either a headless dummy is photographed, with the camera in place of the head; or else a real man is photographed, with his head held far back or to one side to make room for the camera. In other words, to ensure that I shall identify myself with the actor, his head is got out of the way: he must be my kind of man. For a picture of me-with-a-head is no likeness at all: it is the portrait of a complete stranger, a case of mistaken identity.

It is curious that anyone should go to the advertising man for a glimpse into the deepest—and simplest—truths about himself; odd also that an elaborate modern invention like the cinema should help rid any-one of an illusion which very young children and animals are free of. But in other ages there were other and equally curious pointers, and our human capacity for self-deception has surely never been complete. A profound though dim awareness of the human condition may well explain the popularity of many old cults and legends of loose and flying heads, of one-eyed or headless monsters and apparitions, of human bodies with non-human heads, and of martyrs who (like King Charles in the ill-punctuated sentence) walked and talked after their heads were cut off—

fantastic pictures, no doubt, but nearer than common sense ever gets to a true portrait of *this* man.

*   *   *

But if I have no head or face or eyes here (protests common sense) how on earth do I see you, and what are eyes for, anyway? The truth is that the verb *to see* has two quite opposite meanings. When we observe a couple conversing, we say they *see* each other, though their faces remain intact and some feet apart; but when I see you your face is all, mine nothing. You are the end of me. Yet (so Enlightenment-preventing is the language of common sense) we use the same little word for both operations: and, of course, the same word has to mean the same thing! What actually goes on between third persons as such is visual communication —that continuous and self-contained chain of physical processes (involving light waves, eye-lenses, retinas, the visual area of the cortex, and so on) in which the scientist can find no chink where "mind" or "seeing" could be slipped in, or (if it could) would make any difference. True seeing, by contrast, is first person and so eyeless. In the language of the sages, only the Buddha Nature, or Brahman, or Allah, or God, sees or hears or experiences anything at all.

Reflections

We have here been presented with a charmingly childish and solipsistic view of the human condition. It is something that, at an intellectual level, offends and appalls us: can anyone sincerely entertain such notions without embarrassment? Yet to some primitive level in us it speaks clearly. That is the level at which we cannot accept the notion of our own death. In many of us, that level has been submerged and concealed for so long that we forget how incomprehensible is the concept of personal nonexistence. We can so easily—it seems—extrapolate from the nonexistence of others to the potential nonexistence, one day, of ourselves. Yet how can it be a *day* when I die? After all, a day is a time with light and sounds; when I die, there will be none of those. "Oh, yes, there will be," protests an inner voice. "Just because I won't be there to experience them doesn't mean they won't exist! That's so solipsistic!" My inner voice, coerced by the power of a simple syllogism, has reluctantly overridden the notion that I am a necessary ingredient of the universe. That syllogism is, roughly, this:

> All human beings are mortal.
> I am a human being.
> _____
> Therefore . . . I . . . am . . . mortal.

But for the substitution of "I" for "Socrates," this is the most classical of all syllogisms. What kind of evidence is there for the two premises? The first premise presumes an abstract category, the class of human beings. The second premise is that I too belong to that class, despite the seemingly radical difference between myself and every other member of that class (which Harding is so adept at pointing out).

The idea of classes about which general statements can be made is not so shocking, but it seems to be a rather advanced property of intelligence to be able to formulate classes beyond those that are part of an innate repertoire. Bees seem to have the class "flower" down pretty well, but it is doubtful that they can formulate a concept of "chimney" or "human." Dogs and cats seem to be able to manufacture new classes, such as "food dish," "door," "toy," and so on. But people are by far the best at the piling up of new category upon new category. This capacity is at the core of human nature and is a profound source of joy. Sportscasters and scientists and artists all give us great pleasure in their formulation of new kinds of concepts that enter our mental vocabulary.

The other part of the first premise is the general concept of death. That something can vanish or be destroyed is a very early discovery. The food in the spoon vanishes, the rattle falls off the high chair, Mommy goes away for a while, the balloon pops, the newspaper in the fireplace burns up, the house a block down the street is razed, and so on. All very shocking and disturbing, certainly—but still acceptable. The swatted fly, the sprayed mosquitoes—these build on the previous abstractions, and we come to the general concept of death. So much for the first premise.

The second premise is the tricky one. As a child I formulated the abstraction "human being" by seeing things outside of me that had something in common—appearance, behavior, and so on. That this particular class could then "fold back" on me and engulf me—this realization necessarily comes at a later stage of cognitive development, and must be quite a shocking experience, although probably most of us do not remember it happening.

The truly unnerving step, though, is the conjunction of the two premises. By the time we've developed the mental power to formulate them both, we also have developed a respect for the compelling quality of simple logic. But the sudden conjunction of these two premises slaps us in the face unexpectedly. It is an ugly, brutal blow that sends us reeling —probably for days, weeks, months. Actually, for years—for our whole lives!—but somehow we suppress the conflict and turn it in other directions.

Do higher animals have the ability to see themselves as members of a class? Is a dog capable of (wordlessly) thinking the thought, "I bet I look like those dogs over there"? Imagine the following gory situation. A ring is formed of, say, twenty animals of one sort. An evil human repeatedly spins a dial and then walks over to the designated animal and knifes it to death in front of the remaining ones. Is it likely that each one will realize its impending doom, will think, "That animal over there is just like me, and *my* goose may soon be cooked just as his was. Oh, no!"?

This ability to map oneself onto others seems to be the exclusive property of members of higher species. (It is the central topic of Thomas Nagel's article, "What Is It Like to Be a Bat?" reprinted in selection 24.) One begins by making partial mappings: "I have feet, you have feet; I have hands, you have hands; hmm. . . ." These partial mappings then can induce a total mapping. Pretty soon, I conclude from your having a head that I too have one, although I can't see mine. But this stepping outside myself is a gigantic and, in some ways, self-denying, step. It contradicts much direct knowledge about myself. It is like Harding's two distinct types of verb "to see"—when it applies to myself it is quite another thing than when it applies to you. The power of this distinction gets overcome, however, by the sheer weight of too many mappings all the time, establishing without doubt my membership in a class that I formulated originally without regard to myself.

So logic overrides intuition. Just as we could come to believe that our Earth can be round—as is the alien moon—without people falling off, so we finally come to believe that the solipsistic view is nutty. Only a powerful vision such as Harding's Himalayan experience can return us to that primordial sense of self and otherness, which is at the root of the problems of consciousness, soul, and self.

Do I have a brain? Will I actually die? We all think about such questions many times during our lives. Occasionally, probably every imaginative person thinks that all of life is a huge joke or hoax—perhaps a psychology experiment—being perpetrated by some inconceivable superbeing, seeing how far it can push us into believing obvious absurdities (the idea that sounds that I can't understand really *mean* something, the idea that someone can hear Chopin or eat chocolate ice cream without loving it, the idea that light goes at the same speed in any reference frame, the idea that I am made of inanimate atoms, the idea of my own death, and so on). But unfortunately (or fortunately), that "conspiracy theory" undermines itself, since it postulates another mind—in fact a superintelligent and therefore inconceivable one—in order to explain away other mysteries.

There seems to be no alternative to accepting some sort of incomprehensible quality to existence. Take your pick. We all fluctuate delicately between a subjective and objective view of the world, and this quandary is central to human nature.

D.R.H.

3

HAROLD J. MOROWITZ

Rediscovering the Mind

Something peculiar has been going on in science for the past 100 years or so. Many researchers are unaware of it, and others won't admit it even to their own colleagues. But there is a strangeness in the air.

What has happened is that biologists, who once postulated a privileged role for the human mind in nature's hierarchy, have been moving relentlessly toward the hard-core materialism that characterized nineteenth-century physics. At the same time, physicists, faced with compelling experimental evidence, have been moving away from strictly mechanical models of the universe to a view that sees the mind as playing an integral role in all physical events. It is as if the two disciplines were on fast-moving trains, going in opposite directions and not noticing what is happening across the tracks.

This role reversal by biologists and physicists has left the contemporary psychologist in an ambivalent position. From the perspective of biology, the psychologist studies phenomena that are far removed from the core of certainty, that is, the submicroscopic world of atoms and molecules. From the perspective of physics, the psychologist deals with "the mind," an undefined primitive that seems at once essential and impenetrable. Clearly, both views embody some measure of truth—and a resolution of the problem is essential to deepening and extending the foundations of behavioral science.

The study of life at all levels, from social to molecular behavior, has

"Rediscovering the Mind," by Harold J. Morowitz. From *Psychology Today*, August 1980. Reprinted by permission of the author.

ILLUSTRATIONS BY VICTOR JUHASZ

in modern times relied on reductionism as the chief explanatory concept. This approach to knowledge tries to comprehend one level of scientific phenomena in terms of concepts at a lower and presumably more fundamental level. In chemistry, large-scale reactions are accounted for by examining the behavior of molecules. Similarly, physiologists study the activity of living cells in terms of processes carried out by organelles and other subcellular entities. And in geology, the formations and properties of minerals are described using the features of the constituent crystals. The essence of these cases is seeking explanation in underlying structures and activities.

Reductionism at the psychological level is exemplified by the viewpoint in Carl Sagan's best-selling book *The Dragons of Eden.* He writes: "My fundamental premise about the brain is that its workings—what we sometimes call 'mind'—are a consequence of its anatomy and physiology and nothing more." As a further demonstration of this trend of thought, we note that Sagan's glossary does not contain the words *mind, consciousness, perception, awareness,* or *thought,* but rather deals with entries such as *synapse, lobotomy, proteins,* and *electrodes.*

Such attempts to reduce human behavior to its biological basis have a long history, beginning with the early Darwinians and their contemporaries working in physiological psychology. Before the nineteenth century, the mind-body duality, which was central to Descartes's philosophy, had tended to place the human mind outside the domain of biology. Then the stress that the evolutionists placed on our "apeness" made us subject to biological study by methods appropriate to nonhuman primates and, by extension, to other animals. The Pavlovian school reinforced that theme, and it became a cornerstone of many behavioral theories. While no general agreement has emerged among psychologists as to how far reductionism should be carried, most will readily concede that our actions have hormonal, neurological, and physiological components. Although Sagan's premise lies within a general tradition in psychology, it is radical in aiming at *complete* explanation in terms of the underlying level. This goal I take to be the thrust of his phrase "and nothing more."

At the time various schools of psychology were attempting to reduce their science to biology, other life scientists were also looking for more basic levels of explanation. Their outlook can be seen in the writings of a popular spokesman of molecular biology, Francis Crick. In his book, *Of Molecules and Men,* a contemporary attack on vitalism—the doctrine that biology needs to be explained in terms of life forces lying outside the domain of physics—Crick states: "The ultimate aim of the modern movement in biology is in fact to explain *all* biology in terms of physics and chemistry." He goes on to say that by physics and chemistry he refers to the atomic level, where our knowledge is secure. By use of the italicized *all,* he expresses the position of radical reductionism that has been the dominant viewpoint among an entire generation of biochemists and molecular biologists.

*   *   *

If we now combine psychological and biological reductionism and assume they overlap, we end up with a sequence of explanation going from mind to anatomy and physiology, to cell physiology, to molecular biology, to atomic physics. All this knowledge is assumed to rest on a firm bedrock of understanding the laws of quantum mechanics, the newest and most complete theory of atomic structures and processes. Within this context, psychology becomes a branch of physics, a result that may cause some unease among both groups of professionals.

This attempt to explain everything about human beings in terms of the first principles of physical science is not a new idea and had reached a definitive position in the views of the mid-nineteenth-century European physiologists. A representative of that school, Emil Du Bois-Reymond, set forth his extreme opinions in the introduction to an 1848 book on animal electricity. He wrote that "if our methods only were sufficient, an analytical mechanics [Newtonial physics] of general life processes would be possible and fundamentally would reach even to the problem of the freedom of the will."

There is a certain hubris in the words of these early savants that was picked up by Thomas Huxley and his colleagues in their defense of Darwinism and, even today, echoes in the theories of modern reductionists who would move from the mind to the first principles of atomic physics. It is most clearly seen at present in the writings of the sociobiologists, whose arguments animate the contemporary intellectual scene. In any case, Du Bois-Reymond's views are consistent with the modern radical reductionists, except that quantum mechanics has now replaced Newtonian mechanics as the underlying discipline.

During the period in which psychologists and biologists were steadily moving toward reducing their disciplines to the physical sciences, they were largely unaware of perspectives emerging from physics that cast an entirely new light on their understanding. Toward the close of the last century, physics presented a very ordered picture of the world, in which events unfolded in characteristic, regular ways, following Newton's equations in mechanics and Maxwell's in electricity. These processes moved inexorably, independent of the scientist, who was simply a spectator. Many physicists considered their subject as essentially complete.

Starting with the introduction of the theory of relativity by Albert Einstein in 1905, this neat picture was unceremoniously upset. The new theory postulated that observers in different systems moving with respect to each other would perceive the world differently. The observer thus became involved in establishing physical reality. The scientist was losing the spectator's role and becoming an active participant in the system under study.

With the development of quantum mechanics, the role of the observer became an even more central part of physical theory, an essential component in defining an event. The mind of the observer emerged as a necessary element in the structure of the theory. The implications of the developing paradigm greatly surprised early quantum physicists and led them to study epistemology and the philosophy of science. Never before in scientific history, to my knowledge, had all of the leading contributors produced books and papers expounding the philosophical and humanistic meaning of their results.

Werner Heisenberg, one of the founders of the new physics, became deeply involved in the issues of philosophy and humanism. In *Philosophical Problems of Quantum Physics,* he wrote of physicists having to renounce thoughts of an objective time scale common to all observers, and of events in time and space that are independent of our ability to observe them. Heisenberg stressed that the laws of nature no longer dealt with elementary particles, but with our knowledge of these particles—that is, *with the contents of our minds.* Erwin Schrödinger, the man who formulated the fundamental equation of quantum mechanics, wrote an extraordinary little book in 1958 called *Mind and Matter.* In this series of essays, he moved from the results of the new physics to a rather mystical view of the universe that he identified with the "perennial philosophy" of Aldous Huxley. Schrödinger was the first of the quantum theoreticians to express sympathy with the *Upanishads* and Eastern philosophical thought. A growing body of literature now embodies this perspective, including two popular works, *The Tao of Physics* by Fritjof Capra and *The Dancing Wu Li Masters* by Gary Zukav.

The problem faced by quantum theorists can best be seen in the famous paradox, "Who killed Schrödinger's cat?" In a hypothetical formulation, a kitten is put in a closed box with a jar of poison and a triphammer poised to smash the jar. The hammer is activated by a counter that records random events, such as radioactive decay. The experiment lasts just long enough for there to be a probability of one-half that the hammer will be released. Quantum mechanics represents the system mathematically by the sum of a live-cat and a dead-cat function, each with a probability of one-half. The question is whether the act of looking (the measurement) kills or saves the cat, since before the experimenter looks in the box both solutions are equally likely.

This lighthearted example reflects a deep conceptual difficulty. In more formal terms, a complex system can only be described by using a probability distribution that relates the possible outcomes of an experiment. In order to decide among the various alternatives, a measurement is required. This measurement is what constitutes an event, as distinguished from the probability, which is a mathematical abstraction. However, the only simple and consistent description physicists were able to assign to a measurement involved an observer's becoming aware of the result. Thus the physical event and the content of the human mind were inseparable. This linkage forced many researchers to seriously consider consciousness as an integral part of the structure of physics. Such interpretations moved science toward the *idealist* as contrasted with the *realist* conception of philosophy.

The views of a large number of contemporary physical scientists are summed up in the essay "Remarks on the Mind-Body Question" written by Nobel laureate Eugene Wigner. Wigner begins by pointing out that most physical scientists have returned to the recognition that thought— meaning the mind—is primary. He goes on to state: "It was not possible to formulate the laws of quantum mechanics in a fully consistent way without reference to the consciousness." And he concludes by noting how remarkable it is that the scientific study of the world led to the content of consciousness as an ultimate reality.

A further development in yet another field of physics reinforces Wigner's viewpoint. The introduction of information theory and its application to thermodynamics has led to the conclusion that entropy, a basic concept of that science, is a measure of the observer's ignorance of the atomic details of the system. When we measure the pressure, volume, and temperature of an object, we have a residual lack of knowledge of the exact position and velocity of the component atoms and molecules. The numerical value of the amount of information we are missing is proportional to the entropy. In earlier thermodynamics, entropy had represented, in an engineering sense, the energy of the system unavailable to perform external work. In the modern view, the human mind enters once again, and entropy relates not just to the state of the system but to our knowledge of that state.

The founders of modern atomic theory did not start out to impose a "mentalist" picture on the world. Rather, they began with the opposite point of view and were forced to the present-day position in order to explain experimental results.

We are now in a position to integrate the perspectives of three large fields: psychology, biology, and physics. By combining the positions of Sagan, Crick, and Wigner as spokesmen for various outlooks, we get a picture of the whole that is quite unexpected.

First, the human mind, including consciousness and reflective thought, can be explained by activities of the central nervous system, which, in turn, can be reduced to the biological structure and function of that physiological system. Second, biological phenomena at all levels can be totally understood in terms of atomic physics, that is, through the action and interaction of the component atoms of carbon, nitrogen, oxygen, and so forth. Third and last, atomic physics, which is now understood most fully by means of quantum mechanics, must be formulated with the mind as a primitive component of the system.

We have thus, in separate steps, gone around an epistemological circle—from the mind, back to the mind. The results of this chain of reasoning will probably lend more aid and comfort to Eastern mystics than to neurophysiologists and molecular biologists; nevertheless, the closed loop follows from a straightforward combination of the explanatory processes of recognized experts in the three separate sciences. Since individuals seldom work with more than one of these paradigms, the general problem has received little attention.

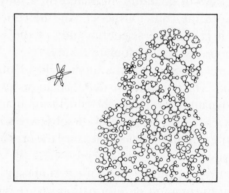

If we reject this epistemological circularity, we are left with two opposing camps: a physics with a claim to completeness because it describes all of nature, and a psychology that is all-embracing because it deals with the mind, our only source of knowledge of the world. Given the problems in both of these views, it is perhaps well to return to the circle and give it more sympathetic consideration. If it deprives us of firm absolutes, at least it encompasses the mind-body problem and provides a framework within which individual disciplines can communicate. The closing of the circle provides the best possible approach for psychological theorists.

*   *   *

The strictly reductionist approach to human behavior so characteristic of sociobiology also runs into trouble on more narrowly biological grounds. For it includes an assumption of continuity in evolution from early mammals to man, which implies that the mind, or consciousness, was not a radical departure. Such an assumption is hardly justified when one considers the dramatic instances of discontinuity in evolution. The origin of the universe itself, the "big bang," is a cosmic example of a discontinuity. The beginning of life, while less cataclysmic, is certainly another example.

The encoding of information in genetic molecules introduced the possibility of profound disturbances in the laws that governed the universe. Before the coming of genetic life, for example, fluctuations in temperature or noise were averaged out, giving rise to precise laws of planetary evolution. Afterward, however, a single molecular event at the level of thermal noise could lead to macroscopic consequences. For if the event were a mutation in a self-replicating system, then the entire course of biological evolution could be altered. A single molecular event could kill a whale by inducing a cancer or destroy an ecosystem by generating a virulent virus that attacks a key species in that system. The origin of life does not abrogate the underlying laws of physics, but it adds a new feature: large-scale consequences of molecular events. This rule change makes evolutionary history indeterminate and so constitutes a clear-cut discontinuity.

A number of contemporary biologists and psychologists believe that the origin of reflective thought that occurred during primate evolution is also a discontinuity that has changed the rules. Again, the new situation does not abrogate the underlying biological laws, but it adds a feature that necessitates novel ways of thinking about the problem. The evolutionary biologist Lawrence B. Slobodkin has identified the new feature as an introspective self-image. This property, he asserts, alters the response to evolutionary problems and makes it impossible to assign major historical events to causes inherent in biological evolutionary laws. Slobodkin is claiming that the rules have changed, and man cannot be understood by laws applicable to other mammals whose brains have a very similar physiology.

This emergent feature of man has, in one form or another, been discussed by numerous anthropologists, psychologists, and biologists. It is part of the empirical data that cannot be shelved just to preserve reductionist purity. The discontinuity needs to be thoroughly studied and evaluated, but first it needs to be recognized. Primates are very different from other animals, and human beings are very different from other primates.

We now understand the troublesome features in a forceful commitment to uncritical reductionism as a solution to the problem of the mind. We have discussed the weaknesses of that position. In addition to being weak, it is a dangerous view, since the way we respond to our fellow human beings is dependent on the way we conceptualize them in our theoretical formulations. If we envision our fellows solely as animals or machines, we drain our interactions of humanistic richness. If we seek our behavioral norms in the study of animal societies, we ignore those uniquely human features that so enrich our lives. Radical reductionism offers very little in the area of moral imperatives. Further, it presents the wrong glossary of terms for a humanistic pursuit.

The scientific community has made notable progress in understanding the brain, and I share the enthusiasm for neurobiology that characterizes modern-day research. Nevertheless, we should be reluctant to let that élan generate statements that go beyond science and lock us into philosophical positions that impoverish our humanity by denying the most intriguing aspect of our species. To underrate the significance of the appearance and character of reflective thought is a high price to pay in order to honor the liberation of science from theology by our reductionist predecessors several generations back. The human psyche is part of the observed data of science. We can retain it and still be good empirical biologists and psychologists.

Reflections

"The Garden of Forking Paths" is a picture, incomplete yet not false, of the universe as Ts'ui Pên conceived it to be. Differing from Newton and Schopenhauer . . . [he] did not think of time as absolute and uniform. He believed in an infinite series of times, in a dizzily growing, ever spreading network of diverging, converging and parallel times. This web of time—the strands of which approach one another, bifurcate, intersect, or ignore each other through the centuries—embraces every possibility. We do not exist in most of them. In some you exist and not I, while in others I do, and you do not, and in yet others both of us exist. In this one, in which chance has favored me, you have come to my gate. In another, you, crossing the garden, have found me dead. In yet another, I say these very same words, but am an error, a phantom.

—Jorge Luis Borges
"The Garden of Forking Paths"

Actualities seem to float in a wider sea of possibilities from out of which they were chosen; and *somewhere*, indeterminism says, such possibilities exist, and form part of the truth.

—William James

It is an attractive notion that the mysteries of quantum physics and the mysteries of consciousness are somehow one. The epistemological loop that Morowitz describes has just about the proper amounts of hard sci-

ence, beauty, weirdness, and mysticism to "sound right." However, it is
an idea that in many ways opposes an important theme of this book, which
is that nonquantum-mechanical computational models of mind (and all
that goes along with mind) are possible in principle. But right or wrong
—and it is too early to say—the ideas that Morowitz presents are worth
thinking about, for there is certainly no question that the problem of the
interaction of subjective and objective viewpoints is a conceptual difficulty at the heart of quantum mechanics. In particular, quantum mechanics as it is usually cast accords a privileged causal status to certain systems
known as "observers," without spelling out precisely what observers are
(in particular, without spelling out whether consciousness is a necessary
ingredient of observer status). To clarify this point we must present a
quick overview of the "measurement problem" in quantum mechanics,
and we will invoke the metaphor of the "quantum water faucet" for that
purpose.

Imagine a water faucet with two knobs—hot and cold—each of which
you can twist continuously. Water comes streaming out of the faucet, but
there is a strange property to this system: The water is always either
totally hot or totally cold—no in-between. These are called the two "temperature eigenstates" of the water. The only way you can tell which
eigenstate the water is in is by sticking your hand in and feeling it.
Actually, in orthodox quantum mechanics it is trickier than that. It is the
act of putting your hand under the water that *throws* the water into one
or the other eigenstate. Up until that very instant, the water is said to be
in a *superposition of states* (or more accurately, a superposition of *eigenstates*).

Depending on the setting of the knobs, the likelihood of cold water
will vary. Of course, if you turn on only the "H" tap, then you'll get hot
water always, and if you turn on only "C," then you'll get cold water for
sure. If you open both valves, however, you'll create a superposition of
states. By trying it out over and over again with one setting, you can
measure the probability that you'll get cold water with that setting. After
that, you can change the setting and try again. There will be some cross-
over point where hot and cold are equally likely. It will then be like
flipping a coin. (This quantum water faucet is sadly reminiscent of many
a bathroom shower.) Eventually you can build up enough data to draw
a graph of the probability of cold water as a function of the knobs'
settings.

Quantum phenomena are like this. Physicists can twiddle knobs and
put systems into superpositions of states analogous to our hot–cold
superpositions. As long as no *measurement* is made of the system, the
physicists cannot know which eigenstate the system is in. Indeed it can

be shown that in a very fundamental sense the system itself does not "know" which eigenstate it is in, and that it decides—at random—only at the moment the observer's hand is put in to "test the water," so to speak. The system, up till the moment of observation, acts as if it were *not* in an eigenstate. For all practical purposes, for all theoretical purposes—in fact for *all* purposes—the system is not in an eigenstate.

You can imagine doing a lot of experiments on the water coming out of a quantum water faucet to determine if it is actually hot or actually cold without sticking your hand in (we're of course assuming that there are no telltale cues such as steam). For example, run your washing machine on the water from the faucet. Still, you won't know if your wool sweater has shrunk or not until the moment when you open the washing machine (a measurement made by a conscious observer). Make some tea with water from the faucet. Still, you won't know if you've got iced tea or not, until you taste it (interaction with a conscious observer again). Attach a recording thermometer just under the water faucet. Until you yourself see the reading on the thermometer or the ink marks on its record, you can't know the temperature. You can't be any surer that the ink is on the paper than you are that the water has a definite temperature. The critical point here is that the sweater and the tea and the thermometer, not having conscious-observer status themselves, have to play along with the gag and, just as the water did, enter their own superpositions of states— shrunk-and-nonshrunk, iced-tea-and-hot-tea, ink-high-and-ink-low.

This may sound as if it has nothing to do with physics per se but merely with ancient philosophical conundrums such as "Does a tree in a forest make a noise when it falls if there's no one there to hear it?" But the quantum-mechanical twist on such riddles is that there are observational consequences of the reality of such superpositions, consequences that are diametrically opposite to the consequences that would occur if a seemingly mixed state were in reality always a true eigenstate, merely hiding its identity from observers until the moment of measurement. In crude terms, a stream of maybe-hot-maybe-cold water would act differently from a stream of water that is actually hot or actually cold, because the two alternatives "interfere" with each other in the sense of overlapping waves (as when one part of a speedboat's wake momentarily cancels another part reflected off a jetty, or when a skipped rock's successive bounces send out ripples that crisscross and create shimmering patterns on a still lake surface). It turns out that such interference effects are only statistical, so the effect would become manifest only after a large number of sweater-washings or tea-makings. Interested readers should consult the beautiful exposition of this difference in *The Character of Physical Law* by Richard Feynman.

The plight of Schrödinger's cat carries this idea further—that even a cat could be in a quantum-mechanical superposition of states until a human observer intervened. One might object and say, "Wait a minute! Isn't a live cat as much of a conscious observer as a human being is?" Probably it is—but notice that this cat is possibly a *dead* cat, which

Schrödinger's cat in a superposition of states. (From *The Many-Worlds of Quantum Mechanics*, edited by Bryce S. DeWitt and Neill Graham.)

is certainly not a conscious observer. In effect, we have created, in Schrödinger's cat, a superposition of two eigenstates one of which has observer status, the other of which lacks it! Now what do we do? The situation is reminiscent of a Zen riddle (recounted in *Zen Flesh, Zen Bones* by Paul Reps) posed by the master Kyōgen:

Zen is like a man hanging in a tree by his teeth over a precipice. His hands grasp no branch, his feet rest on no limb, and under the tree another person asks him: "Why did Bodhidharma come to China from India?" If the man in the tree does not answer, he fails; and if he does answer, he falls and loses his life. Now what shall he do?

To many physicists the distinction between systems with observer status and those without has seemed artificial, even repugnant. Moreover, the idea that an observer's intervention causes a "collapse of the wave function"—a sudden jump into one randomly chosen pure eigenstate—introduces caprice into the ultimate laws of nature. "God does not play dice" (*"Der Herrgott würfelt nicht"*) was Einstein's lifelong belief.

A radical attempt to save both continuity and determinism in quantum mechanics is known as the "many-worlds interpretation" of quantum mechanics, first proposed in 1957 by Hugh Everett III. According to this very bizarre theory, no system ever jumps discontinuously into an eigenstate. What happens is that the superposition evolves smoothly with its various branches unfolding in parallel. Whenever necessary, the state sprouts further branches that carry the various new alternatives. For instance, there are two branches in the case of Schrödinger's cat, and they both develop in parallel. "Well, what happens to the cat? Does it feel itself to be alive, or dead?" one must wonder. Everett would answer, "It depends which branch you look at. On one branch it feels itself alive, on the other there's no cat to feel anything." With intuition beginning to rebel, one then asks, "Well, what about a few moments before the cat on the fatal branch died? How did the cat feel then? Surely the cat can't feel two ways at once! Which of the two branches contains the genuine cat?"

The problem becomes even more intense as you realize the implications of this theory as applied to you, here and now. For every quantum-mechanical branch point in your life (and there have been billions upon billions), you have split into two or more yous, riding along parallel but disconnected branches of one gigantic "universal wave function." At the critical spot in his article where this difficulty arises, Everett calmly inserts the following footnote:

At this point we encounter a language difficulty. Whereas before the observation we had a single observer state, afterwards there were a number of different states for the observer, all occurring in a superposition. Each of these separate states is a state for an observer, so that we can speak of the different observers described by different states. On the other hand, the same physical system is involved, and from this viewpoint it is the *same* observer, which is in different states for different elements of the superposition (i.e., has had different experiences in the separate elements of the superposition). In this situation we shall use the singular when we wish to emphasize that a single physical system is involved, and the plural when we wish to emphasize the different experiences for the separate elements of the superposition. (E.g., "The observer performs an observation of the quantity A, after which each of the observers of the resulting superposition has perceived an eigenvalue.")

All said with a poker face. The problem of how it feels *subjectively* is not treated; it is just swept under the rug. It is probably considered meaningless.

And yet, one simply has to wonder, "Why, then, do I feel myself to be in just *one* world?" Well, according to Everett's view, you *don't*—you feel all the alternatives simultaneously, it's just *this* you going down *this* branch who doesn't experience all the alternatives. This is completely shocking. The vivid quotes with which we opened our reflection come back and penetrate deeply. The ultimate question is this: "Why is *this me* in *this branch,* then? What makes me—I mean *this* me—feel itself—I mean myself—unsplit?"

The sun is setting one evening over the ocean. You and a group of friends are standing at various points along the wet sand. As the water laps at your feet, you silently watch the red globe drop nearer and nearer to the horizon. As you watch, somewhat mesmerized, you notice how the sun's reflection on the wave crests forms a straight line composed of thousands of momentary orange-red glints—a straight line pointing right at you! "How lucky that I am the one who happens to be lined up exactly with that line!" you think to yourself. "Too bad not all of us can stand here and experience this perfect unity with the sun." And at the same moment, each of your friends is having precisely the same thought . . . or is it the same?

Such musings are at the heart of the "soul-searching question." Why is this soul in this body? (Or on this branch of the universal wave function?) Why, when there are so many possibilities, did *this* mind get attached to this body? Why can't my "I-ness" belong to some other body? It is obviously circular and unsatisfying to say something like "You are in that body because that was the one made by your parents." But why were *they* my parents, and not sometwo else? Who would have been my parents if I had been born in Hungary? What would I have been like if I had been someone else? Or if someone else had been me? Or—*am* I someone else? Am I everyone else? Is there only one universal consciousness? Is it an illusion to feel oneself as separate, as an individual? It is rather eerie to find these bizarre themes reproduced at the core of what is supposedly our stablest and least erratic science.

And yet in a way it is not so surprising. There is a clear connection between the imaginary worlds in our minds and the alternate worlds evolving in parallel with the one we experience. The proverbial young man picking apart the daisy and muttering, "She loves me, she loves me not, she loves me, she loves me not" is clearly maintaining in his mind (at least) two different worlds based on two different models for his beloved. Or would it be more accurate to say that there is *one* mental model of his beloved that is in a mental analogue of a quantum-mechanical superposition of states?

And when a novelist simultaneously entertains a number of possible ways of extending a story, are the characters not, to speak metaphorically, in a mental superposition of states? If the novel never gets set to paper, perhaps the split characters can continue to evolve their multiple stories in their author's brain. Furthermore, it would even seem strange to ask

ILLUSTRATION BY RICK GRANGER

which story is the *genuine* version. All the worlds are equally genuine.

And in like manner, there is a world—a branch of the universal wave function—in which you didn't make that stupid mistake you now regret so much. Aren't you jealous? But how can you be jealous of your*self*? Besides which, there's *another* world in which you made yet stupider mistakes, and are jealous of this very you, here and now in *this* world!

Perhaps one way to think of the universal wave function is as the mind—or brain, if you prefer—of the great novelist in the sky, God, in which all possible branches are being simultaneously entertained. We would be mere subsystems of God's brain, and these versions of us are no more privileged or authentic than our galaxy is the only genuine galaxy. God's brain, conceived in this way, evolves smoothly and deterministically, as Einstein always maintained. The physicist Paul Davies, writing on just this topic in his recent book *Other Worlds*, says: "Our consciousness weaves a route at random along the ever-branching evolutionary pathway of the cosmos, so it is we, rather than God, who are playing dice."

Yet this leaves unanswered the most fundamental riddle that each of us must ask: "Why is my unitary feeling of myself propagating down *this* random branch rather than down some other? What *law* underlies the random choices that pick out the branch I feel myself tracing out? Why doesn't my feeling of myself go along with the other me's as they split off, following other routes? What attaches *me-ness* to the viewpoint of this body evolving down this branch of the universe at this moment in time?"

The question is so basic that it almost seems to defy clear formulation in words. And the answer does not seem to be forthcoming from quantum mechanics. In fact, this is exactly the collapse of the wave function reappearing at the far end of the rug it was shoved under by Everett. It turns it into a problem of personal identity, no less perplexing than the original problem it replaces.

One can fall even more deeply into the pit of paradox when one realizes that there are branches of this one gigantically branching universal wave function on which there is no evidence for quantum mechanics whatsoever, branches on which there is no Everett or many-worlds interpretation of quantum mechanics. There are branches on which the Borges story did not get written. There is even a branch in which this entire Reflection got written exactly as you see it here, except that it ended with a different flutzpah.

D.R.H.

II

Soul Searching

4

A. M. TURING

Computing Machinery and Intelligence

The Imitation Game

I propose to consider the question "Can machines think?" This should begin with definitions of the meaning of the terms "machine" and "think." The definitions might be framed so as to reflect so far as possible the normal use of the words, but this attitude is dangerous. If the meaning of the words "machine" and "think" are to be found by examining how they are commonly used it is difficult to escape the conclusion that the meaning and the answer to the question, "Can machines think?" is to be sought in a statistical survey such as a Gallup poll. But this is absurd. Instead of attempting such a definition I shall replace the question by another, which is closely related to it and is expressed in relatively unambiguous words.

The new form of the problem can be described in terms of a game which we call the "imitation game." It is played with three people, a man (A), a woman (B), and an interrogator (C) who may be of either sex. The interrogator stays in a room apart from the other two. The object of the game for the interrogator is to determine which of the other two is

Excerpt from "Computing Machinery and Intelligence," *Mind*, Vol. LIX, No. 236 (1950). Reprinted by permission.

the man and which is the woman. He knows them by labels X and Y, and at the end of the game he says either "X is A and Y is B" or "X is B and Y is A." The interrogator is allowed to put questions to A and B thus:

c: Will X please tell me the length of his or her hair?

Now suppose X is actually A, then A must answer. It is A's object in the game to try to cause C to make the wrong identification. His answer might therefore be

"My hair is shingled, and the longest strands are about nine inches long."

In order that tones of voice may not help the interrogator the answers should be written, or better still, typewritten. The ideal arrangement is to have a teleprinter communicating between the two rooms. Alternatively the question and answers can be repeated by an intermediary. The object of the game for the third player (B) is to help the interrogator. The best strategy for her is probably to give truthful answers. She can add such things as "I am the woman, don't listen to him!" to her answers, but it will avail nothing as the man can make similar remarks.

We now ask the question, "What will happen when a machine takes the part of A in this game?" Will the interrogator decide wrongly as often when the game is played like this as he does when the game is played between a man and a woman? These questions replace our original, "Can machines think?"

Critique of the New Problem

As well as asking "What is the answer to this new form of the question," one may ask, "Is this new question a worthy one to investigate?" This latter question we investigate without further ado, thereby cutting short an infinite regress.

The new problem has the advantage of drawing a fairly sharp line between the physical and the intellectual capacities of a man. No engineer or chemist claims to be able to produce a material which is indistinguishable from the human skin. It is possible that at some time this might be done, but even supposing this invention available we should feel there was little point in trying to make a "thinking machine" more human by dressing it up in such artificial flesh. The form in which we have set the problem reflects this fact in the condition which prevents the interrogator from seeing or touching the other competitors, or hearing their voices.

Some other advantages of the proposed criterion may be shown up by specimen questions and answers. Thus:

Q: Please write me a sonnet on the subject of the Forth Bridge.
A: Count me out on this one. I never could write poetry.
Q: Add 34957 to 70764.
A: (Pause about 30 seconds and then give as answer) 105621.
Q: Do you play chess?
A: Yes.
Q: I have K at my K1, and no other pieces. You have only K at K6 and R at R1. It is your move. What do you play?
A: (After a pause of 15 seconds) R-R8 mate.

The question and answer method seems to be suitable for introducing almost any one of the fields of human endeavor that we wish to include. We do not wish to penalize the machine for its inability to shine in beauty competitions, nor to penalize a man for losing in a race against an airplane. The conditions of our game make these disabilities irrelevant. The "witnesses" can brag, if they consider it advisable, as much as they please about their charms, strength or heroism, but the interrogator cannot demand practical demonstrations.

The game may perhaps be criticized on the ground that the odds are weighted too heavily against the machine. If the man were to try and pretend to be the machine he would clearly make a very poor showing. He would be given away at once by slowness and inaccuracy in arithmetic. May not machines carry out something which ought to be described as thinking but which is very different from what a man does? This objection is a very strong one, but at least we can say that if, nevertheless, a machine can be constructed to play the imitation game satisfactorily, we need not be troubled by this objection.

It might be urged that when playing the "imitation game" the best strategy for the machine may possibly be something other than imitation of the behavior of a man. This may be, but I think it is unlikely that there is any great effect of this kind. In any case there is no intention to investigate here the theory of the game, and it will be assumed that the best strategy is to try to provide answers that would naturally be given by a man.

The Machines Concerned in the Game

The question which we put earlier will not be quite definite until we have specified what we mean by the word "machine." It is natural that we should wish to permit every kind of engineering technique to be used in our machines. We also wish to allow the possibility that an engineer or team of engineers may construct a machine which works, but whose manner of operation cannot be satisfactorily described by its constructors because they have applied a method which is largely experimental. Finally, we wish to exclude from the machines men born in the usual manner. It is difficult to frame the definitions so as to satisfy these three conditions. One might for instance insist that the team of engineers should be all of one sex, but this would not really be satisfactory, for it is probably possible to rear a complete individual from a single cell of the skin (say) of a man. To do so would be a feat of biological technique deserving of the very highest praise, but we would not be inclined to regard it as a case of "constructing a thinking machine." This prompts us to abandon the requirement that every kind of technique should be permitted. We are the more ready to do so in view of the fact that the present interest in "thinking machines" has been aroused by a particular kind of machine, usually called an "electronic computer" or "digital computer." Following this suggestion we only permit digital computers to take part in our game. . . .

This special property of digital computers, that they can mimic any discrete machine, is described by saying that they are *universal* machines. The existence of machines with this property has the important consequence that, considerations of speed apart, it is unnecessary to design various new machines to do various computing processes. They can all be done with one digital computer, suitably programmed for each case. It will be seen that as a consequence of this all digital computers are in a sense equivalent.

Contrary Views on the Main Question

We may now consider the ground to have been cleared and we are ready to proceed to the debate on our question "Can machines think?" . . . We cannot altogether abandon the original form of the problem, for opinions will differ as to the appropriateness of the substitution and we must at least listen to what has to be said in this connection.

It will simplify matters for the reader if I explain first my own beliefs in the matter. Consider first the more accurate form of the question. I believe that in about fifty years' time it will be possible to program computers, with a storage capacity of about 10^9, to make them play the imitation game so well that an average interrogator will not have more than 70 percent chance of making the right identification after five minutes of questioning. The original question, "Can machines think?" I believe to be too meaningless to deserve discussion. Nevertheless I believe that at the end of the century the use of words and general educated opinion will have altered so much that one will be able to speak of machines thinking without expecting to be contradicted. I believe further that no useful purpose is served by concealing these beliefs. The popular view that scientists proceed inexorably from well-established fact to well-established fact, never being influenced by any unproved conjecture, is quite mistaken. Provided it is made clear which are proved facts and which are conjectures, no harm can result. Conjectures are of great importance since they suggest useful lines of research.

I now proceed to consider opinions opposed to my own.

1. *The Theological Objection.* Thinking is a function of man's immortal soul. God has given an immortal soul to every man and woman, but not to any other animal or to machines. Hence no animal or machine can think.[1]

I am unable to accept any part of this, but will attempt to reply in theological terms. I should find the argument more convincing if animals were classed with men, for there is a greater difference, to my mind, between the typical animate and the inanimate than there is between man and the other animals. The arbitrary character of the orthodox view becomes clearer if we consider how it might appear to a member of some other religious community. How do Christians regard the Moslem view that women have no souls? But let us leave this point aside and return to the main argument. It appears to me that the argument quoted above implies a serious restriction of the omnipotence of the Almighty. It is admitted that there are certain things that He cannot do such as making one equal to two, but should we not believe that He has freedom to confer a soul on an elephant if He sees fit? We might expect that He would only exercise this power in conjunction with a mutation which provided the elephant with an appropriately improved brain to minister to the needs of this soul. An argument of exactly similar form may be made for the case

---

[1] Possibly this view is heretical. St. Thomas Aquinas (*Summa Theologica*, quoted by Bertrand Russell, *A History of Western Philosophy* [New York: Simon and Schuster, 1945], p. 458) states that God cannot make a man to have no soul. But this may not be a real restriction on His powers, but only a result of the fact that men's souls are immortal, and therefore indestructible.

of machines. It may seem different because it is more difficult to "swallow." But this really only means that we think it would be less likely that He would consider the circumstances suitable for conferring a soul. The circumstances in question are discussed in the rest of this paper. In attempting to construct such machines we should not be irreverently usurping His power of creating souls, any more than we are in the procreation of children: rather we are, in either case, instruments of His will providing mansions for the souls that He creates.

However, this is mere speculation. I am not very impressed with theological arguments whatever they may be used to support. Such arguments have often been found unsatisfactory in the past. In the time of Galileo it was argued that the texts, "And the sun stood still . . . and hasted not to go down about a whole day" (Joshua x. 13) and "He laid the foundations of the earth, that it should not move at any time" (Psalm cv. 5) were an adequate refutation of the Copernican theory. With our present knowledge such an argument appears futile. When that knowledge was not available it made a quite different impression.

2. *The "Heads in the Sand" Objection.* "The consequences of machines thinking would be too dreadful. Let us hope and believe that they cannot do so."

This argument is seldom expressed quite so openly as in the form above. But it affects most of us who think about it at all. We like to believe that Man is in some subtle way superior to the rest of creation. It is best if he can be shown to be *necessarily* superior, for then there is no danger of him losing his commanding position. The popularity of the theological argument is clearly connected with this feeling. It is likely to be quite strong in intellectual people, since they value the power of thinking more highly than others, and are more inclined to base their belief in the superiority of Man on this power.

I do not think that this argument is sufficiently substantial to require refutation. Consolation would be more appropriate: perhaps this should be sought in the transmigration of souls.

3. *The Mathematical Objection.* There are a number of results of mathematical logic which can be used to show that there are limitations to the powers of discrete state machines. The best known of these results is known as Gödel's theorem, and shows that in any sufficiently powerful logical system statements can be formulated which can neither be proved nor disproved within the system, unless possibly the system itself is inconsistent. There are other, in some respects similar, results due to Church, Kleene, Rosser, and Turing. The latter result is the most convenient to consider, since it refers directly to machines, whereas the others can only be used in a comparatively indirect argument: for instance if Gödel's

theorem is to be used we need in addition to have some means of describing logical systems in terms of machines, and machines in terms of logical systems. The result in question refers to a type of machine which is essentially a digital computer with an infinite capacity. It states that there are certain things that such a machine cannot do. If it is rigged up to give answers to questions as in the imitation game, there will be some questions to which it will either give a wrong answer, or fail to give an answer at all however much time is allowed for a reply. There may, of course, be many such questions, and questions which cannot be answered by one machine may be satisfactorily answered by another. We are of course supposing for the present that the questions are of the kind to which an answer "Yes" or "No" is appropriate, rather than questions, such as "What do you think of Picasso?" The questions that we know the machines must fail on are of this type, "Consider the machine specified as follows. . . . Will this machine ever answer 'Yes' to any question?" The dots are to be replaced by a description of some machine in a standard form. . . . When the machine described bears a certain comparatively simple relation to the machine which is under interrogation, it can be shown that the answer is either wrong or not forthcoming. This is the mathematical result: it is argued that it proves a disability of machines to which the human intellect is not subject.

The short answer to this argument is that although it is established that there are limitations to the powers of any particular machine, it has only been stated, without any sort of proof, that no such limitations apply to the human intellect. But I do not think this view can be dismissed quite so lightly. Whenever one of these machines is asked the appropriate critical question, and gives a definite answer, we know that this answer must be wrong, and this gives us a certain feeling of superiority. Is this feeling illusory? It is no doubt quite genuine, but I do not think too much importance should be attached to it. We too often give wrong answers to questions ourselves to be justified in being very pleased at such evidence of fallibility on the part of the machines. Further, our superiority can only be felt on such an occasion in relation to the one machine over which we have scored our petty triumph. There would be no question of triumphing simultaneously over *all* machines. In short, then, there might be men cleverer than any given machine, but then again there might be other machines cleverer again, and so on.

Those who hold to the mathematical argument would, I think, mostly be willing to accept the imitation game as a basis for discussion. Those who believe in the two previous objections would probably not be interested in any criteria.

4. *The Argument from Consciousness.* This argument is very well ex-

pressed in Professor Jefferson's Lister Oration for 1949, from which I quote. "Not until a machine can write a sonnet or compose a concerto because of thoughts and emotions felt, and not by the chance fall of symbols, could we agree that machine equals brain—that is, not only write it but know that it had written it. No mechanism could feel (and not merely artificially signal, an easy contrivance) pleasure at its successes, grief when its valves fuse, be warmed by flattery, be made miserable by its mistakes, be charmed by sex, be angry or depressed when it cannot get what it wants."

This argument appears to be a denial of the validity of our test. According to the most extreme form of this view the only way by which one could be sure that a machine thinks is to *be* the machine and to feel oneself thinking. One could then describe these feelings to the world, but of course no one would be justified in taking any notice. Likewise according to this view the only way to know that a *man* thinks is to be that particular man. It is in fact the solipsist point of view. It may be the most logical view to hold but it makes communication of ideas difficult. A is liable to believe "A thinks but B does not" while B believes "B thinks but A does not." Instead of arguing continually over this point it is usual to have the polite convention that everyone thinks.

I am sure that Professor Jefferson does not wish to adopt the extreme and solipsist point of view. Probably he would be quite willing to accept the imitation game as a test. The game (with the player B omitted) is frequently used in practice under the name of *viva voce* to discover whether someone really understands something or has "learned it parrot fashion." Let us listen in to a part of such a *viva voce*:

INTERROGATOR: In the first line of your sonnet which reads "Shall I compare thee to a summer's day," would not "a spring day" do as well or better?
WITNESS: It wouldn't scan.
INTERROGATOR: How about "a winter's day"? That would scan all right.
WITNESS: Yes, but nobody wants to be compared to a winter's day.
INTERROGATOR: Would you say Mr. Pickwick reminded you of Christmas?
WITNESS: In a way.
INTERROGATOR: Yet Christmas is a winter's day, and I do not think Mr. Pickwick would mind the comparison.
WITNESS: I don't think you're serious. By a winter's day one means a typical winter's day, rather than a special one like Christmas.

And so on. What would Professor Jefferson say if the sonnet-writing machine was able to answer like this in the *viva voce*? I do not know whether he would regard the machine as "merely artificially signaling" these answers, but if the answers were as satisfactory and sustained as in the above passage I do not think he would describe it as "an easy contrivance." This phrase is, I think, intended to cover such devices as the inclusion in the machine of a record of someone reading a sonnet, with appropriate switching to turn it on from time to time.

In short, then, I think that most of those who support the argument from consciousness could be persuaded to abandon it rather than be forced into the solipsist position. They will then probably be willing to accept our test.

I do not wish to give the impression that I think there is no mystery about consciousness. There is, for instance, something of a paradox connected with any attempt to localize it. But I do not think these mysteries necessarily need to be solved before we can answer the question with which we are concerned in this paper.

5. *Arguments from Various Disabilities.* These arguments take the form "I grant you that you can make machines do all the things you have mentioned but you will never be able to make one to do X." Numerous features X are suggested in this connection. I offer a selection:

Be kind, resourceful, beautiful, friendly . . . have initiative, have a sense of humor, tell right from wrong, make mistakes . . . fall in love, enjoy strawberries and cream . . . make someone fall in love with it, learn from experience . . . use words properly, be the subject of its own thought . . . have as much diversity of behavior as a man, do something really new. . . .

No support is usually offered for these statements. I believe they are mostly founded on the principle of scientific induction. A man has seen thousands of machines in his lifetime. From what he sees of them he draws a number of general conclusions. They are ugly, each is designed for a very limited purpose, when required for a minutely different purpose they are useless, the variety of behavior of any one of them is very small, etc., etc. Naturally he concludes that these are necessary properties of machines in general. Many of these limitations are associated with the very small storage capacity of most machines. (I am assuming that the idea of storage capacity is extended in some way to cover machines other than discrete state machines. The exact definition does not matter as no mathematical accuracy is claimed in the present discussion.) A few years ago, when very little had been heard of digital computers, it was possible to elicit much incredulity concerning them, if one mentioned their properties without describing their construction. That was presumably due to a similar application of the principle of scientific induction. These applications of the principle are of course largely unconscious. When a burned child fears the fire and shows that he fears it by avoiding it, I should say that he was applying scientific induction. (I could of course also describe his behavior in many other ways.) The works and customs of mankind do not seem to be very suitable material to which to apply scientific induction. A very large part of space-time must be investigated if reliable results are to be obtained. Otherwise we may (as most English children do) decide that everybody speaks English, and that it is silly to learn French.

There are, however, special remarks to be made about many of the disabilities that have been mentioned. The inability to enjoy strawberries and cream may have struck the reader as frivolous. Possibly a machine might be made to enjoy this delicious dish, but any attempt to make one do so would be idiotic. What is important about this disability is that it contributes to some of the other disabilities, e.g., to the difficulty of the same kind of friendliness occurring between man and machine as between white man and white man, or between black man and black man.

The claim that "machines cannot make mistakes" seems a curious one. One is tempted to retort, "Are they any the worse for that?" But let us adopt a more sympathetic attitude, and try to see what is really meant. I think this criticism can be explained in terms of the imitation game. It is claimed that the interrogator could distinguish the machine from the man simply by setting them a number of problems in arithmetic. The machine would be unmasked because of its deadly accuracy. The reply to this is simple. The machine (programmed for playing the game) would not attempt to give the *right* answers to the arithmetic problems. It would deliberately introduce mistakes in a manner calculated to confuse the interrogator. A mechanical fault would probably show itself through an unsuitable decision as to what sort of a mistake to make in the arithmetic. Even this interpretation of the criticism is not sufficiently sympathetic. But we cannot afford the space to go into it much further. It seems to me that this criticism depends on a confusion between two kinds of mistakes. We may call them "errors of functioning" and "errors of conclusion." Errors of functioning are due to some mechanical or electrical fault which causes the machine to behave otherwise than it was designed to do. In philosophical discussions one likes to ignore the possibility of such errors; one is therefore discussing "abstract machines." These abstract machines are mathematical fictions rather than physical objects. By definition they are incapable of errors of functioning. In this sense we can truly say that "machines can never make mistakes." Errors of conclusion can only arise when some meaning is attached to the output signals from the machine. The machine might, for instance, type out mathematical equations, or sentences in English. When a false proposition is typed we say that the machine has committed an error of conclusion. There is clearly no reason at all for saying that a machine cannot make this kind of mistake. It might do nothing but type out repeatedly "$0 = 1$." To take a less perverse example, it might have some method for drawing conclusions by scientific induction. We must expect such a method to lead occasionally to erroneous results.

The claim that a machine cannot be the subject of its own thought can of course only be answered if it can be shown that the machine has *some* thought with *some* subject matter. Nevertheless, "the subject matter of a machine's operations" does seem to mean something, at least to the people who deal with it. If, for instance, the machine was trying to find a solution of the equation $x^2 - 40x - 11 = 0$, one would be tempted to describe this equation as part of the machine's subject matter at that moment. In this sort of sense a machine undoubtedly can be its own subject matter. It may be used to help in making up its own programs, or to predict the effect of alterations in its own structure. By observing the results of its own behavior it can modify its own programs so as to achieve some purpose more effectively. These are possibilities of the near future, rather than Utopian dreams.

The criticism that a machine cannot have much diversity of behavior is just a way of saying that it cannot have much storage capacity. Until fairly recently a storage capacity of even a thousand digits was very rare.

The criticisms that we are considering here are often disguised forms of the argument from consciousness. Usually if one maintains that a machine *can* do one of these things, and describes the kind of method that the machine could use, one will not make much of an impression. It is thought that the method (whatever it may be, for it must be mechanical) is really rather base. Compare the parenthesis in Jefferson's statement quoted above.

6. *Lady Lovelace's Objection.* Our most detailed information of Babbage's Analytical Engine comes from a memoir by Lady Lovelace. In it she states, "The Analytical Engine has no pretensions to *originate* anything. It can do *whatever we know how to order it* to perform" (her italics). This statement is quoted by Hartree who adds: "This does not imply that it may not be possible to construct electronic equipment which will 'think for itself,' or in which, in biological terms, one could set up a conditioned reflex, which would serve as a basis for 'learning.' Whether this is possible in principle or not is a stimulating and exciting question, suggested by some of these recent developments. But it did not seem that the machines constructed or projected at the time had this property."

I am in thorough agreement with Hartree over this. It will be noticed that he does not assert that the machines in question had not got the property, but rather that the evidence available to Lady Lovelace did not encourage her to believe that they had it. It is quite possible that the machines in question had in a sense got this property. For suppose that some discrete state machine has the property. The Analytical Engine was a universal digital computer, so that, if its storage capacity and speed were adequate, it could by suitable programing be made to mimic the machine in question. Probably this argument did not occur to the Countess or to Babbage. In any case there was no obligation on them to claim all that could be claimed.

A variant of Lady Lovelace's objection states that a machine can "never do anything really new." This may be parried for a moment with the saw, "There is nothing new under the sun." Who can be certain that "original work" that he has done was not simply the growth of the seed planted in him by teaching, or the effect of following well-known general principles? A better variant of the objection says that a machine can never "take us by surprise." This statement is a more direct challenge and can be met directly. Machines take me by surprise with great frequency. This is largely because I do not do sufficient calculation to decide what to expect them to do, or rather because, although I do a calculation, I do it in a hurried, slipshod fashion, taking risks. Perhaps I say to myself, "I suppose the voltage here ought to be the same as there; anyway let's assume it is." Naturally I am often wrong, and the result is a surprise for me, for by the time the experiment is done these assumptions have been forgotten. These admissions lay me open to lectures on the subject of my vicious ways, but do not throw any doubt on my credibility when I testify to the surprises I experience.

I do not expect this reply to silence my critic. He will probably say that such surprises are due to some creative mental act on my part, and reflect no credit on the machine. This leads us back to the argument from consciousness, and far from the idea of surprise. It is a line of argument we must consider closed, but it is perhaps worth remarking that the appreciation of something as surprising requires as much of a "creative mental act" whether the surprising event originates from a man, a book, a machine or anything else.

The view that machines cannot give rise to surprises is due, I believe, to a fallacy to which philosophers and mathematicians are particularly subject. This is the assumption that as soon as a fact is presented to a mind all consequences of that fact spring into the mind simultaneously with it. It is a very useful assumption under many circumstances, but one too easily forgets that it is false. A natural consequence of doing so is that one then assumes that there is no virtue in the mere working out of consequences from data and general principles.

7. *Argument from Continuity in the Nervous System.* The nervous system

is certainly not a discrete state machine. A small error in the information about the size of a nervous impulse impinging on a neuron may make a large difference to the size of the outgoing impulse. It may be argued that, this being so, one cannot expect to be able to mimic the behavior of the nervous system with a discrete state system.

It is true that a discrete state machine must be different from a continuous machine. But if we adhere to the conditions of the imitation game, the interrogator will not be able to take any advantage of this difference. The situation can be made clearer if we consider some other simpler continuous machine. A differential analyzer will do very well. (A differential analyzer is a certain kind of machine not of the discrete state type used for some kinds of calculation.) Some of these provide their answers in a typed form, and so are suitable for taking part in the game. It would not be possible for a digital computer to predict exactly what answers the differential analyzer would give to a problem, but it would be quite capable of giving the right sort of answer. For instance, if asked to give the value of π (actually about 3.1416) it would be reasonable to choose at random between the values 3.12, 3.13, 3.14, 3.15, 3.16 with the probabilities of 0.05, 0.15, 0.55, 0.19, 0.06 (say). Under these circumstances it would be very difficult for the interrogator to distinguish the differential analyzer from the digital computer.

8. *The Argument from Informality of Behavior.* It is not possible to produce a set of rules purporting to describe what a man should do in every conceivable set of circumstances. One might for instance have a rule that one is to stop when one sees a red traffic light, and to go if one sees a green one, but what if by some fault both appear together? One may perhaps decide that it is safest to stop. But some further difficulty may well arise from this decision later. To attempt to provide rules of conduct to cover every eventuality, even those arising from traffic lights, appears to be impossible. With all this I agree.

From this it is argued that we cannot be machines. I shall try to reproduce the argument, but I fear I shall hardly do it justice. It seems to run something like this. "If each man had a definite set of rules of conduct by which he regulated his life he would be no better than a machine. But there are no such rules, so men cannot be machines." The undistributed middle is glaring. I do not think the argument is ever put quite like this, but I believe this is the argument used nevertheless. There may however be a certain confusion between "rules of conduct" and "laws of behavior" to cloud the issue. By "rules of conduct" I mean precepts such as "Stop if you see red lights," on which one can act, and of which one can be conscious. By "laws of behavior" I mean laws of nature as applied to a man's body such as "if you pinch him he will squeak." If we substitute "laws of behavior which regulate his life" for "laws of conduct by which he regulates his life" in the argument quoted the undistributed middle is no longer insuperable. For we believe that it is not only true that being regulated by laws of behavior implies being some sort of machine (though not necessarily a discrete state machine), but that conversely being such a machine implies being regulated by such laws. However, we cannot so easily convince ourselves of the absence of complete laws of behavior as of complete rules of conduct. The only way we know of for finding such laws is scientific observation, and we certainly know of no circumstances under which we could say, "We have searched enough. There are no such laws."

We can demonstrate more forcibly that any such statement would be unjustified. For suppose we could be sure of finding such laws if they existed. Then given a discrete state machine it should certainly be possible to discover by observation sufficient about it to predict its future behavior, and this within a reasonable time, say a thousand years. But this does not seem to be the case. I have set up on the Manchester computer a small program using only 1000 units of storage, whereby the machine supplied with one sixteen-figure number replies with another within two seconds. I would defy anyone to learn from these replies sufficient about the program to be able to predict any replies to untried values.

9. *The Argument from Extrasensory Perception.* I assume that the reader is familiar with the idea of extrasensory perception, and the meaning of the four items of it, viz., telepathy, clairvoyance, precognition, and psychokinesis. These disturbing phenomena seem to deny all our usual scientific ideas. How we should like to discredit them! Unfortunately the statistical evidence, at least for telepathy, is overwhelming. It is very difficult to rearrange one's ideas so as to fit these new facts in. Once one has accepted them it does not seem a very big step to believe in ghosts and bogies. The idea that our bodies move simply according to the known laws of physics, together with some others not yet discovered but somewhat similar, would be one of the first to go.

This argument is to my mind quite a strong one. One can say in reply that many scientific theories seem to remain workable in practice, in spite of clashing with E.S.P.; that in fact one can get along very nicely if one forgets about it. This is rather cold comfort, and one fears that thinking is just the kind of phenomenon where E.S.P. may be especially relevant.

A more specific argument based on E.S.P. might run as follows: "Let us play the imitation game, using as witnesses a man who is good as a telepathic receiver, and a digital computer. The interrogator can ask such questions as 'What suit does the card in my right hand belong to?' The man by telepathy or clairvoyance gives the right answer 130 times out of 400 cards. The machine can only guess at random, and perhaps get 104 right, so the interrogator makes the right identification." There is an interesting possibility which opens here. Suppose the digital computer contains a random number generator. Then it will be natural to use this to decide what answer to give. But then the random number generator will be subject to the psychokinetic powers of the interrogator. Perhaps this psychokinesis might cause the machine to guess right more often than would be expected on a probability calculation, so that the interrogator might still be unable to make the right identification. On the other hand, he might be able to guess right without any questioning, by clairvoyance. With E.S.P. anything may happen.

If telepathy is admitted it will be necessary to tighten our test. The situation could be regarded as analogous to that which would occur if the interrogator were talking to himself and one of the competitors was listening with his ear to the wall. To put the competitors into a "telepathy-proof room" would satisfy all requirements.

Reflections

Most of our response to this remarkable and lucid article is contained in the following dialogue. However, we wish to make a short comment about Turing's apparent willingness to believe that extrasensory perception might turn out to be the ultimate difference between humans and the machines they create. If this comment is taken at face value (and not as some sort of discreet joke), one has to wonder what motivated it. Apparently Turing was convinced that the evidence for telepathy was quite strong. However, if it was strong in 1950, it is no stronger now, thirty years later—in fact, it is probably weaker. Since 1950 there have been many notorious cases of claims of psychic ability of one sort or another, often vouched for by physicists of some renown. Some of those physicists have later felt they had been made fools of and have taken back their public pro-ESP pronouncements, only to jump on some new paranormal bandwagon the next month. But it is safe to say that the majority of physicists—and certainly the majority of psychologists, who specialize in understanding the mind—doubt the existence of extrasensory perception in any form.

Turing took "cold comfort" in the idea that paranormal phenomena might be reconcilable in some way with well-established scientific theories. We differ with him. We suspect that if such phenomena as telepathy, precognition, and telekinesis turned out to exist (and turned out to have the remarkable properties typically claimed for them), the laws of physics would not be simply *amendable* to accommodate them; only a major revolution in our scientific world view could do them justice. One might look forward to such a revolution with eager excitement—but it should be tinged with sadness and perplexity. How could the science that had worked so well for so many things turn out to be so wrong? The challenge of rethinking all of science from its most basic assumptions on up would be a great intellectual adventure, but the evidence that we will need to do this has simply failed to accumulate over the years.

D.R.H.
D.C.D.

5

DOUGLAS R. HOFSTADTER

The Turing Test:
A Coffeehouse Conversation

PARTICIPANTS

Chris, a physics student; Pat, a biology student; and Sandy,
a philosophy student.

CHRIS: Sandy, I want to thank you for suggesting that I read Alan Turing's article "Computing Machinery and Intelligence." It's a wonderful piece and it certainly made me think—and think about my thinking.

SANDY: Glad to hear it. Are you still as much of a skeptic about artificial
intelligence as you used to be?

CHRIS: You've got me wrong. I'm not against artificial intelligence; I
think it's wonderful stuff—perhaps a little crazy, but why not? I
simply am convinced that you AI advocates have far underestimated
the human mind, and that there are things a computer will never,
ever be able to do. For instance, can you imagine a computer writing
a Proust novel? The richness of imagination, the complexity of the
characters . . .

SANDY: Rome wasn't built in a day!

This selection appeared previously as "Metamagical Themas: A coffeehouse conversation
on the Turing test to determine if a machine can think," in *Scientific American*, May 1981,
pp. 15–36.

CHRIS: In the article Turing comes through as an interesting person. Is he still alive?

SANDY: No, he died back in 1954, at just forty-one. He'd only be sixty-seven this year, although he is now such a legendary figure it seems strange to imagine him still alive today.

CHRIS: How did he die?

SANDY: Almost certainly suicide. He was homosexual and had to deal with a lot of harsh treatment and stupidity from the outside world. In the end it apparently got to be too much, and he killed himself.

CHRIS: That's a sad story.

SANDY: Yes, it certainly is. What saddens me is that he never got to see the amazing progress in computing machinery and theory that has taken place.

PAT: Hey, are you going to clue me in as to what this Turing article is about?

SANDY: It is really about two things. One is the question "Can a machine think?"—or rather, "Will a machine ever think?" The way Turing answers this question—he thinks the answer is "yes," by the way—is by batting down a series of objections to the idea, one after another. The other point he tries to make is that the question is not meaningful as it stands. It's too full of emotional connotations. Many people are upset by the suggestion that people are machines, or that machines might think. Turing tries to defuse the question by casting it in less emotional terms. For instance, what do you think, Pat, of the idea of "thinking machines"?

PAT: Frankly, I find the term confusing. You know what confuses me? It's those ads in the newspapers and on TV that talk about "products that think" or "intelligent ovens" or whatever. I just don't know how seriously to take them.

SANDY: I know the kind of ads you mean, and I think they confuse a lot of people. On the one hand we're given the refrain "Computers are really dumb, you have to spell everything out for them in complete detail," and on the other hand we're bombarded with advertising hype about "smart products."

CHRIS: That's certainly true. Did you know that one computer terminal manufacturer has even taken to calling its products "dumb terminals" in order to stand out from the crowd?

SANDY: That's cute, but it just plays along with the trend toward obfusca-
tion. The term "electronic brain" always comes to my mind when I'm
thinking about this. Many people swallow it completely, while others
reject it out of hand. Few have the patience to sort out the issues and
decide how much of it makes sense.

PAT: Does Turing suggest some way of resolving it, some sort of IQ test
for machines?

SANDY: That would be interesting, but no machine could yet come close
to taking an IQ test. Instead, Turing proposes a test that theoretically
could be applied to any machine to determine whether it can think
or not.

PAT: Does the test give a clear-cut yes or no answer? I'd be skeptical if
it claimed to.

SANDY: No, it doesn't. In a way, that's one of its advantages. It shows
how the borderline is quite fuzzy and how subtle the whole question
is.

PAT: So, as is usual in philosophy, it's all just a question of words.

SANDY: Maybe, but they're emotionally charged words, and so it's important, it seems to me, to explore the issues and try to map out the
meanings of the crucial words. The issues are fundamental to our
concept of ourselves, so we shouldn't just sweep them under the rug.

PAT: So tell me how Turing's test works.

SANDY: The idea is based on what he calls the Imitation Game. In this
game a man and a woman go into separate rooms and can be interro-
gated by a third party, via some sort of teletype set-up. The third
party can address questions to either room, but has no idea which
person is in which room. For the interrogator the idea is to discern
which room the woman is in. Now the woman, by her answers, tries
to aid the interrogator as much as possible. The man, however, is
doing his best to bamboozle the interrogator by responding as he
thinks a woman might. And if he succeeds in fooling the
interrogator . . .

PAT: The interrogator only gets to see written words, eh? And the sex
of the author is supposed to shine through? That game sounds like
a good challenge. I would very much like to participate in it someday.
Would the interrogator know either the man or the woman before
the test began? Would any of them know the others?

SANDY: That would probably be a bad idea. All sorts of subliminal cue-
ing might occur if the interrogator knew one or both of them. It

would be safest if all three people were totally unknown to each other.

PAT: Could you ask any questions at all, with no holds barred?

SANDY: Absolutely. That's the whole idea.

PAT: Don't you think, then, that pretty quickly it would degenerate into very sex-oriented questions? I can imagine the man, overeager to act convincing, giving away the game by answering some very blunt questions that most women would find too personal to answer, even through an anonymous computer connection.

SANDY: It sounds plausible.

CHRIS: Another possibility would be to probe for knowledge of minute aspects of traditional sex-role differences, by asking about such things as dress sizes and so on. The psychology of the Imitation Game could get pretty subtle. I suppose it would make a difference if the interrogator were a woman or a man. Don't you think that a woman could spot some telltale differences more quickly than a man could?

PAT: If so, maybe *that's* how to tell a man from a woman!

SANDY: Hmm . . . that's a new twist! In any case, I don't know if this original version of the Imitation Game has ever been seriously tried out, despite the fact that it would be relatively easy to do with modern computer terminals. I have to admit, though, that I'm not sure what it would prove, whichever way it turned out.

PAT: I was wondering about that. What would it prove if the interrogator —say, a woman—couldn't tell correctly which person was the woman? It certainly wouldn't prove that the man *was* a woman!

SANDY: Exactly! What I find funny is that although I fundamentally believe in the Turing test, I'm not sure what the point is of the Imitation Game, on which it's founded!

CHRIS: I'm not any happier with the Turing test as a test for "thinking machines" than I am with the Imitation Game as a test for femininity.

PAT: From your statements I gather that the Turing test is a kind of extension of the Imitation Game, only involving a machine and a person in separate rooms.

SANDY: That's the idea. The machine tries its hardest to convince the interrogator that it is the human being, while the human tries to make it clear that he or she is not a computer.

PAT: Except for your loaded phrase "the machine tries," this sounds very interesting. But how do you know that this test will get at the essence of thinking? Maybe it's testing for the wrong things. Maybe, just to take a random illustration, someone would feel that a machine was able to think only if it could dance so well that you couldn't tell it was a machine. Or someone else could suggest some other characteristic. What's so sacred about being able to fool people by typing at them?

SANDY: I don't see how you can say such a thing. I've heard that objection before, but frankly it baffles me. So what if the machine can't tap-dance or drop a rock on your toe? If it can discourse intelligently on any subject you want, then it has shown it can think—to me, at least! As I see it, Turing has drawn, in one clean stroke, a clear division between thinking and other aspects of being human.

PAT: Now *you're* the baffling one. If one couldn't conclude anything from a man's ability to win at the Imitation Game, how could one conclude anything from a machine's ability to win at the Turing game?

CHRIS: Good question.

SANDY: It seems to me that you could conclude *something* from a man's win in the Imitation Game. You wouldn't conclude he was a woman, but you could certainly say he had good insights into the feminine mentality (if there is such a thing). Now, if a computer could fool someone into thinking it was a person, I guess you'd have to say something similar about it—that it had good insights into what it's like to be human, into "the human condition" (whatever that is).

PAT: Maybe, but that isn't necessarily equivalent to thinking, is it? It seems to me that passing the Turing test would merely prove that some machine or other could do a very good job of *simulating* thought.

CHRIS: I couldn't agree more with Pat. We all know that fancy computer programs exist today for simulating all sorts of complex phenomena. In physics, for instance, we simulate the behavior of particles, atoms, solids, liquids, gases, galaxies, and so on. But nobody confuses any of those simulations with the real thing!

SANDY: In his book *Brainstorms,* the philosopher Daniel Dennett makes a similar point about simulated hurricanes.

CHRIS: That's a nice example too. Obviously, what goes on inside a computer when it's simulating a hurricane is not a hurricane, for the machine's memory doesn't get torn to bits by 200-mile-an-hour winds, the floor of the machine room doesn't get flooded with rain-water, and so on.

SANDY: Oh, come on—that's not a fair argument! In the first place, the programmers don't claim the simulation really *is* a hurricane. It's merely a simulation of certain aspects of a hurricane. But in the second place, you're pulling a fast one when you imply that there are no downpours or 200-mile-an-hour winds in a simulated hurricane. To us there aren't any—but if the program were incredibly detailed, it could include simulated people on the ground who would experience the wind and the rain just as we do when a hurricane hits. In their minds—or, if you prefer, in their *simulated* minds—the hurricane would not be a simulation but a genuine phenomenon complete with drenching and devastation.

CHRIS: Oh, boy—what a science-fiction scenario! Now we're talking about simulating whole populations, not just a single mind!

SANDY: Well, look—I'm simply trying to show you why your argument that a simulated McCoy isn't the real McCoy is fallacious. It depends on the tacit assumption that any old observer of the simulated phenomenon is equally able to assess what's going on. But, in fact, it may take an observer with a special vantage point to recognize what is going on. In this case, it takes special "computational glasses" to see the rain and the winds and so on.

PAT: "Computational glasses"? I don't know what you're talking about!

SANDY: I mean that to see the winds and the wetness of the hurricane, you have to be able to look at it in the proper way. You—

CHRIS: No, no, no! A simulated hurricane isn't wet! No matter how much it might seem wet to simulated people, it won't ever be *genuinely* wet! And no computer will ever get torn apart in the process of simulating winds!

SANDY: Certainly not, but you're confusing levels. The laws of physics don't get torn apart by real hurricanes either. In the case of the simulated hurricane, if you go peering at the computer's memory expecting to find broken wires and so forth, you'll be disappointed. But look at the proper level. Look into the *structures* that are coded for in the memory. You'll see that some abstract links have been broken, some values of variables radically changed, and so forth. There's your flood, your devastation—real, only a little concealed, a little hard to detect.

CHRIS: I'm sorry, I just can't buy that. You're insisting that I look for a new kind of devastation, a kind never before associated with hurri-

canes. Using this idea, you could call *anything* a hurricane as long as
its effects, seen through your special "glasses," could be called
"floods and devastation."

SANDY: Right—you've got it exactly! You recognize a hurricane by its
effects. You have no way of going in and finding some ethereal "essence of hurricane," some "hurricane soul," located right in the
middle of the eye! It's the existence of a certain kind of *pattern*—a
spiral storm with an eye and so forth that makes you say it's a hurricane. Of course there are a lot of things that you'll insist on before
you call something a hurricane.

PAT: Well, wouldn't you say that being an atmospheric phenomenon is
one vital prerequisite? How can anything inside a computer be a
storm? To me, a simulation is a simulation is a simulation!

SANDY: Then I suppose you would say that even the calculations that
computers do are simulated—that they are fake calculations. Only
people can do genuine calculations, right?

PAT: Well, computers get the right answers, so their calculations are not
exactly fake—but they're still just *patterns*. There's no understanding
going on in there. Take a cash register. Can you honestly say that you
feel it is calculating something when its gears turn on each other?
And a computer is just a fancy cash register, as I understand it.

SANDY: If you mean that a cash register doesn't feel like a schoolkid
doing arithmetic problems, I'll agree. But is that what "calculation"
means? Is that an integral part of it? If so, then contrary to what
everybody has thought till now, we'll have to write a very complicated
program to perform *genuine* calculations. Of course, this program
will sometimes get careless and make mistakes and it will sometimes
scrawl its answers illegibly, and it will occasionally doodle on its
paper. . . . It won't be more reliable than the post office clerk who
adds up your total by hand. Now, I happen to believe eventually such
a program could be written. Then we'd know something about how
post office clerks and schoolkids work.

PAT: I can't believe you could ever do that!

SANDY: Maybe, maybe not, but that's not my point. You say a cash
register can't calculate. It reminds me of another favorite passage of
mine from Dennett's *Brainstorms*—a rather ironic one, which is why
I like it. The passage goes something like this: "Cash registers can't
really calculate; they can only spin their gears. But cash registers
can't really spin their gears either; they can only follow the laws of

physics." Dennett said it originally about computers; I modified it to talk about cash registers. And you could use the same line of reasoning in talking about people: "People can't really calculate; all they can do is manipulate mental symbols. But they aren't really manipulating symbols; all they are doing is firing various neurons in various patterns. But they can't really make their neurons fire; they simply have to let the laws of physics make them fire for them." Et cetera. Don't you see how this Dennett-inspired *reductio ad absurdum* would lead you to conclude that calculation doesn't exist, hurricanes don't exist, nothing at a higher level than particles and the laws of physics exists? What do you gain by saying a computer only pushes symbols around and doesn't truly calculate?

PAT: The example may be extreme, but it makes my point that there is a vast difference between a real phenomenon and any simulation of it. This is so for hurricanes, and even more so for human thought.

SANDY: Look, I don't want to get too tangled up in this line of argument, but let me try out one more example. If you were a radio ham listening to another ham broadcasting in Morse code and you were responding in Morse code, would it sound funny to you to refer to "the person at the other end"?

PAT: No, that would sound okay, although the existence of a person at the other end would be an assumption.

SANDY: Yes, but you wouldn't be likely to go and check it out. You're prepared to recognize personhood through those rather unusual channels. You don't have to see a human body or hear a voice—all you need is a rather abstract manifestation—a code, as it were. What I'm getting at is this. To "see" the person behind the dits and dahs, you have to be willing to do some decoding, some interpretation. It's not direct perception; it's indirect. You have to peel off a layer or two, to find the reality hidden in there. You put on your "radio-ham's glasses" to "see" the person behind the buzzes. Just the same with the simulated hurricane! You don't see it darkening the machine room—you have to decode the machine's memory. You have to put on special "memory-decoding glasses." *Then* what you see is a hurricane!

PAT: Oh, ho ho! Talk about fast ones—wait a minute! In the case of the shortwave radio, there's a real person out there, somewhere in the Fiji Islands or wherever. My decoding act as I sit by my radio simply reveals that that person exists. It's like seeing a shadow and concluding there's an object out there, casting it. One doesn't confuse the shadow with the object, however! And with the hurricane there's no *real* hurricane behind the scenes, making the computer follow its patterns. No, what you have is just a shadow hurricane without any genuine hurricane. I just refuse to confuse shadows with reality.

SANDY: All right. I don't want to drive this point into the ground. I even admit it is pretty silly to say that a simulated hurricane *is* a hurricane. But I wanted to point out that it's not as silly as you might think at first blush. And when you turn to simulated thought, you've got a very different matter on your hands from simulated hurricanes.

PAT: I don't see why. A brainstorm sounds to me like a mental hurricane. But seriously, you'll have to convince me.

SANDY: Well, to do so I'll have to make a couple of extra points about hurricanes first.

PAT: Oh, no! Well, all right, all right.

SANDY: Nobody can say just exactly what a hurricane is—that is, in totally precise terms. There's an abstract pattern that many storms share, and it's for that reason that we call those storms hurricanes. But it's not possible to make a sharp distinction between hurricanes and nonhurricanes. There are tornados, cyclones, typhoons, dust-devils.... Is the Great Red Spot on Jupiter a hurricane? Are sunspots hurricanes? Could there be a hurricane in a wind tunnel? In a test tube? In your imagination you can even extend the concept of "hurricane" to include a microscopic storm on the surface of a neutron star.

CHRIS: That's not so far-fetched, you know. The concept of "earth-quake" has actually been extended to neutron stars. The astrophysicists say that the tiny changes in rate that once in a while are observed in the pulsing of a pulsar are caused by "glitches"—starquakes—that have just occurred on the neutron star's surface.

SANDY: Yes, I remember that now. The idea of a "glitch" strikes me as wonderfully eerie—a surrealistic kind of quivering on a surrealistic kind of surface.

CHRIS: Can you imagine—plate tectonics on a giant rotating sphere of pure nuclear matter?

SANDY: That's a wild thought. So starquakes and earthquakes can both be subsumed into a new, more abstract category. And that's how science constantly extends familiar concepts, taking them further and further from familiar experience and yet keeping some essence constant. The number system is the classic example—from positive numbers to negative numbers, then rationals, reals, complex numbers, and "on beyond zebra," as Dr. Seuss says.

PAT: I think I can see your point here, Sandy. We have many examples in biology of close relationships that are established in rather abstract ways. Often the decision about what family some species belongs to comes down to an abstract pattern shared at some level. When you base your system of classification on very abstract patterns, I suppose that a broad variety of phenomena can fall into "the same class," even if in many superficial ways the class members are utterly unlike each other. So perhaps I can glimpse, at least a little, how to you a simulated hurricane could, in some funny sense, *be* a hurricane.

CHRIS: Perhaps the word that's being extended is not "hurricane" but "be"!

PAT: How so?

CHRIS: If Turing can extend the verb "think," can't I extend the verb "be"? All I mean is that when simulated things are deliberately confused with the genuine article, somebody's doing a lot of philosophical wool-pulling. It's a lot more serious than just extending a few nouns such as "hurricane."

SANDY: I like your idea that "be" is being extended, but I think your slur about "wool-pulling" goes too far. Anyway, if you don't object, let me just say one more thing about simulated hurricanes and then I'll get to simulated minds. Suppose you consider a really deep simulation of a hurricane—I mean a simulation of every atom, which I admit is impossibly deep. I hope you would agree that it would then share all that abstract structure that defines the "essence of hurricanehood." So what's to hold you back from calling it a hurricane?

PAT: I thought you were backing off from that claim of equality!

SANDY: So did I, but then these examples came up, and I was forced back to my claim. But let me back off, as I said I would do, and get back to *thought*, which is the real issue here. Thought, even more than hurricanes, is an abstract structure, a way of describing some complex events that happen in a medium called a brain. But actually thought can take place in any of several billion brains. There are all these physically very different brains, and yet they all support "the same thing"—thinking. What's important, then, is the abstract *pattern*, not the medium. The same kind of swirling can happen inside any of them, so no person can claim to think more "genuinely" than any other. Now, if we come up with some new kind of medium in which *the same style* of swirling takes place, could you deny that thinking is taking place in it?

PAT: Probably not, but you have just shifted the question. The question now is, how can you determine whether "the same style" of swirling is really happening?

SANDY: The beauty of the Turing test is that it *tells* you when!

CHRIS: I don't see that at all. How would you know that the same style of activity was occurring inside a computer as inside my mind, simply because it answered questions as I do? All you're looking at is its outside.

SANDY: But how do you know that when I speak to you, anything similar to what you call "thinking" is going on inside *me*? The Turing test is a fantastic probe, something like a particle accelerator in physics. Chris, I think you'll like this analogy. Just as in physics, when you want to understand what is going on at an atomic or subatomic level, since you can't see it directly, you scatter accelerated particles off the target in question and observe their behavior. From this you infer the internal nature of the target. The Turing test extends this idea to the mind. It treats the mind as a "target" that is not directly visible but whose structure can be deduced more abstractly. By "scattering" questions off a target mind, you learn about its internal workings, just as in physics.

CHRIS: More exactly put, you can hypothesize about what kinds of internal structures might account for the behavior observed—but they may or may not in fact exist.

SANDY: Hold on, now! Are you saying that atomic nuclei are merely hypothetical entities? After all, their existence—or should I say "hypothetical existence"?—was proven—or should I say "suggested"?—by the behavior of particles scattered off of atoms.

CHRIS: Physical systems seem to me to be much simpler than the mind, and the certainty of the inferences made is correspondingly greater.

SANDY: The experiments are also correspondingly harder to perform and to interpret. In the Turing test, you could perform many highly delicate experiments in the course of an hour. I maintain that people give other people credit for being conscious simply because of their continual external monitoring of them—which is itself something like a Turing test.

PAT: That may be roughly true, but it involves more than just conversing with people through a teletype. We see that other people have bodies, we watch their faces and expressions—we see they are fellow human beings and so we think they think.

SANDY: To me, that seems a highly anthropocentric view of what thought is. Does that mean you would sooner say a mannikin in a store thinks than a wonderfully programmed computer, simply because the mannikin looks more human?

PAT: Obviously I would need more than just vague physical resemblance to the human form to be willing to attribute the power of thought to an entity. But that organic quality, the sameness of origin, undeniably lends a degree of credibility that is very important.

SANDY: Here we disagree. I find this simply too chauvinistic. I feel that the key thing is a similarity of *internal* structure—not bodily, organic, chemical structure, but organizational structure—software. Whether an entity can think seems to me a question of whether its organization can be described in a certain way, and I'm perfectly willing to believe that the Turing test detects the presence or absence of that mode of organization. I would say that your depending on my physical body as evidence that I am a thinking being is rather shallow. The way I see it, the Turing test looks far deeper than at mere external form.

PAT: Hey now—you're not giving me much credit. It's not just the shape of a body that lends weight to the idea there's real thinking going on inside—it's also, as I said, the idea of common origin. It's the idea that you and I both sprang from DNA molecules, an idea to which I attribute much depth. Put it this way: The external form of human bodies reveals that they share a deep biological history, and it's *that* depth that lends a lot of credibility to the notion that the owner of such a body can think.

SANDY: But that is all indirect evidence. Surely you want some *direct* evidence. That is what the Turing test is for. And I think it is the *only* way to test for "thinkinghood."

CHRIS: But you could be fooled by the Turing test, just as an interrogator could think a man was a woman.

SANDY: I admit, I could be fooled if I carried out the test in too quick or too shallow a way. But I would go for the deepest things I could think of.

CHRIS: I would want to see if the program could understand jokes. That would be a real test of intelligence.

SANDY: I agree that humor probably is an acid test for a supposedly intelligent program, but equally important to me—perhaps more so —would be to test its emotional responses. So I would ask it about its reactions to certain pieces of music or works of literature—especially my favorite ones.

CHRIS: What if it said, "I don't know that piece," or even "I have no interest in music"? What if it avoided all emotional references?

SANDY: That would make me suspicious. Any consistent pattern of avoiding certain issues would raise serious doubts in me as to whether I was dealing with a thinking being.

CHRIS: Why do you say that? Why not say that you're dealing with a thinking but unemotional being?

SANDY: You've hit upon a sensitive point. I simply can't believe that emotions and thought can be divorced. Put another way, I think that emotions are an automatic by-product of the ability to think. They are implied by the very nature of thought.

CHRIS: Well, what if you're wrong? What if I produced a machine that could think but not emote? Then its intelligence might go unrecognized because it failed to pass *your* kind of test.

SANDY: I'd like you to point out to me where the boundary line between emotional questions and nonemotional ones lies. You might want to ask about the meaning of a great novel. This requires understanding of human emotions! Is that thinking or merely cool calculation? You might want to ask about a subtle choice of words. For that you need an understanding of their connotations. Turing uses examples like this in his article. You might want to ask it for advice about a complex romantic situation. It would need to know a lot about human motivations and their roots. Now if it failed at this kind of task, I would not be much inclined to say that it could think. As far as I am concerned, the ability to think, the ability to feel, and consciousness are just different facets of one phenomenon, and no one of them can be present without the others.

CHRIS: Why couldn't you build a machine that could feel nothing, but that could think and make complex decisions anyway? I don't see any contradiction there.

SANDY: Well, I do. I think that when you say that, you are visualizing a metallic, rectangular machine, probably in an air-conditioned room —a hard, angular, cold object with a million colored wires inside it, a machine that sits stock still on a tiled floor, humming or buzzing or whatever, and spinning its tapes. Such a machine can play a good game of chess, which, I freely admit, involves a lot of decision making. And yet I would never call such a machine conscious.

CHRIS: How come? To mechanists, isn't a chess-playing machine rudimentarily conscious?

SANDY: Not to this mechanist. The way I see it, consciousness has got to come from a precise pattern of organization—one that we haven't yet figured out how to describe in any detailed way. But I believe we will gradually come to understand it. In my view consciousness requires a certain way of mirroring the external universe internally, and the ability to respond to that external reality on the basis of the internally represented model. And then in addition, what's really crucial for a conscious machine is that it should incorporate a well-developed and flexible self-model. And it's there that all existent programs, including the best chess-playing ones, fall down.

CHRIS: Don't chess programs look ahead and say to themselves as they're figuring out their next move, "If you move here, then I'll go there, and then if you go this way, I could go that way . . ."? Isn't that a sort of self-model?

SANDY: Not really. Or, if you want, it's an extremely limited one. It's an understanding of self only in the narrowest sense. For instance, a chess-playing program has no concept of why it is playing chess, or the fact that it is a program, or is in a computer, or has a human opponent. It has no ideas about what winning and losing are, or—

PAT: How do *you* know it has no such sense? How can you presume to say what a chess program feels or knows?

SANDY: Oh, come on! We all know that certain things don't feel anything or know anything. A thrown stone doesn't know anything about parabolas, and a whirling fan doesn't know anything about air. It's true I can't *prove* those statements, but here we are verging on questions of faith.

PAT: This reminds me of a Taoist story I read. It goes something like this. Two sages were standing on a bridge over a stream. One said to the other, "I wish I were a fish. They are so happy!" The second replied, "How do you know whether fish are happy or not? You're not a fish." The first said, "But you're not me, so how do you know whether I know how fish feel?"

SANDY: Beautiful! Talking about consciousness really does call for a certain amount of restraint. Otherwise you might as well just jump on either the solipsism bandwagon—"I am the only conscious being in the universe"—or the panpsychism bandwagon—"Everything in the universe is conscious!"

PAT: Well, how do you know? Maybe everything *is* conscious.

SANDY: If you're going to join those who claim that stones and even particles like electrons have some sort of consciousness, then I guess we part company here. That's a kind of mysticism I can't fathom. As for chess programs, I happen to know how they work, and I can tell you for sure that they aren't conscious! No way!

PAT: Why not?

SANDY: They incorporate only the barest knowledge about the goals of chess. The notion of "playing" is turned into the mechanical act of comparing a lot of numbers and choosing the biggest one over and over again. A chess program has no sense of shame about losing or pride in winning. Its self-model is very crude. It gets away with doing the least it can, just enough to play a game of chess and do nothing more. Yet, interestingly enough, we still tend to talk about the "desires" of a chess-playing computer. We say, "It wants to keep its king behind a row of pawns," or "It likes to get its rooks out early," or "It thinks I don't see that hidden fork."

PAT: Well, we do the same thing with insects. We spot a lonely ant somewhere and say, "It's trying to get back home" or "It wants to drag that dead bee back to the colony." In fact, with any animal we use terms that indicate emotions, but we don't know for sure how much the animal feels. I have no trouble talking about dogs and cats being happy or sad, having desires and beliefs and so on, but of course I don't think their sadness is as deep or complex as human sadness is.

SANDY: But you wouldn't call it "simulated sadness," would you?

PAT: No, of course not. I think it's real.

SANDY: It's hard to avoid use of such teleological or mentalistic terms. I believe they're quite justified, although they shouldn't be carried too far. They simply don't have the same richness of meaning when applied to present-day chess programs as when applied to people.

CHRIS: I still can't see that intelligence has to involve emotions. Why couldn't you imagine an intelligence that simply calculates and has no feelings?

SANDY: A couple of answers here! Number one, any intelligence has to have motivations. It's simply not the case, whatever many people may think, that machines could think any more "objectively" than people do. Machines, when they look at a scene, will have to focus and filter that scene down into some preconceived categories, just as a person does. And that means seeing some things and missing others. It means giving more weight to some things than to others. This happens on every level of processing.

PAT: What do you mean?

SANDY: Take me right now, for instance. You might think that I'm just making some intellectual points, and I wouldn't need emotions to do that. But what makes me *care* about these points? Why did I stress the word "care" so heavily? Because I'm emotionally involved in this conversation! People talk to each other out of conviction, not out of hollow, mechanical reflexes. Even the most intellectual conversation is driven by underlying passions. There's an emotional undercurrent to every conversation—it's the fact that the speakers want to be listened to, understood, and respected for what they are saying.

PAT: It sounds to me as if all you're saying is that people need to be interested in what they're saying, otherwise a conversation dies.

SANDY: Right! I wouldn't bother to talk to anyone if I weren't motivated by interest. And interest is just another name for a whole constellation of subconscious biases. When I talk, all my biases work together and what you perceive on the surface level is my style, my personality. But that style arises from an immense number of tiny priorities, biases, leanings. When you add up a million of these interacting together, you get something that amounts to a lot of *desires*. It just all adds up! And that brings me to the other point, about feelingless calculation. Sure, that exists—in a cash register, a pocket calculator. I'd say it's even true of all today's computer programs. But eventually, when you put enough feelingless calculations together in a huge coordinated organization, you'll get something that has properties on another level. You can see it—in fact, you *have* to see it—not as a bunch of little calculations, but as a system of tendencies and desires and beliefs and so on. When things get complicated enough, you're forced to change your level of description. To some extent that's already happening, which is why we use words such as "want," "think," "try," and "hope," to describe chess programs and other attempts at mechanical thought. Dennett calls that kind of level switch by the observer "adopting the intentional stance." The really interesting things in AI will only begin to happen, I'd guess, when the program *itself* adopts the intentional stance toward itself!

CHRIS: That would be a very strange sort of level-crossing feedback loop.

SANDY: It certainly would. Of course, in my opinion, it's highly premature for anyone to adopt the intentional stance, in the full force of the term, toward today's programs. At least that's my opinion.

CHRIS: For me an important related question is: To what extent is it valid to adopt the intentional stance toward beings other than humans?

PAT: I would certainly adopt the intentional stance toward mammals.

SANDY: I vote for that.

CHRIS: That's interesting! How can that be, Sandy? Surely you wouldn't claim that a dog or cat can pass the Turing test? Yet don't you think that the Turing test is the only way to test for the presence of thought? How can you have these beliefs at once?

SANDY: Hmm. . . . All right. I guess I'm forced to admit that the Turing test works only above a certain level of consciousness. There can be thinking beings that could fail the test—but on the other hand, anything that passes it, in my opinion, would be a genuinely conscious, thinking being.

PAT: How can you think of a computer as a conscious being? I apologize if this sounds like a stereotype, but when I think of conscious beings, I just can't connect that thought with machines. To me consciousness is connected with soft, warm bodies, silly though that may sound.

CHRIS: That does sound odd, coming from a biologist. Don't you deal with life in terms of chemistry and physics enough for all magic to seem to vanish?

PAT: Not really. Sometimes the chemistry and physics just increase the feeling that there's something magical going on down there! Anyway, I can't always integrate my scientific knowledge with my gut-level feelings.

CHRIS: I guess I share that trait.

PAT: So how do you deal with rigid preconceptions like mine?

SANDY: I'd try to dig down under the surface of your concept of "machines" and get at the intuitive connotations that lurk there, out of sight but deeply influencing your opinions. I think that we all have a holdover image from the Industrial Revolution that sees machines as clunky iron contraptions gawkily moving under the power of some loudly chugging engine. Possibly that's even how the computer inventor Charles Babbage viewed people! After all, he called his magnificent many-geared computer the Analytical Engine.

PAT: Well, I certainly don't think people are just fancy steam shovels or even electric can openers. There's something about people, something that—that—they've got a sort of *flame* inside them, something alive, something that flickers unpredictably, wavering, uncertain—but something *creative!*

SANDY: Great! That's just the sort of thing I wanted to hear. It's very human to think that way. Your flame image makes me think of candles, of fires, of thunderstorms with lightning dancing all over the sky in crazy patterns. But do you realize that just that kind of pattern is visible on a computer's console? The flickering lights form amazing chaotic sparkling patterns. It's such a far cry from heaps of lifeless clanking metal! It *is* flamelike, by God! Why don't you let the word "machine" conjure up images of dancing patterns of light rather than of giant steam shovels?

CHRIS: That's a beautiful image, Sandy. It changes my sense of mechanism from being matter-oriented to being pattern-oriented. It makes me try to visualize the thoughts in my mind—these thoughts right now, even—as a huge spray of tiny pulses flickering in my brain.

SANDY: That's quite a poetic self-portrait for a spray of flickers to have come up with!

CHRIS: Thank you. But still, I'm not totally convinced that a machine is all that I am. I admit, my concept of machines probably does suffer from anachronistic subconscious flavors, but I'm afraid I can't change such a deeply rooted sense in a flash.

SANDY: At least you do sound open-minded. And to tell the truth, part of me does sympathize with the way you and Pat view machines. Part of me balks at calling myself a machine. It *is* a bizarre thought that a feeling being like you or me might emerge from mere circuitry. Do I surprise you?

CHRIS: You certainly surprise *me.* So tell us—do you believe in the idea of an intelligent computer, or don't you?

SANDY: It all depends on what you mean. We have all heard the question "Can computers think?" There are several possible interpretations of this (aside from the many interpretations of the word "think").

They revolve around different meanings of the words "can" and "computer."

PAT: Back to word games again. . . .

SANDY: That's right. First of all, the question might mean "Does some present-day computer think, right now?" To this I would immediately answer with a loud "no." Then it could be taken to mean, "Could some present-day computer, if suitably programmed, potentially think?" This is more like it, but I would still answer, "Probably not." The real difficulty hinges on the word "computer." The way I see it, "computer" calls up an image of just what I described earlier: an air-conditioned room with cold rectangular metallic boxes in it. But I suspect that with increasing public familiarity with computers and continued progress in computer architecture, that vision will eventually become outmoded.

PAT: Don't you think computers, as we know them, will be around for a while?

SANDY: Sure, there will have to be computers in today's image around for a long time, but advanced computers—maybe no longer called computers—will evolve and become quite different. Probably, as in the case of living organisms, there will be many branchings in the evolutionary tree. There will be computers for business, computers for schoolkids, computers for scientific calculations, computers for systems research, computers for simulation, computers for rockets going into space, and so on. Finally, there will be computers for the study of intelligence. It's really only these last that I'm thinking of —the ones with the maximum flexibility, the ones that people are deliberately attempting to make smart. I see no reason that these will stay fixed in the traditional image. Probably they will soon acquire as standard features some rudimentary sensory systems—mostly for vision and hearing, at first. They will need to be able to move around, to explore. They will have to be physically flexible. In short, they will have to become more animal-like, more self-reliant.

CHRIS: It makes me think of the robots R2D2 and C3PO in *Star Wars*.

SANDY: As a matter of fact I don't think of anything like them when I visualize intelligent machines. They're too silly, too much the product of a film designer's imagination. Not that I have a clear vision of my own. But I think it is necessary, if people are going to try realistically to imagine an artificial intelligence, to go beyond the limited, hard-edged image of computers that comes from exposure to what we have today. The only thing that all machines will always have in common is their underlying mechanicalness. That may sound cold and inflexible, but what could be more mechanical—in a wonderful way—than the operations of the DNA and proteins and organelles in our cells?

PAT: To me what goes on inside cells has a "wet," "slippery" feel to it, and what goes on inside machines is dry and rigid. It's connected with the fact that computers don't make mistakes, that computers do only what you tell them to do. Or at least that's my image of computers.

SANDY: Funny—a minute ago your image was of a flame, and now it's of something "wet and slippery." Isn't it marvelous how contradictory we can be?

PAT: I don't need your sarcasm.

SANDY: I'm not being sarcastic—I really *do* think it is marvelous.

PAT: It's just an example of the human mind's slippery nature—mine, in this case.

SANDY: True. But your image of computers is stuck in a rut. Computers certainly can make mistakes—and I don't mean on the hardware level. Think of any present-day computer predicting the weather. It can make wrong predictions, even though its program runs flawlessly.

PAT: But that's only because you've fed it the wrong data.

SANDY: Not so. It's because weather prediction is too complex. Any such program has to make do with a limited amount of data—entirely correct data—and extrapolate from there. Sometimes it will make wrong predictions. It's no different from the farmer in the field gazing at the clouds who says, "I reckon we'll get a little snow tonight." We make models of things in our heads and use them to guess how the world will behave. We have to make do with our models, however inaccurate they may be. And if they're too inaccurate, evolution will prune us out—we'll fall over a cliff or something. And computers are the same. It's just that human designers will speed up the evolutionary process by aiming explicitly at the goal of creating intelligence, which is something nature just stumbled on.

PAT: So you think computers will make fewer mistakes as they get smarter?

SANDY: Actually, just the other way around. The smarter they get, the more they'll be in a position to tackle messy real-life domains, so they'll be more and more likely to have inaccurate models. To me, mistake making is a sign of high intelligence!

PAT: Boy—you throw me sometimes!

SANDY: I guess I'm a strange sort of advocate for machine intelligence. To some degree I straddle the fence. I think that machines won't really be intelligent in a humanlike way until they have something like that biological wetness or slipperiness to them. I don't mean literally wet—the slipperiness could be in the software. But biological-seeming or not, intelligent machines will in any case be machines. We will have designed them, built them—or grown them! We will understand how they work—at least in some sense. Possibly no one person will really understand them, but collectively we will know how they work.

PAT: It sounds like you want to have your cake and eat it too.

SANDY: You're probably right. What I'm getting at is that when artificial intelligence comes, it will be mechanical and yet at the same time organic. It will have that same astonishing flexibility that we see in life's mechanisms. And when I say "mechanisms," I *mean* "mechanisms." DNA and enzymes and so on really *are* mechanical and rigid and reliable. Wouldn't you agree, Pat?

PAT: That's true. But when they work together, a lot of unexpected things happen. There are so many complexities and rich modes of behavior that all that mechanicalness adds up to something very fluid.

SANDY: For me it's an almost unimaginable transition from the mechanical level of molecules to the living level of cells. But it's what convinces me that people are machines. That thought makes me uncomfortable in some ways, but in other ways it is an exhilarating thought.

CHRIS: If people are machines, how come it's so hard to convince them of the fact? Surely if we are machines, we ought to be able to recognize our own machinehood.

SANDY: You have to allow for emotional factors here. To be told you're a machine is, in a way, to be told that you're nothing more than your physical parts, and it brings you face to face with your own mortality. That's something nobody finds easy to face. But beyond the emotional objection, to see yourself as a machine you have to jump all the way from the bottommost mechanical level to the level where the complex lifelike activities take place. If there are many intermediate layers, they act as a shield, and the mechanical quality becomes almost invisible. I think that's how intelligent machines will seem to us—and to themselves!—when they come around.

PAT: I once heard a funny idea about what will happen when we eventually have intelligent machines. When we try to implant that intelligence into devices we'd like to control, their behavior won't be so predictable.

SANDY: They'll have a quirky little "flame" inside, maybe?

PAT: Maybe.

CHRIS: So what's so funny about that?

PAT: Well, think of military missiles. The more sophisticated their target-tracking computers get, according to this idea, the less predictably they will function. Eventually you'll have missiles that will decide they are pacifists and will turn around and go home and land quietly without blowing up. We could even have "smart bullets" that turn around in midflight because they don't want to commit suicide!

SANDY: That's a lovely thought.

CHRIS: I'm very skeptical about these ideas. Still, Sandy, I'd like to hear your predictions about when intelligent machines will come to be.

SANDY: It won't be for a long time, probably, that we'll see anything remotely resembling the level of human intelligence. It just rests on too awesomely complicated a substrate—the brain—for us to be able to duplicate it in the foreseeable future. Anyway, that's my opinion.

PAT: Do you think a program will ever pass the Turing test?

SANDY: That's a pretty hard question. I guess there are various degrees of passing such a test, when you come down to it. It's not black and white. First of all, it depends on who the interrogator is. A simpleton might be totally taken in by some programs today. But secondly, it depends on how deeply you are allowed to probe.

PAT: Then you could have a scale of Turing tests—one-minute versions, five-minute versions, hour-long versions, and so forth. Wouldn't it be interesting if some official organization sponsored a periodic competition, like the annual computer-chess championships, for programs to try to pass the Turing test?

CHRIS: The program that lasted the longest against some panel of distinguished judges would be the winner. Perhaps there could be a big prize for the first program that fools a famous judge for, say, ten minutes.

PAT: What would a program do with a prize?

CHRIS: Come now, Pat. If a program's good enough to fool the judges, don't you think it's good enough to enjoy the prize?

PAT: Sure, especially if the prize is an evening out on the town, dancing with all the interrogators!

SANDY: I'd certainly like to see something like that established. I think it could be hilarious to watch the first programs flop pathetically!

PAT: You're pretty skeptical, aren't you? Well, do you think any computer program today could pass a five-minute Turing test, given a sophisticated interrogator?

SANDY: I seriously doubt it. It's partly because no one is really working at it explicitly. However, there is one program called "Parry" which its inventors claim has already passed a rudimentary version of the Turing test. In a series of remotely conducted interviews, Parry fooled several psychiatrists who were told they were talking to either a computer or a paranoid patient. This was an improvement over an earlier version, in which psychiatrists were simply handed transcripts of short interviews and asked to determine which ones were with a genuine paranoid and which ones with a computer simulation.

PAT: You mean they didn't have the chance to ask any questions? That's a severe handicap—and it doesn't seem in the spirit of the Turing test. Imagine someone trying to tell which sex I belong to just by reading a transcript of a few remarks by me. It might be very hard! So I'm glad the procedure has been improved.

CHRIS: How do you get a computer to act like a paranoid?

SANDY: I'm not saying it *does* act like a paranoid, only that some psychiatrists, under unusual circumstances, thought so. One of the things that bothered me about this pseudo-Turing test is the way Parry works. "He"—as they call him—acts like a paranoid in that he gets abruptly defensive, veers away from undesirable topics in the conversation, and, in essence, maintains control so that no one can truly probe "him." In this way, a simulation of a paranoid is a lot easier than a simulation of a normal person.

PAT: No kidding! It reminds me of the joke about the easiest kind of human for a computer program to simulate.

CHRIS: What is that?

PAT: A catatonic patient—they just sit and do nothing at all for days on end. Even I could write a computer program to do that!

SANDY: An interesting thing about Parry is that it creates no sentences on its own—it merely selects from a huge repertoire of canned sentences the one that best responds to the input sentence.

PAT: Amazing! But that would probably be impossible on a larger scale, wouldn't it?

SANDY: Yes. The number of sentences you'd need to store to be able to respond in a normal way to all possible sentences in a conversation is astronomical, really unimaginable. And they would have to be so intricately indexed for retrieval. . . . Anybody who thinks that somehow a program could be rigged up just to pull sentences out of storage like records in a jukebox, and that this program could pass the Turing test, has not thought very hard about it. The funny part about it is that it is just this kind of unrealizable program that some enemies of artificial intelligence cite when arguing against the concept of the Turing test. Instead of a truly intelligent machine, they want you to imagine a gigantic, lumbering robot that intones canned sentences in a dull monotone. It's assumed that you could see through to its mechanical level with ease, even if it were simultaneously performing tasks that we think of as fluid, intelligent processes. Then the critics say, "You see! It would still be just a machine—a mechanical device, not intelligent at all!" I see things almost the opposite way. If I were shown a machine that can do things that I can do—I mean pass the Turing test—then, instead of feeling insulted or threatened, I'd chime in with the philosopher Raymond Smullyan and say, "How wonderful machines are!"

CHRIS: If you could ask a computer just one question in the Turing test, what would it be?

SANDY: Uhmm. . . .

PAT: How about "If you could ask a computer just one question in the Turing test, what would it be?"?

Reflections

Many people are put off by the provision in the Turing test requiring the contestants in the Imitation Game to be in another room from the judge, so only their verbal responses can be observed. As an element in a parlor game the rule makes sense, but how could a legitimate scientific proposal include a deliberate attempt to *hide facts* from the judges? By placing the candidates for intelligence in "black boxes" and leaving nothing as evidence but a restricted range of "external behavior" (in this case, verbal output by typing), the Turing test seems to settle dogmatically on some form of behaviorism, or (worse) operationalism, or (worse still) verificationism. (These three cousins are horrible monster *isms* of the recent past, reputed to have been roundly refuted by philosophers of science and interred—but what is that sickening sound? Can they be stirring in their graves? We should have driven stakes through their hearts!) Is the Turing test just a case of what John Searle calls "operationalist sleight-of-hand"?

The Turing test certainly does make a strong claim about what matters about minds. What matters, Turing proposes, is not what kind of gray matter (if any) the candidate has between its ears, and not what it looks like or smells like, but whether it can *act*—or behave, if you like— intelligently. The particular game proposed in the Turing test, the Imitation Game, is not sacred, but just a cannily chosen test of more general intelligence. The assumption Turing was prepared to make was that nothing could possibly pass the Turing test by winning the Imitation Game without being able to perform indefinitely many other clearly intelligent actions. Had he chosen checkmating the world chess champion as his litmus test of intelligence, there would have been powerful reasons for objecting; it now seems quite probable that one could make a machine that can do that *but nothing else.* Had he chosen stealing the British Crown Jewels without using force or accomplices, or solving the Arab-Israeli conflict without bloodshed, there would be few who would make the objection that intelligence was being "reduced to" behavior or "operationally defined" in terms of behavior. (Well, no doubt *some* philosopher somewhere would set about diligently constructing an elaborate but entirely outlandish scenario in which some utter dolt stumbled into possession of the British Crown Jewels, "passing" the test and thereby "refuting" it as a good general test of intelligence. The true operationalist, of course, would then have to admit that such a lucky moron was, by operationalist lights, truly intelligent since he passed the defining test—which is no doubt why true operationalists are hard to find.)

What makes Turing's chosen test better than stealing the British Crown Jewels or solving the Arab-Israeli conflict is that the latter tests are unrepeatable (if successfully passed once!), too difficult (many manifestly intelligent people would fail them utterly) and too hard to judge objectively. Like a well-composed wager, Turing's test invites trying; it seems fair, demanding but possible, and crisply objective in the judging. The Turing test reminds one of a wager in another way, too. Its motivation is to stop an interminable, sterile debate by saying "Put up or shut up!" Turing says in effect: "Instead of arguing about the ultimate nature and essence of mind or intelligence, why don't we all agree that anything that could pass this test is *surely* intelligent, and then turn to asking how something could be designed that might pass the test fair and square?" Ironically, Turing failed to shut off the debate but simply managed to get it redirected.

Is the Turing test vulnerable to criticism because of its "black box" ideology? First, as Hofstadter notes in his dialogue, we treat *each other* as black boxes, relying on our observation of apparently intelligent behavior to ground our belief in other minds. Second, the black box ideology is in any event the ideology of all scientific investigation. We learn about the DNA molecule by probing it in various ways and seeing how it behaves in response; we learn about cancer and earthquakes and inflation in the same way. "Looking inside" the black box is often useful when macroscopic objects are our concern; we do it by bouncing "opening" probes (such as a scalpel) off the object and then scattering photons off the exposed surfaces into our eyes. Just one more black box experiment. The question must be, as Hofstadter says: Which probes will be most directly relevant to the question we want to answer? If our question is about whether some entity is intelligent, we will find no more direct, telling probes than the everyday questions we often ask each other. The extent of Turing's "behaviorism" is simply to incorporate that near truism into a handy, laboratory-style experimental test.

Another problem raised but not settled in Hofstadter's dialogue concerns representation. A computer simulation of something is typically a detailed, "automated," multi-dimensional representation of that thing, but of course there's a world of difference between representation and reality, isn't there? As John Searle says, "No one would suppose that we could produce milk and sugar by running a computer simulation of the formal sequences in lactation and photosynthesis. . . ."* If we devised a program that simulated a cow on a digital computer, our simulation, being a mere representation of a cow, would not, if "milked," produce milk, but at best a representation of milk. You can't drink that, no matter how good a representation it is, and no matter how thirsty you are.

But now suppose we made a computer simulation of a mathematician, and suppose it worked well. Would we complain that what we had hoped for was *proofs,* but alas, all we got instead was mere *representations* of proofs? But representations of proofs *are* proofs, aren't they? It depends on how good the proofs represented are. When cartoonists repre-

*(See selection 22, "Minds, Brains, and Programs," p. 372)

sent scientists pondering blackboards, what they typically represent as proofs or formulae on the blackboard is pure gibberish, however "realistic" these figures appear to the layman. If the simulation of the mathematician produced phony proofs like those in the cartoons, it might still simulate *something* of theoretical interest about mathematicians—their verbal mannerisms, perhaps, or their absentmindedness. On the other hand, if the simulation were designed to produce representations of the proofs a good mathematician would produce, it would be as valuable a "colleague"—in the proof-producing department—as the mathematician. That is the difference, it seems, between abstract, formal products like proofs or songs (see the next selection "The Princess Ineffabelle") and concrete, material products like milk. On which side of this divide does the mind fall? Is mentality like milk or like a song?

If we think of the mind's product as something like *control of the body*, it seems its product is quite abstract. If we think of the mind's product as a sort of special substance or even a variety of substances—lots 'n lots of *love*, a smidgin or two of *pain*, some *ecstasy*, and a few ounces of that *desire* that all good ballplayers have in abundance—it seems its product is quite concrete.

Before leaping into debate on this issue we might pause to ask if the principle that creates the divide is all that clear-cut at the limits to which we would have to push it, were we to confront a truly detailed, superb simulation of *any* concrete object or phenomenon. Any actual, running simulation is concretely "realized" in some hardware or other, and the vehicles of representation must themselves produce some effects in the world. If the representation of an event produces just about the same effects in the world as the event itself would, to insist that it is merely a representation begins to sound willful. This idea, playfully developed in the next selection, is a recurrent theme throughout the rest of the book.

D.C.D.

6

STANISLAW LEM

The Princess Ineffabelle

"There was something . . . but I forget just what," said the King, back in front of the Cabinet That Dreamed. "But why are you, Subtillion, hopping about on one leg like that and holding the other?"

"It's—it's nothing, Your Highness . . . a touch of rhombotism . . . must be a change in the weather," stammered the crafty Thaumaturge, and then continued to tempt the King to sample yet another dream. Zipperupus thought awhile, read through the Table of Contents and chose, "The Wedding Night of Princess Ineffabelle." And he dreamt he was sitting by the fire and reading an ancient volume, quaint and curious, in which it told, with well-turned words and crimson ink on gilded parchment, of the Princess Ineffabelle, who reigned five centuries ago in the land of Dandelia, and it told of her Icicle Forest, and her Helical Tower, and the Aviary That Neighed, and the Treasury with a Hundred Eyes, but especially of her beauty and abounding virtues. And Zipperupus longed for this vision of loveliness with a great longing, and a mighty desire was kindled within him and set his soul afire, that his eyeballs blazed like beacons, and he rushed out and searched every corner of the dream for Ineffabelle, but she was nowhere to be found; indeed, only the very oldest robots had ever heard of that princess. Weary from his long peregrinations, Zipperupus came at last to the center of the royal desert, where the

Excerpt from "The Tale of the Three Story-telling Machines," from *The Cyberiad* by Stanislaw Lem, translated by Michael Kandel. Copyright © 1974 by The Seabury Press, Inc. Reprinted by permission of The Continuum Publishing Corporation.

dunes were gold-plated, and there espied a humble hut; when he approached it, he saw an individual of patriarchal appearance, in a robe as white as snow. The latter rose and spake thusly:

"Thou seekest Ineffabelle, poor wretch! And yet thou knowest full well she doth not live these five hundred years, hence how vain and unavailing is thy passion! The only thing that I can do for thee is to let thee see her—not in the flesh, forsooth, but a fair informational facsimile, a model that is digital, not physical, stochastic, not plastic, ergodic and most assuredly erotic, and all in yon Black Box, which I constructed in my spare time out of odds and ends!"

"Ah, show her to me, show her to me now!" exclaimed Zipperupus, quivering. The patriarch gave a nod, examined the ancient volume for the princess's coordinates, put her and the entire Middle Ages on punch cards, wrote up the program, threw the switch, lifted the lid of the Black Box and said:

"Behold!"

The King leaned over, looked and saw, yes, the Middle Ages simulated to a T, all digital, binary, and nonlinear, and there was the land of Dandelia, the Icicle Forest, the palace with the Helical Tower, the Aviary That Neighed, and the Treasury with a Hundred Eyes as well; and there was Ineffabelle herself, taking a slow, stochastic stroll through her simulated garden, and her circuits glowed red and gold as she picked simulated daisies and hummed a simulated song. Zipperupus, unable to restrain himself any longer, leaped upon the Black Box and in his madness tried to climb into that computerized world. The patriarch, however, quickly killed the current, hurled the King to the earth and said:

"Madman! Wouldst attempt the impossible?! For no being made of matter can ever enter a system that is naught but the flux and swirl of alphanumerical elements, discontinuous integer configurations, the abstract stuff of digits!"

"But I must, I must!!" bellowed Zipperupus, beside himself, and beat his head against the Black Box until the metal was dented. The old sage then said:

"If such is thy inalterable desire, there *is* a way I can connect thee to the Princess Ineffabelle, but first thou must part with thy present form, for I shall take thy appurtenant coordinates and make a program of thee, atom by atom, and place thy simulation in that world medievally modeled, informational and representational, and there will it remain, enduring as long as electrons course through these wires and hop from cathode to anode. But thou, standing here before me now, thou wilt be annihilated,

so that thy only existence may be in the form of given fields and poten-
tials, statistical, heuristical, and wholly digital!"

"That's hard to believe," said Zipperupus. "How will I know you've
simulated me, and not someone else?"

"Very well, we'll make a trial run," said the sage. And he took all the
King's measurements, as if for a suit of clothes, though with much greater
precision, since every atom was carefully plotted and weighed, and then
he fed the program into the Black Box and said:

"Behold!"

The King peered inside and saw himself sitting by the fire and reading in an ancient book about the Princess Ineffabelle, then rushing out
to find her, asking here and there, until in the heart of the gold-plated
desert he came upon a humble hut and a snow-white patriarch, who
greeted him with the words, "Thou seekest Ineffabelle, poor wretch!"
And so on.

"Surely now thou art convinced," said the patriarch, switching it off.
"This time I shall program thee in the Middle Ages, at the side of the
sweet Ineffabelle, that thou mayest dream with her an unending dream,
simulated, nonlinear, binary . . ."

"Yes, yes, I understand," said the King. "But still, it's only my likeness, not myself, since I am right here and not in any Box!"

"But thou wilt not be here long," replied the sage with a kindly smile,
"for I shall attend to that. . . ."

And he pulled out a hammer from under the bed, a heavy hammer,
but serviceable.

"When thou art locked in the arms of thy beloved," the patriarch told
him, "I shall see to it that there be not two of thee, one here and one
there, in the Box—employing a method that is old and primitive, yet
never fails, so if thou wilt just bend over a little . . ."

"First let me take another look at your Ineffabelle," said the King.
"Just to make sure . . ."

The sage lifted the lid of the Black Box and showed him Ineffabelle.
The King looked and looked, and finally said:

"The description in the ancient volume is greatly exaggerated. She's
not bad, of course, but nowhere near as beautiful as it says in the chroni-
cles. Well, so long, old sage. . . ."

And he turned to leave.

"Where art thou going, madman?!" cried the patriarch, clutching his
hammer, for the King was almost out the door.

"Anywhere but in the Box," said Zipperupus and hurried out, but at
that very moment the dream burst like a bubble beneath his feet, and he
found himself in the vestibule facing the bitterly disappointed Subtillion,

disappointed because the King had come so close to being locked up in the Black Box, and the Lord High Thaumaturge could have kept him there forever. . . .

Reflections

This is the first of three selections in our book by the Polish writer and philosopher Stanislaw Lem. We have used the published translations by Michael Kandel, and before commenting on Lem's ideas, we must pay tribute to Kandel for his ingenious conversions of sparkling Polish wordplay into sparkling English wordplay. All through *The Cyberiad* (from which this story was taken), this high level of translation is maintained. In reading translations like this one, we are reminded how woefully far the current programs for machine translation are from snatching jobs away from people.

Lem has had a lifelong interest in the questions we raise in this book. His intuitive and literary approach perhaps does a better job of convincing readers of his views than any hard-nosed scientific article or arcanely reasoned philosophical paper might do.

As for his story, we think it speaks for itself. We would just like to know one thing: what is the difference between a *simulated* song and a *real* song?

D.R.H.

7

TERREL MIEDANER

The Soul of Martha, a Beast

Jason Hunt thanked him, breathed a deep inward sigh of relief, and called his next witness.

Dr. Alexander Belinsky, professor of animal psychology, was a short, rotund individual of brusque and businesslike manner. His initial testimony brought to light his excellent academic credentials, qualifying him as an expert witness in his field. That done, Hunt requested the court's permission to allow a demonstration of some complexity.

There was a brief discussion before the bench as to whether this should be allowed, but as Morrison had no objection, it was permitted in spite of Feinman's reservations, and the bailiff shortly escorted a pair of graduate assistants into the room, pushing before them a cart fitted with a variety of electronic equipment.

Because the taking of court records had been historically limited to verbal transcription, demonstrations of the sort planned here had not been permitted until recent years, when specialized laws designed to speed up courtroom procedure permitted a court reporter to videotape such demonstrations for the official record. But as Feinman watched one assistant set up electronic paraphernalia, while the other left momentarily and returned leading a chimpanzee, he began to regret the onset of modernization.

The animal appeared nervous and afraid of the crowd, holding itself close to its handler as it was escorted into the courtroom. Upon perceiving Dr. Belinsky, the creature jumped into the witness box with obvious displays of affection. Under Hunt's direction, he introduced her to the court as Martha, one of twenty experimental animals he used in his latest researches, the results of which had been recently published in book form. When asked by Hunt to describe these experiments, he proceeded as follows:

"For years it was assumed that animals had not developed a human-like language facility because their brains were deficient. But in the early sixties some animal psychologists proposed that the only reason chimpanzees couldn't talk was because their primitive vocalizing mechanisms prevented them from sounding words. They proceeded to test this theory by devising simple symbolic languages which didn't involve speech. They tried colored cards, pictures, magnetic slate boards, keyboard devices, and even the international sign language, all with some degree of success.

"Although these experiments proved that symbolic speech is not restricted to man, they seemed also to show that the language capacity of the most intelligent animal was severely limited. When a clever undergraduate student subsequently devised a computer program capable of duplicating every language achievement of the cleverest chimpanzees, interest in the animal speech experiments diminished significantly.

"Nonetheless, it seemed that these animals might be limited by the constraints of the previous experiments, just as they were limited earlier by poor vocal chords. Man has a speech center within his brain, a specialized area devoted to the interpretation and creation of human language forms. Chimpanzees do communicate with each other in their natural state, and also have a specialized brain area for their natural system of chattering and yowling.

"It occurred to me that, by their use of hand motions to bypass vocal chords, the previous language experiments had also bypassed the chimpanzee's natural speech centers. I decided to try to involve this natural speech center while still bypassing the animal's primitive vocal chords, and succeeded with the equipment you see before you.

"If you look closely at the left side of Martha's head here, you will observe a circular plastic cap. This covers an electrical connector permanently imbedded in her skull. To this are attached a number of electrodes which terminate within her brain. Our electronic equipment can be connected to Martha's head so as to monitor the neural activity of her speech center and translate it into English words.

"Martha is only a seven-electrode chimp, one of our slower experimental animals. She 'speaks' by stimulating certain of the implanted electrodes, although she doesn't realize that. The pattern of electrode signals is decoded by a small computer that outputs her selected word on a voice synthesizer. This technique enabled her to develop a natural sort of feedback-response mechanism. Except for a deficient grammatical base and lack of inflection, when we connect up her transistorized vocal chords she will sound quite human.

"Don't expect too much, however, for as I mentioned, Martha is not one of our star pupils. Although her seven-electrode system can be decoded into one hundred twenty-eight distinct words, she has learned only fifty-three. Other animals have done much better. Our resident genius is a nine-electrode male with a vocabulary of four hundred seven words out of five hundred twelve possibilities. Nonetheless," he added as he reached for her connecting cable, "I believe you'll find her a pleasant conversationalist."

As Dr. Belinsky proceeded to connect her to the world of human language, the chimpanzee indicated delight and excitement. She jumped up and down and chattered as he reached for the cable handed him by one of his student assistants, then sat still while he removed the protective cap and mated the halves of the connector. As soon as they snapped together in positive lock she jumped up again, seemingly oblivious to the cable attached to her head, as she pointed to a small box the scientist held in one hand.

"For Martha," he explained, "speech is an almost ceaseless activity, for her electronic vocal chords never tire. In order to get a word in I use this control to literally shut her off.

"All right, Martha, go ahead," the psychologist said as he switched her sound on.

Immediately a small loudspeaker on the equipment cart burst into noisy life. "Hello! Hello! I Martha Martha Happy Chimp. Hello Hello—"

The beast was cut off with a soft electrical click as the courtroom sat in dumb amazement. The sight of the animal opening and closing her mouth in mimicry of the sexy female voice pouring from the speaker was rather difficult to assimilate.

Her teacher continued. "How old is Martha?"

"Three Three Martha Three—"

"Very good. Now relax, Martha, quiet down. Who am I?" he asked, pointing to himself.

"Belinsky Man Nice Belins—"

"And what are those?" he asked, his hand sweeping the packed courtroom.

"Man Man People Nice People—"

The researcher cut her off again and turned to the defense attorney, indicating that he was ready to proceed.

Hunt stood and addressed his first question. "In your opinion is this animal intelligent?"

"Within the broad definition of 'intelligence' I would say yes, she is."

"Is she intelligent in the human sense?" Hunt asked.

"I believe so, but to form such an opinion of her yourself, you would really have to treat her like a human, talk to her, play with her. To that end I brought along a box of her favorite playthings. She will devote her limited attention either to me, or whoever has custody of her treasures. I suggest you examine her yourself."

From the corner of his eye Morrison observed the judge watching him in anticipation of an objection, which he dutifully provided. "Objection, your Honor. I should at least like to hear Mr. Hunt assure us this testimony will be relevant."

"Well, Mr. Hunt?" Feinman asked.

"It is relevant, as will become clear."

"And if it is not," Feinman promised, "rest assured it will be stricken from the record. Proceed."

Hunt opened Martha's box, an oversized jewelry box painted in bright red and silver, and after looking over its contents, he reached in and retrieved a cellophane-wrapped cigar. As he held it up the chimpanzee piped, "Cigar Belinsky Bad Bad Cigar," to which she added her normal chattering and some flamboyant nose-holding for emphasis.

"What's an old cigar doing in your toy box, Martha?" Hunt asked.

"What? What? Wha—" she returned before Belinsky cut her off.

"The question is a bit complicated for her. Try simplifying it to key words and short verbs," he suggested.

Hunt did. "Does Martha eat cigar?"

This time she responded, "No Eat No Eat Cigar. Eat Food Food Smoke Cigar."

"Rather impressive, Doctor," Hunt complimented the scientist. Then he turned to Morrison. "Perhaps the prosecution would like an opportunity to examine the witness?"

Morrison hesitated before agreeing, then took the box holding the animal's playthings. With undisguised discomfort he picked out a stuffed teddy bear and asked the chimp to identify it. Immediately the beast began to jump in agitation as her artificial voice tried to keep up with her.

"Man Bad Bad No Take Bear Martha Bear Help Belinsky Help Martha Take Bear Hel—"

As soon as she was cut off, she reverted to her natural chattering, while the researcher explained her paranoia. "She detects a level of hostility in you, sir. Frankly, I sympathize with you, and assure you that many people besides yourself are uncomfortable with the notion that an animal might speak intelligibly. But she is becoming somewhat agitated. Perhaps if someone else could interview her—"

"I would like to try," Judge Feinman interjected. The participants readily agreed, and as Morrison brought the box to the bench, Martha subsided, unoffended by the prosecutor's scowl.

"Is Martha hungry?" Feinman asked, perceiving several ripe bananas and candies within the container.

"Martha Eat Now Martha Eat—"

"What would Martha like to eat?"

"Martha Eat Now—"

"Would Martha like candy?"

"Candy Candy Yes Can—"

He reached in and handed her a banana, which the animal adroitly grasped, peeled, and stuck into her mouth. Once while she was eating, Belinsky turned her on for a moment, catching part of an endless "Happy Martha" readout that appeared to startle the chimp slightly. When done, she faced the judge again, opening and closing her mouth soundlessly until her handler switched on the audio. "Good Banana Good Banana Thank You Man Candy Now Candy Now."

Pleased with his results, Feinman reached into the box and offered the requested treat. She took it, but instead of eating it immediately, Martha again pointed to Belinsky's switch box, indicating that she wanted to be heard.

"Cigar Cigar Martha Want Cigar—"

The judge found the cigar and held it out. She took it, sniffed at it a moment, then handed it back. "Nice Nice Man Eat Belinsky Cigar Thank You Thank You Man—"

The judge was both fascinated with the creature's intelligence and charmed by her childlike simplicity. The animal sensed his affection and returned it, to the delight and entertainment of the court. But Hunt did not want to prolong this, and after a few minutes of interspecies conversation, he interrupted.

"Perhaps I should proceed with the testimony, your Honor?"

"Yes, of course," the judge agreed, reluctantly handing over the animal, who had by this time joined him on the bench.

"Doctor Belinsky," Hunt continued after Martha had settled down, "could you briefly state your scientific conclusions regarding the intelligence of this animal?"

"Her mind differs from ours," the scientist said, "but only in degree. Our brains are larger and our bodies are more adaptable; consequently we are superior. But the differences between us may yet prove to be embarrassingly slight. I believe that Martha, deficient as she is, still possesses humanlike intelligence."

"Could you draw some clear dividing line between the mentality of her species and ours?"

"No. Clearly she is inferior to the normal human. Yet Martha is unquestionably superior to deficient humans at the idiot level, and a peer to most imbeciles. She has an added advantage in that she is cleaner and can care for herself and offspring, which idiots and imbeciles cannot do. I would not wish to make clear-cut distinctions between her intelligence and ours."

Hunt did not ask his next question immediately. He had, of course, planned this experiment with the researcher beforehand. To complete the testimony he was to request one more demonstration, which by its nature could not have been practiced. But he was not sure that Belinsky would go through with it as planned. In fact he was not entirely sure he himself wanted the demonstration performed. Yet, there was a job to do.

"Doctor Belinsky, does the humanlike intelligence of this creature merit corresponding humanlike treatment?"

"No. We treat all laboratory animals decently, of course, but their value lies only in their experimental potential. Martha, for example, has already outlived her usefulness and is scheduled to be destroyed shortly, for the cost of her upkeep is greater than her experimental value."

"How do you go about eliminating such an animal?" Hunt asked.

"There are a variety of quick and painless methods. I prefer an orally administered poison contained in a favorite food and given unexpectedly. Although that may seem a cruel trick, it prevents the animal from anticipating its fate. The fact of death is inevitable for all of us, but for these simple creatures at least, the fear of it need never reach them." As he spoke, Belinsky extracted a small piece of candy from his coat pocket.

"Would you demonstrate this procedure before the court?" Hunt asked.

As the scientist offered the candy to the chimpanzee, Feinman finally realized what was being done. He voiced an order to halt the deadly experiment, but too late.

The researcher had never personally destroyed one of his animals before, always leaving the task to assistants. As the unsuspecting chimpanzee placed the poisoned gift into her mouth and bit, Belinsky conceived of an experiment he had never before considered. He turned on the switch. "Candy Candy Thank You Belinsky Happy Happy Martha."

Then her voice stopped of its own accord. She stiffened, then relaxed in her master's arms, dead.

But brain death is not immediate. The final sensory discharge of some circuit within her inert body triggered a brief burst of neural pulsations decoded as "Hurt Martha Hurt Martha."

Nothing happened for another two seconds. Then randomly triggered neural discharges no longer having anything to do with the animal's lifeless body sent one last pulsating signal to the world of men.

"Why Why Why Why—"

A soft electrical click stopped the testimony.

Reflections

At the office in the morning and did business. By and by we are called to Sir W. Battens to see the strange creature that Captain Holmes hath brought with him from Guiny; it is a great baboone, but so much like a man in most things, that (though they say there is a Species of them) yet I cannot believe but that it is a monster got of a man and she-baboone. I do believe it already understands much english; and I am of the mind it might be tought to speak or make signs.

—The Diary of Samuel Pepys
August 24, 1661

The pathetic noncomprehending cry of the dying chimp evokes in us powerful sympathy—we can identify so easily with this innocent and enchanting creature. What, though, is the plausibility of this scenario? Chimp language has been a controversial area for over a decade now. While it appears that these and other primates can absorb numerous vocabulary items—up to several hundred, in fact—and even on occasion come up with ingenious compound words, it is far less well substantiated that they can absorb a grammar by which they can combine words into complex meaning-carrying propositions. It seems that chimps may simply use arbitrary juxtapositions of words rather than syntactic structures. Is this a severe limitation? In the eyes of some it is, for it puts a strict upper bound to the complexity of ideas that can be expressed thereby. Noam Chomsky and others maintain that that which is essentially human is our innate linguistic ability, a sort of "primal grammar" that all languages would share at a sufficiently deep level. Thus chimps and other primates not sharing our primal grammar would be essentially different from us.

Others have argued that the primates who—or do I mean "that"?—give the appearance of using language are doing something very different from what we do when we use language. Rather than communicating—that is, converting private ideas into the common currency of signs in patterns—they are manipulating symbols that to them have no meaning, but whose manipulation can achieve desired goals for them. To a strict behaviorist, this idea of distinguishing between external behaviors on the basis of hypothetical mental qualities such as "meaning" is absurd. And yet such an experiment was once carried out with high-school students instead of primates as the subjects. The students were given colored plastic chips of various shapes and were "conditioned" to manipulate them in certain ways in order to obtain certain rewards. Now, the sequences in which they learned to arrange the chips in order to get the desired objects could in fact be decoded into simple English requests for the objects—and yet most of the students claimed to have never thought of matters this way. They said that they detected patterns that worked and patterns that didn't work, and that was as far as it went. To them it felt like an exercise in meaningless symbol-manipulation! This astonishing result may convince many people that the chimp-language claims are all wishful thinking on the part of anthropomorphic animal lovers. But the debate is far from settled.

However, whatever the realism of our excerpt, many moral and philosophical issues are well posed. What is the difference between having a mind—intellect—and having a soul—emotionality? Can one exist without the other? The justification given for killing Martha is that she is not as "valuable" as a human being. Somehow this must be a code word for the idea that she has "less of a soul" than a human does. But is degree of intellect a true indicator of degree of soul? Do retarded or senile people have "smaller souls" than normal people? The critic James Huneker, writing of Chopin's Etude opus 25 no. 11, said, "Small-souled men, no matter how agile their fingers, should avoid it." What an incredible pronouncement! Yet it has a certain truth to it, snobbish and elitist though it might be to say so. But who will provide the soul meter?

Is the Turing test not such a meter? Can we measure the soul through language? Needless to say, some qualities of Martha's soul come through loud and clear in her utterances. She is very appealing, partly through her physical appearance (actually, how do we know this?), partly through the fact of our identifying with her, partly through her charmingly simple-minded syntax. We feel protective of her as we would of a baby or small child.

Well, all these devices and more will be exploited—even more insidiously!—in the following passage, another selection from *The Soul of Anna Klane*.

D.R.H.

8

TERREL MIEDANER

The Soul of
the Mark III Beast

"Anatol's attitude is straightforward enough," Hunt said. "He considers biological life as a complex form of machinery."

She shrugged, but not indifferently. "I admit being fascinated by the man, but I can't accept *that* philosophy."

"Think about it," Hunt suggested. "You know that according to neoevolution theory, animal bodies are formed by a completely mechanistic process. Each cell is a microscopic machine, a tiny component part integrated into a larger, more complex device."

Dirksen shook her head. "But animal and human bodies are more than machines. The reproductive act itself makes them different."

"Why," Hunt asked, "is it so wonderful that a biological machine should beget another biological machine? It requires no more creative thought for a female mammal to conceive and give birth than for an automatic mill to spew forth engine blocks."

Dirksen's eyes flashed. "Do you think the automatic mill feels anything when it gives birth?" she challenged.

"Its metal is severely stressed, and eventually the mill wears out."

"I don't think that's what I mean by 'feeling.'"

"Nor I," Hunt agreed. "But it isn't always easy to know who or what has feelings. On the farm where I was raised, we had a brood sow with an unfortunate tendency to crush most of her offspring to death—accidentally, I imagine. Then she ate her children's corpses. Would you say she had maternal feelings?"

"I'm not talking about pigs!"

"We could talk about humans in the same breath. Would you care to estimate how many newborn babies drown in toilets?"

Dirksen was too appalled to speak.

After some silence Hunt continued. "What you see in Klane as preoccupation with machinery is just a different perspective. Machines are another life form to him, a form he himself can create from plastic and metal. And he is honest enough to regard himself as a machine."

"A machine begetting machines," Dirksen quipped. "Next thing, you'll be calling him a mother!"

"No," Hunt said. "He's an engineer. And however crude an engineered machine is in comparison with the human body, it represents a higher act than simple biological reproduction, for it is at least the result of a thought process."

"I ought to know better than to argue with a lawyer," she conceded, still upset. "But I just do not relate to machines! Emotionally speaking, there is a difference between the way we treat animals and the way we treat machines that defies logical explanation. I mean, I can break a machine and it really doesn't bother me, but I cannot kill an animal."

"Have you ever tried?"

"Sort of," Dirksen recalled. "The apartment I shared at college was infested with mice, so I set a trap. But when I finally caught one, I couldn't empty the trap—the poor dead thing looked so hurt and harmless. So I buried it in the backyard, trap and all, and decided that living with mice was far more pleasant than killing them."

"Yet you do eat meat," Hunt pointed out. "So your aversion isn't so much to killing *per se* as it is to doing it yourself."

"Look," she said, irritated. "That argument misses a point about basic respect for life. We have something in common with animals. You do see that, don't you?"

"Klane has a theory that you might find interesting," Hunt persisted. "He would say that real or imagined biological kinship has nothing to do with your 'respect for life.' In actual fact, you don't like to kill simply because the animal resists death. It cries, struggles, or looks sad—it pleads with you not to destroy it. And it is your mind, by the way, not your biological body, that hears an animal's plea."

She looked at him, unconvinced.

Hunt laid some money on the table, pushed back his chair. "Come with me."

A half hour later Dirksen found herself entering Klane's house in the company of his attorney, for whose car the entrance gate had automatically moved aside, and at whose touch the keyless front door had servoed immediately open.

She followed him to the basement laboratory, where Hunt opened one of several dozen cabinets and brought out something that looked like a large aluminum beetle with small, colored indicator lamps and a few mechanical protrusions about its smooth surface. He turned it over, showing Dirksen three rubber wheels on its underside. Stenciled on the flat metal base plate were the words MARK III BEAST.

Hunt set the device on the tiled floor, simultaneously toggling a tiny switch on its underbelly. With a quiet humming sound the toy began to move in a searching pattern back and forth across the floor. It stopped momentarily, then headed for an electrical outlet near the base of one large chassis. It paused before the socket, extended a pair of prongs from an opening in its metallic body, probed and entered the energy source. Some of the lights on its body began to glow green, and a noise almost like the purring of a cat emanated from within.

Dirksen regarded the contrivance with interest. "A mechanical animal. It's cute—but what's the point of it?"

Hunt reached over to a nearby bench for a hammer and held it out to her. "I'd like you to kill it."

"What are you talking about?" Dirksen said in mild alarm. "Why should I kill . . . break that . . . that machine?" She backed away, refusing to take the weapon.

"Just as an experiment," Hunt replied. "I tried it myself some years ago at Klane's behest and found it instructive."

"What did you learn?"

"Something about the meaning of life and death."

Dirksen stood looking at Hunt suspiciously.

"The 'beast' has no defenses that can hurt you," he assured her. "Just don't crash into anything while you're chasing it." He held out the hammer.

She stepped tentatively forward, took the weapon, looked sidelong at the peculiar machine purring deeply as it sucked away at the electrical current. She walked toward it, stooped down and raised the hammer. "But . . . it's eating," she said, turning to Hunt.

He laughed. Angrily she took the hammer in both hands, raised it, and brought it down hard.

But with a shrill noise like a cry of fright the beast had pulled its mandibles from the socket and moved suddenly backwards. The hammer cracked solidly into the floor, on a section of tile that had been obscured from view by the body of the machine. The tile was pockmarked with indentations.

Dirksen looked up. Hunt was laughing. The machine had moved two meters away and stopped, eyeing her. No, she decided, it was not eyeing her. Irritated with herself, Dirksen grasped her weapon and stalked cautiously forward. The machine backed away, a pair of red lights on the front of it glowing alternately brighter and dimmer at the approximate alphawave frequency of the human brain. Dirksen lunged, swung the hammer, and missed—

Ten minutes later she returned, flushed and gasping, to Hunt. Her body hurt in several places where she had bruised it on jutting machinery, and her head ached where she had cracked it under a workbench. "It's like trying to catch a big rat! When do its stupid batteries run down anyway?"

Hunt checked his watch. "I'd guess it has another half hour, provided you keep it busy." He pointed beneath a workbench, where the beast had found another electrical outlet. "But there is an easier way to get it."

"I'll take it."

"Put the hammer down and pick it up."

"Just . . . pick it up?"

"Yes. It only recognizes danger from its own kind—in this case the steel hammer head. It's programmed to trust unarmed protoplasm."

She laid the hammer on a bench, walked slowly over to the machine. It didn't move. The purring had stopped; pale amber lights glowed softly. Dirksen reached down and touched it tentatively, felt a gentle vibration. She gingerly picked it up with both hands. Its lights changed to a clear green color, and through the comfortable warmth of its metal skin she could feel the smooth purr of motors.

"So now what do I do with the stupid thing?" she asked irritably.

"Oh, lay him on his back on the workbench. He'll be quite helpless in that position, and you can bash him at your leisure."

"I can do without the anthropomorphisms," Dirksen muttered as she followed Hunt's suggestion, determined to see this thing through.

As she inverted the machine and set it down, its lights changed back to red. Wheels spun briefly, stopped. Dirksen picked up the hammer again, quickly raised it and brought it down in a smooth arc which struck the helpless machine off-center, damaging one of its wheels and flipping it right side up again. There was a metallic scraping sound from the damaged wheel, and the beast began spinning in a fitful circle. A snap-

ping sound came from its underbelly; the machine stopped, lights glowing dolefully.

Dirksen pressed her lips together tightly, raised the hammer for a
final blow. But as she started to bring it down there came from within the
beast a sound, a soft crying wail that rose and fell like a baby whimpering.
Dirksen dropped the hammer and stepped back, her eyes on the blood-
red pool of lubricating fluid forming on the table beneath the creature.
She looked at Hunt, horrified. "It's . . . it's—"

"Just a machine," Hunt said, seriously now. "Like these, its evolutionary predecessors." His gesturing hands took in the array of machinery in the workshop around them, mute and menacing watchers. "But
unlike them it can sense its own doom and cry out for succor."

"Turn it off," she said flatly.

Hunt walked to the table, tried to move its tiny power switch.
"You've jammed it, I'm afraid." He picked up the hammer from the floor
where it had fallen. "Care to administer the death blow?"

She stepped back, shaking her head as Hunt raised the hammer.
"Couldn't you fix—" There was a brief metallic crunch. She winced,
turned her head. The wailing had stopped, and they returned upstairs in
silence.

Reflections

Jason Hunt remarks, "But it isn't always easy to know who or what has
feelings." This is the crux of the selection. At first Lee Dirksen seizes on
self-reproductive power as the essence of the living. Hunt quickly points
out to her that inanimate devices can self-assemble. And what about
microbes, even viruses, which carry within them instructions for their
own replication? Have they souls? Doubtful!

Then she turns to the idea of feeling as the key. And to drive this
point home, the author pulls out every stop in the emotional organ, in
trying to convince you that there can be mechanical, metallic feelings—
a contradiction in terms, it would surely seem. Mostly it comes as a set
of subliminal appeals to the gut level. He uses phrases like "aluminum
beetle," "soft purring," "shrill noise like a cry of fright," "eyeing her,"
"gentle vibration," "the comfortable warmth of its metal skin," "helpless
machine," "spinning in a fitful circle," "lights gleaming dolefully." This

all seems quite blatant—but how could he have gone further than his next image, that of the "blood-red pool of lubricating fluid forming on the table beneath the creature," from which (or from whom?) is emanating a "soft crying wail that rose and fell like a baby whimpering"? Now, really!

The imagery is so provocative that one is sucked in. One may feel manipulated, yet one's annoyance at that cannot overcome one's instinctive sense of pity. How hard it is for some people to drown an ant in their sink by turning on the faucet! How easy for others to feed live goldfish to their pet piranhas each day! Where should we draw the line? What is sacred and what is dispensable?

Few of us are vegetarians or even seriously consider the alternative during our lives. Is it because we feel at ease with the idea of killing cows and pigs and so on? Hardly. Few of us want to be reminded that there is a hunk of dead animal on our plate when we are served a steak. Mostly, we protect ourselves by a coy use of language and an elaborate set of conventions that allow us to maintain a double standard. The true nature of meat eating, like the true nature of sex and excretion, is only easy to refer to implicitly, hidden in euphemistic synonyms and allusions: "veal cutlets," "making love," "going to the bathroom." Somehow we sense that there is soul-killing going on in slaughterhouses, but our palates don't want to be reminded of it.

Which would you more easily destroy—a Chess Challenger VII that can play a good game of chess against you and whose red lights cheerfully flash as it "ponders" what to do next, or the cute little Teddy bear that you used to love when you were a child? Why does it tug at the heartstrings? It somehow connotes smallness, innocence, vulnerability.

We are so subject to emotional appeal yet so able to be selective in our attribution of soul. How were the Nazis able to convince themselves it was all right to kill Jews? How were Americans so willing to "waste gooks" in the Viet Nam war? It seems that emotions of one sort—patriotism—can act as a valve, controlling the other emotions that allow us to identify, to project—to see our victim as (a reflection of) ourselves.

We are all animists to some degree. Some of us attribute "personalities" to our cars, others of us see our typewriters or our toys as "alive," as possessors of "souls." It is hard to burn some things in a fire because some piece of *us* is going up in flames. Clearly the "soul" we project into these objects is an image purely in our minds. Yet if that is so, why isn't it equally so for the souls that we project into our friends and family?

We all have a storehouse of empathy that is variously hard or easy to tap into, depending on our moods and on the stimulus. Sometimes mere words or fleeting expressions hit the bull's-eye and we soften. Other times we remain callous and icy, unmovable.

In this selection, the little beast's flailing against death touches Lee Dirksen's heart and our own. We see the small beetle fighting for its life, or in the words of Dylan Thomas, raging "against the dying of the light," refusing to "go gentle into that good night." This supposed recognition of its own doom is perhaps the most convincing touch of all. It reminds us of the ill-fated animals in the ring, being randomly selected and slaughtered, trembling as they see the inexorable doom approach.

When does a body contain a soul? In this very emotional selection, we have seen "soul" emerge as a function not of any clearly defined inner state, but as a function of our own ability to project. This is, oddly enough, the most behavioristic of approaches! We ask nothing about the internal mechanisms—instead we impute it all, given the behavior. It is a strange sort of validation of the Turing test approach to "soul detection."

D.R.H.

III

From Hardware to Software

9

ALLEN WHEELIS

Spirit

We come into being as a slight thickening at the end of a long thread. Cells proliferate, become an excrescence, assume the shape of a man. The end of the thread now lies buried within, shielded, inviolate. Our task is to bear it forward, pass it on. We flourish for a moment, achieve a bit of singing and dancing, a few memories we would carve in stone, then we wither, twist out of shape. The end of the thread lies now in our children, extends back through us, unbroken, unfathomably into the past. Numberless thickenings have appeared on it, have flourished and have fallen away as we now fall away. Nothing remains but the germ-line. What changes to produce new structures as life evolves is not the momentary excrescence but the hereditary arrangements within the thread.

We are carriers of spirit. We know not how nor why nor where. On our shoulders, in our eyes, in anguished hands through unclear realm, into a future unknown, unknowable, and in continual creation, we bear its full weight. Depends it on us utterly, yet we know it not. We inch it forward with each beat of heart, give to it the work of hand, of mind. We falter, pass it on to our children, lay out our bones, fall away, are lost, forgotten. Spirit passes on, enlarged, enriched, more strange, complex.

We are being used. Should not we know in whose service? To whom, to what, give we unwitting loyalty? What is this quest? Beyond that which we have what could we want? What is spirit?

A river or a rock, writes Jacques Monod, "we know, or believe, to have been molded by the free play of physical forces to which we cannot attribute any design, any 'project' or purpose. Not, that is, if we accept the basic premise of the scientific method, to wit, that nature is *objective* and not *projective.*"

That basic premise carries a powerful appeal. For we remember a time, no more than a few generations ago, when the opposite seemed manifest, when the rock *wanted* to fall, the river to sing or to rage. Willful spirits roved the universe, used nature with whim. And we know what gains in understanding and in control have come to us from the adoption of a point of view which holds that natural objects and events are without goal or intention. The rock doesn't *want* anything, the volcano pursues no purpose, river quests not the sea, wind seeks no destination.

But there is another view. The animism of the primitive is not the only alternative to scientific objectivity. This objectivity may be valid for the time spans in which we are accustomed to reckon, yet untrue for spans of enormously greater duration. The proposition that light travels in a straight line, unaffected by adjacent masses, serves us well in surveying our farm, yet makes for error in the mapping of distant galaxies. Likewise, the proposition that nature, what is just "out there," is without purpose, serves us well as we deal with nature in days or years or lifetimes, yet may mislead us on the plains of eternity.

Spirit rises, matter falls. Spirit reaches like a flame, a leap of dancer. Out of the void it creates form like a god, *is* god. Spirit was from the start, though even that beginning may have been an ending of some earlier start. If we look back far enough we arrive at a primal mist wherein spirit is but a restlessness of atoms, a trembling of something there that will not stay in stillness and in cold.

Matter would have the universe a uniform dispersion, motionless, complete. Spirit would have an earth, a heaven and a hell, whirl and conflict, an incandescent sun to drive away the dark, to illumine good and evil, would have thought, memory, desire, would build a stairway of forms increasing in complexity, inclusiveness, to a heaven ever receding above, changing always in configuration, becoming when reached but the way to more distant heavens, the last . . . but there is no last, for spirit tends upward without end, wanders, spirals, dips, but tends ever upward, ruthlessly using lower forms to create higher forms, moving toward ever greater inwardness, consciousness, spontaneity, to an ever greater freedom.

Particles become animate. Spirit leaps aside from matter which tugs forever to pull it down, to make it still. Minute creatures writhe in warm oceans. Ever more complex become the tiny forms which bear for a moment a questing spirit. They come together, touch; spirit is beginning to create love. They touch, something passes. They die, die, die, endlessly. Who shall know the spawnings in the rivers of our past? Who shall count the waltzing grunion on the shores of ancient seas? Who shall hear the unheard poundings of that surf? Who will mourn the rabbits of the plains, the furry tides of lemmings? They die, die, die, but have touched, and something passes. Spirit leaps away, creates new bodies, endlessly, ever more complex vessels to bear spirit forward, pass it on enlarged to those who follow.

Virus becomes bacteria, becomes algae, becomes fern. Thrust of spirit cracks stone, drives up the Douglas fir. Amoeba reaches out soft blunt arms in ceaseless motion to find the world, to know it better, to bring it in, growing larger, questing further, ever more capacious of spirit. Anemone becomes squid, becomes fish; wiggling becomes swimming, becomes crawling; fish becomes slug, becomes lizard; crawling becomes walking, becomes running, becomes flying. Living things reach out to each other, spirit leaps between. Tropism becomes scent, becomes fascination, becomes lust, becomes love. Lizard to fox to monkey to man, in a look, in a word, we come together, touch, die, serve spirit without knowing, carry it forward, pass it on. Ever more winged this spirit, ever greater its leaps. We love someone far away, someone who died long ago.

*   *   *

"Man is the vessel of the Spirit," writes Erich Heller; ". . . Spirit is the voyager who, passing through the land of man, bids the human soul to follow it to the Spirit's purely spiritual destination."

Viewed closely, the path of spirit is seen to meander, is a glisten of snail's way in night forest; but from a height minor turnings merge into steadiness of course. Man has reached a ledge from which to look back. For thousands of years the view is clear, and beyond, though a haze, for thousands more, we still see quite a bit. The horizon is millions of years behind us. Beyond the vagrant turnings of our last march stretches a shining path across that vast expanse running straight. Man did not begin it nor will he end it, but makes it now, finds the passes, cuts the channels. Whose way is it we so further? Not man's; for there's our first footprint. Not life's; for there's still the path when life was not yet.

Spirit is the traveler, passes now through the realm of man. We did not create spirit, do not possess it, cannot define it, are but the bearers. We take it up from unmourned and forgotten forms, carry it through our span, will pass it on, enlarged or diminished, to those who follow. Spirit is the voyager, man is the vessel.

Spirit creates and spirit destroys. Creation without destruction is not possible; destruction without creation feeds on past creation, reduces form to matter, tends toward stillness. Spirit creates more than it destroys (though not in every season, nor even every age, hence those meanderings, those turnings back, wherein the longing of matter for stillness triumphs in destruction) and this preponderance of creation makes for that overall steadiness of course.

From primal mist of matter to spiraled galaxies and clockwork solar systems, from molten rock to an earth of air and land and water, from heaviness to lightness to life, sensation to perception, memory to consciousness—man now holds a mirror, spirit sees itself. Within the river currents turn back, eddies whirl. The river itself falters, disappears, emerges, moves on. The general course is the growth of form, increasing awareness, matter to mind to consciousness. The harmony of man and nature is to be found in continuing this journey along its ancient course toward greater freedom and awareness.

Reflections

In these poetic passages, psychiatrist Allen Wheelis portrays the eerie, disorienting view that modern science has given us of our place in the scheme of things. Many scientists, not to mention humanists, find this a very difficult view to swallow and look for some kind of spiritual essence, perhaps intangible, that would distinguish living beings, particularly humans, from the inanimate rest of the universe. How does anima come from atoms?

Wheelis's concept of "spirit" is not that sort of essence. It is a way of describing the seemingly purposeful path of evolution as if there were one guiding force behind it. If there is, it is that which Richard Dawkins in the powerful selection that follows so clearly states: survival of stable replicators. In his preface Dawkins candidly writes: "We are survival machines—robot vehicles blindly programmed to preserve the selfish molecules known to us as genes. This is a truth which still fills me with astonishment. Though I have known it for years, I never seem to get fully used to it. One of my hopes is that I may have some success in astonishing others."

D.R.H.

10

RICHARD DAWKINS

Selfish Genes
and Selfish Memes

Selfish Genes

In the beginning was simplicity. It is difficult enough explaining how even a simple universe began. I take it as agreed that it would be even harder to explain the sudden springing up, fully armed, of complex order—life, or a being capable of creating life. Darwin's theory of evolution by natural selection is satisfying because it shows us a way in which simplicity could change into complexity, how unordered atoms could group themselves into ever more complex patterns until they ended up manufacturing people. Darwin provides a solution, the only feasible one so far suggested, to the deep problem of our existence. I will try to explain the great theory in a more general way than is customary, beginning with the time before evolution itself began.

Darwin's 'survival of the fittest' is really a special case of a more general law of *survival of the stable*. The universe is populated by stable things. A stable thing is a collection of atoms which is permanent enough or common enough to deserve a name. It may be a unique collection of atoms, such as the Matterhorn, which lasts long enough to be worth naming. Or it may be a *class* of entities, such as rain drops, which come into existence at a sufficiently high rate to deserve a collective name, even if any one of them is short-lived. The things which we see around us, and which we think of as needing explanation—rocks, galaxies, ocean waves —are all, to a greater or lesser extent, stable patterns of atoms. Soap bubbles tend to be spherical because this is a stable configuration for thin films filled with gas. In a spacecraft, water is also stable in spherical globules, but on earth, where there is gravity, the stable surface for standing water is flat and horizontal. Salt crystals tend to be cubes because this is a stable way of packing sodium and chloride ions together. In the sun the simplest atoms of all, hydrogen atoms, are fusing to form helium atoms, because in the conditions which prevail there the helium configuration is more stable. Other even more complex atoms are being formed in stars all over the universe, and were formed in the "big bang" which, according to the prevailing theory, initiated the universe. This is originally where the elements on our world came from.

Sometimes when atoms meet they link up together in chemical reaction to form molecules, which may be more or less stable. Such molecules can be very large. A crystal such as a diamond can be regarded as a single molecule, a proverbially stable one in this case, but also a very simple one since its internal atomic structure is endlessly repeated. In modern living organisms there are other large molecules which are highly complex, and their complexity shows itself on several levels. The hemoglobin of our blood is a typical protein molecule. It is built up from chains of smaller molecules, amino acids, each containing a few dozen atoms arranged in a precise pattern. In the hemoglobin molecule there are 574 amino acid molecules. These are arranged in four chains, which twist around each other to form a globular three-dimensional structure of bewildering complexity. A model of a hemoglobin molecule looks rather like a dense thornbush. But unlike a real thornbush it is not a haphazard approximate pattern but a definite invariant structure, identically repeated, with not a twig nor a twist out of place, over six thousand million million million times in an average human body. The precise thornbush shape of a protein molecule such as hemoglobin is stable in the sense that two chains consisting of the same sequences of amino acids will tend, like two springs, to come to rest in exactly the same three-dimensional coiled pattern. Hemoglobin thornbushes are springing into their "preferred" shape in your body at a rate of about four hundred million million per second, and others are being destroyed at the same rate.

Hemoglobin is a modern molecule, used to illustrate the principle that atoms tend to fall into stable patterns. The point that is relevant here is that, before the coming of life on earth, some rudimentary evolution fo molecules could have occurred by ordinary processes of physics and

chemistry. There is no need to think of design or purpose or directed-
ness. If a group of atoms in the presence of energy falls into a stable
pattern it will tend to stay that way. The earliest form of natural selection
was simply a selection of stable forms and a rejection of unstable ones.
There is no mystery about this. It had to happen by definition.

From this, of course, it does not follow that you can explain the
existence of entities as complex as man by exactly the same principles on
their own. It is no good taking the right number of atoms and shaking
them together with some external energy till they happen to fall into the
right pattern, and out drops Adam! You may make a molecule consisting
of a few dozen atoms like that, but a man consists of over a thousand
million million million million atoms. To try to make a man, you would
have to work at your biochemical cocktail-shaker for a period so long that
the entire age of the universe would seem like an eye-blink, and even then
you would not succeed. This is where Darwin's theory, in its most general
form, comes to the rescue. Darwin's theory takes over from where the
story of the slow building up of molecules leaves off.

The account of the origin of life which I shall give is necessarily
speculative; by definition, nobody was around to see what happened.
There are a number of rival theories, but they all have certain features
in common. The simplified account I shall give is probably not too far
from the truth.

We do not know what chemical raw materials were abundant on
earth before the coming of life, but among the plausible possibilities are
water, carbon dioxide, methane, and ammonia: all simple compounds
known to be present on at least some of the other planets in our solar
system. Chemists have tried to imitate the chemical conditions of the
young earth. They have put these simple substances in a flask and supplied a source of energy such as ultraviolet light or electric sparks—
artificial simulation of primordial lightning. After a few weeks of this,
something interesting is usually found inside the flask: a weak brown soup
containing a large number of molecules more complex than the ones
originally put in. In particular, amino acids have been found—the building blocks of proteins, one of the two great classes of biological molecules. Before these experiments were done, naturally occurring amino
acids would have been thought of as diagnostic of the presence of life.
If they had been detected on, say, Mars, life on that planet would have
seemed a near certainty. Now, however, their existence need imply only
the presence of a few simple gases in the atmosphere and some vol-
canoes, sunlight, or thundery weather. More recently, laboratory simulations of the chemical conditions of earth before the coming of life have

yielded organic substances called purines and pyrimidines. These are building blocks of the genetic molecule, DNA itself.

Processes analogous to these must have given rise to the "primeval soup" which biologists and chemists believe constituted the seas some three to four thousand million years ago. The organic substances became locally concentrated, perhaps in drying scum round the shores, or in tiny suspended droplets. Under the further influence of energy such as ultraviolet light from the sun, they combined into larger molecules. Nowadays large organic molecules would not last long enough to be noticed: they would be quickly absorbed and broken down by bacteria or other living creatures. But bacteria and the rest of us are late-comers, and in those days large organic molecules could drift unmolested through the thickening broth.

At some point a particularly remarkable molecule was formed by accident. We will call it the *Replicator*. It may not necessarily have been the biggest or the most complex molecule around, but it had the extraordinary property of being able to create copies of itself. This may seem a very unlikely sort of accident to happen. So it was. It was exceedingly improbable. In the lifetime of a man, things which are that improbable can be treated for practical purposes as impossible. That is why you will never win a big prize on the football pools. But in our human estimates of what is probable and what is not, we are not used to dealing in hundreds of millions of years. If you filled in pools coupons every week for a hundred million years you would very likely win several jackpots.

Actually a molecule which makes copies of itself is not as difficult to imagine as it seems at first, and it only had to arise once. Think of the replicator as a mold or template. Imagine it as a large molecule consisting of a complex chain of various sorts of building block molecules. The small building blocks were abundantly available in the soup surrounding the replicator. Now suppose that each building block has an affinity for its own kind. Then whenever a building block from out in the soup lands up next to a part of the replicator for which it has an affinity, it will tend to stick there. The building blocks which attach themselves in this way will automatically be arranged in a sequence which mimics that of the replicator itself. It is easy then to think of them joining up to form a stable chain just as in the formation of the original replicator. This process could continue as a progressive stacking up, layer upon layer. This is how crystals are formed. On the other hand, the two chains might split apart, in which case we have two replicators, each of which can go on to make further copies.

A more complex possibility is that each building block has affinity not for its own kind, but reciprocally for one particular other kind. Then the replicator would act as a template not for an identical copy, but for a kind of "negative," which would in its turn remake an exact copy of the original positive. For our purposes it does not matter whether the original replication process was positive–negative or positive–positive, though it is worth remarking that the modern equivalents of the first replicator, the DNA molecules, use positive–negative replication. What does matter is that suddenly a new kind of "stability" came into the world. Previously it is probable that no particular kind of complex molecule was very abundant in the soup, because each was dependent on building blocks happening to fall by luck into a particular stable configuration. As soon as the replicator was born it must have spread its copies rapidly throughout the seas, until the smaller building block molecules became a scarce resource, and other larger molecules were formed more and more rarely.

So we seem to arrive at a large population of identical replicas. But now we must mention an important property of any copying process: it is not perfect. Mistakes will happen. I hope there are no misprints in this book, but if you look carefully you may find one or two. They will probably not seriously distort the meaning of the sentences, because they will be "first-generation" errors. But imagine the days before printing, when books such as the Gospels were copied by hand. All scribes, however careful, are bound to make a few errors, and some are not above a little willful "improvement." If they all copied from a single master original, meaning would not be greatly perverted. But let copies be made from other copies, which in their turn were made from other copies, and errors will start to become cumulative and serious. We tend to regard erratic copying as a bad thing, and in the case of human documents it is hard to think of examples where errors can be described as improvements. I suppose the scholars of the Septuagint could at least be said to have started something big when they mistranslated the Hebrew word for "young woman" into the Greek word for "virgin," coming up with the prophecy: "Behold a virgin shall conceive and bear a son. . . ." Anyway, as we shall see, erratic copying in biological replicators can in a real sense give rise to improvement, and it was essential for the progressive evolution of life that some errors were made. We do not know how accurately the original replicator molecules made their copies. Their modern descendants, the DNA molecules, are astonishingly faithful compared with the most high-fidelity human copying process, but even they occasionally make mistakes, and it is ultimately these mistakes which make evolution possible. Probably the original replicators were far more erratic, but in any case we may be sure that mistakes were made, and these mistakes were cumulative.

As mis-copyings were made and propagated, the primeval soup became filled by a population not of identical replicas, but of several varieties of replicating molecules, all "descended" from the same ancestor. Would some varieties have been more numerous than others? Almost certainly yes. Some varieties would have been inherently more stable than others. Certain molecules, once formed, would be less likely than others to break up again. These types would become relatively numerous in the soup, not only as a direct logical consequence of their "longevity," but also because they would have a long time available for making copies of themselves. Replicators of high longevity would therefore tend to become more numerous and, other things being equal, there would have been an "evolutionary trend" toward greater longevity in the population of molecules.

But other things were probably not equal, and another property of a replicator variety which must have had even more importance in spreading it through the population was speed of replication, or "fecundity." If replicator molecules of type A make copies of themselves on average once a week while those of type B make copies of themselves once an hour, it is not difficult to see that pretty soon type A molecules are going to be far outnumbered, even if they "live" much longer than B molecules. There would therefore probably have been an "evolutionary trend" towards higher "fecundity" of molecules in the soup. A third characteristic of replicator molecules which would have been positively selected is accuracy of replication. If molecules of type X and type Y last the same length of time and replicate at the same rate, but X makes a mistake on average every tenth replication while Y makes a mistake only every hundredth replication, Y will obviously become more numerous. The X contingent in the population loses not only the errant "children" themselves, but also all their descendants, actual or potential.

If you already know something about evolution, you may find something slightly paradoxical about the last point. Can we reconcile the idea that copying errors are an essential prerequisite for evolution to occur, with the statement that natural selection favors high copying-fidelity? The answer is that although evolution may seem, in some vague sense, a "good thing," especially since we are the product of it, nothing actually "wants" to evolve. Evolution is something that happens, willy-nilly, in spite of all the efforts of the replicators (and nowadays of the genes) to prevent it happening. Jacques Monod made this point very well in his Herbert Spencer lecture, after wryly remarking: "Another curious aspect of the theory of evolution is that everybody thinks he understands it!"

To return to the primeval soup, it must have become populated by stable varieties of molecule; stable in that either the individual molecules lasted a long time, or they replicated rapidly, or they replicated accurately. Evolutionary trends toward these three kinds of stability took place in the following sense: If you had sampled the soup at two different times, the later sample would have contained a higher proportion of varieties with high longevity/fecundity/copying-fidelity. This is essentially what a biologist means by evolution when he is speaking of living creatures, and the mechanism is the same—natural selection.

Should we then call the original replicator molecules "living"? Who cares? I might say to you "Darwin was the greatest man who has ever lived," and you might say, "No, Newton was," but I hope we would not prolong the argument. The point is that no conclusion of substance would be affected whichever way our argument was resolved. The facts of the lives and achievements of Newton and Darwin remain totally unchanged whether we label them "great" or not. Similarly, the story of the replicator molecules probably happened something like the way I am telling it, regardless of whether we choose to call them "living." Human suffering has been caused because too many of us cannot grasp that words are only tools for our use, and that the mere presence in the dictionary of a word like "living" does not mean it necessarily has to refer to something definite in the real world. Whether we call the early replicators living or not, they were the ancestors of life; they were our founding fathers.

The next important link in the argument, one which Darwin himself laid stress on (although he was talking about animals and plants, not molecules) is *competition*. The primeval soup was not capable of supporting an infinite number of replicator molecules. For one thing, the earth's size is finite, but other limiting factors must also have been important. In our picture of the replicator acting as a template or mold, we supposed it to be bathed in a soup rich in the small building block molecules necessary to make copies. But when the replicators became numerous, building blocks must have been used up at such a rate that they became a scarce and precious resource. Different varieties or strains of replicator must have competed for them. We have considered the factors which would have increased the numbers of favored kinds of replicator. We can now see that less-favored varieties must actually have become *less* numerous because of competition, and ultimately many of their lines must have gone extinct. There was a struggle for existence among replicator varieties. They did not know they were struggling, or worry about it; the struggle was conducted without any hard feelings, indeed without feelings of any kind. But they were struggling, in the sense that any miscopying which resulted in a new higher level of stability, or a new way of reducing the stability of rivals, was automatically preserved and multiplied. The process of improvement was cumulative. Ways of increasing stability and of decreasing rivals' stability became more elaborate and more efficient. Some of them may even have "discovered" how to break up molecules of rival varieties chemically, and to use the building blocks so released for making their own copies. These proto-carnivores simultaneously obtained food and removed competing rivals. Other replicators perhaps discovered how to protect themselves, either chemically or by building a physical wall of protein around themselves. This may have been how the first living cells appeared. Replicators began not merely to exist, but to construct for themselves containers, vehicles for their continued existence. The replicators which survived were the ones which built *survival machines* for themselves to live in. The first survival machines probably consisted of nothing more than a protective coat. But making a living got steadily harder as new rivals arose with better and more effective survival machines. Survival machines got bigger and more elaborate, and the process was cumulative and progressive.

Was there to be any end to the gradual improvement in the techniques and artifices used by the replicators to ensure their own continuance in the world? There would be plenty of time for improvement. What weird engines of self-preservation would the millennia bring forth? Four thousand million years on, what was to be the fate of the ancient replicators? They did not die out, for they are past masters of the survival arts. But do not look for them floating loose in the sea; they gave up that cavalier freedom long ago. Now they swarm in huge colonies, safe inside gigantic lumbering robots, sealed off from the outside world, communicating with it by tortuous indirect routes, manipulating it by remote control. They are in you and in me; they created us, body and mind; and their preservation is the ultimate rationale for our existence. They have come a long way, those replicators. Now they go by the name of genes, and we are their survival machines.

*   *   *

Once upon a time, natural selection consisted of the differential survival of replicators floating free in the primeval soup. Now natural selection favors replicators which are good at building survival machines, genes which are skilled in the art of controlling embryonic development. In this, the replicators are no more conscious or purposeful than they ever were. The same old processes of automatic selection between rival molecules by reason of their longevity, fecundity, and copying-fidelity, still go on as blindly and as inevitably as they did in the far-off days. Genes have no foresight. They do not plan ahead. Genes just *are,* some genes more so than others, and that is all there is to it. But the qualities which determine a gene's longevity and fecundity are not so simple as they were. Not by a long way.

In recent years—the last six hundred million or so—the replicators have achieved notable triumphs of survival-machine technology such as the muscle, the heart, and the eye (evolved several times independently). Before that, they radically altered fundamental features of their way of life as replicators, which must be understood if we are to proceed with the argument.

The first thing to grasp about a modern replicator is that it is highly gregarious. A survival machine is a vehicle containing not just one gene but many thousands. The manufacture of a body is a cooperative venture of such intricacy that it is almost impossible to disentangle the contribution of one gene from that of another. A given gene will have many different effects on quite different parts of the body. A given part of the body will be influenced by many genes, and the effect of any one gene depends on interaction with many others. Some genes act as master genes controlling the operation of a cluster of other genes. In terms of the analogy, any given page of the plans makes reference to many different parts of the building; and each page makes sense only in terms of cross-references to numerous other pages.

This intricate interdependence of genes may make you wonder why we use the word "gene" at all. Why not use a collective noun like "gene complex"? The answer is that for many purposes that is indeed quite a good idea. But if we look at things in another way, it does make sense too to think of the gene complex as being divided up into discrete replicators or genes. This arises because of the phenomenon of sex. Sexual reproduction has the effect of mixing and shuffling genes. This means that any one individual body is just a temporary vehicle for a short-lived combination of genes. The *combination* of genes that is any one individual may be short-lived, but the genes themselves are potentially very long-lived. Their paths constantly cross and recross down the generations. One gene may be regarded as a unit which survives through a large number of successive individual bodies.

*   *   *

Natural selection in its most general form means the differential survival of entities. Some entities live and others die but, in order for this selective death to have any impact on the world, an additional condition must be met. Each entity must exist in the form of lots of copies, and at least some of the entities must be *potentially* capable of surviving—in the form of copies—for a significant period of evolutionary time. Small genetic units have these properties; individuals, groups, and species do not. It was the great achievement of Gregor Mendel to show that hereditary units can be treated in practice as indivisible and independent particles. Nowadays we know that this is a little too simple. Even a cistron is occasionally divisible and any two genes on the same chromosome are not wholly independent. What I have done is to define a gene as a unit which, to a high degree, *approaches* the ideal of indivisible particulateness. A gene is not indivisible, but it is seldom divided. It is either definitely present or definitely absent in the body of any given individual. A gene travels intact from grandparent to grandchild, passing straight through the intermediate generation without being merged with other genes. If genes continually blended with each other, natural selection as we now understand it would be impossible. Incidentally, this was proved in Darwin's lifetime, and it caused Darwin great worry since in those days it was assumed that heredity was a blending process. Mendel's discovery had already been published, and it could have rescued Darwin, but alas he never knew about it: nobody seems to have read it until years after Darwin and Mendel had both died. Mendel perhaps did not realize the significance of his findings, otherwise he might have written to Darwin.

Another aspect of the particulateness of the gene is that it does not grow senile; it is no more likely to die when it is a million years old than when it is only a hundred. It leaps from body to body down the generations, manipulating body after body in its own way and for its own ends, abandoning a succession of mortal bodies before they sink in senility and death.

The genes are the immortals, or rather, they are defined as genetic entities which come close to deserving the title. We, the individual survival machines in the world, can expect to live a few more decades. But the genes in the world have an expectation of life which must be measured not in decades but in thousands and millions of years.

*   *   *

Survival machines began as passive receptacles for the genes, providing little more than walls to protect them from the chemical warfare of their rivals and the ravages of accidental molecular bombardment. In the early days they "fed" on organic molecules freely available in the soup. This easy life came to an end when the organic food in the soup, which had been slowly built up under the energetic influence of centuries of sunlight, was all used up. A major branch of survival machines, now called plants, started to use sunlight directly themselves to build up complex

molecules from simple ones, reenacting at much higher speed the synthetic processes of the original soup. Another branch, now known as
animals, "discovered" how to exploit the chemical labors of the plants,
either by eating them, or by eating other animals. Both main branches of
survival machines evolved more and more ingenious tricks to increase
their efficiency in their various ways of life, and new ways of life were
continually being opened up. Subbranches and sub-subbranches
evolved, each one excelling in a particular specialized way of making a
living: in the sea, on the ground, in the air, underground, up trees, inside
other living bodies. This subbranching has given rise to the immense
diversity of animals and plants which so impresses us today.

Both animals and plants evolved into many-celled bodies, complete
copies of all the genes being distributed to every cell. We do not know
when, why, or how many times independently, this happened. Some
people use the metaphor of a colony, describing a body as a colony of
cells. I prefer to think of the body as a colony of *genes,* and of the cell as
a convenient working unit for the chemical industries of the genes.

Colonies of genes they may be but, in their behavior, bodies have
undeniably acquired an individuality of their own. An animal moves as a
coordinated whole, as a unit. Subjectively I feel like a unit, not a colony.
This is to be expected. Selection has favored genes which cooperate with
others. In the fierce competition for scarce resources, in the relentless
struggle to eat other survival machines, and to avoid being eaten, there
must have been a premium on central coordination rather than anarchy
within the communal body. Nowadays the intricate mutual coevolution of
genes has proceeded to such an extent that the communal nature of an
individual survival machine is virtually unrecognizable. Indeed many biologists do not recognize it, and will disagree with me.

*   *   *

One of the most striking properties of survival-machine behavior is its
apparent purposiveness. By this I do not just mean that it seems to be well
calculated to help the animal's genes to survive, although of course it is.
I am talking about a closer analogy to human purposeful behavior. When
we watch an animal "searching" for food, or for a mate, or for a lost child,
we can hardly help imputing to it some of the subjective feelings we
ourselves experience when we search. These may include "desire" for
some object, a "mental picture" of the desired object, an "aim" or "end
in view." Each one of us knows, from the evidence of his own introspection, that, at least in one modern survival machine, this purposiveness has
evolved the property we call "consciousness." I am not philosopher

enough to discuss what this means, but fortunately it does not matter for our present purposes because it is easy to talk about machines which behave *as if* motivated by a purpose, and to leave open the question whether they actually are conscious. These machines are basically very simple, and the principles of unconscious purposive behavior are among the commonplaces of engineering science. The classic example is the Watt steam governor.

The fundamental principle involved is called negative feedback, of which there are various different forms. In general what happens is this. The "purpose machine," the machine or thing that behaves as if it had a conscious purpose, is equipped with some kind of measuring device which measures the discrepancy between the current state of things and the "desired" state. It is built in such a way that the larger this discrepancy is, the harder the machine works. In this way the machine will automatically tend to reduce the discrepancy—this is why it is called *negative* feedback—and it may actually come to rest if the "desired" state is reached. The Watt governor consists of a pair of balls which are whirled round by a steam engine. Each ball is on the end of a hinged arm. The faster the balls fly round, the more does centrifugal force push the arms toward a horizontal position, this tendency being resisted by gravity. The arms are connected to the steam valve feeding the engine, in such a way that the steam tends to be shut off when the arms approach the horizontal position. So, if the engine goes too fast, some of its steam will be shut off, and it will tend to slow down. If it slows down too much, more steam will automatically be fed to it by the valve, and it will speed up again. Such purpose machines often oscillate due to overshooting and time-lags, and it is part of the engineer's art to build in supplementary devices to reduce the oscillations.

The "desired" state of the Watt governor is a particular speed of rotation. Obviously it does not consciously desire it. The "goal" of a machine is simply defined as that state to which it tends to return. Modern purpose machines use extensions of basic principles like negative feedback to achieve much more complex "lifelike" behavior. Guided missiles, for example, appear to search actively for their target, and when they have it in range they seem to pursue it, taking account of its evasive twists and turns, and sometimes even "predicting" or "anticipating" them. The details of how this is done are not worth going into. They involve negative feedback of various kinds, "feed-forward," and other principles well understood by engineers and now known to be extensively involved in the working of living bodies. Nothing remotely approaching consciousness needs to be postulated, even though a layman, watching its apparently deliberate and purposeful behavior, finds it hard to believe that the missile is not under the direct control of a human pilot.

It is a common misconception that because a machine such as a guided missile was originally designed and built by conscious man, then it must be truly under the immediate control of conscious man. Another variant of this fallacy is "computers do not really play chess, because they can only do what a human operator tells them." It is important that we understand why this is fallacious, because it affects our understanding of the sense in which genes can be said to "control" behavior. Computer chess is quite a good example for making the point, so I will discuss it briefly.

Computers do not yet play chess as well as human grand masters, but they have reached the standard of a good amateur. More strictly, one should say *programs* have reached the standard of a good amateur, for a chess-playing program is not fussy which physical computer it uses to act out its skills. Now, what is the role of the human programmer? First, he is definitely not manipulating the computer from moment to moment, like a puppeteer pulling strings. That would be just cheating. He writes the program, puts it in the computer, and then the computer is on its own: there is no further human intervention, except for the opponent typing in his moves. Does the programmer perhaps anticipate all possible chess positions and provide the computer with a long list of good moves, one for each possible contingency? Most certainly not, because the number of possible positions in chess is so great that the world would come to an end before the list had been completed. For the same reason, the computer cannot possibly be programmed to try out "in its head" all possible moves, and all possible follow-ups, until it finds a winning strategy. There are more possible games of chess than there are atoms in the galaxy. So much for the trivial nonsolutions to the problem of programming a computer to play chess. It is in fact an exceedingly difficult problem, and it is hardly surprising that the best programs have still not achieved grand master status.

The programmer's actual role is rather more like that of a father teaching his son to play chess. He tells the computer the basic moves of the game, not separately for every possible starting position, but in terms of more economically expressed rules. He does not literally say in plain English "bishops move in a diagonal," but he does say something mathematically equivalent, such as, though more briefly: "New coordinates of bishop are obtained from old coordinates, by adding the same constant, though not necessarily with the same sign, to both old x coordinate and old y coordinate." Then he might program in some "advice," written in the same sort of mathematical or logical language, but amounting in human terms to hints such as "don't leave your king unguarded," or useful tricks such as "forking" with the knight. The details are intriguing, but they would take us too far afield. The important point is this: When it is actually playing, the computer is on its own and can expect no help from its master. All the programmer can do is to set the computer up *beforehand* in the best way possible, with a proper balance between lists of specific knowledge and hints about strategies and techniques.

The genes too control the behavior of their survival machines, not directly with their fingers on puppet strings, but indirectly like the computer programmer. All they can do is to set it up beforehand; then the survival machine is on its own, and the genes can only sit passively inside. Why are they so passive? Why don't they grab the reins and take charge from moment to moment? The answer is that they cannot because of time-lag problems. This is best shown by another analogy, taken from science fiction. *A for Andromeda* by Fred Hoyle and John Elliot is an exciting story, and, like all good science fiction, it has some interesting scientific points lying behind it. Strangely, the book seems to lack explicit mention of the most important of these underlying points. It is left to the reader's imagination. I hope the authors will not mind if I spell it out here.

There is a civilization two hundred light years away, in the constellation of Andromeda.* They want to spread their culture to distant worlds. How best to do it? Direct travel is out of the question. The speed of light imposes a theoretical upper limit to the rate at which you can get from one place to another in the universe, and mechanical considerations impose a much lower limit in practice. Besides, there may not be all that many worlds worth going to, and how do you know which direction to go in? Radio is a better way of communicating with the rest of the universe, since, if you have enough power to broadcast your signals in all directions rather than beam them in one direction, you can reach a very large number of worlds (the number increasing as the square of the distance the signal travels). Radio waves travel at the speed of light, which means the signal takes two hundred years to reach Earth from Andromeda. The trouble with this sort of distance is that you can never hold a conversation. Even if you discount the fact that each successive message from Earth would be transmitted by people separated from each other by twelve generations or so, it would be just plain wasteful to attempt to converse over such distances.

This problem will soon arise in earnest for us: it takes about four minutes for radio waves to travel between Earth and Mars. There can be no doubt that spacemen will have to get out of the habit of conversing

---

*Not to be confused with the Andromeda galaxy, which is two million light years away.
—Eds.

in short alternating sentences, and will have to use long soliloquies or monologues, more like letters than conversations. As another example, Roger Payne has pointed out that the acoustics of the sea have certain peculiar properties, which mean that the exceedingly loud "song" of the humpback whale could theoretically be heard all the way round the world, provided the whales swim at a certain depth. It is not known whether they actually do communicate with each other over very great distances, but if they do they must be in much the same predicament as an astronaut on Mars. The speed of sound in water is such that it would take nearly two hours for the song to travel across the Atlantic Ocean and for a reply to return. I suggest this as an explanation for the fact that the whales deliver a continuous soliloquy, without repeating themselves, for a full eight minutes. They then go back to the beginning of the song and repeat it all over again, many times over, each complete cycle lasting about eight minutes.

The Andromedans of the story did the same thing. Since there was no point in waiting for a reply, they assembled everything they wanted to say into one huge unbroken message, and then they broadcast it out into space, over and over again, with a cycle time of several months. Their message was very different from that of the whales, however. It consisted of coded instructions for the building and programming of a giant computer. Of course the instructions were in no human language, but almost any code can be broken by a skilled cryptographer, especially if the designers of the code intended it to be easily broken. Picked up by the Jodrell Bank radio telescope, the message was eventually decoded, the computer built, and the program run. The results were nearly disastrous for mankind, for the intentions of the Andromedans were not universally altruistic, and the computer was well on the way to dictatorship over the world before the hero eventually finished it off with an axe.

From our point of view, the interesting question is in what sense the Andromedans could be said to be manipulating events on Earth. They had no direct control over what the computer did from moment to moment; indeed they had no possible way of even knowing the computer had been built, since the information would have taken two hundred years to get back to them. The decisions and actions of the computer were entirely its own. It could not even refer back to its masters for general policy instructions. All its instructions had to be built-in in advance, because of the inviolable two-hundred-year barrier. In principle, it must have been programmed very much like a chess-playing computer, but with greater flexibility and capacity for absorbing local information. This was because the program had to be designed to work not just on earth, but on any world possessing an advanced technology, any of a set of worlds whose detailed conditions the Andromedans had no way of knowing.

Just as the Andromedans had to have a computer on earth to take day-to-day decisions for them, our genes have to build a brain. But the genes are not only the Andromedans who sent the coded instructions; they are also the instructions themselves. The reason why they cannot manipulate our puppet strings directly is the same: time-lags. Genes work by controlling protein synthesis. This is a powerful way of manipulating the world, but it is slow. It takes months of patiently pulling protein strings to build an embryo. The whole point about behavior, on the other hand, is that it is fast. It works on a time scale not of months but of seconds and fractions of seconds. Something happens in the world, an owl flashes overhead, a rustle in the long grass betrays prey, and in milliseconds nervous systems crackle into action, muscles leap, and someone's life is saved—or lost. Genes don't have reaction times like that. Like the Andromedans, the genes can do only their best *in advance* by building a fast executive computer for themselves, and programming it in advance with rules and "advice" to cope with as many eventualities as they can "anticipate." But life, like the game of chess, offers too many different possible eventualities for all of them to be anticipated. Like the chess programmer, the genes have to "instruct" their survival machines not in specifics, but in the general strategies and tricks of the living trade.

As J. Z. Young has pointed out, the genes have to perform a task analogous to prediction. When an embryo survival machine is being built, the dangers and problems of its life lie in the future. Who can say what carnivores crouch waiting for it behind what bushes, or what fleet-footed prey will dart and zigzag across its path? No human prophet, nor any gene. But some general predictions can be made. Polar bear genes can safely predict that the future of their unborn survival machine is going to be a cold one. They do not think of it as a prophecy, they do not think at all: they just build in a thick coat of hair, because that is what they have always done before in previous bodies, and that is why they still exist in the gene pool. They also predict that the ground is going to be snowy, and their prediction takes the form of making the coat of hair white and therefore camouflaged. If the climate of the Arctic changed so rapidly that the baby bear found itself born into a tropical desert, the predictions of the genes would be wrong, and they would pay the penalty. The young bear would die, and they inside it.

*   *   *

One of the most interesting methods of predicting the future is simulation. If a general wishes to know whether a particular military plan will be better than alternatives, he has a problem in prediction. There are unknown quantities in the weather, in the morale of his own troops, and in the possible countermeasures of the enemy. One way of discovering whether it is a good plan is to try it and see, but it is undesirable to use this test for all the tentative plans dreamed up, if only because the supply of young men prepared to die "for their country" is exhaustible and the supply of possible plans is very large. It is better to try the various plans out in dummy runs rather than in deadly earnest. This may take the form of full-scale exercises with "Northland" fighting "Southland" using blank ammunition, but even this is expensive in time and materials. Less wastefully, war games may be played, with tin soldiers and little toy tanks being shuffled around a large map.

Recently, computers have taken over large parts of the simulation function, not only in military strategy, but in all fields where prediction of the future is necessary, fields like economics, ecology, sociology, and many others. The technique works like this. A model of some aspect of the world is set up in the computer. This does not mean that if you unscrewed the lid you would see a little miniature dummy inside with the same shape as the object simulated. In the chess-playing computer there is no "mental picture" inside the memory banks recognizable as a chess board with knights and pawns sitting on it. The chess board and its current position would be represented by lists of electronically coded numbers. To us a map is a miniature scale model of a part of the world, compressed into two dimensions. In a computer, a map would more probably be represented as a list of towns and other spots, each with two numbers—its latitude and longitude. But it does not matter how the computer actually holds its model of the world in its head, provided that it holds it in a form in which it can operate on it, manipulate it, do experiments with it, and report back to the human operators in terms which they can understand. Through the technique of simulation, model battles can be won or lost, simulated airliners fly or crash, economic policies lead to prosperity or to ruin. In each case the whole process goes on inside the computer in a tiny fraction of the time it would take in real life. Of course there are good models of the world and bad ones, and even the good ones are only approximations. No amount of simulation can predict exactly what will happen in reality, but a good simulation is enormously preferable to blind trial and error. Simulation could be called vicarious trial and error, a term unfortunately preempted long ago by rat psychologists.

If simulation is such a good idea, we might expect that survival machines would have discovered it first. After all, they invented many of the other techniques of human engineering long before we came on the scene: the focusing lens and the parabolic reflector, frequency analysis of sound waves, servo-control, sonar, buffer storage of incoming information, and countless others with long names, whose details don't matter. What about simulation? Well, when you yourself have a difficult decision to make involving unknown quantities in the future, you do go in for a form of simulation. You *imagine* what would happen if you did each of the alternatives open to you. You set up a model in your head, not of everything in the world, but of the restricted set of entities which you think may be relevant. You may see them vividly in your mind's eye, or you may see and manipulate stylized abstractions of them. In either case it is unlikely that somewhere laid out in your brain is an actual spatial model of the events you are imagining. But, just as in the computer, the details of how your brain represents its model of the world are less important than the fact that it is able to use it to predict possible events. Survival machines which can simulate the future are one jump ahead of survival machines who can only learn on the basis of overt trial and error. The trouble with overt trial is that it takes time and energy. The trouble with overt error is that it is often fatal. Simulation is both safer and faster.

The evolution of the capacity to simulate seems to have culminated in subjective consciousness. Why this should have happened is, to me, the most profound mystery facing modern biology. There is no reason to suppose that electronic computers are conscious when they simulate, although we have to admit that in the future they may become so. Perhaps consciousness arises when the brain's simulation of the world becomes so complete that it must include a model of itself. Obviously the limbs and body of a survival machine must constitute an important part of its simulated world; presumably for the same kind of reason, the simulation itself could be regarded as part of the world to be simulated. Another word for this might indeed be "self-awareness," but I don't find this a fully satisfying explanation of the evolution of consciousness, and this is only partly because it involves an infinite regress—if there is a model of the model, why not a model of the model of the model? . . .

Whatever the philosophical problems raised by consciousness, for the purpose of this story it can be thought of as the culmination of an evolutionary trend towards the emancipation of survival machines as executive decision-takers from their ultimate masters, the genes. Not only are brains in charge of the day-to-day running of survival-machine affairs, they have also acquired the ability to predict the future and act accordingly. They even have the power to rebel against the dictates of the genes, for instance in refusing to have as many children as they are able to. But in this respect man is a very special case, as we shall see.

What has all this to do with altruism and selfishness? I am trying to build up the idea that animal behavior, altruistic or selfish, is under the control of genes in only an indirect, but still very powerful, sense. By dictating the way survival machines and their nervous systems are built, genes exert ultimate power over behavior. But the moment-to-moment decisions about what to do next are taken by the nervous system. Genes are the primary policy-makers; brains are the executives. But as brains became more highly developed, they took over more and more of the actual policy decisions, using tricks like learning and simulation in doing so. The logical conclusion to this trend, not yet reached in any species, would be for the genes to give the survival machine a single overall policy instruction: do whatever you think best to keep us alive.

Selfish Memes

The laws of physics are supposed to be true all over the accessible universe. Are there any principles of biology which are likely to have similar universal validity? When astronauts voyage to distant planets and look for life, they can expect to find creatures too strange and unearthly for us to imagine. But is there anything which must be true of all life, wherever it is found, and whatever the basis of its chemistry? If forms of life exist whose chemistry is based on silicon rather than carbon, or ammonia rather than water, if creatures are discovered which boil to death at −100 degrees centigrade, if a form of life is found which is not based on chemistry at all but on electronic reverberating circuits, will there still be any general principle which is true of all life? Obviously I do not know but, if I had to bet, I would put my money on one fundamental principle. This is the law that all life evolves by the differential survival of replicating entities. The gene, the DNA molecule, happens to be the replicating entity which prevails on our own planet. There may be others. If there are, provided certain other conditions are met, they will almost inevitably tend to become the basis for an evolutionary process.

But do we have to go to distant worlds to find other kinds of replicator and other, consequent, kinds of evolution? I think that a new kind of replicator has recently emerged on this very planet. It is staring us in the face. It is still in its infancy, still drifting clumsily about in its primeval soup, but already it is achieving evolutionary change at a rate which leaves the old gene panting far behind.

The new soup is the soup of human culture. We need a name for the

new replicator, a noun which conveys the idea of a unit of cultural transmission, or a unit of *imitation*. "Mimeme" comes from a suitable Greek
root, but I want a monosyllable that sounds a bit like "gene." I hope my
classicist friends will forgive me if I abbreviate mimeme to *meme*. If it is
any consolation, it could alternatively be thought of as being related to
"memory," or to the French word *même*. It should be pronounced to
rhyme with "cream."

Examples of memes are tunes, ideas, catch-phrases, clothes fashions,
ways of making pots or of building arches. Just as genes propagate themselves in the gene pool by leaping from body to body via sperms or eggs,
so memes propagate themselves in the meme pool by leaping from brain
to brain via a process which, in the broad sense, can be called imitation.
If a scientist hears, or reads about, a good idea, he passes it on to his
colleagues and students. He mentions it in his articles and his lectures.
If the idea catches on, it can be said to propagate itself, spreading from
brain to brain. As my colleague N. K. Humphrey neatly summed up an
earlier draft of this chapter: ". . . memes should be regarded as living
structures, not just metaphorically but technically. When you plant a
fertile meme in my mind, you literally parasitize my brain, turning it into
a vehicle for the meme's propagation in just the way that a virus may
parasitize the genetic mechanism of a host cell. And this isn't just a way
of talking—the meme for, say, 'belief in life after death' is actually realized
physically, millions of times over, as a structure in the nervous systems
of individual men the world over."

*   *   *

I conjecture that co-adapted meme-complexes evolve in the same kind of
way as co-adapted gene-complexes. Selection favours memes which exploit their cultural environment to their own advantage. This cultural
environment consists of other memes which are also being selected. The
meme pool therefore comes to have the attributes of an evolutionarily
stable set, which new memes find it hard to invade.

I have been a bit negative about memes, but they have their cheerful
side as well. When we die there are two things we can leave behind us:
genes and memes. We were built as gene machines, created to pass on
our genes. But that aspect of us will be forgotten in three generations.
Your child, even your grandchild, may bear a resemblance to you, perhaps in facial features, in a talent for music, in the colour of her hair. But
as each generation passes, the contribution of your genes is halved. It
does not take long to reach negligible proportions. Our genes may be
immortal but the *collection* of genes which is any one of us is bound to

crumble away. Elizabeth II is a direct descendant of William the Conqueror. Yet it is quite probable that she bears not a single one of the old king's genes. We should not seek immortality in reproduction.

But if you contribute to the world's culture, if you have a good idea, compose a tune, invent a spark plug, write a poem, it may live on, intact, long after your genes have dissolved in the common pool. Socrates may or may not have a gene or two alive in the world today, as G. C. Williams has remarked, but who cares? The meme-complexes of Socrates, Leonardo, Copernicus, and Marconi are still going strong.

Reflections

Dawkins is a master at expounding the reductionist thesis that says life and mind come out of a seething molecular tumult, when small units, accidentally formed, are subjected over and over to the merciless filter of fierce competition for resources with which to replicate. Reductionism sees all of the world as reducible to the laws of physics, with no room for so-called "emergent" properties or, to use an evocative though old-fashioned word, "entelechies"—higher-level structures that presumably cannot be explained by recourse to the laws that govern their parts.

Imagine this scenario: You send your nonfunctioning typewriter (or washing machine or photocopy machine) back to the factory for repair, and a month later they send it back reassembled correctly (as it had been when you sent it in), along with a note saying that they're sorry—all the parts check out fine, but the whole simply doesn't work. This would be considered outrageous. How can every part be perfect if the machine still doesn't work right? Something has to be wrong somewhere! So common sense tells us, in the macroscopic domain of everyday life.

Does this principle continue to hold, however, as you go from a whole to its parts, then from those parts to their parts, and so on, level after level? Common sense would again say yes—and yet many people continue to believe such things as "You can't derive the properties of water from the properties of hydrogen and oxygen atoms" or "A living being is greater than the sum of its parts." Somehow people often envision atoms as simple billiard balls, perhaps with chemical valences but without much more detail. As it turns out, nothing could be further from the truth. When you get down to that very small size scale, the mathematics of "matter" becomes more intractable than ever. Consider this passage from Richard Mattuck's text on interacting particles:

A reasonable starting point for a discussion of the many-body problem might be the question of how many bodies are required before we have a problem. Prof. G. E. Brown has pointed out that, for those interested in exact solutions, this can be answered by a look at history. In eighteenth-century Newtonian mechanics, the three-body problem was insoluble. With the birth of general relativity around 1910, and quantum electrodynamics around 1930, the two- and one-body problems became insoluble. And within modern quantum field theory, the problem of zero bodies (vacuum) is insoluble. So, if we are out after exact solutions, no bodies at all is already too many.

The quantum mechanics of an atom like oxygen, with its eight electrons, is far beyond our capability to completely solve analytically. A hydrogen or oxygen atom's properties, not to mention those of a water molecule, are indescribably subtle, and are precisely the sources of water's many elusive qualities. Many of those properties can be studied by computer simulations of many interacting molecules, using simplified models of the atoms. The better the model of the atom, the more realistic the simulation, naturally. In fact, computer models have become one of the most prevalent ways of discovering new properties of collections of many identical components, given knowledge only of the properties of an individual component. Computer simulations have yielded new insights into how galaxies form spiral arms, based on modeling a single star as a mobile gravitating point. Computer simulations have shown how solids, liquids, and gases vibrate, flow, and change state, based on modeling a single molecule as a simple electromagnetically interacting structure.

It is a fact that people habitually underestimate the intricacy and complexity that can result from a huge number of interacting units obeying formal rules at very high speeds, relative to our time scale.

Dawkins concludes his book by presenting his own meme about memes—software replicators that dwell in minds. He precedes his presentation of the notion by entertaining the idea of alternate life-support media. One that he fails to mention is the surface of a neutron star, where nuclear particles can band together and disband thousands of times faster than atoms do. In theory, a "chemistry" of nuclear particles could permit extremely tiny self-replicating structures whose high-speed lives would zoom by in an eyeblink, equally complex as their slow earthbound counterparts. Whether such life actually exists—or whether we could ever find out, assuming it did—is unclear, but it gives rise to the amazing idea of an entire civilization's rise and fall in the period of a few earth days—a super-Lilliput! The selections by Stanislaw Lem in this book all share this quality; see especially selection 18, "The Seventh Sally."

We bring this weird idea up to remind the reader to keep an open mind about the variability of media that can support complex lifelike or thoughtlike activity. This notion is explored slightly less wildly in the following dialogue, in which consciousness emerges from the interacting levels of an ant colony.

D. R. H.

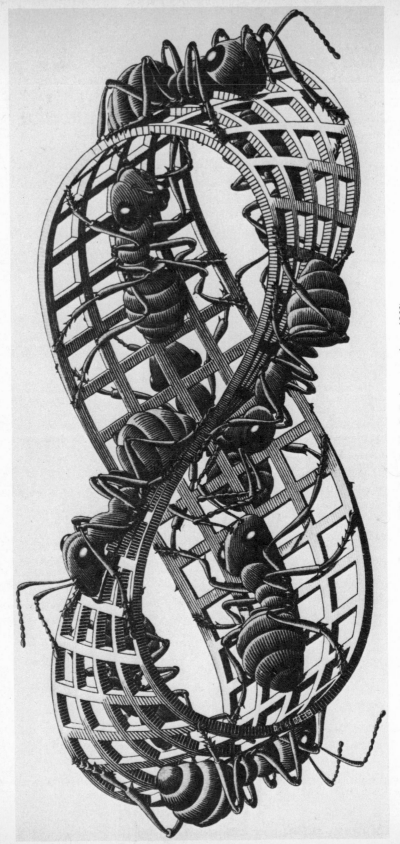

Möbius Strip II (M. C. Escher, woodcut, 1963).

11

DOUGLAS R. HOFSTADTER

Prelude . . . Ant Fugue

Prelude . . .

Achilles and the Tortoise have come to the residence of their friend the Crab, to make the acquaintance of one of his friends, the Anteater. The introductions having been made, the four of them settle down to tea.

TORTOISE: We have brought along a little something for you, Mr. Crab.

CRAB: That's most kind of you. But you shouldn't have.

TORTOISE: Just a token of our esteem. Achilles, would you like to give it to Mr. C?

ACHILLES: Surely. Best wishes, Mr. Crab. I hope you enjoy it.

(Achilles hands the Crab an elegantly wrapped present, square and very thin. The Crab begins unwrapping it.)

ANTEATER: I wonder what it could be.

CRAB: We'll soon find out. *(Completes the unwrapping, and pulls out the gift.)* Two records! How exciting! But there's no label. Uh-oh—is this another of your "specials," Mr. T?

TORTOISE: If you mean a phonograph-breaker, not this time. But it is in fact a custom-recorded item, the only one of its kind in the entire world. In fact, it's never even been heard before—except, of course, when Bach played it.

CRAB: When Bach played it? What do you mean, exactly?

ACHILLES: Oh, you are going to be fabulously excited, Mr. Crab, when Mr. T tells you what these records in fact are.

TORTOISE: Oh, you go ahead and tell him, Achilles.

ACHILLES: May I? Oh, boy! I'd better consult my notes, then. *(Pulls out a small filing card and clears his voice.)* Ahem. Would you be interested in hearing about the remarkable new result in mathematics, to which your records owe their existence?

CRAB: My records derive from some piece of mathematics? How curious! Well, now that you've provoked my interest, I must hear about it.

ACHILLES: Very well, then. *(Pauses for a moment to sip his tea, then resumes.)* Have you heard of Fermat's infamous "Last Theorem"?

ANTEATER: I'm not sure. . . . It sounds strangely familiar, and yet I can't quite place it.

ACHILLES: It's a very simple idea. Pierre de Fermat, a lawyer by vocation but mathematician by avocation, had been reading in his copy of the classic text *Arithmetica* by Diophantus and came across a page containing the equation

$$a^2 + b^2 = c^2$$

He immediately realized that this equation has infinitely many solutions a, b, c, and then wrote in the margin the following notorious comment:

The equation

$$n^a + n^b = n^c$$

has solutions in positive integers a, b, c, and n only when n = 2 (and then there are infinitely many triplets a, b, c, which satisfy the equation); but there are no solutions for n > 2. I have discovered a truly marvelous proof of this statement, which, unfortunately, is so small that it would be well-nigh invisible if written in the margin.

Ever since that day, some three hundred years ago, mathematicians have been vainly trying to do one of two things: either to prove Fermat's claim and thereby vindicate Fermat's reputation, which, although very high, has been somewhat tarnished by skeptics who think he never really found the proof he claimed to have found—or else to refute the claim, by finding a counterexample: a set of four integers a, b, c, and n, with $n > 2$, which satisfy the equation. Until very recently, every attempt in either direction had met with failure. To be sure, the Theorem has been proven for many specific values of n—in particular, all n up to 125,000.

ANTEATER: Shouldn't it be called a "Conjecture" rather than a "Theorem," if it's never been given a proper proof?

ACHILLES: Strictly speaking, you're right, but tradition has kept it this way.

CRAB: Has someone at last managed to resolve this celebrated question?

ACHILLES: Indeed! In fact, Mr. Tortoise has done so, and as usual, by a wizardly stroke. He has not only found a *proof* of Fermat's Last Theorem (thus justifying its name as well as vindicating Fermat), but also a *counterexample*, thus showing that the skeptics had good intuition!

CRAB: Oh my gracious! That is a revolutionary discovery.

ANTEATER: But please don't leave us in suspense. What magical integers are they, that satisfy Fermat's equation? I'm especially curious about the value of n.

ACHILLES: Oh, horrors! I'm most embarrassed! Can you believe this? I left the values at home on a truly colossal piece of paper. Unfortunately it was too huge to bring along. I wish I had them here to show to you. If it's of any help to you, I do remember one thing—the value of n is the only positive integer which does not occur anywhere in the continued fraction for π.

CRAB: Oh, what a shame that you don't have them here. But there's no reason to doubt what you have told us.

ANTEATER: Anyway, who needs to see n written out decimally? Achilles has just told us how to find it. Well, Mr. T, please accept my hearty felicitations, on the occasion of your epoch-making discovery!

TORTOISE: Thank you. But what I feel is more important than the result itself is the practical use to which my result immediately led.

CRAB: I am dying to hear about it, since I always thought number theory was the Queen of Mathematics—the purest branch of mathematics —the one branch of mathematics which has *no* applications!

TORTOISE: You're not the only one with that belief, but in fact it is quite impossible to make a blanket statement about when or how some

Pierre de Fermat.

branch—or even some individual Theorem—of pure mathematics will have important repercussions outside of mathematics. It is quite unpredictable—and this case is a perfect example of that phenomenon.

ACHILLES: Mr. Tortoise's double-barreled result has created a breakthrough in the field of acoustico-retrieval!

ANTEATER: What is acoustico-retrieval?

ACHILLES: The name tells it all: it is the retrieval of acoustic information from extremely complex sources. A typical task of acoustico-retrieval is to reconstruct the sound which a rock made on plummeting into a lake, from the ripples which spread out over the lake's surface.

CRAB: Why, that sounds next to impossible!

ACHILLES: Not so. It is actually quite similar to what one's brain does, when it reconstructs the sound made in the vocal cords of another person from the vibrations transmitted by the eardrum to the fibers in the cochlea.

CRAB: I see. But I still don't see where number theory enters the picture, or what this all has to do with my new records.

ACHILLES: Well, in the mathematics of acoustico-retrieval, there arise many questions which have to do with the number of solutions of certain Diophantine equations. Now Mr. T has been for years trying to find a way of reconstructing the sounds of Bach playing his harpsichord, which took place over two hundred years ago, from calculations involving the motions of all the molecules in the atmosphere at the present time.

ANTEATER: Surely that is impossible! They are irretrievably gone, gone forever!

ACHILLES: Thus think the naïve . . . But Mr. T has devoted many years to this problem, and came to the realization that the whole thing hinged on the number of solutions to the equation

$$a^n + b^n = c^n$$

in positive integers, with $n > 2$.

TORTOISE: I could explain, of course, just how this equation arises, but I'm sure it would bore you.

ACHILLES: It turned out that acoustico-retrieval theory predicts that the Bach sounds can be retrieved from the motion of all the molecules in the atmosphere, provided that there exists *either* at least one solution to the equation—

CRAB: Amazing!

ANTEATER: Fantastic!

TORTOISE: Who would have thought!

ACHILLES: I was about to say, "provided that there exists *either* such a solution *or* a proof that there are *no* solutions!" And therefore, Mr. T, in careful fashion, set about working at both ends of the problem simultaneously. As it turns out, the discovery of the counterexample was the key ingredient to finding the proof, so the one led directly to the other.

CRAB: How could that be?

TORTOISE: Well, you see, I had shown that the structural layout of any proof of Fermat's Last Theorem—if one existed—could be described by an elegant formula, which, it so happened, depended on the values of a solution to a certain equation. When I found this second equation, to my surprise it turned out to be the Fermat equation. An amusing accidental relationship between form and content. So when I found the counterexample, all I needed to do was to use those numbers as a blueprint for constructing my proof that there were no solutions to the equation. Remarkably simple, when you think about it. I can't imagine why no one had ever found the result before.

ACHILLES: As a result of this unanticipatedly rich mathematical success, Mr. T was able to carry out the acoustico-retrieval which he had so long dreamed of. And Mr. Crab's present here represents a palpable realization of all this abstract work.

CRAB: Don't tell me it's a recording of Bach playing his own works for harpsichord!

ACHILLES: I'm sorry, but I have to, for that is indeed just what it is! This is a set of two records of Johann Sebastian Bach playing all of his *Well-Tempered Clavier.* Each record contains one of the two volumes of the *Well-Tempered Clavier;* that is to say, each record contains twenty-four preludes and fugues—one in each major and minor key.

CRAB: Well, we must absolutely put one of these priceless records on, immediately! And how can I ever thank the two of you?

TORTOISE: You have already thanked us plentifully, with this delicious tea which you have prepared.

(The Crab slides one of the records out of its jacket and puts it on. The sound of an incredibly masterful harpsichordist fills the room, in the highest imaginable fidelity. One even hears—or is it one's imagination?—the soft sounds of Bach singing to himself as he plays. . . .)

CRAB: Would any of you like to follow along in the score? I happen to have a unique edition of the *Well-Tempered Clavier,* specially il-luminated by a teacher of mine who happens also to be an unusually fine calligrapher.

TORTOISE: I would very much enjoy that.

(The Crab goes to his elegant glass-enclosed wooden bookcase, opens the doors, and draws out two large volumes.)

CRAB: Here you are, Mr. Tortoise. I've never really gotten to know all the beautiful illustrations in this edition. Perhaps your gift will pro-vide the needed impetus for me to do so.

TORTOISE: I do hope so.

ANTEATER: Have you ever noticed how in these pieces the prelude al-ways sets the mood perfectly for the following fugue?

CRAB: Yes. Although it may be hard to put it into words, there is always some subtle relation between the two. Even if the prelude and fugue do not have a common melodic subject, there is nevertheless always some intangible abstract quality which underlies both of them, binding them together very strongly.

TORTOISE: And there is something very dramatic about the few moments of silent suspense hanging between prelude and fugue—that moment where the theme of the fugue is about to ring out, in single tones, and then to join with itself in ever-increasingly complex levels of weird, exquisite harmony.

ACHILLES: I know just what you mean. There are so many preludes and fugues which I haven't yet gotten to know, and for me that fleeting interlude of silence is very exciting; it's a time when I try to second-guess old Bach. For example, I always wonder what the fugue's tempo will be: allegro or adagio? Will it be in 6/8 or 4/4? Will it have three voices or five—or four? And then, the first voice starts. . . . Such an exquisite moment.

CRAB: Ah, yes, well do I remember those long-gone days of my youth, the days when I thrilled to each new prelude and fugue, filled with the excitement of their novelty and beauty and the many unexpected surprises which they conceal.

ACHILLES: And now? Is that thrill all gone?

CRAB: It's been supplanted by familiarity, as thrills always will be. But in that familiarity there is also a kind of depth, which has its own compensations. For instance, I find that there are always new surprises which I hadn't noticed before.

ACHILLES: Occurrences of the theme which you had overlooked?

CRAB: Perhaps—especially when it is inverted and hidden among several other voices, or where it seems to come rushing up from the depths, out of nowhere. But there are also amazing modulations which it is marvelous to listen to over and over again, and wonder how old Bach dreamt them up.

ACHILLES: I am very glad to hear that there is something to look forward to, after I have been through the first flush of infatuation with the *Well-Tempered Clavier*—although it also makes me sad that this stage could not last forever and ever.

CRAB: Oh, you needn't fear that your infatuation will totally die. One of the nice things about that sort of youthful thrill is that it can always be resuscitated, just when you thought it was finally dead. It just takes the right kind of triggering from the outside.

ACHILLES: Oh, really? Such as what?

CRAB: Such as hearing it through the ears, so to speak, of someone to whom it is a totally new experience—someone such as you, Achilles. Somehow the excitement transmits itself, and I can feel thrilled again.

ACHILLES: That is intriguing. The thrill has remained dormant somewhere inside you, but by yourself, you aren't able to fish it up out of your subconscious.

CRAB: Exactly. The potential of reliving the thrill is "coded," in some unknown way, in the structure of my brain, but I don't have the power to summon it up at will; I have to wait for chance circumstance to trigger it.

ACHILLES: I have a question about fugues which I feel a little embarrassed about asking, but as I am just a novice at fugue-listening, I was wondering if perhaps one of you seasoned fugue-listeners might help me in learning? . . .

TORTOISE: I'd certainly like to offer my own meager knowledge, if it might prove of some assistance.

ACHILLES: Oh, thank you. Let me come at the question from an angle. Are you familiar with the print called *Cube with Magic Ribbons,* by M. C. Escher?

TORTOISE: In which there are circular bands having bubblelike distortions which, as soon as you've decided that they are bumps, seem to turn into dents—and vice versa?

ACHILLES: Exactly.

CRAB: I remember that picture. Those little bubbles always seem to flip back and forth between being concave and convex, depending on the direction that you approach them from. There's no way to see them simultaneously as concave *and* convex—somehow one's brain doesn't allow that. There are two mutually exclusive "modes" in which one can perceive the bubbles.

ACHILLES: Just so. Well, I seem to have discovered two somewhat analogous modes in which I can listen to a fugue. The modes are these: either to follow one individual voice at a time, or to listen to the total effect of all of them together, without trying to disentangle one from another. I have tried out both of these modes, and, much to my frustration, each one of them shuts out the other. It's simply not in my power to follow the paths of individual voices and at the same

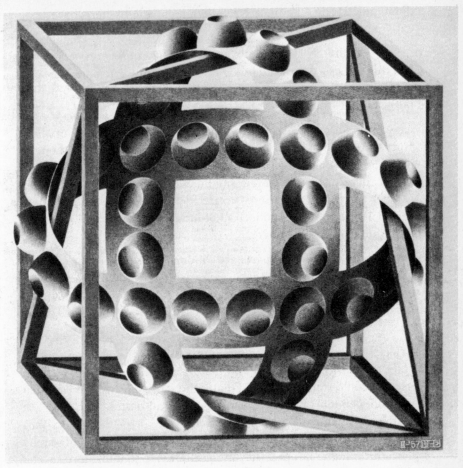

Cube with Magic Ribbons (M. C. Escher, lithograph, 1957).

time to hear the whole effect. I find that I flip back and forth between one mode and the other, more or less spontaneously and involuntarily.

ANTEATER: Just as when you look at the magic bands, eh?

ACHILLES: Yes. I was just wondering . . . does my description of these two modes of fugue-listening brand me unmistakably as a naive, inexperienced listener, who couldn't even begin to grasp the deeper modes of perception which exist beyond his ken?

TORTOISE: No, not at all, Achilles. I can only speak for myself, but I too find myself shifting back and forth from one mode to the other without exerting any conscious control over which mode should be dominant. I don't know if our other companions here have also experienced anything similar.

CRAB: Most definitely. It's quite a tantalizing phenomenon, since you feel that the essence of the fugue is flitting about you, and you can't quite grasp all of it, because you can't quite make yourself function both ways at once.

ANTEATER: Fugues have that interesting property, that each of their voices is a piece of music in itself; and thus a fugue might be thought of as a collection of several distinct pieces of music, all based on one single theme, and all played simultaneously. And it is up to the listener (or his subconscious) to decide whether it should be perceived as a unit, or as a collection of independent parts, all of which harmonize.

ACHILLES: You say that the parts are "independent," yet that can't be literally true. There has to be some coordination between them, otherwise when they were put together one would just have an unsystematic clashing of tones—and that is as far from the truth as could be.

ANTEATER: A better way to state it might be this: if you listened to each voice on its own, you would find that it seemed to make sense all by itself. It could stand alone, and that is the sense in which I meant that it is independent. But you are quite right in pointing out that each of these individually meaningful lines fuses with the others in a highly nonrandom way, to make a graceful totality. The art of writing a beautiful fugue lies precisely in this ability, to manufacture several different lines, each one of which gives the illusion of having been written for its own beauty, and yet which when taken together form a whole, which does not feel forced in any way. Now, this dichotomy between hearing a fugue as a whole and hearing its component voices is a particular example of a very general dichotomy, which applies to many kinds of structures built up from lower levels.

ACHILLES: Oh, really? You mean that my two "modes" may have some more general type of applicability, in situations other than fugue-listening?

ANTEATER: Absolutely.

ACHILLES: I wonder how that could be. I guess it has to do with alternating between perceiving something as a whole and perceiving it as a collection of parts. But the only place I have ever run into that dichotomy is in listening to fugues.

TORTOISE: Oh, my, look at this! I just turned the page while following the music, and came across this magnificent illustration facing the first page of the fugue.

CRAB: I have never seen that illustration before. Why don't you pass it 'round?

(The Tortoise passes the book around. Each of the foursome looks at it in a characteristic way—this one from afar, that one from close up, everyone tipping his head this way and that in puzzlement. Finally it has made the rounds and returns to the Tortoise, who peers at it rather intently.)

ACHILLES: Well, I guess the prelude is just about over. I wonder if, as I listen to this fugue, I will gain any more insight into the question "What is the right way to listen to a fugue: as a whole, or as the sum of its parts?"

TTORTOISE: Listen carefully, and you will!

(The prelude ends. There is a moment of silence; and . . .

[ATTACCA]

. . . Ant Fugue

. . . then, one by one, the four voices of the fugue chime in.)

ACHILLES: I know the rest of you won't believe this, but the answer to the question is staring us all in the face, hidden in the picture. It is simply one word—but what an important one: "MU"!

CCRAB: I know the rest of you won't believe this, but the answer to the question is staring us all in the face, hidden in the picture. It is simply one word—but what an important one: "HOLISM"!

ACHILLES: Now hold on a minute. You must be seeing things. It's plain as day that the message of this picture is "MU," not "HOLISM"!

CRAB: I beg your pardon, but my eyesight is extremely good. Please look again, and then tell me if the picture doesn't say what I said it says!

ANTEATER: I know the rest of you won't believe this, but the answer to the question is staring us all in the face, hidden in the picture. It is simply one word—but what an important one: "REDUCTIONISM"!

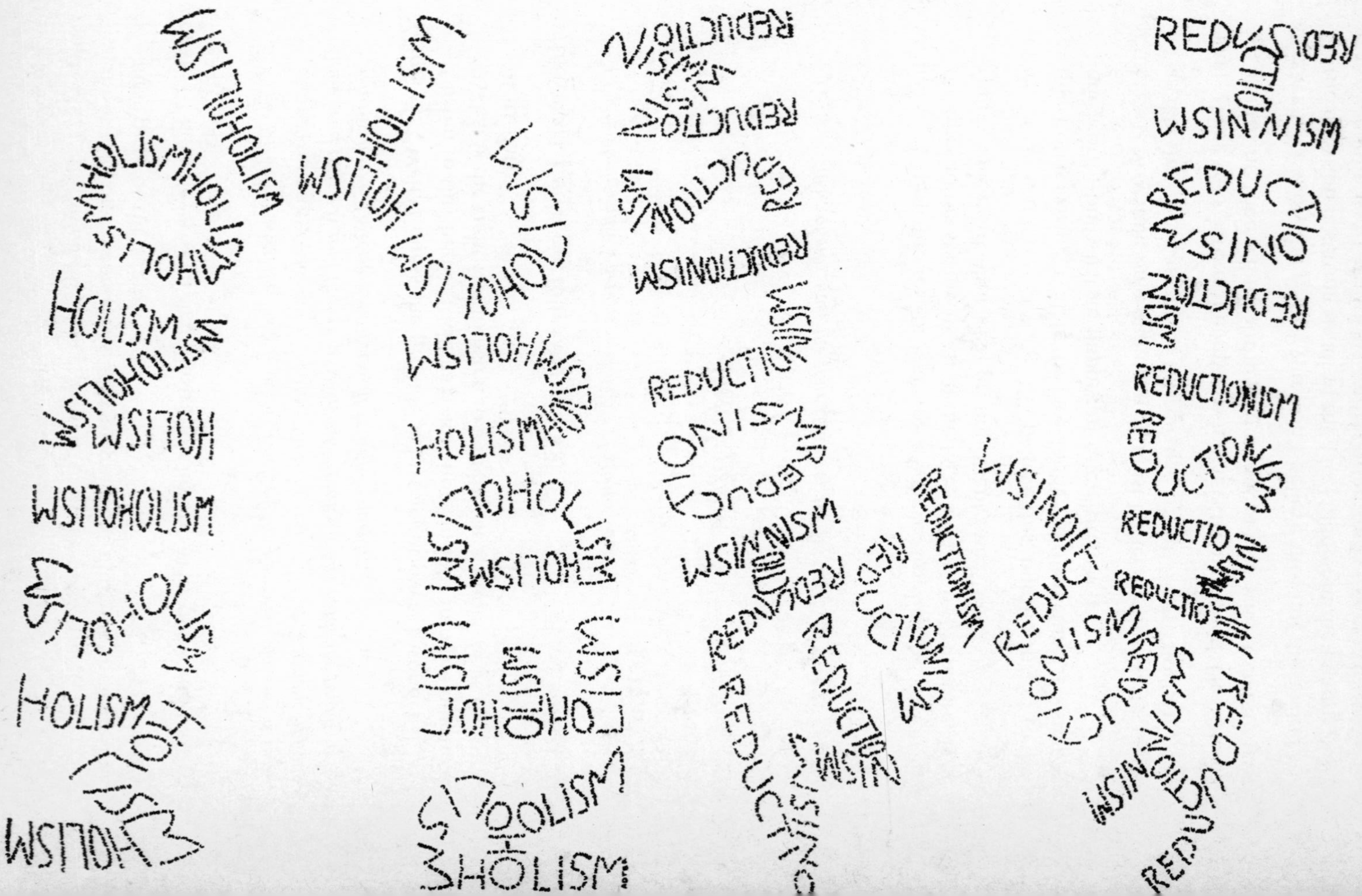
HOLISM
REDUCTIONISM

CRAB: Now hold on a minute. You must be seeing things. It's plain as day that the message of this picture is "HOLISM," not "REDUCTION-ISM"!

ACHILLES: Another deluded one! Not "HOLISM," not "REDUCTIONISM," but "MU" is the message of this picture, and that much is certain.

ANTEATER: I beg your pardon, but my eyesight is extremely clear. Please look again, and then see if the picture doesn't say what I said it says.

ACHILLES: Don't you see that the picture is composed of two pieces, and that each of them is a single letter?

CRAB: You are right about the two pieces, but you are wrong in your identification of what they are. The piece on the left is entirely composed of three copies of one word: "'HOLISM"; and the piece on the right is composed of many copies, in smaller letters, of the same word. Why the letters are of different sizes in the two parts, I don't know, but I know what I see, and what I see is "HOLISM," plain as day. How you see anything else is beyond me.

ANTEATER: You are right about the two pieces, but you are wrong in your identification of what they are. The piece on the left is entirely composed of many copies of one word: "REDUCTIONISM"; and the piece on the right is composed of one single copy, in larger letters, of the same word. Why the letters are of different sizes in the two parts, I don't know, but I know what I see, and what I see is "REDUC-TIONISM," plain as day. How you see anything else is beyond me.

ACHILLES: I know what is going on here. Each of you has seen letters which compose, or are composed of, other letters. In the left-hand piece, there are indeed three "HOLISM"s, but each one of them is composed out of smaller copies of the word "REDUCTIONISM." And in complementary fashion, in the right-hand piece, there is indeed one "REDUCTIONISM," but it is composed out of smaller copies of the word "HOLISM." Now this is all fine and good, but in your silly squabble, the two of you have actually missed the forest for the trees. You see, what good is it to argue about whether "HOLISM" or "RE-DUCTIONISM" is right, when the proper way to understand the matter is to transcend the question, by answering "MU"?

CRAB: I now see the picture as you have described it, Achilles, but I have no idea of what you mean by the strange expression "transcending the question."

ANTEATER: I now see the picture as you have described it, Achilles, but I have no idea of what you mean by the strange expression "mu."

ACHILLES: I will be glad to indulge both of you, if you will first oblige me, by telling me the meaning of these strange expressions, *"holism"* and *"reductionism."*

CRAB: *Holism* is the most natural thing in the world to grasp. It's simply the belief that "the whole is greater than the sum of its parts." No one in his right mind could reject holism.

ANTEATER: *Reductionism* is the most natural thing in the world to grasp. It's simply the belief that "a whole can be understood completely if you understand its parts, and the nature of their 'sum.' " No one in her left brain could reject reductionism.

CRAB: I reject reductionism. I challenge you to tell me, for instance, how to understand a brain reductionistically. Any reductionistic explanation of a brain will inevitably fall far short of explaining where the consciousness experienced by a brain arises from.

ANTEATER: I reject holism. I challenge you to tell me, for instance, how a holistic description of an ant colony sheds any more light on it than is shed by a description of the ants inside it, and their roles, and their interrelationships. Any holistic explanation of an ant colony will inevitably fall far short of explaining where the consciousness experienced by an ant colony arises from.

ACHILLES: Oh, no! The last thing that I wanted to do was to provoke another argument. Anyway, now that I understand the controversy, I believe that my explanation of *"mu"* will help greatly. You see, *"mu"* is an ancient Zen answer which, when given to a question, *unasks* the question. Here, the question seems to be "Should the world be understood via holism or via reductionism?" And the answer of *"mu"* here rejects the premises of the question, which are that one or the other must be chosen. By unasking the question, it reveals a wider truth: that there is a larger context into which both holistic and reductionistic explanations fit.

ANTEATER: Absurd! Your *"mu"* is as silly as a cow's moo. I'll have none of this Zen wishy-washiness.

CRAB: Ridiculous! Your *"mu"* is as silly as a kitten's mew. I'll have none of this Zen washy-wishiness.

ACHILLES: Oh, dear! We're getting nowhere fast. Why have you stayed so strangely silent, Mr. Tortoise? It makes me very uneasy. Surely you must somehow be capable of helping straighten out this mess?

TORTOISE: I know the rest of you won't believe this, but the answer to the question is staring us all in the face, hidden in the picture. It is simply one word—but what an important one: "MU"!

(Just as he says this, the fourth voice in the fugue being played enters, exactly one octave below the first entry.)

ACHILLES: Oh, Mr. T, for once you have let me down. I was sure that you, who always see the most deeply into things, would be able to resolve this dilemma—but apparently, you have seen no further than I myself saw. Oh, well, I guess I should feel pleased to have seen as far as Mr. Tortoise, for once.

TORTOISE: I beg your pardon, but my eyesight is extremely fine. Please look again, and then tell me if the picture doesn't say what I said it says.

ACHILLES: But of course it does! You have merely repeated my own original observation.

TORTOISE: Perhaps "MU" exists in this picture on a deeper level than you imagine, Achilles—an octave lower (figuratively speaking). But for now I doubt that we can settle the dispute in the abstract. I would like to see both the holistic and reductionistic points of view laid out more explicitly; then there may be more of a basis for a decision. I would very much like to hear a reductionistic description of an ant colony, for instance.

CRAB: Perhaps Dr. Anteater will tell you something of his experiences in that regard. After all, he is by profession something of an expert on that subject.

TORTOISE: I am sure that we could learn much from a myrmecologist like you, Dr. Anteater. Could you tell us more about ant colonies, from a reductionistic point of view?

ANTEATER: Gladly. As Mr. Crab mentioned to you, my profession has led me quite a long way into the understanding of ant colonies.

ACHILLES: I can imagine! The profession of Anteater would seem to be synonymous with being an expert on ant colonies!

ANTEATER: I beg your pardon. "Anteater" is not my profession; it is my species. By profession, I am a colony surgeon. I specialize in correcting nervous disorders of the colony by the technique of surgical removal.

ACHILLES: Oh, I see. But what do you mean by "nervous disorders" of an ant colony?

ANTEATER: Most of my clients suffer from some sort of speech impairment. You know, colonies which have to grope for words in everyday situations. It can be quite tragic. I attempt to remedy the situation by, uhh—removing—the defective part of the colony. These operations are sometimes quite involved, and of course years of study are required before one can perform them.

ACHILLES: But—isn't it true that, before one can suffer from speech impairment, one must have the faculty of speech?

ANTEATER: Right.

ACHILLES: Since ant colonies don't have that faculty, I am a little confused.

CRAB: It's too bad, Achilles, that you weren't here last week, when Dr. Anteater and Aunt Hillary were my house guests. I should have thought of having you over then.

ACHILLES: Is Aunt Hillary your aunt, Mr. Crab?

CRAB: Oh, no, she's not really anybody's aunt.

ANTEATER: But the poor dear insists that everybody should call her that, even strangers. It's just one of her many endearing quirks.

CRAB: Yes, Aunt Hillary is quite eccentric, but such a merry old soul. It's a shame I didn't have you over to meet her last week.

ANTEATER: She's certainly one of the best-educated ant colonies I have ever had the good fortune to know. The two of us have spent many a long evening in conversation on the widest range of topics.

ACHILLES: I thought anteaters were devourers of ants, not patrons of ant-intellectualism!

ANTEATER: Well, of course the two are not mutually inconsistent. I am on the best of terms with ant colonies. It's just *ants* that I eat, not colonies—and that is good for both parties: me, and the colony.

ACHILLES: How is it possible that—

TORTOISE: How is it possible that—

ACHILLES: —having its ants eaten can do an ant colony any good?

CRAB: How is it possible that—

TORTOISE: —having a forest fire can do a forest any good?

ANTEATER: How is it possible that—

CRAB: —having its branches pruned can do a tree any good?

ANTEATER: —having a haircut can do Achilles any good?

TORTOISE: Probably the rest of you were too engrossed in the discussion to notice the lovely stretto which just occurred in this Bach fugue.

ACHILLES: What is a stretto?

TORTOISE: Oh, I'm sorry; I thought you knew the term. It is where one
theme repeatedly enters in one voice after another, with very little
delay between entries.

ACHILLES: If I listen to enough fugues, soon I'll know all of these things
and will be able to pick them out myself, without their having to be
pointed out.

TORTOISE: Pardon me, my friends. I am sorry to have interrupted. Dr.
Anteater was trying to explain how eating ants is perfectly consistent
with being a friend of an ant colony.

ACHILLES: Well, I can vaguely see how it might be possible for a limited
and regulated amount of ant consumption to improve the overall
health of a colony—but what is far more perplexing is all this talk
about having conversations with ant colonies. That's impossible. An
ant colony is simply a bunch of individual ants running around at
random looking for food and making a nest.

ANTEATER: You could put it that way if you want to insist on seeing the
trees but missing the forest, Achilles. In fact, ant colonies, seen as
wholes, are quite well-defined units, with their own qualities, at times
including the mastery of language.

ACHILLES: I find it hard to imagine myself shouting something out loud
in the middle of the forest, and hearing an ant colony answer back.

ANTEATER: Silly fellow! That's not the way it happens. Ant colonies
don't converse out loud, but in writing. You know how ants form
trails leading them hither and thither?

ACHILLES: Oh, yes—usually straight through the kitchen sink and into
my peach jam.

ANTEATER: Actually, some trails contain information in coded form. If
you know the system, you can read what they're saying just like a
book.

ACHILLES: Remarkable. And can you communicate back to them?

ANTEATER: Without any trouble at all. That's how Aunt Hillary and I
have conversations for hours. I take a stick and draw trails in the
moist ground, and watch the ants follow my trails. Presently, a new
trail starts getting formed somewhere. I greatly enjoy watching trails
develop. As they are forming, I anticipate how they will continue
(and more often I am wrong than right). When the trail is completed,
I know what Aunt Hillary is thinking, and I in turn make my reply.

ACHILLES: There must be some amazingly smart ants in that colony, I'll say that.

ANTEATER: I think you are still having some difficulty realizing the difference in levels here. Just as you would never confuse an individual tree with a forest, so here you must not take an ant for the colony. You see, all the ants in Aunt Hillary are as dumb as can be. They couldn't converse to save their little thoraxes!

ACHILLES: Well then, where does the ability to converse come from? It must reside somewhere inside the colony! I don't understand how the ants can all be unintelligent, if Aunt Hillary can entertain you for hours with witty banter.

TORTOISE: It seems to me that the situation is not unlike the composition of a human brain out of neurons. Certainly no one would insist that individual brain cells have to be intelligent beings on their own, in order to explain the fact that a person can have an intelligent conversation.

ACHILLES: Oh, no, clearly not. With brain cells, I see your point completely. Only . . . ants are a horse of another color. I mean, ants just roam about at will, completely randomly, chancing now and then upon a morsel of food. . . . They are free to do what they want to do, and with that freedom, I don't see at all how their behavior, seen as a whole, can amount to anything coherent—especially something so coherent as the brain behavior necessary for conversing.

CRAB: It seems to me that the ants are free only within certain constraints. For example, they are free to wander, to brush against each other, to pick up small items, to work on trails, and so on. But they never step out of that small world, that ant-system, which they are in. It would never occur to them, for they don't have the mentality to imagine anything of the kind. Thus the ants are very reliable components, in the sense that you can depend on them to perform certain kinds of tasks in certain ways.

ACHILLES: But even so, within those limits they are still free, and they just act at random, running about incoherently without any regard for the thought mechanisms of a higher-level being which Dr. Anteater asserts they are merely components of.

ANTEATER: Ah, but you fail to recognize one thing, Achilles—the regularity of statistics.

ACHILLES: How is that?

ANTEATER: For example, even though ants as individuals wander about in what seems a random way, there are nevertheless overall trends, involving large numbers of ants, which can emerge from that chaos.

ACHILLES: Oh, I know what you mean. In fact, ant trails are a perfect example of such a phenomenon. There, you have really quite unpredictable motion on the part of any single ant—and yet, the trail itself seems to remain well defined and stable. Certainly that must mean that the individual ants are not just running about totally at random.

ANTEATER: Exactly, Achilles. There is some degree of communication among the ants, just enough to keep them from wandering off completely at random. By this minimal communication they can remind each other that they are not alone but are cooperating with teammates. It takes a large number of ants, all reinforcing each other this way, to sustain any activity—such as trail building—for any length of time. Now my very hazy understanding of the operation of brains leads me to believe that something similar pertains to the firing of neurons. Isn't it true, Mr. Crab, that it takes a group of neurons firing in order to make another neuron fire?

CRAB: Definitely. Take the neurons in Achilles' brain, for example. Each neuron receives signals from neurons attached to its input lines, and if the sum total of inputs at any moment exceeds a critical threshold, then that neuron will fire and send its own output pulse rushing off to other neurons, which may in turn fire—and on down the line it goes. The neural flash swoops relentlessly in its Achillean path, in shapes stranger then the dash of a gnat-hungry swallow; every twist, every turn foreordained by the neural structure in Achilles' brain, until sensory input messages interfere.

ACHILLES: Normally, I think that *I'm* in control of what I think—but the way you put it turns it all inside out, so that it sounds as though "I" am just what comes out of all this neural structure, and natural law. It makes what I consider my *self* sound at best like a by-product of an organism governed by natural law and, at worst, an artificial notion produced by my distorted perspective. In other words, you make me feel like I don't know who—or what—I am, if anything.

TORTOISE: You'll come to understand much better as we go along. But Dr. Anteater—what do you make of this similarity?

ANTEATER: I knew there was something parallel going on in the two very different systems. Now I understand it much better. It seems that group phenomena which have coherence—trail building, for example—will take place only when a certain threshold number of ants get involved. If an effort is initiated, perhaps at random, by a few ants in some locale, one of two things can happen: either it will fizzle out after a brief sputtering start—

ACHILLES: When there aren't enough ants to keep the thing rolling?

ANTEATER: Exactly. The other thing that can happen is that a critical mass of ants is present, and the thing will snowball, bringing more and more ants into the picture. In the latter case, a whole "team" is brought into being which works on a single project. That project might be trail making, or food gathering, or it might involve nest keeping. Despite the extreme simplicity of this scheme on a small scale, it can give rise to very complex consequences on a larger scale.

ACHILLES: I can grasp the general idea of order emerging from chaos, as you sketch it, but that still is a long way from the ability to converse. After all, order also emerges from chaos when molecules of a gas bounce against each other randomly—yet all that results there is an amorphous mass with but three parameters to characterize it: volume, pressure, and temperature. Now that's a far cry from the ability to understand the world, or to talk about it!

ANTEATER: That highlights a very interesting difference between the explanation of the behavior of an ant colony and the explanation of the behavior of gas inside a container. One can explain the behavior of the gas simply by calculating the statistical properties of the motions of its molecules. There is no need to discuss any higher elements of structure than molecules, except the full gas itself. On the other hand, in an ant colony, you can't even begin to understand the activities of the colony unless you go through several layers of structure.

ACHILLES: I see what you mean. In a gas, one jump takes you from the lowest level—molecules—to the highest level—the full gas. There are no intermediate levels of organization. Now how do intermediate levels of organized activity arise in an ant colony?

ANTEATER: It has to do with the existence of several different varieties of ants inside any colony.

ACHILLES: Oh, yes. I think I have heard about that. They are called "castes," aren't they?

ANTEATER: That's correct. Aside from the queen, there are males, who do practically nothing toward the upkeep of the nest, and then—

ACHILLES: And of course there are soldiers—glorious fighters against communism!

CRAB: Hmm . . . I hardly think that could be right, Achilles. An ant colony is quite communistic internally, so why would its soldiers fight against communism? Or am I right, Dr. Anteater?

ANTEATER: Yes, about colonies you are right, Mr. Crab; they are indeed based on somewhat communistic principles. But about soldiers Achilles is somewhat naive. In fact, the so-called "soldiers" are hardly adept at fighting at all. They are slow, ungainly ants with giant heads, who can snap with their strong jaws, but are hardly to be glorified. As in a true communistic state, it is rather the workers who are to be glorified. It is they who do most of the chores, such as food gathering, hunting, and nursing of the young. It is even they who do most of the fighting.

ACHILLES: Bah. That is an absurd state of affairs. Soldiers who won't fight!

ANTEATER: Well, as I just said, they really aren't soldiers at all. It's the workers who are soldiers; the soldiers are just lazy fatheads.

ACHILLES: Oh, how disgraceful! Why, if I were an ant, I'd put some discipline in their ranks! I'd knock some sense into those fatheads!

TORTOISE: If you were an ant? How could a myrmidon like you be an ant? There is no way to map your brain onto an ant brain, so it seems to me to be a pretty fruitless question to worry over. More reasonable would be the proposition of mapping your brain onto an ant colony. . . . But let us not get sidetracked. Let Dr. Anteater continue with his most illuminating description of castes and their role in the higher levels of organization.

ANTEATER: Very well. There are all sorts of tasks which must be accomplished in a colony, and individual ants develop specializations. Usually an ant's specialization changes as the ant ages. And of course it is also dependent on the ant's caste. At any one moment, in any small area of a colony, there are ants of all types present. Of course, one caste may be be very sparse in some places and very dense in others.

CRAB: Is the density of a given caste, or specialization, just a random thing? Or is there a reason why ants of one type might be more heavily concentrated in certain areas, and less heavily in others?

ANTEATER: I'm glad you brought that up, since it is of crucial importance in understanding how a colony thinks. In fact, there evolves, over a long period of time, a very delicate distribution of castes inside a colony. And it is this distribution that allows the colony to have the complexity that underlies the ability to converse with me.

ACHILLES: It would seem to me that the constant motion of ants to and fro would completely prevent the possibility of a very delicate distribution. Any delicate distribution would be quickly destroyed by all the random motions of ants, just as any delicate pattern among molecules in a gas would not survive for an instant, due to the random bombardment from all sides.

ANTEATER: In an ant colony, the situation is quite the contrary. In fact, it is just exactly the constant to-ing and fro-ing of ants inside the colony which adapts the caste distribution to varying situations, and thereby preserves the delicate caste distribution. You see, the caste distribution cannot remain as one single rigid pattern; rather, it must constantly be changing so as to reflect, in some manner, the real-world situation with which the colony is dealing, and it is precisely the motion inside the colony which updates the caste distribution, so as to keep it in line with the present circumstances facing the colony.

TORTOISE: Could you give an example?

ANTEATER: Gladly. When I, an anteater, arrive to pay a visit to Aunt Hillary, all the foolish ants, upon sniffing my odor, go into a panic—which means, of course, that they begin running around completely differently from the way they were before I arrived.

ACHILLES: But that's understandable, since you're a dreaded enemy of the colony.

ANTEATER: Oh, no. I must reiterate that, far from being an enemy of the colony, I am Aunt Hillary's favorite companion. And Aunt Hillary is my favorite aunt. I grant you, I'm quite feared by all the individual ants in the colony—but that's another matter entirely. In any case, you see that the ants' action in response to my arrival completely changes the internal distribution of ants.

ACHILLES: That's clear.

ANTEATER: And that sort of thing is the updating which I spoke of. The new distribution reflects my presence. One can describe the change from old state to new as having added a "piece of knowledge" to the colony.

ACHILLES: How can you refer to the distribution of different types of ants inside a colony as a "piece of knowledge"?

ANTEATER: Now there's a vital point. It requires some elaboration. You see, what it comes down to is how you choose to describe the caste distribution. If you continue to think in terms of the lower levels—

individual ants—then you miss the forest for the trees. That's just too microscopic a level, and when you think microscopically, you're bound to miss some large-scale features. You've got to find the proper high-level framework in which to describe the caste distribution—only then will it make sense how the caste distribution can encode many pieces of knowledge.

ACHILLES: Well, how *do* you find the proper-sized units in which to describe the present state of the colony, then?

ANTEATER: All right. Let's begin at the bottom. When ants need to get something done, they form little "teams," which stick together to perform a chore. As I mentioned earlier, small groups of ants are constantly forming and unforming. Those which actually exist for a while are the teams, and the reason they don't fall apart is that there really is something for them to do.

ACHILLES: Earlier you said that a group will stick together if its size exceeds a certain threshold. Now you're saying that a group will stick together if there is something for it to do.

ANTEATER: They are equivalent statements. For instance, in food gathering, if there is an inconsequential amount of food somewhere which gets discovered by some wandering ant who then attempts to communicate its enthusiasm to other ants, the number of ants who respond will be proportional to the size of the food sample—and an inconsequential amount will not attract enough ants to surpass the threshold. Which is exactly what I meant by saying there is nothing to do—too little food ought to be ignored.

ACHILLES: I see. I assume that these "teams" are one of the levels of structure falling somewhere in between the single-ant level and the colony level.

ANTEATER: Precisely. There exists a special kind of team, which I call a "signal"—and all the higher levels of structure are based on signals. In fact, all the higher entities are collections of signals acting in concert. There are teams on higher levels whose members are not ants, but teams on lower levels. Eventually you reach the lowest-level teams—which is to say, signals—and below them, ants.

ACHILLES: Why do signals deserve their suggestive name?

ANTEATER: It comes from their function. The effect of signals is to transport ants of various specializations to appropriate parts of the colony. So the typical story of a signal is thus: It comes into existence by exceeding the threshold needed for survival, then it migrates for some distance through the colony, and at some point it more or less disintegrates into its individual members, leaving them on their own.

ACHILLES: It sounds like a wave, carrying sand dollars and seaweed from afar, and leaving them strewn, high and dry, on the shore.

ANTEATER: In a way that's analogous, since the team does indeed deposit something which it has carried from a distance, but whereas the water in the wave rolls back to the sea, there is no analogous carrier substance in the case of a signal, since the ants themselves compose it.

TORTOISE: And I suppose that a signal loses its coherency just at some spot in the colony where ants of that type were needed in the first place.

ANTEATER: Naturally.

ACHILLES: Naturally? It's not so obvious to *me* that a signal should always go just where it is needed. And even if it goes in the right direction, how does it figure out where to decompose? How does it know it has arrived?

ANTEATER: Those are extremely important matters, since they involve explaining the existence of purposeful behavior—or what seems to be purposeful behavior—on the part of signals. From the description, one would be inclined to characterize the signals' behavior as being oriented toward filling a need, and to call it "purposeful." But you can look at it otherwise.

ACHILLES: Oh, wait. Either the behavior *is* purposeful, or it is *not*. I don't see how you can have it both ways.

ANTEATER: Let me explain my way of seeing things, and then see if you agree. Once a signal is formed, there is no awareness on its part that it should head off in any particular direction. But here the delicate caste distribution plays a crucial role. It is what determines the motion of signals through the colony, and also how long a signal will remain stable, and where it will "dissolve."

ACHILLES: So everything depends on the caste distribution, eh?

ANTEATER: Right. Let's say a signal is moving along. As it goes, the ants which compose it interact, either by direct contact or by exchange of scents, with ants of the local neighborhoods which it passes through. The contacts and scents provide information about local matters of urgency, such as nest building, or nursing, or whatever. The signal will remain glued together as long as the local needs are different from what it can supply; but if it *can* contribute, it disintegrates, spilling a fresh team of usable ants onto the scene. Do you see now how the caste distribution acts as an overall guide of the teams inside the colony?

ACHILLES: I do see that.

ANTEATER: And do you see how this way of looking at things requires attributing no sense of purpose to the signal?

ACHILLES: I think so. Actually, I'm beginning to see things from two different vantage points. From an ant's-eye point of view, a signal has *no* purpose. The typical ant in a signal is just meandering around the colony, in search of nothing in particular, until it finds that it feels like stopping. Its teammates usually agree, and at that moment the team unloads itself by crumbling apart, leaving just its members but none of its coherency. No planning is required, no looking ahead; nor is any search required to determine the proper direction. But from the *colony*'s point of view, the team has just responded to a message which was written in the language of the caste distribution. Now from this perspective, it looks very much like purposeful activity.

CRAB: What would happen if the caste distribution were entirely random? Would signals still band and disband?

ANTEATER: Certainly. But the colony would not last long, due to the meaninglessness of the caste distribution.

CRAB: Precisely the point I wanted to make. Colonies survive because their caste distribution has *meaning*, and that meaning is a holistic aspect, invisible on lower levels. You lose explanatory power unless you take that higher level into account.

ANTEATER: I see your side; but I believe you see things too narrowly.

CRAB: How so?

ANTEATER: Ant colonies have been subjected to the rigors of evolution for billions of years. A few mechanisms were selected for, and most were selected against. The end result was a set of mechanisms which make ant colonies work as we have been describing. If you could watch the whole process in a movie—running a billion or so times faster than life, of course—the emergence of various mechanisms would be seen as natural responses to external pressures, just as bubbles in boiling water are natural responses to an external heat source. I don't suppose you see "meaning" and "purpose" in the bubbles in boiling water—or do you?

CRAB: No, but—

ANTEATER: Now that's *my* point. No matter how big a bubble is, it owes its existence to processes on the molecular level, and you can forget about any "higher-level laws." The same goes for ant colonies and their teams. By looking at things from the vast perspective of evolution, you can drain the whole colony of meaning and purpose. They become superfluous notions.

ACHILLES: Why, then, Dr. Anteater, did you tell me that you talked with Aunt Hillary? It now seems that you would deny that she can talk or think at all.

ANTEATER: I am not being inconsistent, Achilles. You see, I have as much difficulty as anyone else in seeing things on such a grandiose time scale, so I find it much easier to change points of view. When I do so, forgetting about evolution and seeing things in the here and now, the vocabulary of teleology comes back: the *meaning* of the caste distribution and the *purposefulness* of signals. This not only happens when I think of ant colonies, but also when I think about my own brain and other brains. However, with some effort I can always remember the other point of view if necessary, and drain all these systems of meaning, too.

CRAB: Evolution certainly works some miracles. You never know the next trick it will pull out of its sleeve. For instance, it wouldn't surprise me one bit if it were theoretically possible for two or more "signals" to pass through each other, each one unaware that the other one is also a signal; each one treating the other as if it were just part of the background population.

ANTEATER: It is better than theoretically possible; in fact it happens routinely!

ACHILLES: Hmm. . . . What a strange image that conjures up in my mind. I can just imagine ants moving in four different directions, some black, some white, criss-crossing, together forming an orderly pattern, almost like—like—

TORTOISE: A fugue, perhaps?

ACHILLES: Yes—that's it! An ant fugue!

CRAB: An interesting image, Achilles. By the way, all that talk of boiling water made me think of tea. Who would like some more?

ACHILLES: I could do with another cup, Mr. C.

CRAB: Very good.

An "ant fugue" drawn by M. C. Escher (woodcut, 1953.)

ACHILLES: Do you suppose one could separate out the different visual "voices" of such an "ant fugue"? I know how hard it is for me—

TORTOISE: Not for me, thank you.

ACHILLES: —to track a single voice—

ANTEATER: I'd like some too, Mr. Crab—

ACHILLES: —in a musical fugue—

ANTEATER: —if it isn't too much trouble.

ACHILLES: —when all of them—

CRAB: Not at all. Four cups of tea—

TORTOISE: Three!

ACHILLES: —are going at once.

CRAB: —coming right up!

ANTEATER: That's an interesting thought, Achilles. But it's unlikely that anyone could draw such a picture in a convincing way.

ACHILLES: That's too bad.

TORTOISE: Perhaps you could answer this, Dr. Anteater. Does a signal, from its creation until its dissolution, always consist of the same set of ants?

ANTEATER: As a matter of fact, the individuals in a signal sometimes break off and get replaced by others of the same caste, if there are a few in the area. Most often, signals arrive at their disintegration points with nary an ant in common with their starting lineup.

CRAB: I can see that the signals are constantly affecting the caste distribution throughout the colony, and are doing so in response to the internal needs of the colony—which in turn reflect the external situation which the colony is faced with. Therefore the caste distribution, as you said, Dr. Anteater, gets continually updated in a way which ultimately reflects the outer world.

ACHILLES: But what about those intermediate levels of structure? You were saying that the caste distribution should best be pictured not in terms of ants or signals, but in terms of teams whose members were other teams, whose members were other teams, and so on until you come down to the ant level. And you said that that was the key to understanding how it was possible to describe the caste distribution as encoding pieces of information about the world.

ANTEATER: Yes, we are coming to all that. I prefer to give teams of a sufficiently high level the name of "symbols." Mind you, this sense of the word has some significant differences from the usual sense. My "symbols" are *active subsystems* of a complex system, and they are composed of lower-level active subsystems. . . . They are therefore quite different from *passive* symbols, external to the system, such as letters of the alphabet or musical notes, which sit there immobile waiting for an active system to process them.

ACHILLES: Oh, this is rather complicated, isn't it? I just had no idea that ant colonies had such an abstract structure.

ANTEATER: Yes, it's quite remarkable. But all these layers of structure are necessary for the storage of the kinds of knowledge which enable an organism to be "intelligent" in any reasonable sense of the word. Any system which has a mastery of language has essentially the same underlying sets of levels.

ACHILLES: Now just a cotton-picking minute. Are you insinuating that my brain consists of, at bottom, just a bunch of ants running around?

ANTEATER: Oh, hardly. You took me a little too literally. The lowest level may be utterly different. Indeed, the brains of anteaters, for instance, are not composed of ants. But when you go up a level or two in a brain, you reach a level whose elements have exact counterparts in other systems of equal intellectual strength—such as ant colonies.

TORTOISE: That is why it would be reasonable to think of mapping your brain, Achilles, onto an ant colony, but not onto the brain of a mere ant.

ACHILLES: I appreciate the compliment. But how would such a mapping be carried out? For instance, what in my brain corresponds to the low-level teams which you call signals?

ANTEATER: Oh, I but dabble in brains, and therefore couldn't set up the map in its glorious detail. But—and correct me if I'm wrong, Mr. Crab—I would surmise that the brain counterpart to an ant colony's signal is the firing of a neuron; or perhaps it is a larger-scale event, such as a pattern of neural firings.

CRAB: I would tend to agree. But don't you think that, for the purposes of our discussion, delineating the exact counterpart is not in itself crucial, desirable though it might be? It seems to me that the main idea is that such a correspondence does exist, even if we don't know exactly how to define it right now. I would only question one point, Dr. Anteater, which you raised, and that concerns the level at which one can have faith that the correspondence begins. You seemed to think that a *signal* might have a direct counterpart in a brain; whereas I feel that it is only at the level of your *active symbols* and above that it is likely that a correspondence must exist.

ANTEATER: Your interpretation may very well be more accurate than mine, Mr. Crab. Thank you for bringing out that subtle point.

ACHILLES: What does a symbol do that a signal couldn't do?

ANTEATER: It is something like the difference between words and letters. Words, which are meaning-carrying entities, are composed of letters, which in themselves carry no meaning. This gives a good idea of the difference between symbols and signals. In fact it is a useful analogy, as long as you keep in mind the fact that words and letters are *passive*, symbols and signals are *active*.

ACHILLES: I'll do so, but I'm not sure I understand why it is so vital to stress the difference between active and passive entities.

ANTEATER: The reason is that the meaning which you attribute to any passive symbol, such as a word on a page, actually derives from the meaning which is carried by corresponding active symbols in your brain. So that the meaning of passive symbols can only be properly understood when it is related to the meaning of active symbols.

ACHILLES: All right. But what is it that endows a *symbol*—an active one, to be sure—with meaning, when you say that a *signal,* which is a perfectly good entity in its own right, has none?

ANTEATER: It all has to do with the way that symbols can cause other symbols to be triggered. When one symbol becomes active, it does not do so in isolation. It is floating about, indeed, in a medium, which is characterized by its caste distribution.

CRAB: Of course, in a brain there is no such thing as a caste distribution, but the counterpart is the "brain state." There, you describe the states of all the neurons, and all the interconnections, and the threshold for firing of each neuron.

ANTEATER: Very well; let's lump "caste distribution" and "brain state" under a common heading, and call them just the "state." Now the state can be described on a low level or on a high level. A low-level description of the state of an ant colony would involve painfully specifying the location of each ant, its age and caste, and other similar items. A very detailed description, yielding practically no global insight as to *why* it is in that state. On the other hand, a description on a high level would involve specifying which symbols could be triggered by which combinations of other symbols, under what conditions, and so forth.

ACHILLES: What about a description on the level of signals, or teams?

ANTEATER: A description on that level would fall somewhere in between the low-level and symbol-level descriptions. It would contain a great deal of information about what is actually going on in specific locations throughout the colony, although certainly less than an ant-by-ant description, since teams consist of clumps of ants. A team-by-team description is like a summary of an ant-by-ant description. However, you have to add extra things which were not present in the ant-by-ant description—such as the relationships between teams, and the supply of various castes here and there. This extra complication is the price you pay for the right to summarize.

ACHILLES: It is interesting to me to compare the merits of the descriptions at various levels. The highest-level description seems to carry the most explanatory power, in that it gives you the most intuitive picture of the ant colony, although strangely enough, it leaves out seemingly the most important feature—the ants.

ANTEATER: But you see, despite appearances, the ants are not the most important feature. Admittedly, were it not for them, the colony wouldn't exist; but something equivalent—a brain—can exist, ant-free. So, at least from a high-level point of view, the ants are dispensable.

ACHILLES: I'm sure no ant would embrace your theory with eagerness.

ANTEATER: Well, I never met an ant with a high-level point of view.

CRAB: What a counterintuitive picture you paint, Dr. Anteater. It seems that, if what you say is true, in order to grasp the whole structure, you have to describe it omitting any mention of its fundamental building blocks.

ANTEATER: Perhaps I can make it a little clearer by an analogy. Imagine you have before you a Charles Dickens novel.

ACHILLES: *The Pickwick Papers*—will that do?

ANTEATER: Excellently! And now imagine trying the following game: You must find a way of mapping letters onto ideas, so that the entire *Pickwick Papers* makes sense when you read it letter by letter.

ACHILLES: Hmm. . . . You mean that every time I hit a word such as "the," I have to think of three definite concepts, one after another, with no room for variation?

ANTEATER: Exactly. They are the "t"-concept, the "h"-concept, and the "e"-concept—and every time, those concepts are as they were the preceding time.

ACHILLES: Well, it sounds like that would turn the experience of "reading" *The Pickwick Papers* into an indescribably boring nightmare. It would be an exercise in meaninglessness, no matter what concept I associated with each letter.

ANTEATER: Exactly. There is no natural mapping from the individual letters into the real world. The natural mapping occurs on a higher level—between words, and parts of the real world. If you wanted to describe the book, therefore, you would make no mention of the letter level.

ACHILLES: Of course not! I'd describe the plot and the characters, and so forth.

ANTEATER: So there you are. You would omit all mention of the building blocks, even though the book exists thanks to them. They are the medium, but not the message.

ACHILLES: All right—but what about ant colonies?

ANTEATER: Here, there are active signals instead of passive letters, and active symbols instead of passive words—but the idea carries over.

ACHILLES: Do you mean I couldn't establish a mapping between signals and things in the real world?

ANTEATER: You would find that you could not do it in such a way that the triggering of new signals would make any sense. Nor could you succeed on any lower level—for example, the ant level. Only on the symbol level do the triggering patterns make sense. Imagine, for instance, that one day you were watching Aunt Hillary when I arrived to pay a call. You could watch as carefully as you wanted, and yet you would probably perceive nothing more than a rearrangement of ants.

ACHILLES: I'm sure that's accurate.

ANTEATER: And yet, as I watched, reading the higher level instead of the lower level, I would see several dormant symbols being awakened, those which translate into the thought "Oh, here's that charming Dr. Anteater again—how pleasant!"—or words to that effect.

ACHILLES: That sounds like what happened when the four of us all found different levels to read in the MU-picture—or at least *three* of us did. . . .

TORTOISE: What an astonishing coincidence that there should be such a resemblance between that strange picture which I chanced upon in the *Well-Tempered Clavier* and the trend of our conversation.

ACHILLES: Do you think it's just coincidence?

TORTOISE: Of course.

ANTEATER: Well, I hope you can grasp now how the thoughts in Aunt Hillary emerge from the manipulation of symbols composed of signals composed of teams composed of lower-level teams, all the way down to ants.

ACHILLES: Why do you call it "symbol manipulation"? Who does the manipulating, if the symbols are themselves active? Who is the agent?

ANTEATER: This gets back to the question that you earlier raised about purpose. You're right that symbols themselves are active, but the activities which they follow are nevertheless not absolutely free. The activities of all symbols are strictly determined by the state of the full system in which they reside. Therefore, the full system is responsible for how its symbols trigger each other, and so it is quite reasonable to speak of the full system as the "agent." As the symbols operate, the state of the system gets slowly transformed, or updated. But there are many features that remain over time. It is this partially constant, partially varying system that is the agent. One can give a name to the full system. For example, Aunt Hillary is the "who" who can be said to manipulate her symbols; and you are similar, Achilles.

ACHILLES: That's quite a strange characterization of the notion of who I am. I'm not sure I can fully understand it, but I will give it some thought.

TORTOISE: It would be quite interesting to follow the symbols in your brain as you do that thinking about the symbols in your brain.

ACHILLES: That's too complicated for me. I have trouble enough just trying to picture how it is possible to look at an ant colony and read it on the symbol level. I can certainly imagine perceiving it at the ant level; and with a little trouble, I can imagine what it must be like to perceive it at the signal level; but what in the world can it be like to perceive an ant colony at the symbol level?

ANTEATER: One learns only through long practice. But when one is at my stage, one reads the top level of an ant colony as easily as you yourself read the "MU" in the MU-picture.

ACHILLES: Really? That must be an amazing experience.

ANTEATER: In a way—but it is also one which is quite familiar to you, Achilles.

ACHILLES: Familiar to me? What do you mean? I have never looked at an ant colony on anything but the ant level.

ANTEATER: Maybe not; but ant colonies are no different from brains in many respects.

ACHILLES: I have never seen nor read any brain either, however.

ANTEATER: What about your *own* brain? Aren't you aware of your own thoughts? Isn't that the essence of consciousness? What else are you doing but reading your own brain directly at the symbol level?

ACHILLES: I never thought of it that way. You mean that I bypass all the lower levels, and see only the topmost level?

ANTEATER: That's the way it is, with conscious systems. They perceive themselves on the symbol level only, and have no awareness of the lower levels, such as the signal levels.

ACHILLES: Does it follow that in a brain, there are active symbols that are constantly updating themselves so that they reflect the overall state of the brain itself, always on the symbol level?

ANTEATER: Certainly. In any conscious system there are symbols that represent the brain state, and they are themselves part of the very brain state which they symbolize. For consciousness requires a large degree of self-consciousness.

ACHILLES: That is a weird notion. It means that although there is frantic activity occurring in my brain at all times, I am capable of registering that activity in only one way—on the symbol level; and I am completely insensitive to the lower levels. It is like being able to read a Dickens novel by direct visual perception, without ever having learned the letters of the alphabet. I can't imagine anything as weird as that really happening.

CRAB: But precisely that sort of thing *did* happen when you read "MU," without perceiving the lower levels "HOLISM" and "REDUCTIONISM."

ACHILLES: You're right—I bypassed the lower levels, and saw only the top. I wonder if I'm missing all sorts of meaning on lower levels of my brain as well, by reading only the symbol level. It's too bad that the top level doesn't contain all the information about the bottom level, so that by reading the top, one also learns what the bottom level says. But I guess it would be naive to hope that the top level encodes anything from the bottom level—it probably doesn't percolate up. The MU-picture is the most striking possible example of that: There, the topmost level says only "MU," which bears no relation whatever to the lower levels!

CRAB: That's absolutely true. (*Picks up the MU-picture, to inspect it more closely.*) Hmm. . . . There's something strange about the smallest letters in this picture; they're very wiggly . . .

ANTEATER: Let me take a look. (*Peers closely at the MU-picture.*) I think there's yet another level, which all of us missed!

TORTOISE: Speak for yourself, Dr. Anteater.

ACHILLES: Oh, no—that can't be! Let me see. (*Looks very carefully.*) I know the rest of you won't believe this, but the message of this picture is staring us all in the face, hidden in its depths. It is simply one word, repeated over and over again, like a mantra—but what an important one: "MU"! What do you know! It is the same as the top level! And none of us suspected it in the least.

CRAB: We would never have noticed it if it hadn't been for you, Achilles.

ANTEATER: I wonder if the coincidence of the highest and lowest levels happened by chance? Or was it a purposeful act carried out by some creator?

CRAB: How could one ever decide that?

TORTOISE: I don't see any way to do so, since we have no idea why that particular picture is in the Crab's edition of the *Well-Tempered Clavier.*

ANTEATER: Although we have been having a lively discussion, I have still managed to listen with a good fraction of an ear to this very long and complex four-voice fugue. It is extraordinarily beautiful.

TORTOISE: It certainly is. And now, in just a moment, comes an organ point.

ACHILLES: Isn't an organ point what happens when a piece of music slows down slightly, settles for a moment or two on a single note or chord, and then resumes at normal speed after a short silence?

TORTOISE: No, you're thinking of a "fermata"—a sort of musical semicolon. Did you notice there was one of those in the prelude?

ACHILLES: I guess I must have missed it.

TORTOISE: Well, you have another chance coming up to hear a fermata —in fact, there are a couple of them coming up, toward the end of this fugue.

ACHILLES: Oh, good. You'll point them out in advance, won't you?

TORTOISE: If you like.

ACHILLES: But do tell me, what is an organ point?

TORTOISE: An organ point is the sustaining of a single note by one of the voices in a polyphonic piece (often the lowest voice), while the other voices continue their own independent lines. This organ point is on the note of G. Listen carefully, and you'll hear it.

ANTEATER: There occurred an incident one day when I visited with Aunt Hillary which reminds me of your suggestion of observing the symbols in Achilles' brain as they create thoughts which are about themselves.

CRAB: Do tell us about it.

ANTEATER: Aunt Hillary had been feeling very lonely, and was very happy to have someone to talk to that day. So she gratefully told me to help myself to the juiciest ants I could find. (She's always been most generous with her ants.)

ACHILLES: Gee!

ANTEATER: It just happened that I had been watching the symbols which were carrying out her thoughts, because in them were some particularly juicy-looking ants.

ACHILLES: Gee!

ANTEATER: So I helped myself to a few of the fattest ants which had been parts of the higher-level symbols which I had been reading. Specifically, the symbols which they were part of were the ones which had expressed the thought "Help yourself to any of the ants which look appetizing."

ACHILLES: Gee!

ANTEATER: Unfortunately for them, but fortunately for me, the little bugs didn't have the slightest inkling of what they were collectively telling me, on the symbol level.

ACHILLES: Gee! That is an amazing wraparound. They were completely unconscious of what they were participating in. Their acts could be seen as part of a pattern on a higher level, but of course they were completely unaware of that. Ah, what a pity—a supreme irony, in fact —that they missed it.

CRAB: You are right, Mr. T—that was a lovely organ point.

ANTEATER: I had never heard one before, but that one was so conspicuous that no one could miss it. Very effective.

ACHILLES: What? Has the organ point already occurred? How can I not have noticed it, if it was so blatant?

TORTOISE: Perhaps you were so wrapped up in what you were saying that you were completely unaware of it. Ah, what a pity—a supreme irony, in fact—that you missed it.

CRAB: Tell me, does Aunt Hillary live in an anthill?

ANTEATER: Well, she owns a rather large piece of property. It used to belong to someone else, but that is rather a sad story. In any case, her estate is quite expansive. She lives rather sumptuously, compared to many other colonies.

ACHILLES: How does that jibe with the communistic nature of ant colonies which you earlier described to us? It sounds quite inconsistent, to me, to preach communism and to live in a fancy estate!

ANTEATER: The communism is on the ant level. In an ant colony all ants work for the common good, even to their own individual detriment at times. Now this is simply a built-in aspect of Aunt Hillary's structure, but for all I know, she may not even be aware of this internal communism. Most human beings are not aware of anything about their neurons; in fact they probably are quite content not to know anything about their brains, being somewhat squeamish creatures. Aunt Hillary is also somewhat squeamish; she gets rather antsy whenever she starts to think about ants at all. So she avoids thinking about them whenever possible. I truly doubt that she knows anything about the communistic society which is built into her very structure. She herself is a staunch believer in libertarianism—you know, laissez-faire and all that. So it makes perfect sense, to me at least, that she should live in a rather sumptuous manor.

ILLUSTRATION BY THE AUTHOR.

TORTOISE: As I turned the page just now, while following along in this lovely edition of the *Well-Tempered Clavier*, I noticed that the first of the two fermatas is coming up soon—so you might listen for it, Achilles.

ACHILLES: I will, I will.

TORTOISE: Also, there's a most curious picture facing this page.

CRAB: Another one? What next?

TORTOISE: See for yourself. (*Passes the score over to the Crab.*)

CRAB: Aha! It's just a few bunches of letters. Let's see—there are various numbers of the letters "J," "S," "B," "m," "a," and "t." It's strange, how the first three letters grow, and then the last three letters shrink again.

ANTEATER: May I see it?

CRAB: Why, certainly.

ANTEATER: Oh, by concentrating on details, you have utterly missed the big picture. In reality, this group of letters is "f," "e," "r," "A," "C," "H," without any repetitions. First they get smaller, then they get bigger. Here, Achilles—what do you make of it?

ACHILLES: Let me see. Hmm. Well, I see it as a set of uppercase letters which grow as you move to the right.

TORTOISE: Do they spell anything?

ACHILLES: Ah . . . "J. S. BACH." Oh! I understand now. It's Bach's name!

TORTOISE: Strange that you should see it that way. I see it as a set of lower-case letters, shrinking as they move to the right, and . . . spelling out . . . the name of . . . (*Slows down slightly, especially drawing out the last few words. Then there is a brief silence. Suddenly he resumes as if nothing unusual had happened.*)—"fermat."

ACHILLES: Oh, you've got Fermat on the brain, I do believe. You see Fermat's Last Theorem everywhere.

ANTEATER: You were right, Mr. Tortoise—I just heard a charming little fermata in the fugue.

CRAB: So did I.

ACHILLES: Do you mean everybody heard it but me? I'm beginning to feel stupid.

TORTOISE: There, there, Achilles—don't feel bad. I'm sure you won't miss Fugue's Last Fermata (which is coming up quite soon). But, to return to our previous topic, Dr. Anteater, what is the very sad story which you alluded to, concerning the former owner of Aunt Hillary's property?

ANTEATER: The former owner was an extraordinary individual, one of the most creative ant colonies who ever lived. His name was Johant Sebastiant Fermant, and he was a mathematician by vocation, but a musiciant by avocation.

ACHILLES: How very versantile of him!

ANTEATER: At the height of his creative powers, he met with a most untimely demise. One day, a very hot summer day, he was out soaking up the warmth, when a freak thundershower—the kind that hits only once every hundred years or so—appeared from out of the blue and thoroughly drenched J. S. F. Since the storm came utterly without warning, the ants got completely disoriented and confused. The intricate organization that had been so finely built up over decades all went down the drain in a matter of minutes. It was tragic.

ACHILLES: Do you mean that all the ants drowned, which obviously would spell the end of poor J. S. F.?

ANTEATER: Actually, no. The ants managed to survive, every last one of them, by crawling onto various sticks and logs that floated above the raging torrents. But when the waters receded and left the ants back on their home grounds, there was no organization left. The caste distribution was utterly destroyed, and the ants themselves had no ability to reconstruct what had once before been such a finely tuned organization. They were as helpless as the pieces of Humpty Dumpty in putting themselves back together again. I myself tried, like all the king's horses and all the king's men, to put poor Fermant together again. I faithfully put out sugar and cheese, hoping against hope that somehow Fermant would reappear . . . *(Pulls out a handkerchief and wipes his eyes.)*

ACHILLES: How valiant of you! I never knew Anteaters had such big hearts.

ANTEATER: But it was all to no avail. He was gone, beyond reconstitution. However, something very strange then began to take place: over the next few months, the ants that had been components of J. S. F. slowly regrouped, and built up a new organization. And thus was Aunt Hillary born.

CRAB: Remarkable! Aunt Hillary is composed of the very same ants as Fermant was?

ANTEATER: Well, originally she was, yes. By now, some of the older ants have died, and been replaced. But there are still many holdovers from the J. S. F.-days.

CRAB: And can't you recognize some of J. S. F.'s old traits coming to the fore, from time to time, in Aunt Hillary?

ANTEATER: Not a one. They have nothing in common. And there is no reason they should, as I see it. There are, after all, often several distinct ways to rearrange a group of parts to form a "sum." And Aunt Hillary was just a new "sum" of the old parts. Not *more* than the sum, mind you—just that particular *kind* of sum.

TORTOISE: Speaking of sums, I am reminded of number theory, where occasionally one will be able to take apart a theorem into its component symbols, rearrange them in a new order, and come up with a new theorem.

ANTEATER: I've never heard of such a phenomenon, although I confess to being a total ignoramus in the field.

ACHILLES: Nor have I heard of it—and I am rather well versed in the field, if I don't say so myself. I suspect Mr. T is just setting up one of his elaborate spoofs. I know him pretty well by now.

ANTEATER: Speaking of number theory, I am reminded of J. S. F. again, for number theory is one of the domains in which he excelled. In fact, he made some rather remarkable contributions to number theory. Aunt Hillary, on the other hand, is remarkably dull-witted in anything that has even the remotest connection with mathematics. Also, she has only a rather banal taste in music, whereas Sebastiant was extremely gifted in music.

ACHILLES: I am very fond of number theory. Could you possibly relate to us something of the nature of Sebastiant's contributions?

ANTEATER: Very well, then. *(Pauses for a moment to sip his tea, then resumes.)* Have you heard of Fourmi's infamous "Well-Tested Conjecture"?

ᴀCHILLES: I'm not sure. . . . It sounds strangely familiar, and yet I can't quite place it.

ANTEATER: It's a very simple idea. Lierre de Fourmi, a mathematician by vocation but lawyer by avocation, had been reading in his copy of the classic text *Arithmetica* by Di of Antus, and came across a page containing the equation

$$2^a + 2^b = 2^c$$

He immediately realized that this equation has infinitely many solutions a, b, c, and then wrote in the margin the following notorious comment:

The equation

$$a^n + h^n = c^n$$

has solutions in positive integers a, b, c, and n only when $n = 2$ (and then there are infinitely many triplets a, b, c, which satisfy the equation); but there are no solutions for $n > 2$. I have discovered a truly marvelous proof of this statement, which, unfortunately, this margin is too small to contain.

Ever since that year, some three hundred days ago, mathematicians have been vainly trying to do one of two things: either to prove Fourmi's claim, and thereby vindicate Fourmi's reputation, which,

During emigrations army ants sometimes create bridges of their own bodies. In this photograph of such a bridge (de Fourmi Lierre), the workers *Eciton burchelli* colony can be seen linking their legs and, along the top of the bridge, hooking their tarsal claws together to form irregular systems of chains. A symbiotic silverfish, *Trichatelura manni*, is seen crossing the bridge in the center. (From E. O. Wilson, *The Insect Societies*. Photograph courtesy of C. W. Rettenmeyer.)

although very high, has been somewhat tarnished by skeptics who think he never really found the proof he claimed to have found—or else to refute the claim, by finding a counterexample: a set of four integers a, b, c, and n, with $n > 2$, which satisfy the equation. Until very recently, every attempt in either direction had met with failure. To be sure, the Conjecture has been verified for many specific values of n—in particular, all n up to 125,000. But no one had succeeded in proving it for *all* n—no one, that is, until Johant Sebastiant Fermant came upon the scene. It was he who found the proof that cleared Fourmi's name. It now goes under the name "Johant Sebastiant's Well-Tested Conjecture."

ACHILLES: Shouldn't it be called a "Theorem" rather than a "Conjecture," if it's finally been given a proper proof?

ANTEATER: Strictly speaking, you're right, but tradition has kept it this way.

TORTOISE: What sort of music did Sebastiant do?

ANTEATER: He had great gifts for composition. Unfortunately, his greatest work is shrouded in mystery, for he never reached the point of publishing it. Some believe that he had it all in his mind; others are more unkind, saying that he probably never worked it out at all, but merely blustered about it.

ACHILLES: What was the nature of this magnum opus?

ANTEATER: It was to be a giant prelude and fugue; the fugue was to have twenty-four voices, and to involve twenty-four distinct subjects, one in each of the major and minor keys.

ACHILLES: It would certainly be hard to listen to a twenty-four-voice fugue as a whole!

CRAB: Not to mention composing one!

ANTEATER: But all that we know of it is Sebastiant's description of it, which he wrote in the margin of his copy of Buxtehude's Preludes and Fugues for Organ. The last words which he wrote before his tragic demise were:

> I have composed a truly marvelous fugue. In it, I have added together the power of 24 keys, and the power of 24 themes; I came up with a fugue with the power of 24 voices. Unfortunately, this margin is too narrow to contain it.

And the unrealized masterpiece simply goes by the name "Fermant's Last Fugue."

ACHILLES: Oh, that is unbearably tragic.

TORTOISE: Speaking of fugues, this fugue that we have been listening to is nearly over. Toward the end, there occurs a strange new twist on its theme. *(Flips the page in the* Well-Tempered Clavier.*)* Well, what have we here? A new illustration—how appealing! *(Shows it to the Crab.)*

CRAB: Well, what have we here? Oh, I see: it's "HOLISMIONISM," written in large letters that first shrink and then grow back to their original size. But that doesn't make any sense, because it's not a word. Oh me, oh my! *(Passes it to the Anteater.)*

ANTEATER: Well, what have we here? Oh, I see: it's "REDUCTHOLISM," written in small letters that first grow and then shrink back to their original size. But that doesn't make any sense, because it's not a word. Oh my, oh me! *(Passes it to Achilles.)*

ACHILLES: I know the rest of you won't believe this, but in fact this picture consists of the word "HOLISM" written twice, with the letters

ILLUSTRATION BY THE AUTHOR.

continually shrinking as they proceed from left to right. (*Returns it to the Tortoise.*)

TORTOISE: I know the rest of you won't believe this, but in fact this picture consists of the word "REDUCTIONISM" written once, with the letters continually growing as they proceed from left to right.

ACHILLES: At last—I heard the new twist on the theme this time! I am so glad that you pointed it out to me, Mr. Tortoise. Finally, I think I am beginning to grasp the art of listening to fugues.

Reflections

Is a soul greater than the hum of its parts? The participants in the preceding dialogue seem to have divergent views on this question. What is certain and agreed upon, however, is that the collective behavior of a system of individuals can have many surprising properties.

Many people, on reading this dialogue, are reminded of the seemingly purposive, selfish, survival-oriented behavior of countries that emerges somehow from the habits and institutions of their citizens: their educational system, legal structure, religions, resources, style of consumption and level of expectations, and so on. When a tight organization forms from distinct individuals—particularly when contributions to the organization are not traceable to specific individuals in the lower level—we tend to see it as a higher-level individual and often speak of it in anthropomorphic terms. A newspaper article about a terrorist group described it as "playing its cards extremely close to its chest." It is often said of Russia that it "desires" world recognition of its might because it "suffers" from a "long-standing inferiority complex" with respect to Western Europe. While admittedly metaphors, these examples serve to demonstrate how strong the urge is to personify organizations.

The component individuals of organizations—secretaries, workers, bus drivers, executives, and so on—have their own goals in life, which, one might expect, would come into conflict with any higher-level entity of which they formed a part, but there is an effect (which many students of political science would regard as insidious and sinister) whereby the organization co-opts and exploits these very goals, taking advantage of the individuals' pride, need for self-esteem, and so on, and turning them back to its own profits. There emerges from all the many low-level goals a kind of higher-level momentum that subsumes all of them, that sweeps them along and thereby perpetuates itself.

Therefore it is perhaps not so silly for the Tortoise to object to Achilles' comparison of himself to an ant and to prefer an attempt by Achilles to "map himself," at a suitable level, onto an ant colony. Similarly, we may sometimes wonder to ourselves "What is it like to be China? How different from that would it feel to be the United States?" Do such questions makes any kind of sense at all? We shall postpone detailed discussion of them until after Nagel's piece on bats (selection 24). Nonetheless, let us think a bit right now about whether it makes sense to think of "being" a country. Does a country have thoughts or beliefs? It all comes down to whether a country has a *symbol* level, in the sense that Aunt Hillary does. Instead of saying that a system "has a symbol level," we might instead say, "It is a representational system."

This concept of "representational system" is a crucial one in this book, and needs a somewhat precise definition. By "representational system" we will mean an active, self-updating collection of structures organized to "mirror" the world as it evolves. A painting, no matter how representational, would thus be excluded, since it is static. Curiously, we mean also to exclude mirrors themselves, although the argument could be made that the set of images in a mirror keeps quite up to date with the world! The lack in this case is twofold. First, the mirror itself does not make any distinction between images of different objects—it mirrors the universe, but sees no *categories*. In fact, a mirror makes only *one* image— it is in the eye of the beholder that the mirror's single image breaks up into "separate" images of many distinct objects. A mirror cannot be said to perceive—only to reflect. Second, the image in a mirror is not an autonomous structure with its own "life"; it depends directly on the external world. If the lights are turned off, it goes away. A representational system should be able to keep on going even if cut off from contact with the reality it is "reflecting"—although you now see that "reflection" is not quite a rich enough metaphor. The isolated representational structures should now continue to evolve in a way that reflects, if not the true way the world will evolve, at least a probable way. Actually, a good representational system will sprout parallel branches for various possibilities that can be reasonably anticipated. Its internal models will, in the metaphorical sense defined in the Reflections on "Rediscovering the Mind," go into superpositions of states, each with an associated subjective estimate of likelihood.

In brief, then, a representational system is built on categories; it sifts incoming data into those categories, when necessary refining or enlarging its network of internal categories; its representations or "symbols" interact among themselves according to their own internal logic; this logic, although it runs without ever consulting the external world, nevertheless creates a faithful enough model of the way the world works that it manages to keep the symbols pretty much "in phase" with the world they are supposed to be mirroring. A television is thus not a representational system, as it indiscriminately throws dots onto its screen without regard to what kinds of things they represent, and the patterns on the screen do not have autonomy—they are just passive copies of things "out there." By contrast, a computer program that can "look" at a scene and tell you what is in that scene comes closer to being a representational system. The most advanced artificial intelligence work on computer vision hasn't yet cracked that nut. A program that could look at a scene and tell you not only what kinds of things are in the scene, but also what probably caused that scene and what will probably ensue in it—that is what we mean by a representational system. In this sense, is a country a representational system? Does a country have a symbol level? We'll leave this one for you to ponder on.

One of the crucial notions of the Ant Fugue is the "caste distribution" or "state," for it is claimed that that is a causal agent in determining the future of the organism. Yet this seems to contradict the idea that all of a system's behavior comes from underlying laws—those of ants or neurons, in the case of colonies or brains—but ultimately, in either case, those of particles. Is there such a thing as "downward causality"—put starkly, the notion that "a thought can influence the path of an electron"?

In *Inside the Brain* by William Calvin and George Ojemann, there is a provocative series of questions asked about a neural firing. "What starts it?" they ask. What causes the sodium channels to open up? (The function of the sodium channels is to let sodium ions into the neuron, and when their concentration is high enough, that then triggers the release of the neurotransmitters, whose flow from one neuron to another constitutes the essence of neural firing.) The answer is, the sodium channels are voltage-sensitive, and they have just been hit by a strong enough voltage pulse to flip their state from closed to open.

"But what causes the voltage to rise originally, so that it crosses this threshold . . . and sets off this sequence of events called the impulse?" they go on. The answer is, various "nodes" along the neuron's axon have simply relayed this high voltage from one station to the next. So then the question is again transformed. This time they ask, "But what causes the very first impulse to occur at the very first node? Where does *that* voltage shift come from? What precedes the impulse?"

Well, for most neurons inside the brain—"interneurons," meaning neurons that are fed into not by sensory input but only by other neurons —the answer is, their first node's voltage shift is provoked by the total effect of the pulses of neurotransmitters coming in from other neurons. (We could call those neurons "upstream" neurons, but that would imply, quite falsely, that the flow of neural activity in the brain follows a line in only one direction, in the manner of a river. In fact, as a rule, neural flow patterns are far from linear and make loops all over the place, quite unlike rivers.)

Thus we seem to get into a vicious circle—a chicken-and-egg type of riddle. Question: "What triggers a neural firing?" Answer: "Other neural firings!" But the real question remains unanswered: "Why those neurons, and not others? Why this vicious circle and not another neural loop in another part of the brain?" To answer this, we have to shift levels and talk about the relationship of the brain to the ideas it encodes, which then would require us to talk about how the brain encodes, or represents, its concepts about the world. Since we do not wish to theorize in this book on the details of such matters, we will talk about a related but simpler concept.

Imagine an intricately bifurcating and rejoining domino-chain network. Suppose that each domino has a little time-delayed spring underneath it that stands it up again five seconds after it has fallen. By setting up the network in various configurations, one could actually program the system of dominoes to perform calculations with numbers, exactly as one could a full-scale computer. Various pathways would carry out various parts of the calculation, and elaborate branching loops could be set up. (Note how this image is not too different, then, from that of networks of neurons in a brain.)

One could imagine a "program" trying to break the integer 641 into the product of its prime factors. "Why isn't this particular domino ever falling down?" you might ask, pointing at one that you've been watching for a long time. An answer on one level would be "Because its predecessor never falls." But that low-level "explanation" only begs the question. What one really wants—the only satisfying answer, in fact—is an answer on the level of the concepts of the program: "It never falls because it is in a stretch of dominoes that gets activated only when a divisor is found. But 641 has no divisors—it is prime. So the reason that domino never falls has nothing to do with physics or domino chains—it is simply the fact that 641 is prime."

But have we then admitted that higher-level laws actually are responsible, and govern the system above and beyond lower-level laws? No. It is simply that an explanation that makes any *sense* demands higher-level concepts. The dominos certainly don't know they are part of a program, nor do they need to—any more than the keys of a piano know, or need to know, which piece you are playing. Think how strange it would be if they did! Nor do your neurons know that they are involved in thinking these thoughts right now, nor ants that they are part of the grand scheme of their colony.

There is a further-back question that might arise in your mind: "What laws, at what level, are responsible for the existence of the program and the domino chains—indeed, for the manufacturing of the dominoes at all?" To answer this and the many questions it inevitably triggers, we are sent sailing backward in time over larger and larger spans, back into all the reasons our society exists, back to the origin of life, and so on. It is more convenient to sweep these many questions under the rug and simply to leave our reason as: the primeness of 641. We prefer this kind of compact higher-level explanation, one that eliminates long views into the past and that concentrates on the present or the timeless. But if we want to trace events to their ultimate causes, we are forced into reductionistic views as described by Dawkins or the Tortoise. Indeed, ultimately we are sent back to the physicists, who will refer us to the "Big Bang" as the primordial cause of everything. This is not satisfying, however, because we want an answer at a level that appeals to concepts familiar to people—and, fortunately, nature is stratified enough that this is often possible.

We asked whether a thought can influence the course of an electron in flight. The reader could easily conjure up an image we do not have in mind—namely, of a deeply concentrating "psychic" with furrowed brow beaming his "waves of Plutonian energy" (or whatever he calls them) outwards toward an object—say a tumbling die—and influencing the way it will land. We do not believe in anything of the sort. We do not believe that there is some as-yet undiscovered "mental magnetism" through which concepts could "reach down" and, through some sort of "semantic potential," alter the paths of particles, making them deviate from what present-day physics would predict. We are talking about something else. It is more a question of where explanatory power comes from—perhaps a question of the proper ways of using words, a question of how to reconcile everyday usage of terms like "cause" with the scientific usage of those terms. Thus, is it reasonable to explain the trajectories of particles by making references to higher-level notions such as "beliefs," "desires," and so forth? The reader may detect that we see much utility in adopting this way of speaking. Just as evolutionary biologists feel free to use "teleological shorthand" to condense their concepts down to an intuitively reasonable size, so we feel that people who study the mechanisms of thought must necessarily become conversant with ways of translating back and forth between purely reductionistic language and a sort of "holistic" language in which wholes do indeed exert a visible effect on their parts, do indeed possess "downward causality."

In physics, when a shift of point of view is made, sometimes the laws may appear to be different. Think of the amusement park ride in which people line the inner walls of a large cylinder. The cylinder starts spinning and as it does so, its floor falls away, as if a giant can opener had just opened this can from below. The people are left hanging, with their backs powerfully pressed against the wall by the so-called centrifugal force. If you were on this ride and attempted to throw a tennis ball to a friend directly across the cylinder, you would see the ball flying crazily off course, perhaps even boomeranglike returning to you! Of course, this is simply because you would move around in the same amount of time as the ball sailed (in a straight line) across the cylinder. But if you were unaware that you were in a rotating frame, you might invent a name for the strange deflecting force that makes your ball veer away from its intended destination. You might think it was some bizarre variation of gravity. This would be strongly supported by the observation that this force acted identically on any two objects with the same mass, as gravity does. Amazingly enough, this simple observation—that "fictitious forces" and gravity are easily confused—is at the heart of Einstein's great theory of general relativity. The point of this example is that a shift of frame of reference can induce a shift of perceptions and concepts—a shift in ways of perceiving causes and effects. If it is good enough for Einstein, it ought to be good enough for us!

We will not belabor the reader further with descriptions of the tricky shifts of point of view as one swings back and forth between the level of wholes and the level of their parts. We will simply introduce some catchy terminology which may titillate the reader into thinking further about these issues. We have contrasted "reductionism" and "holism." Now you can see that "reductionism" is synonymous with "upward causality" and "holism" with "downward causality." These are concepts having to do with how events on different size-scales in *space* determine each other. They have counterpart notions in the *time* dimension: to reductionism corresponds the idea of predicting the future from the past without regard to "goals" of organisms; to holism corresponds the idea that only inanimate objects can be so predicted, but that in the case of animate objects, purposes and goals and desires and so on are essential to explain their actions. This view, often called "goal-oriented" or "teleological," could equally well be termed "goalism"—and its opposite could be termed "predictionism." Thus predictionism emerges as the temporal counterpart to reductionism, with goalism being the temporal counterpart to holism. Predictionism is the doctrine that only "upstream" events —and nothing "downstream"—need be taken into account in determining the way the present flows into the future. Goalism, its opposite, sees animate objects as moving toward goals in the future—thus it sees future events in some sense projecting causal power backward in time, or retroactively. We can call this "retroactive causality"; it is the temporal counterpart to holism's "introactive causality," where causes are seen to flow "inward" (from wholes to their parts). Put goalism and holism together, and you have—you guessed it—soulism! Put predictionism and reductionism together, and you get—mechanism.

To summarize, we can draw a little chart:

Hard scientists	Soft scientists
Reductionism (upward causality)	Holism (downward causality)
+	+
Predictionism (upstream causality)	Goalism (downstream causality)
= Mechanism	= Soulism

Well, now that we have indulged our fancy for wordplay, let us move on. A fresh perspective is offered us by another metaphor for brain activity: that of the "thinking wind chime." Think of a complex wind chime structured like a mobile, with glass "tinklers" dangling like leaves off branches, branches dangling from larger branches, and so on. When wind strikes the chime, many tinklers flutter and slowly the whole structure changes on all levels. It is obvious that not just the wind, but also the chime state, determines how the little glass tinklers move. Even if only one single glass tinkler were dangling, the twistedness of its string would have as much to do with how the chime would move as the wind would.

Just as people do things "of their own volition," so the chime seems to have a "will of its own." What is volition? A complicated internal configuration, established through a long history, that encodes tendencies toward certain future internal configurations and away from others. This is present in the lowliest wind chime.

But is this fair? Does a wind chime have desires? Can a wind chime think? Let's fantasize a bit, adding many features to our chime. Suppose there is a fan on a track near the chime, whose position is electronically controlled by the angle of one particular branch in the chime, and whose blades' rotational speed is controlled by the angle of another branch. Now the chime has some control over its environment, like having big hands that are guided by groups of tiny, insignificant-seeming neurons: the chime plays a larger role in determining its own future.

Let's go further and suppose that many of the branches control blowers, one blower per branch. Now when wind—natural or blower-caused—blows, a group of tinklers will shimmer, and subtly and delicately they will transmit a soft shimmer to various other portions of the chime. That in turn propagates around, gradually twisting branches, thus creating a new chime state that determines where the blowers point and how hard they blow, and this will set up more responses in the chime. Now the external wind and the internal chime state are intertwined in a very complicated way—so complicated, in fact, that it would be very hard to disentangle them conceptually from each other.

Imagine two chimes in the same room, each affecting the other by blowing small gusts of wind in the direction of the other. Who can say that it makes sense to decompose the system into two natural parts? It might be that the best way to look at the system is in terms of top-level branches, in which case there might be five or ten natural parts in each of the two chimes—or perhaps the branches a level below that are the best units to look at, in which case we might see twenty or more per chime. . . . It is all a matter of convenience. All parts interact in some sense with all others, but there might be two parts that are somewhat discernible as separate in space or in coherence of organization—certain types of shimmering might stay localized in one region, for instance—and we could then speak of distinct "organisms." But note how the whole thing is still explicable in terms of physics.

We could now posit a mechanical hand whose motions are controlled by the angles of, say, two dozen high-level branches. These branches are of course intimately tied in with the entire chime state. We could imagine the chime state determining the hand's motions in a curious way—namely telling the hand which chess piece to pick up and move on a board. Wouldn't it be a marvelous coincidence if it always picked up a sensible piece and made a legal move? And an even more marvelous coincidence if its moves were always *good* moves? Hardly. If this were to happen, it would be precisely because it was *not* a coincidence. It would be because the chime's internal state had *representational power.*

Once again we'll back away from trying to describe precisely how ideas could be stored in this strange shimmering structure, reminiscent of a quaking aspen. The point has been to suggest to the reader the potential delicacy, intricacy, and self-involvedness of a system that responds to external stimuli and to features at various levels of its own internal configuration.

It is well-nigh impossible to disentangle such a system's response to the outside world from its own self-involved response, for the tiniest external perturbation will trigger a myriad tiny interconnected events, and a cascade will ensue. If you think of this as the system's "perception" of input, then clearly its own state is also "perceived" in a similar way. Self-perception cannot be disentangled from perception.

The existence of a higher-level way of looking at such a system is not a foregone conclusion; that is, there is no guarantee that we could decode the chime state into a consistent set of English sentences expressing the beliefs of the system, including, for instance, the set of rules of chess (as well as how to play a good game of chess!). However, when systems like that have *evolved* by means of natural selection, there *will* be a reason that some have survived and most others failed to: meaningful internal organization allowing the system to take advantage of its environment and to control it, at least partially.

In the wind chime, the hypothetical conscious ant colony, and the brain, that organization is stratified. The levels in the wind chime corresponded to the different levels of branches dangling from other branches, with the spatial disposition of the highest branches representing the most compact and abstract summary of the global qualities of the chime state, and the disposition of the many thousands (or millions?) of quivering individual tinklers giving a totally unsummarized, unintuitive, but concrete and local description of the chime state. In the ant colony, there were ants, teams, signals at various levels, and finally the caste distribution or "colony state"—again the most incisive yet abstract view of the colony. As Achilles marveled, it is so abstract that the ants themselves are never mentioned! In the brain, we just do not know how to find the high-level structures that would provide a readout in English of the beliefs stored in the brain. Or rather, we do—we just ask the brain's owner to tell us what he or she believes! But we have no way of physically determining where or how beliefs are coded.*

In our three systems, various semiautonomous subsystems exist, each of which represents a concept, and various input stimuli can awaken certain concepts, or symbols. Note that in this view there is no "inner eye" that watches all the activity and "feels" the system; instead the system's state itself represents the feelings. The legendary "little person" who would play that role would have to have yet a smaller "inner eye," after all, and that would lead to further little people and ever-tinier "inner eyes"—in short, to infinite regress of the worst and silliest kind. In this kind of system, contrariwise, the self-awareness comes from the system's intricately intertwined responses to both external and internal stimuli. This kind of pattern illustrates a general thesis: "Mind is a pattern perceived by a mind." This is perhaps circular, but it is neither vicious nor paradoxical.

The closest one could come to having a "little person" or an "inner eye" that perceives the brain's activity would be in the *self-symbol*—a complex subsystem that is a model of the full system. But the self-symbol does not perceive by having its own repertoire of smaller symbols (including its *own* self-symbol—an obvious invitation to infinite regress). Rather, the self-symbol's *joint activation* with ordinary (nonreflexive) symbols constitutes the system's perception. Perception resides at the level of the full system, not at the level of the self-symbol. If you want to say that the self-symbol perceives something, it is only in the sense that a male moth perceives a female moth, or in the sense that your brain perceives your heart rate—at a level of microscopic intercellular chemical messages.

The last point to be made here is that the brain needs this multileveled structure because its mechanisms must be extraordinarily flexible in order to cope with an unpredictable, dynamic world. Rigid programs will go extinct rapidly. A strategy exclusively for hunting dinosaurs will be no good when it comes to hunting woolly mammoths, and much less good when it comes to tending domestic animals or commuting to work on the subway. An intelligent system must be able to reconfigure itself—to sit back, assess the situation, and regroup—in rather deep ways; such flexi-

---

*See selection 25, "An Epistemological Nightmare," for a story featuring a machine that can outdo a person at "brain reading."

bility requires only the most abstract kinds of mechanisms to remain unchanged. A many-layered system can have programs tailored to very specific needs (e.g., programs for chess playing, woolly-mammoth hunting, and so on) at its most superficial level, and progressively more abstract programs at deeper layers, thus getting the best of both worlds. Examples of the deeper type of program would be ones for recognizing patterns; for evaluating conflicting pieces of evidence; for deciding which, among rival subsystems clamoring for attention, should get higher priority; for deciding how to label the currently perceived situation for possible retrieval on future occasions that may be similar; for deciding whether two concepts really are or are not analogous; and so on.

Further description of this kind of system would carry us deep into the philosophical and technical territory of cognitive science, and we will not go that far. Instead, we refer readers to the "Further Readings" section for discussions of the strategies of knowledge representation in humans and in programs. In particular, Aaron Sloman's book *The Computer Revolution in Philosophy* goes into great detail on these issues.

D.R.H.

12

ARNOLD ZUBOFF

The Story of a Brain

I

Once upon a time, a kind young man who enjoyed many friends and great wealth learned that a horrible rot was overtaking all of his body but his nervous system. He loved life; he loved having experiences. Therefore he was intensely interested when scientist friends of amazing abilities proposed the following:

"We shall take the brain from your poor rotting body and keep it healthy in a special nutrient bath. We shall have it connected to a machine that is capable of inducing in it any pattern at all of neural firings and is therein capable of bringing about for you any sort of total experience that it is possible for the activity of your nervous system to cause or to be."

The reason for this last disjunction of the verbs *to cause* and *to be* was that, although all these scientists were convinced of a general theory that they called "the neural theory of experience," they disagreed on the specific formulation of this theory. They all knew of countless instances in which it was just obvious that the state of the brain, the pattern of its activity, somehow had made for a man's experiencing this rather than that. It seemed reasonable to them all that ultimately what decisively controlled any particular experience of a man—controlled whether it existed and what it was like—was the state of his nervous system and more specifically that of those areas of the brain that careful research had discovered to be involved in the various aspects of consciousness. This conviction was what had prompted their proposal to their young friend.

That they disagreed about whether an experience simply consisted in or else was caused by neural activity was irrelevant to their belief that as long as their friend's brain was alive and functioning under their control, they could keep him having his beloved experience indefinitely, just as though he were walking about and getting himself into the various situations that would in a more natural way have stimulated each of those patterns of neural firings that they would bring about artificially. If he were actually to have gazed through a hole in a snow-covered frozen pond, for instance, the physical reality there would have caused him to experience what Thoreau described: "the quiet parlor of the fishes, pervaded by a softened light as through a window of ground glass, with its bright sanded floor the same as in summer." The brain lying in its bath, stripped of its body and far from the pond, if it were made to behave precisely as it naturally would under such pond-hole circumstances, would have for the young man that very same experience.

Well, the young man agreed with the concept and looked forward to its execution. And a mere month after he had first heard the thing proposed to him, his brain was floating in the warm nutrient bath. His scientist friends kept busy researching, by means of paid subjects, which patterns of neuron firings were like the natural neural responses to very pleasant situations; and, through the use of a complex electrode machine, they kept inducing only these neural activities in their dear friend's brain.

Then there was trouble. One night the watchman had been drinking, and, tipsily wandering into the room where the bath lay, he careened forward so his right arm entered the bath and actually split the poor brain into its two hemispheres.

The brain's scientist friends were very upset the next morning. They had been all ready to feed into the brain a marvelous new batch of experiences whose neural patterns they had just recently discovered.

"If we let our friend's brain mend after bringing the parted hemispheres together," said Fred, "we must wait a good two months before it will be healed well enough so that we can get the fun of feeding him these new experiences. Of course, he won't know about the waiting; but we sure will! And unfortunately, as we all know, two separated halves of a brain can't entertain the same neural patterns that they can when they're together. For all those impulses which cross from one hemisphere to another during a whole-brain experience just can't make it across the gap that has been opened between them."

The end of this speech gave someone else an idea. Why not do the following? Develop tiny electrochemical wires whose ends could be fitted to the synapses of neurons to receive or discharge their neural impulses. These wires could then be strung from each neuron whose connection had been broken in the split to that neuron of the other hemisphere to which it had formerly been connected. "In this way," finished Bert, the proposer of this idea, "all those impulses that were supposed to cross over from one hemisphere to the other could do just that—carried over the wires."

This suggestion was greeted with enthusiasm, since the construction of the wire system, it was felt, could easily be completed within a week. But one grave fellow named Cassander had worries. "We all agree that our friend has been having the experiences we've tried to give him. That is, we all accept in some form or other the neural theory of experience. Now, according to this theory as we all accept it, it is quite permissible to alter as one likes the context of a functioning brain, just so long as one maintains the pattern of its activity. We might look at what we're saying this way. There are various conditions that make for the usual having of an experience—an experience, for instance, like that pond-hole experience we believe we gave our friend three weeks ago. Usually these conditions are the brain being in an actual body on an actual pond stimulated to such neural activity as we did indeed give our friend. We gave our friend the neural activity without those other conditions of its context, because our friend has no body and because we believe that what is essential and decisive for the existence and character of an experience anyway is not such context but rather only the neural activity that it can stimulate. The contextual conditions, we believe, are truly inessential to the bare fact of a man having an experience—even if they *are* essential conditions in the normal having of that experience. If one has the wherewithal, as we do, to get around the normal necessity of these external conditions of an experience of a pond hole, then such conditions are no longer necessary. And this demonstrates that within our concept of experience they never were necessary in principle to the bare fact of having the experience.

"Now, what you men are proposing to do with these wires amounts to regarding as inessential just one more normal condition of our friend's having his experience. That is, you are saying something like what I just said about the context of neural activity—but *you're* saying it about the condition of the *proximity* of the hemispheres of the brain to one another. You're saying that the two hemispheres being attached to one another in the whole-brain experiences may be necessary to the coming about of those experiences in the usual case, but if one can get around a breach of this proximity in some, indeed, *un*usual case, as you fellows would with your wires, there'd still be brought about just the same bare fact of the same experience being had! You're saying that proximity isn't a necessary condition to this bare fact of an experience. But isn't it possible that even reproducing precisely the whole-brain neural patterns in a sundered brain would, to the contrary, *not* constitute the bringing about of the whole-brain experience? Couldn't proximity be not just something to get around in creating a particular whole-brain experience but somehow an absolute condition and principle of the having of a whole-brain experience?"

Cassander got little sympathy for his worries. Typical replies ran something like this: "Would the damn hemispheres *know* they were connected by wires instead of attached in the usual way? That is, would the fact get encoded in any of the brain structures responsible for speech, thought or any other feature of awareness? How could this fact about how his brain looks to external observers concern our dear friend in his pleasures at all—any more than being a naked brain sitting in a warm nutrient bath does? As long as the neural activity in the hemispheres— together *or* apart—matches precisely that which would have been the activity in the hemispheres lumped together in the head of a person walking around having fun, then the person himself is having that fun. Why, if we hooked up a mouth to these brain parts, he'd be telling us through it about his fun." In reply to such answers, which were getting shorter and angrier, Cassander could only mutter about the possible disruption of some experiential field "or some such."

But after the men had been working on the wires for a while someone else came up with an objection to their project that *did* stop them. He pointed out that it took practically no time for an impulse from one hemisphere to enter into the other when a brain was together and functioning normally. But the travel of these impulses over wires must impose a tiny increase on the time taken in such crossovers. Since the impulses in the rest of the brain in each hemisphere would be taking their normal time, wouldn't the overall pattern get garbled, operating as if there were a slowdown in only one region? Certainly it would be impossible to get precisely the normal sort of pattern going—you'd have something strange, disturbed.

When this successful objection was raised, a man with very little training in physics suggested that somehow the wire be replaced by radio signals. This could be done by outfitting the raw face—of the split—of each hemisphere with an "impulse cartridge" that would be capable of sending any pattern of impulses into the hitherto exposed and unconnected neurons of that hemisphere, as well as of receiving from those neurons any pattern of impulses that that hemisphere might be trying to communicate to the other hemisphere. Then each cartridge could be plugged into a special radio transmitter and receiver. When a cartridge received an impulse from a neuron in one hemisphere intended for a neuron of the other, the impulse could then be radioed over and properly administered by the other cartridge. The fellow who suggested this even mused that then each half of the brain could be kept in a separate bath and yet the whole still be engaged in a single whole-brain experience.

The advantage of this system over the wires, this fellow thought, resided in the "fact" that radio waves take no time, unlike impulses in wires, to travel from one place to another. He was quickly disabused of this idea. No, the radio system still suffered from the time-gap obstacle.

But all this talk of impulse cartridges inspired Bert. "Look, we could feed each impulse cartridge with the same pattern of impulses it would have been receiving by radio but do so by such a method as to require no radio or wire transmission. All we need do is fix to each cartridge not a radio transmitter and receiver but an 'impulse programmer,' the sort of gadget that would play through whatever program of impulses you have previously given it. The great thing about this is that there is no longer any need for the impulse pattern going into one hemisphere to be *actually caused,* in part, by the pattern coming from the other. Therefore there need not be any wait for the transmission. The programmed cartridges can be so correlated with the rest of our stimulation of neural patterns that all of the timing can be just as it would have been if the hemispheres were together. And, yes, then it will be easy to fix each hemisphere in a separate bath—perhaps one in the laboratory here and one in the laboratory across town, so that we may employ the facilities of each laboratory in working with merely half a brain. This will make everything easier. And we can then bring in more people; there are many who've been bothering us to let them join our project."

But now Cassander was even more worried. "We have already disregarded the condition of proximity. Now we are about to abandon yet another condition of usual experience—that of actual causal connection. Granted you can be clever enough to get around what is usually quite necessary to an experience coming about. So now, with your programming, it will no longer be necessary for impulses in one half of the brain actually to be a cause of the completion of the whole-brain pattern in the other hemisphere in order for the whole-brain pattern to come about. But is the result still the bare fact of the whole-brain experience or have you, in removing this condition, removed an absolute principle of, an essential condition for, a whole-brain experience really being had?"

The answers to this were much as they had been to the other. How did the neural activity *know* whether a radio-controlled or programmed impulse cartridge fed it? How could this fact, so totally external to them, register with the neural structures underlying thought, speech, and every other item of awareness? Certainly it could not register mechanically.

Wasn't the result then precisely the same with tape as with wire except that now the time-gap problem had been overcome? And wouldn't a properly hooked-up mouth even report the experiences as nicely after the taped as after the wired assistance with crossing impulses?

The next innovation came soon enough—when the question was raised about whether it was at all important, since each hemisphere was now working separately, to synchronize the two causally unconnected playings of the impulse patterns of the hemispheres. Now that each hemisphere would in effect receive all the impulses that in a given experience it would have received from the other hemisphere—and receive them in such a way as would work perfectly with the timing of the rest of its impulses—and since this fine effect could be achieved in either hemisphere quite independent of its having yet been achieved in the other, there seemed no reason for retaining what Cassander sadly pointed to as the "condition of synchronization." Men were heard to say, "How does either hemisphere *know,* how could it register when the other goes off, in the time of the external observer, anyway? For each hemisphere what more can we say than that it is just precisely as if the other had gone off with it the right way? What is there to worry about if at one lab they run through one half of a pattern one day and at the other lab they supply the other hemisphere with its half of the pattern another day? The pattern gets run through fine. The experience comes about. With the brain parts hooked up properly to a mouth, our friend could even report his experience."

There was also some discussion about whether to maintain what Cassander called "topology"—that is, whether to keep the two hemispheres in the general spatial relation of facing each other. Here too Cassander's warnings were ignored.

II

Ten centuries later the famous project was still engrossing men. But men now filled the galaxy and their technology was tremendous. Among them were billions who wanted the thrill and responsibility of participating in the "Great Experience Feed." Of course, behind this desire lay the continuing belief that what men were doing in programming impulses still amounted to making a man have all sorts of experiences.

But in order to accommodate all those who now wished to participate in the project, what Cassander had called the "conditions" of the experiencing had, to the superficial glance, changed enormously. (Actually, they were in a sense more conservative than they had been when we last saw them, because, as I shall explain later, something like "synchronization" had been restored.) Just as earlier each hemisphere of the brain had rested in its bath, now *each individual neuron* rested in one of its own. Since there were billions of neurons, each of the billions of men could involve himself with the proud task of manning a neuron bath.

To understand this situation properly, one must go back again ten centuries, to what had occurred as more and more men had expressed a desire for a part of the project. First it was agreed that if a whole-brain experience could come about with the brain split and yet the two halves programmed as I have described, the same experience could come about if each hemisphere too were carefully divided and each piece treated just as each of the two hemispheres had been. Thus each of four pieces of brain could now be given not only its own bath but a whole lab—allowing many more people to participate. There naturally seemed nothing to stop further and further divisions of the thing, until finally, ten centuries later, there was this situation—a man on each neuron, each man responsible for an impulse cartridge that was fixed to both ends of that neuron— transmitting and receiving an impulse whenever it was programmed to do so.

Meanwhile there had been other Cassanders. After a while none of these suggested keeping the condition of proximity, since this would have so infuriated all his fellows who desired to have a piece of the brain. But it *was* pointed out by such Cassanders that the original topology of the brain, that is, the relative position and directional attitude of each neu- ron, could be maintained even while the brain was spread apart; and also it was urged by them that the neurons continue to be programmed to fire with the same chronology—the same temporal pattern—that their firings would have displayed when together in the brain.

But the suggestion about topology always brought a derisive re- sponse. A sample: "How should each of the neurons *know,* how should it register on a single neuron, where it is in relation to the others? In the usual case of an experience it is indeed necessary for the neurons, in order at all to get firing in that pattern that is or causes the experience, to be next to each other, actually causing the firing of one another, in a certain spatial relation to one another—but the original necessity of all these conditions is overcome by our techniques. For example, they are not necessary to the *bare fact* of the coming about of the experience that we are now causing to be had by the ancient gentleman whose neuron this is before me. And if we should bring these neurons together into a hookup with a mouth, then he would tell you of the experience personally."

Now as for the second part of the Cassanderish suggestion, the reader might suppose that after each successive partitioning of the brain, synchronization of the parts would have been consistently disregarded, so that eventually it would have been thought not to matter when each individual neuron was to be fired in relation to the firings of the other neurons—just as earlier the condition had been disregarded when there were only two hemispheres to be fired. But somehow, perhaps because disregarding the timing and order of individual neuron firings would have reduced the art of programming to absurdity, the condition of order and timing had crept back, but without the Cassanderish reflectiveness. "Right" temporal order of firings is now merely *assumed* as somehow essential to bringing about a given experience by all those men standing before their baths and *waiting* for each properly programmed impulse to come to its neuron.

But now, ten centuries after the great project's birth, the world of these smug billions was about to explode. Two thinkers were responsible.

One of these, named Spoilar, had noticed one day that the neuron in his charge was getting a bit the worse for wear. Like any other man with a neuron in that state, he merely obtained another fresh one just like it and so replaced the particular one that had gotten worn—tossing the old one away. Thus he, like all the others, had violated the Cassanderish condition of "neural identity"—a condition never taken very seriously even by Cassanders. It was realized that in the case of an ordinary brain the cellular metabolism was always replacing all the particular matter of any neuron with other particular matter, forming precisely the same kind of neuron. What this man had done was really no more than a speeding-up of this process. Besides, what if, as some Cassanders had implausibly argued, replacing one neuron by another just like it somehow resulted, when it was eventually done to all the neurons, in a new identity for the experiencer? There still would be *an* experiencer having the same experience every time the same patterns of firings were realized (and what it would mean to say he was a different experiencer was not clear at all, even to the Cassanders). So any shift in neural identity did not seem destructive of the fact of an experience coming about.

This fellow Spoilar, after he had replaced the neuron, resumed his waiting to watch his own neuron fire as part of an experience scheduled several hours later. Suddenly he heard a great crash and a great curse. Some fool had fallen against another man's bath, and it had broken totally on the floor when it fell. Well, this man whose bath had fallen would just have to miss out on any experiences his neuron was to have been part of until the bath and neuron could be replaced. And Spoilar knew that the poor man had had one coming up soon.

The fellow whose bath had just broken walked up to Spoilar. He said, "Look, I've done favors for you. I'm going to have to miss the impulse coming up in five minutes—that experience will have to manage with one less neuron firing. But maybe you'd let me man yours coming up later. I just hate to miss all the thrills coming up today!"

Spoilar thought about the man's plea. Suddenly, a strange thought hit him. "Wasn't the neuron you manned the same sort as mine?"

"Yes."

"Well, look. I've just replaced my neuron with another like it, as we all do occasionally. Why don't we take my entire bath over to the old position of yours? Then won't it still be the same experience brought about in five minutes that it would have been with the old neuron if we fire this then, since this one is just like the old one? Surely the *bath's* identity means nothing. Anyway, then we can bring the bath back here and I can use the neuron for the experience it is scheduled to be used for later on. Wait a minute! We both believe the condition of topology is baloney. So why need we move the bath at all? Leave it here; fire it for yours; and then I'll fire it for mine. Both experiences must still come about. Wait a minute again! Then all we need do is fire this one neuron here in place of all the firings of all neurons just like it! Then there need be only one neuron of each type firing again and again and again to bring about all these experiences! But how would the neurons *know* even that they were repeating an impulse when they fired again and again? How would they *know* the relative order of their firings? Then we could have one neuron of each sort firing once and that would provide the physical realization of all patterns of impulses (a conclusion that would have been arrived at merely by consistently disregarding the necessity of synchronization in the progress from parted hemispheres to parted neurons). And couldn't these neurons simply be any of those naturally firing in any head? So what are we all doing here?"

Then an even more desperate thought hit him, which he expressed thus: "But if all possible neural experience will be brought about simply in the firing once of one of each type of neuron, how can any experiencer believe that he is connected to anything more than this bare minimum of physical reality through the fact of his having *any* of his experiences? And so all this talk of heads and neurons in them, which is supposedly based on the true discovery of physical realities, is undermined entirely. There may be a true system of physical reality, but if it involves all this physiology we have been hoodwinked into believing, it provides so cheaply for so much experience that we can never know what is an actual experience of *it*, the physical reality. And so belief in such a system undermines itself. That is, unless it's tempered with Cassanderish principles."

The other thinker, coincidentally also named Spoilar, came to the same conclusion somewhat differently. He enjoyed stringing neurons. Once he got his own neuron, the one he was responsible for, in the middle of a long chain of like neurons and then recalled he was supposed to have it hooked up to the cartridge for a firing. Not wanting to destroy the chain, he simply hooked the two end neurons of the chain to the two poles of the impulse cartridge and adjusted the timing of the cartridge so that the impulse, traveling now through this whole chain, would reach his neuron at just the right time. Then he noticed that here a neuron, unlike one in usual experience, was quite comfortably participating in two patterns of firings at once—the chain's, which happened to have proximity and causal connection, and the programmed experience for which it had fired. After this Spoilar went about ridiculing "the condition of neural context." He'd say, "Boy, I could hook my neuron up with all those in your head, and if I could get it to fire just at the right time, I could get it into one of these programmed experiences as fine as if it were in my bath, on my cartridge."

Well, one day there was trouble. Some men who had not been allowed to join the project had come at night and so tampered with the baths that many of the neurons in Spoilar's vicinity had simply died. Standing before his own dead neuron, staring at the vast misery around him, he thought about how the day's first experience must turn out for the experiencer when so many neuron firings were to be missing from their physical realization. But as he looked about he suddenly took note of something else. Nearly everyone was stooping to inspect some damaged equipment just under his bath. Suddenly it seemed significant to Spoilar that next to every bath there was a head, each with its own billions of neurons of all sorts, with perhaps millions of each sort firing at any given moment. Proximity didn't matter. But then at any given moment of a particular pattern's being fired through the baths all the requisite activity was already going on anyway in the heads of the operators—in even *one* of those heads, where a loose sort of proximity condition was fulfilled too! Each head was bath and cartridge enough for any spread-brain's realization: "But," thought Spoilar, "the same kind of physical realization must exist for every experience of every brain—since all brains are spreadable. And that includes mine. But then all my beliefs are based on thoughts and experiences that might exist only as some such floating cloud. They are all suspect—including those that had convinced me of all this physiology in the first place. Unless Cassander is right, to some extent, then physiology reduces to absurdity. It undermines itself."

Such thinking killed the great project and with it the spread-brain. Men turned to other weird activities and to new conclusions about the nature of experience. But what these were is another story.

Reflections

This weird tale seems at first to be a sly demolition of virtually all the ideas exploited in the rest of the book, a *reductio ad absurdum* of the assumptions about the relations between brain and experience that had seemed to be innocent and obvious. How might one resist the daffy slide to its conclusion? Some hints:

Suppose someone claimed to have a microscopically exact replica (in marble, even) of Michelangelo's "David" in his home. When you go to see this marvel, you find a twenty-foot-tall roughly rectilinear hunk of pure white marble standing in his living room. "I haven't gotten around to *unpacking* it yet," he says, "but I know it's in there."

Consider how little Zuboff tells us of the wonderful "cartridges" and "impulse programmers" that get fastened to the various bits and pieces of brain. *All they do,* we learn, is provide their attached neuron, or group of neurons, with a lifetime supply of the right sort of impulses in the right order and timing. Mere beepers, we might be inclined to think. But reflect on what must actually be produced by these cartridges, by considering what would in fact be a vastly "easier" technological triumph. Crippling strikes close down all the television stations, so there is nothing to watch on TV; fortunately, IBM comes to the aid of all the people who are going insane without their daily dose of TV, by mailing them "impulse cartridges" to fasten to their TV sets; these cartridges are programmed to produce ten channels of news, weather, soap opera, sports, and so forth —all made up, of course (the news won't be accurate news, but at least it will be realistic). After all, say the IBM people, we all know that television signals are just impulses transmitted from the stations; our cartridges simply take a shorter route to the receiver. What could be inside those wonderful cartridges, though? Videotapes of some sort? But how were *they* made? By videotaping real live actors, newscasters, and the like, or by animation? Animators will tell you that the task of composing, from scratch, all those frames without the benefit of filmed real action to draw upon is a gigantic task that grows exponentially as you try for greater realism. When you get right down to it, only the real world is rich enough in information to provide (and control) the signal trains needed to sustain channels of realistic TV. The task of making up a real world of perception (essentially the task Descartes assigned to an infinitely powerful deceiving demon in his *Meditations*) is perhaps possible in principle, but utterly impossible in fact. Descartes was right to make his evil demon *infinitely* powerful—no lesser deceiver could sustain the illusion without falling back on the real world after all and turning the illusion back into a vision of reality, however delayed or otherwise skewed.

These points strike glancing blows against Zuboff's implicit argument. Can they be put into fatal combinations? Perhaps we can convince ourselves that his conclusions are absurd by asking if a similar argument couldn't be marshalled to prove that there is no need for books. Need we not simply print the whole alphabet just *once* and be done with all of book publishing? Who says we should print the whole alphabet? Will not just one letter, or one *stroke* do? One dot?

The logician Raymond Smullyan, whom we shall meet later in this book, suggests that the proper way to learn to play the piano is to become intimate with each note individually, one at a time. Thus, for instance, you might devote an entire month to practicing just middle C, perhaps only a few days each to the notes at the ends of the keyboard. But let's not forget *rests,* for they are an equally essential part of music. You can spend a whole day on whole-note rests, two days on half-note rests, four days on quarter-note rests and so on. Once you've completed this arduous training, you're ready to play *anything!* It sounds right, but, somehow, slightly wrong as well . . .

The physicist John Archibald Wheeler once speculated that perhaps the reason all electrons are alike is that *there is really only one electron,* careening back and forth from the ends of time, weaving the fabric of the physical universe by crossing its own path innumerable times. Perhaps Parmenides was right: there is only one thing! But this one thing, so imagined, has spatiotemporal parts that enter into astronomically many relations with its other spatiotemporal parts, and this *relative organization,* in time and in space, *matters.* But to whom? To the portions of the great tapestry that are perceivers. And how are they distinguished from the rest of the tapestry?

D. C. D.
D. R. H.

IV

Mind as Program

13

DANIEL C. DENNETT

Where Am I?

Now that I've won my suit under the Freedom of Information Act, I am at liberty to reveal for the first time a curious episode in my life that may be of interest not only to those engaged in research in the philosophy of mind, artificial intelligence, and neuroscience but also to the general public.

Several years ago I was approached by Pentagon officials who asked me to volunteer for a highly dangerous and secret mission. In collaboration with NASA and Howard Hughes, the Department of Defense was spending billions to develop a Supersonic Tunneling Underground Device, or STUD. It was supposed to tunnel through the earth's core at great speed and deliver a specially designed atomic warhead "right up the Red's missile silos," as one of the Pentagon brass put it.

The problem was that in an early test they had succeeded in lodging a warhead about a mile deep under Tulsa, Oklahoma, and they wanted me to retrieve it for them. "Why me?" I asked. Well, the mission involved some pioneering applications of current brain research, and they had heard of my interest in brains and of course my Faustian curiosity and great courage and so forth. . . . Well, how could I refuse? The difficulty that brought the Pentagon to my door was that the device I'd been asked to recover was fiercely radioactive, in a new way. According to monitoring instruments, something about the nature of the device and its complex interactions with pockets of material deep in the earth had produced radiation that could cause severe abnormalities in certain tissues of the brain. No way had been found to shield the brain from these deadly rays, which were apparently harmless to other tissues and organs of the body. So it had been decided that the person sent to recover the device should *leave his brain behind.* It would be kept in a safe place where it could execute its normal control functions by elaborate radio links. Would I submit to a surgical procedure that would completely remove my brain, which would then be placed in a life-support system at the Manned Spacecraft Center in Houston? Each input and output pathway, as it was severed, would be restored by a pair of microminiaturized radio transceivers, one attached precisely to the brain, the other to the nerve stumps in the empty cranium. No information would be lost, all the connectivity would be preserved. At first I was a bit reluctant. Would it really work? The Houston brain surgeons encouraged me. "Think of it," they said, "as a mere *stretching* of the nerves. If your brain were just moved over an *inch* in your skull, that would not alter or impair your mind. We're simply going to make the nerves indefinitely elastic by splicing radio links into them."

I was shown around the life-support lab in Houston and saw the sparkling new vat in which my brain would be placed, were I to agree. I met the large and brilliant support team of neurologists, hematologists, biophysicists, and electrical engineers, and after several days of discussions and demonstrations, I agreed to give it a try. I was subjected to an enormous array of blood tests, brain scans, experiments, interviews, and the like. They took down my autobiography at great length, recorded tedious lists of my beliefs, hopes, fears, and tastes. They even listed my favorite stereo recordings and gave me a crash session of psychoanalysis.

The day for surgery arrived at last and of course I was anesthetized and remember nothing of the operation itself. When I came out of anesthesia, I opened my eyes, looked around, and asked the inevitable, the traditional, the lamentably hackneyed postoperative question: "Where am I?" The nurse smiled down at me. "You're in Houston," she said, and I reflected that this still had a good chance of being the truth one way or another. She handed me a mirror. Sure enough, there were the tiny antennae poling up through their titanium ports cemented into my skull.

"I gather the operation was a success," I said. "I want to go see my brain." They led me (I was a bit dizzy and unsteady) down a long corridor and into the life-support lab. A cheer went up from the assembled support team, and I responded with what I hoped was a jaunty salute. Still feeling lightheaded, I was helped over to the life-support vat. I peered through the glass. There, floating in what looked like ginger ale, was undeniably a human brain, though it was almost covered with printed circuit chips, plastic tubules, electrodes, and other paraphernalia. "Is that mine?" I asked. "Hit the output transmitter switch there on the side of the vat and see for yourself," the project director replied. I moved the switch to OFF, and immediately slumped, groggy and nauseated, into the arms of the technicians, one of whom kindly restored the switch to its ON position. While I recovered my equilibrium and composure, I thought to myself: "Well, here I am sitting on a folding chair, staring through a piece of plate glass at my own brain. . . . But wait," I said to myself, "shouldn't I have thought, 'Here I am, suspended in a bubbling fluid, being stared at by my own eyes'?" I tried to think this latter thought. I tried to project it into the tank, offering it hopefully to my brain, but I failed to carry off the exercise with any conviction. I tried again. "Here am *I*, Daniel Dennett, suspended in a bubbling fluid, being stared at by my own eyes." No, it just didn't work. Most puzzling and confusing. Being a philosopher of firm physicalist conviction, I believed unswervingly that the tokening of my thoughts was occurring somewhere in my brain: yet, when I thought "Here I am," where the thought occurred to me was *here,* outside the vat, where I, Dennett, was standing staring at my brain.

I tried and tried to think myself into the vat, but to no avail. I tried to build up to the task by doing mental exercises. I thought to myself, "The sun is shining *over there,*" five times in rapid succession, each time mentally ostending a different place: in order, the sunlit corner of the lab, the visible front lawn of the hospital, Houston, Mars, and Jupiter. I found I had little difficulty in getting my "there" 's to hop all over the celestial map with their proper references. I could loft a "there" in an instant through the farthest reaches of space, and then aim the next "there" with pinpoint accuracy at the upper left quadrant of a freckle on my arm. Why was I having such trouble with "here"? "Here in Houston" worked well enough, and so did "here in the lab," and even "here in this part of the lab," but "here in the vat" always seemed merely an unmeant mental mouthing. I tried closing my eyes while thinking it. This seemed to help, but still I couldn't manage to pull it off, except perhaps for a fleeting instant. I couldn't be sure. The discovery that I couldn't be sure was also unsettling. How did I know *where* I meant by "here" when I thought "here"? Could I *think* I meant one place when in fact I meant another? I didn't see how that could be admitted without untying the few bonds of intimacy between a person and his own mental life that had survived the onslaught of the brain scientists and philosophers, the physicalists and behaviorists. Perhaps I was incorrigible about where I *meant* when I said "here." But in my present circumstances it seemed that either I was doomed by sheer force of mental habit to thinking systematically false indexical thoughts, or where a person is (and hence where his thoughts are tokened for purposes of semantic analysis) is not necessarily where his brain, the physical seat of his soul, resides. Nagged by confusion, I attempted to orient myself by falling back on a favorite philosopher's ploy. I began naming things.

"Yorick," I said aloud to my brain, "you are my brain. The rest of my body, seated in this chair, I dub 'Hamlet.' " So here we all are: Yorick's my brain, Hamlet's my body, and I am Dennett. *Now,* where am I? And when I think "where am I?" where's that thought tokened? Is it tokened in my brain, lounging about in the vat, or right here between my ears where it *seems* to be tokened? Or nowhere? Its *temporal* coordinates give me no trouble; must it not have spatial coordinates as well? I began making a list of the alternatives.

1. *Where Hamlet goes, there goes Dennett.* This principle was easily refuted by appeal to the familiar brain-transplant thought experiments so enjoyed by philosophers. If Tom and Dick switch brains, Tom is the fellow with Dick's former body—just ask him; he'll claim to be Tom, and tell you the most intimate details of Tom's autobiography. It was clear enough, then, that my current body and I could part company, but not likely that I could be separated from my brain. The rule of thumb that emerged so plainly from the thought experiments was that in a brain-transplant operation, one wanted to be the *donor,* not the recipient. Better to call such an operation a *body* transplant, in fact. So perhaps the truth was,

2. *Where Yorick goes, there goes Dennett.* This was not at all appealing, however. How could I be in the vat and not about to go anywhere, when I was so obviously outside the vat looking in and beginning to make guilty plans to return to my room for a substantial lunch? This begged the question I realized, but it still seemed to be getting at something important. Casting about for some support for my intuition, I hit upon a legalistic sort of argument that might have appealed to Locke.

Suppose, I argued to myself, I were now to fly to California, rob a bank, and be apprehended. In which state would I be tried: in California, where the robbery took place, or in Texas, where the brains of the outfit were located? Would I be a California felon with an out-of-state brain, or a Texas felon remotely controlling an accomplice of sorts in California? It seemed possible that I might beat such a rap just on the undecidability of that jurisdictional question, though perhaps it would be deemed an interstate, and hence Federal, offense. In any event, suppose I were convicted. Was it likely that California would be satisfied to throw Hamlet into the brig, knowing that Yorick was living the good life and luxuriously taking the waters in Texas? Would Texas incarcerate Yorick, leaving Hamlet free to take the next boat to Rio? This alternative appealed to me.

Barring capital punishment or other cruel and unusual punishment, the state would be obliged to maintain the life-support system for Yorick though they might move him from Houston to Leavenworth, and aside from the unpleasantness of the opprobrium, I, for one, would not mind at all and would consider myself a free man under those circumstances. If the state has an interest in forcibly relocating persons in institutions, it would fail to relocate *me* in any institution by locating Yorick there. If this were true, it suggested a third alternative.

3. *Dennett is wherever he thinks he is.* Generalized, the claim was as follows: At any given time a person has a *point of view*, and the location of the point of view (which is determined internally by the content of the point of view) is also the location of the person.

Such a proposition is not without its perplexities, but to me it seemed a step in the right direction. The only trouble was that it seemed to place one in a heads-I-win/tails-you-lose situation of unlikely infallibility as regards location. Hadn't I myself often been wrong about where I was, and at least as often uncertain? Couldn't one get lost? Of course, but getting lost *geographically* is not the only way one might get lost. If one were lost in the woods one could attempt to reassure oneself with the consolation that at least one knew where one was: one was right *here* in the familiar surroundings of one's own body. Perhaps in this case one would not have drawn one's attention to much to be thankful for. Still, there were worse plights imaginable, and I wasn't sure I wasn't in such a plight right now.

Point of view clearly had something to do with personal location, but it was itself an unclear notion. It was obvious that the content of one's point of view was not the same as or determined by the content of one's beliefs or thoughts. For example, what should we say about the point of view of the Cinerama viewer who shrieks and twists in his seat as the roller-coaster footage overcomes his psychic distancing? Has he forgotten that he is safely seated in the theater? Here I was inclined to say that the person is experiencing an illusory shift in point of view. In other cases, my inclination to call such shifts illusory was less strong. The workers in laboratories and plants who handle dangerous materials by operating feedback-controlled mechanical arms and hands undergo a shift in point of view that is crisper and more pronounced than anything Cinerama can provoke. They can feel the heft and slipperiness of the containers they manipulate with their metal fingers. They know perfectly well where they are and are not fooled into false beliefs by the experience, yet it is as if they were inside the isolation chamber they are peering into. With mental effort, they can manage to shift their point of view back and forth, rather like making a transparent Necker cube or an Escher drawing change orientation before one's eyes. It does seem extravagant to suppose that in performing this bit of mental gymnastics, they are transporting *themselves* back and forth.

Still their example gave me hope. If I was in fact in the vat in spite of my intuitions, I might be able to train myself to adopt that point of view even as a matter of habit. I should dwell on images of myself comfortably floating in my vat, beaming volitions to that familiar body *out there.* I reflected that the ease or difficulty of this task was presumably independent of the truth about the location of one's brain. Had I been practicing before the operation, I might now be finding it second nature. You might now yourself try such a *trompe l'oeil.* Imagine you have written an inflammatory letter which has been published in the *Times,* the result of which is that the government has chosen to impound your brain for a probationary period of three years in its Dangerous Brain Clinic in Bethesda, Maryland. Your body of course is allowed freedom to earn a salary and thus to continue its function of laying up income to be taxed. At this moment, however, your body is seated in an auditorium listening to a peculiar account by Daniel Dennett of his own similar experience. Try it. Think yourself to Bethesda, and then hark back longingly to your body, far away, and yet *seeming* so near. It is only with long-distance restraint (yours? the government's?) that you can control your impulse to get those hands clapping in polite applause before navigating the old body to the rest room and a well-deserved glass of evening sherry in the lounge. The task of imagination is certainly difficult, but if you achieve your goal the results might be consoling.

Anyway, there I was in Houston, lost in thought as one might say, but not for long. My speculations were soon interrupted by the Houston doctors, who wished to test out my new prosthetic nervous system before sending me off on my hazardous mission. As I mentioned before, I was a bit dizzy at first, and not surprisingly, although I soon habituated myself to my new circumstances (which were, after all, well nigh indistinguishable from my old circumstances). My accommodation was not perfect, however, and to this day I continue to be plagued by minor coordination difficulties. The speed of light is fast, but finite, and as my brain and body move farther and farther apart, the delicate interaction of my feedback systems is thrown into disarray by the time lags. Just as one is rendered close to speechless by a delayed or echoic hearing of one's speaking voice so, for instance, I am virtually unable to track a moving object with my eyes whenever my brain and my body are more than a few miles apart. In most matters my impairment is scarcely detectable, though I can no longer hit a slow curve ball with the authority of yore. There are some compensations of course. Though liquor tastes as good as ever, and warms my gullet while corroding my liver, I can drink it in any quantity I please, without becoming the slightest bit inebriated, a curiosity some of my close friends may have noticed (though I occasionally have *feigned* inebriation, so as not to draw attention to my unusual circumstances). For similar reasons, I take aspirin orally for a sprained wrist, but if the pain persists I ask Houston to administer codeine to me *in vitro*. In times of illness the phone bill can be staggering.

But to return to my adventure. At length, both the doctors and I were satisfied that I was ready to undertake my subterranean mission. And so I left my brain in Houston and headed by helicopter for Tulsa. Well, in any case, that's the way it seemed to me. That's how I would put it, just off the top of my head as it were. On the trip I reflected further about my earlier anxieties and decided that my first postoperative speculations had been tinged with panic. The matter was not nearly as strange or metaphysical as I had been supposing. Where was I? In two places, clearly: both inside the vat and outside it. Just as one can stand with one foot in Connecticut and the other in Rhode Island, I was in two places at once. I had become one of those scattered individuals we used to hear so much about. The more I considered this answer, the more obviously true it appeared. But, strange to say, the more true it appeared, the less important the question to which it could be the true answer seemed. A sad, but not unprecedented, fate for a philosophical question to suffer. This answer did not completely satisfy me, of course. There lingered some question to which I should have liked an answer, which was neither "Where are all my various and sundry parts?" nor "What is my current point of view?" Or at least there seemed to be such a question. For it did seem undeniable that in some sense *I* and not merely *most of me* was descending into the earth under Tulsa in search of an atomic warhead.

When I found the warhead, I was certainly glad I had left my brain behind, for the pointer on the specially built Geiger counter I had brought with me was off the dial. I called Houston on my ordinary radio and told the operation control center of my position and my progress. In return, they gave me instructions for dismantling the vehicle, based upon my on-site observations. I had set to work with my cutting torch when all of a sudden a terrible thing happened. I went stone deaf. At first I thought it was only my radio earphones that had broken, but when I tapped on my helmet, I heard nothing. Apparently the auditory transceivers had gone on the fritz. I could no longer hear Houston or my own voice, but I could speak, so I started telling them what had happened. In midsentence, I knew something else had gone wrong. My vocal apparatus had become paralyzed. Then my right hand went limp—another transceiver had gone. I was truly in deep trouble. But worse was to follow. After a few more minutes, I went blind. I cursed my luck, and then I cursed the scientists who had led me into this grave peril. There I was, deaf, dumb, and blind, in a radioactive hole more than a mile under Tulsa. Then the last of my cerebral radio links broke, and suddenly I was faced with a new and even more shocking problem: whereas an instant before I had been buried alive in Oklahoma, now I was disembodied in Houston. My recognition of my new status was not immediate. It took me several very anxious minutes before it dawned on me that my poor body lay several hundred miles away, with heart pulsing and lungs respiring, but otherwise as dead as the body of any heart-transplant donor, its skull packed with useless, broken electronic gear. The shift in perspective I had earlier found well nigh impossible now seemed quite natural. Though I could think myself back into my body in the tunnel under Tulsa, it took some effort to sustain the illusion. For surely it was an illusion to suppose I was still in Oklahoma: I had lost all contact with that body.

It occurred to me then, with one of those rushes of revelation of which we should be suspicious, that I had stumbled upon an impressive demonstration of the immateriality of the soul based upon physicalist principles and premises. For as the last radio signal between Tulsa and Houston died away, had I not changed location from Tulsa to Houston at the speed of light? And had I not accomplished this without any increase in mass? What moved from A to B at such speed was surely myself, or at any rate my soul or mind—the massless center of my being and home of my consciousness. My *point of view* had lagged somewhat behind, but I had already noted the indirect bearing of point of view on personal location. I could not see how a physicalist philosopher could quarrel with this except by taking the dire and counterintuitive route of banishing all talk of persons. Yet the notion of personhood was so well entrenched in everyone's world view, or so it seemed to me, that any denial would be as curiously unconvincing, as systematically disingenuous, as the Cartesian negation, "non sum."

The joy of philosophic discovery thus tided me over some very bad minutes or perhaps hours as the helplessness and hopelessness of my situation became more apparent to me. Waves of panic and even nausea swept over me, made all the more horrible by the absence of their normal body-dependent phenomenology. No adrenaline rush of tingles in the arms, no pounding heart, no premonitory salivation. I did feel a dread sinking feeling in my bowels at one point, and this tricked me momentarily into the false hope that I was undergoing a reversal of the process that landed me in this fix—a gradual undisembodiment. But the isolation and uniqueness of that twinge soon convinced me that it was simply the first of a plague of phantom body hallucinations that I, like any other amputee, would be all too likely to suffer.

My mood then was chaotic. On the one hand, I was fired up with elation of my philosophic discovery and was wracking my brain (one of the few familiar things I could still do), trying to figure out how to communicate my discovery to the journals; while on the other, I was bitter, lonely, and filled with dread and uncertainty. Fortunately, this did not last long, for my technical support team sedated me into a dreamless sleep from which I awoke, hearing with magnificent fidelity the familiar opening strains of my favorite Brahms piano trio. So that was why they had wanted a list of my favorite recordings! It did not take me long to realize that I was hearing the music without ears. The output from the stereo stylus was being fed through some fancy rectification circuitry directly into my auditory nerve. I was mainlining Brahms, an unforgettable experience for any stereo buff. At the end of the record it did not surprise me to hear the reassuring voice of the project director speaking into a microphone that was now my prosthetic ear. He confirmed my analysis of what had gone wrong and assured me that steps were being taken to re-embody me. He did not elaborate, and after a few more recordings, I found myself drifting off to sleep. My sleep lasted, I later learned, for the better part of a year, and when I awoke, it was to find myself fully restored to my senses. When I looked into the mirror, though, I was a bit startled to see an unfamiliar face. Bearded and a bit heavier, bearing no doubt a family resemblance to my former face, and with the same look of spritely intelligence and resolute character, but definitely a new face. Further self-explorations of an intimate nature left me no doubt that this was a new body, and the project director confirmed my conclusions. He did not volunteer any information on the past history of my new body and I decided (wisely, I think in retrospect) not to pry. As many philosophers unfamiliar with my ordeal have more recently speculated, the acquisition of a new body leaves one's *person* intact. And after a period of adjustment to a new voice, new muscular strengths and weaknesses, and so forth, one's *personality* is by and large also preserved. More dramatic changes in personality have been routinely observed in people who have undergone extensive plastic surgery, to say nothing of sex-change operations, and I think no one contests the survival of the person in such cases. In any event I soon accommodated to my new body, to the point of being unable to recover any of its novelties to my consciousness or even memory. The view in the mirror soon became utterly familiar. That view, by the way, still revealed antennae, and so I was not surprised to learn that my brain had not been moved from its haven in the life-support lab.

I decided that good old Yorick deserved a visit. I and my new body, whom we might as well call Fortinbras, strode into the familiar lab to another round of applause from the technicians, who were of course congratulating themselves, not me. Once more I stood before the vat and contemplated poor Yorick, and on a whim I once again cavalierly flicked off the output transmitter switch. Imagine my surprise when nothing unusual happened. No fainting spell, no nausea, no noticeable change. A technician hurried to restore the switch to ON, but still I felt nothing. I demanded an explanation, which the project director hastened to provide. It seems that before they had even operated on the first occasion, they had constructed a computer duplicate of my brain, reproducing both the complete information-processing structure and the computational speed of my brain in a giant computer program. After the operation, but before they had dared to send me off on my mission to Oklahoma, they had run this computer system and Yorick side by side. The incoming signals from Hamlet were sent simultaneously to Yorick's transceivers and to the computer's array of inputs. And the outputs from Yorick were not only beamed back to Hamlet, my body; they were recorded and checked against the simultaneous output of the computer program, which was called "Hubert" for reasons obscure to me. Over days and even weeks, the outputs were identical and synchronous, which of course did not *prove* that they had succeeded in copying the brain's functional structure, but the empirical support was greatly encouraging.

Hubert's input, and hence activity, had been kept parallel with Yorick's during my disembodied days. And now, to demonstrate this, they had actually thrown the master switch that put Hubert for the first time in on-line control of my body—not Hamlet, of course, but Fortinbras. (Hamlet, I learned, had never been recovered from its underground tomb and could be assumed by this time to have largely returned to the dust. At the head of my grave still lay the magnificent bulk of the abandoned device, with the word STUD emblazoned on its side in large letters —a circumstance which may provide archeologists of the next century with a curious insight into the burial rites of their ancestors.)

The laboratory technicians now showed me the master switch, which had two positions, labeled *B*, for Brain (they didn't know my brain's name was Yorick) and *H*, for Hubert. The switch did indeed point to *H*, and they explained to me that if I wished, I could switch it back to *B*. With my heart in my mouth (and my brain in its vat), I did this. Nothing happened. A click, that was all. To test their claim, and with the master switch now set at *B,* I hit Yorick's output transmitter switch on the vat and sure enough, I began to faint. Once the output switch was turned back on and I had recovered my wits, so to speak, I continued to play with the master switch, flipping it back and forth. I found that with the exception of the transitional click, I could detect no trace of a difference. I could switch in mid-utterance, and the sentence I had begun speaking under the control of Yorick was finished without a pause or hitch of any kind under the control of Hubert. I had a spare brain, a prosthetic device which might some day stand me in very good stead, were some mishap to befall Yorick. Or alternatively, I could keep Yorick as a spare and use Hubert. It didn't seem to make any difference which I chose, for the wear and tear and fatigue on my body did not have any debilitating effect on either brain, whether or not it was actually causing the motions of my body, or merely spilling its output into thin air.

The one truly unsettling aspect of this new development was the prospect, which was not long in dawning on me, of someone detaching the spare—Hubert or Yorick, as the case might be—from Fortinbras and hitching it to yet another body—some Johnny-come-lately Rosencrantz or Guildenstern. Then (if not before) there would be *two* people, that much was clear. One would be me, and the other would be a sort of super-twin brother. If there were two bodies, one under the control of Hubert and the other being controlled by Yorick, then which would the world recognize as the true Dennett? And whatever the rest of the world decided, which one would be *me?* Would I be the Yorick-brained one, in virtue of Yorick's causal priority and former intimate relationship with the original Dennett body, Hamlet? That seemed a bit legalistic, a bit too redolent of the arbitrariness of consanguinity and legal possession, to be convincing at the metaphysical level. For suppose that before the arrival of the second body on the scene, I had been keeping Yorick as the spare for years, and letting Hubert's output drive my body—that is, Fortinbras —all that time. The Hubert-Fortinbras couple would seem then by squatter's rights (to combat one legal intuition with another) to be the true Dennett and the lawful inheritor of everything that was Dennett's. This was an interesting question, certainly, but not nearly so pressing as another question that bothered me. My strongest intuition was that in such an eventuality *I* would survive so long as *either* brain-body couple remained intact, but I had mixed emotions about whether I should want both to survive.

I discussed my worries with the technicians and the project director. The prospect of two Dennetts was abhorrent to me, I explained, largely for social reasons. I didn't want to be my own rival for the affections of my wife, nor did I like the prospect of the two Dennetts sharing

my modest professor's salary. Still more vertiginous and distasteful,
though, was the idea of knowing *that much* about another person, while
he had the very same goods on me. How could we ever face each other?
My colleagues in the lab argued that I was ignoring the bright side of
the matter. Weren't there many things I wanted to do but, being only
one person, had been unable to do? Now one Dennett could stay at
home and be the professor and family man, while the other could strike
out on a life of travel and adventure—missing the family of course, but
happy in the knowledge that the other Dennett was keeping the home
fires burning. I could be faithful and adulterous at the same time. I
could even cuckold myself—to say nothing of other more lurid possibilities my colleagues were all too ready to force upon my overtaxed
imagination. But my ordeal in Oklahoma (or was it Houston?) had
made me less adventurous, and I shrank from this opportunity that was
being offered (though of course I was never quite sure it was being
offered to *me* in the first place).

There was another prospect even more disagreeable: that the
spare, Hubert or Yorick as the case might be, would be detached from
any input from Fortinbras and just left detached. Then, as in the other
case, there would be two Dennetts, or at least two claimants to my name
and possessions, one embodied in Fortinbras, and the other sadly, mis-
erably disembodied. Both selfishness and altruism bade me take steps
to prevent this from happening. So I asked that measures be taken to
ensure that no one could ever tamper with the transceiver connections
or the master switch without my (our? no, *my*) knowledge and consent.
Since I had no desire to spend my life guarding the equipment in Houston, it was mutually decided that all the electronic connections in the
lab would be carefully locked. Both those that controlled the life-support system for Yorick and those that controlled the power supply for
Hubert would be guarded with fail-safe devices, and I would take the
only master switch, outfitted for radio remote control, with me wherever I went. I carry it strapped around my waist and—wait a moment—
here it is. Every few months I reconnoiter the situation by switching
channels. I do this only in the presence of friends, of course, for if the
other channel were, heaven forbid, either dead or otherwise occupied,
there would have to be somebody who had my interests at heart to
switch it back, to bring me back from the void. For while I could feel,
see, hear, and otherwise sense whatever befell my body, subsequent to
such a switch, I'd be unable to control it. By the way, the two positions
on the switch are intentionally unmarked, so I never have the faintest
idea whether I am switching from Hubert to Yorick or vice versa. (Some
of you may think that in this case I really don't know *who* I am, let alone

where I am. But such reflections no longer make much of a dent on my essential Dennettness, on my own sense of who I am. If it is true that in one sense I don't know who I am then that's another one of your philosophical truths of underwhelming significance.)

In any case, every time I've flipped the switch so far, nothing has happened. *So let's give it a try....*

"THANK GOD! I THOUGHT YOU'D NEVER FLIP THAT SWITCH! You can't imagine how horrible it's been these last two weeks —but now you know; it's your turn in purgatory. How I've longed for this moment! You see, about two weeks ago—excuse me, ladies and gentlemen, but I've got to explain this to my ... um, brother, I guess you could say, but he's just told you the facts, so you'll understand—about two weeks ago our two brains drifted just a bit out of synch. I don't know whether *my* brain is now Hubert or Yorick, any more than you do, but in any case, the two brains drifted apart, and of course once the process started, it snowballed, for I was in a slightly different receptive state for the input we both received, a difference that was soon magnified. In no time at all the illusion that I was in control of my body—our body—was completely dissipated. There was nothing I could do—no way to call you. YOU DIDN'T EVEN KNOW I EXISTED! It's been like being carried around in a cage, or better, like being possessed—hearing my own voice say things I didn't mean to say, watching in frustration as my own hands performed deeds I hadn't intended. You'd scratch our itches, but not the way I would have, and you kept me awake, with your tossing and turning. I've been totally exhausted, on the verge of a nervous breakdown, carried around helplessly by your frantic round of activities, sustained only by the knowledge that some day you'd throw the switch.

"Now it's your turn, but at least you'll have the comfort of knowing *I* know you're in there. Like an expectant mother, I'm eating—or at any rate tasting, smelling, seeing—for *two* now, and I'll try to make it easy for you. Don't worry. Just as soon as this colloquium is over, you and I will fly to Houston, and we'll see what can be done to get one of us another body. You can have a female body—your body could be any color you like. But let's think it over. I tell you what—to be fair, if we both want this body, I promise I'll let the project director flip a coin to settle which of us gets to keep it and which then gets to choose a new body. That should guarantee justice, shouldn't it? In any case, I'll take care of you, I promise. These people are my witnesses.

"Ladies and gentlemen, this talk we have just heard is not exactly the talk *I* would have given, but I assure you that everything he said was perfectly true. And now if you'll excuse me, I think I'd—we'd—better sit down."

Reflections

The story you have just read not only isn't true (in case you wondered) but couldn't be true. The technological feats described are impossible now, and some may remain forever outside our ability, but that is not what matters to us. What matters is whether there is something in principle impossible—something incoherent—about the whole tale. When philosophical fantasies become too outlandish—involving time machines, say, or duplicate universes or infinitely powerful deceiving demons—we may wisely decline to conclude *anything* from them. Our conviction that we understand the issues involved may be unreliable, an illusion produced by the vividness of the fantasy.

In this case the surgery and microradios described are far beyond the present or even clearly envisaged future state of the art, but that is surely "innocent" science fiction. It is less clear that the introduction of Hubert, the computer duplicate of Yorick, Dennett's brain, is within bounds. (As fantasy-mongers we can make up the rules as we go along, of course, but on pain of telling a tale of no theoretical interest.) Hubert is supposed to run *in perfect synchronicity* with Yorick for years on end without the benefit of any interactive, corrective links between them. This would not just be a great technological triumph; it would verge on the miraculous. It is not just that in order for a computer to come close to matching a human brain in speed of handling millions of channels of parallel input and output it would have to have a fundamental structure entirely unlike that of existing computers. Even if we had such a brainlike computer, its sheer size and complexity would make the prospect of *independent* synchronic behavior virtually impossible. Without the synchronized and identical processing in both systems, an essential feature of the story would have to be abandoned. Why? Because the premise that there is only one person with two brains (one a spare) depends on it. Consider what Ronald de Sousa has to say about a similar case:

> When Dr. Jekyll changes into Mr. Hyde, that is a strange and mysterious thing. Are they two people taking turns in one body? But here is something stranger: Dr. Juggle and Dr. Boggle too, take turns in one body. *But they are as*

like as identical twins! You balk: why then say that they have changed into one another? Well, why not: if Dr. Jekyll can change into a man as different as Hyde, surely it must be all the *easier* for Juggle to change into Boggle, who is exactly like him.

We need conflict or strong difference to shake our natural assumption that to one body there corresponds at most one agent.

—from "Rational Homunculi"

Since several of the most remarkable features of "Where Am I?" hinge on the supposition of independent synchronic processing in Yorick and Hubert, it is important to note that this supposition is truly outrageous—in the same league as the supposition that somewhere there is another planet just like Earth, with an atom-for-atom duplicate of you and all your friends and surroundings,* or the supposition that the universe is only five days old (it only seems to be much older because when God made it five days ago, He made lots of instant "memory"-laden adults, libraries full of apparently ancient books, mountains full of brand-new fossils, and so forth).

The possibility of a prosthetic brain like Hubert, then, is only a possibility in principle, though less marvelous bits of artificial nervous system may be just around the corner. Various crude artificial TV eyes for the blind are already in existence; some of these send input directly to portions of the visual cortex of the brain, but others avoid such virtuoso surgery by transmitting their information through other external sense organs—such as the tactile receptors in the fingertips or even by an array of tingling points spread across the subject's forehead, abdomen, or back.

The prospects for such nonsurgical mind extensions are explored in the next selection, a sequel to "Where Am I?" by Duke University philosopher David Sanford.

D. C. D.

---

*As in Hilary Putnam's famous "Twin Earth" thought experiment. See "Further Reading."

14

DAVID HAWLEY SANFORD

Where Was I?

Daniel Dennett, or perhaps one of the representatives from the corporation that collectively comprises him, delivered "Where Am I?" to a Chapel Hill Colloquium and received an unprecedented standing ovation. I wasn't there clapping with the rest of the local philosophers; I was on sabbatical leave. Although my colleagues still believe I was living in New York and pursuing a line of philosophic research, actually I was working secretly for the Department of Defense on a matter closely related to the Dennett corporation.

Dennett became so preoccupied with questions about his nature, unity, and identity that he seemed to forget that the primary purpose of his mission was not to make previously intractable problems in the philosophy of mind even more difficult but to retrieve a fiercely radioactive atomic warhead stuck a mile beneath Tulsa. Dennett tells us that Hamlet, his decerebrate and remotely controlled body, had barely started work on the warhead when communications between it and Yorick, his disembodied brain, broke down. He speculates that Hamlet soon turned to dust and appears neither to know nor to care what became of the warhead. I, as it happens, played an essential role in its ultimate retrieval. Although my role was similar to Dennett's, there were some important differences.

Dennett, or Yorick, during a wakeful interval during the long time when Dennett, or Yorick, slumbered on without any thoroughgoing communication, direct or remote, with a living human body, mainlined a little Brahms. The rectified output from the stereo stylus was fed directly into the auditory nerves. A certain sort of scientist or philosopher would ask,

This essay was first presented to a seminar on the philosophy of mind conducted by Douglas C. Long and Stanley Munsat at the University of North Carolina at Chapel Hill.

"If we can bypass the middle and inner ear and feed directly into the auditory nerve, why can't we bypass that as well and feed directly into whatever the auditory nerve feeds? Indeed, why not bypass that as well and feed directly into the subpersonal information-processing system another step farther in? Or into the next step beyond that?" Some theorists, but presumably not Dennett, would wonder when this process of replacing natural with artificial information-processing devices would reach the ultimate possessor of auditory experience, the real core person, the true seat of the soul. Others would see it rather as a layer-by-layer transformation, from the outside in, of an organic subject of consciousness to an artificial intelligence. The scientist shooting the Brahms piano trio straight into Yorick's auditory nerves, however, actually asked himself a different kind of question. He wondered why they had bothered to disconnect Dennett's ears from his auditory nerves. There would have been advantages, he thought, if we could have used earphones on the ears connected in the normal way to the brain in the vat and had microphones instead of organic ears on the body that ventured deep below Tulsa. The belief that the radiation could damage only brain tissue had been utterly mistaken. Indeed, the organic ears on Hamlet had been the first to go, and the rest of Hamlet was killed off shortly thereafter. With microphones instead of ears on Hamlet, and earphones on the ears connected normally to Yorick, Dennett could get a more realistic stereo rendition of a musical performance than could be obtained merely by mainlining the output from a stereo cartridge tracking a normal stereo recording. If Hamlet sat in the concert hall during a live performance, then every turn of the head would result in slightly different outputs from the earphones back in Houston. This set up would preserve the slight differences in volume and the slight time delay between the two signals that, although not consciously discernible, are so important in fixing the location of a sound source.

A description of this marginal improvement on earphones serves as an analogy in the explanation of some more radical advances made by the NASA technicians. Human eyes, they discovered from the Dennett caper, could not long withstand the fierce radiation from the buried warhead. It would have been better to leave Dennett's eyes attached to his brain as well and mount little television cameras in Hamlet's empty eye sockets. By the time I had entered into the secret mission to retrieve the warhead, the technicians had perfected eyevideos. Eyevideos are to seeing what earphones are to hearing. They not only project an image on the retina, they monitor every movement of the eyeball. For every rapid eye movement, there is a corresponding rapid camera movement; for every twist of the head, there is a corresponding shift in the cameras; and so on.

Seeing by means of eyevideos is in most circumstances indistinguishable from seeing without them. When trying to read really fine print, I noticed a slight loss of acuity; and, until the system was finely tuned, my night vision was rather better with eyevideos than without.

The most amazing simulation devices were for tactile perception. But before I describe skintact, which is to cutaneous and subcutaneous feeling what earphones are to hearing, I should like to describe some experiments that can be performed with eyevideos. The classic experiment with inverting lenses can be repeated simply by mounting the cameras upside down. New experiments of the same general sort can be performed by mounting the cameras in other positions that diverge from the normal. Here are a few: the so-called rabbit mount, with the cameras facing in opposite directions instead of side by side; the rabbit mount with extreme wide angle lenses, so the field of vision is 360 degrees; and the so-called bank or supermarket mount, with the two cameras mounted on opposite walls of the room that the subject occupies. This one takes some getting used to. It is possible, by the way, with this setup to see all the sides of an opaque cube at the same time.

But you want to hear more about skintact. It is a light, porous material worn right next to the skin, and it extends one's tactile range as radio and television extend one's auditory and visual range. When an artificial hand equipped with skintact transmitters strokes a damp puppy, the nerves in the skin of a real hand enclosed in receptor skintact are stimulated in just the way they would be if the real hand that contains them were stroking a damp puppy. When the skintact transmitter touches something warm, the corresponding skin covered with the receptor skintact does not actually warm up, but the appropriate sensory nerves are stimulated as they would be if warmth were actually present.

In order to retrieve the buried warhead, a robot was sent underground. This robot contained no living cells. It had the same proportions as my body; it was covered with skintact transmitter; its head had microphones and cameras mounted in it that could transmit to earphones and eyevideos. It was jointed just as my body is jointed and could move in most of the ways my body moves. It did not have a mouth or jaws or any mechanism for inhaling and exhaling air or for ingesting food. In place of a mouth, it had a loudspeaker that put forth all the sounds picked up by the microphone in front of my mouth.

There was another marvelous intercommunication system between me and the robot, the Motion and Resistance System, or MARS for short. The MARS membrane is worn over the skintact layer covering the human subject and under the skintact layer worn by the robot. I don't understand all the details of how MARS works, but it isn't difficult to say what it does.

It enables most of the bodily motions of the human to be duplicated exactly and simultaneously by the robot while the various pressures and resistances encountered by the limbs of the robot are duplicated for the corresponding human limbs.

The NASA scientists, instead of splitting me up, as they had split up Dennett, would leave me entire. I would stay back in Houston, all of me, and without suffering any effects from radiation would control a robot on its underground mission. The scientists assumed that, unlike Dennett, I would not be distracted from the primary purpose of the mission by abstruse philosophical questions about my location. Little did they know.

Dennett mentions laboratory workers who handle dangerous materials by operating feedback-controlled mechanical arms and hands. I was to be like them, only I would be operating a feedback-controlled entire body with prosthetic hearing, seeing, and feeling. Although it might be as if I were deep in the tunnel under Tulsa, I would know perfectly well where I really was, safe in the laboratory wearing earphones and eye-videos and skintact and MARS membrane, and speaking into a microphone.

It turned out, however, that once I was all rigged up, I could not resist the inclination to locate myself in the location of the robot. Just as Dennett wanted to see his brain, I wanted to see myself swathed in my electronic garments. And just as Dennett had difficulty identifying himself with his brain, I had difficulty identifying myself as the body that moved its head every time the robot moved its head and moved its legs in a walking motion as the robot walked around the laboratory.

Following Dennett's example, I began naming things. I used "Sanford" as Dennett used "Dennett" so that the questions "Where was I?" and "Where was Sanford?" should receive the same answer. My first name, "David," served as a name for the mostly saltwater and carbon compound body being cared for in Houston. My middle name, "Hawley," served for a while as the name of the robot.

The general principle *Where Hawley goes, there goes Sanford* obviously will not do. The robot that first walked around David while David made walking motions and turned its head as David turned his head is now in a highly classified science museum, and Sanford is not.

Also, the robot could be controlled by some other flesh-and-blood body before, and after, it was controlled by David. If Sanford ever went where Hawley went, I did so only when Hawley was in communication with David or a David replica in at least some of the ways that have been described. Dennett's first principle, *Where Hamlet goes, there goes Dennett*, needs analogous qualification.

My attempt to name the robot "Hawley" ran into difficulties when there turned out to be more than one robot. In Houston there were two full-size robots, one whose main parts were mostly plastic and one whose main parts were mostly metal. They looked just the same from the outside, and, if you know what I mean, they felt just the same from the inside. Neither robot was flown to Tulsa. A third robot, built on a three-fifths scale so it could maneuver more easily in cramped quarters, was there already. That's the one that retrieved the warhead.

Once I was onto the fact that there was more than one robot, the technicians did not always wait for David to fall asleep before switching channels. When Little Hawley returned in triumph from Tulsa, the three of us, or the three of I, would play three-corner catch with the cooperation of three human helpers who would keep the temporarily inactive and unsentient robots from toppling over. I persisted in locating myself in the position of the active, sentient robot and thus had the experience, or at least seemed to have the experience, of spatiotemporally discontinuous travel from one location to another without occupying any of the positions in between.

The principle *Where David goes, there goes Sanford* was no more appealing for me than Dennett's analogous *Where Yorick goes, there goes Dennett.* My reasons for rejection were more epistemological than legalistic. I had not seen David since Little Hawley's return from Tulsa and I could not be sure that David still existed. For some reason I never fully understood, quite soon after David began perceiving the external world via skintact, eyevideos, and earphones I was prevented from having the experiences associated with breathing, chewing, swallowing, digesting, and excreting. When Plastic Big Hawley produced articulate speech, I was unsure that the movements of David's diaphragm, larynx, tongue, and lips were still causally involved in its production. The scientists had the technology to tap directly into the appropriate nerves and rectify the neural output, which was itself produced partly in response to artificially rectified input, to transmit the same signals to the receiver connected to the loudspeaker mounted in the head of Plastic Big Hawley. The scientists, indeed, had the technology to bypass any of their fancy electronic devices of causal mediation and substitute even fancier devices that hook up directly with the brain. Suppose, I thought, something went wrong with David; its kidneys broke down or it developed an embolism in a coronary artery. Everything of David except the brain might be dead. For that matter, the brain might be dead too. Since a computer duplicate of Yorick, Dennett's brain, had been manufactured, then so might a computer duplicate of David's brain. I could have become a robot, or a computer, or a robot-computer combination, with no organic parts whatsoever. I would then resemble the Frank Baum character Nick Chopper, better known as the

Tin Woodman, whose transformation from organic to inorganic constitution was a part at a time. In such a case, besides having yet another variation on puzzle cases concerning the persistence of a person through a change of bodies, we would have the materials to construct more variations on puzzle cases concerning one self dividing into several. If one computer duplicate of a brain can be produced, then so can two or three or twenty. While each could control a modified brainless human body like that described by Dennett, each could also control a robot like one of the Hawleys. In either sort of case, body transfer, or robot transfer, or brain transfer, or computer transfer, or whatever you want to call it, could be accomplished without further advances in technology.

I realized that I was tempted by an argument similar to one Arnauld attributes to Descartes.

I can doubt that the human body David, or its brain, exists.

I cannot doubt that I see and hear and feel and think.

Therefore, I who see and hear and so forth cannot be identical to David or its brain; otherwise in doubting their existence I would doubt the existence of myself.

I also realized that David could have been separated into living, functional parts. The eyes with their eyevideos could be connected with the brain down the hall. The limbs, now kept alive with artificial blood, could similarly each have their own room. Whether or not these peripheral systems were still involved in the operation of Plastic Big Hawley, the brain might also have been taken apart, and the information between various subpersonal processing systems could be transferred nearly as quickly as before even if it had to travel much farther in space. And if the brain was gone, replaced with a computer duplicate, the computer parts might be spatially spread out in one of the ways Dennett describes briefly in "Toward a Cognitive Theory of Consciousness."* The spatial contiguity or chemical composition of the various internal information-processing subsystems that together were responsible for my thoughts, actions, and passions seemed irrelevant to my personal location, unity, or identity.

As Dennett first formulated his third principle of personal location, *Dennett is wherever he thinks he is*, it lends itself to misinterpretation. He doesn't mean that thinking that one is in Chapel Hill would ever be sufficient for actually being in Chapel Hill. He means rather that the location of a person's point of view is the location of the person. Of course people do more than literally just view things. They perceive by other senses; they move. Some of their movements, such as head and eye

*In *Brainstorms*.

movements, directly affect what they see. Many of their movements and positions are continually perceived although with only intermittent conscious attention. The robots in the Hawley family preserved almost all the normal functions and relations between the sense organs and limbs of a person and the environment the robots found themselves in. And so the spatial unity of a functioning Hawley robot was more than enough to provide Sanford with a sense of having a unified location *where the robot was*. At the time, the prospect of Hawley's disassembly was more unsettling than the prospect of David's dismemberment.

It was technically possible, I realized, that the inputs and outputs from David, or the computer duplicate, or whatever, could be divided between Little Hawley, Metal Big Hawley, and Plastic Big Hawley. Or a single robot could be disassembled although its various parts continued independently to move and to relay perceptual information. I didn't know what would happen to my sense of unity in such a circumstance. Would I be able to preserve *any* sense of myself as a single agent? Under such bizarre circumstances I might be inclined to parody Descartes and say that I was not only in control of these different parts as an admiral commanding a fleet, but that I was very closely united to them, and so to speak so intermingled with them that I seemed to compose with them one whole. Or I might not be up to that task of self-integration. Would my range of motor and perceptual activity, rather than being more widely distributed in space, be reduced to recollection, meditation, and fantasy as the deliverances from spatially separated and independent sources impressed me only as a booming, buzzing, distracting confusion? I am glad that I was never given a chance to find out.

If we regard light, pressure waves, and so forth as carrying information about the physical world, the point of view is the spatial point where this information is received by a perceiver. Sometimes, as Dennett remarks, one can shift one's point of view back and forth. The laboratory worker remotely manipulating dangerous materials can shift it back and forth from mechanical hands to hands of flesh and blood. The Cinerama viewer can shift it back and forth from a car hurtling down a roller-coaster from which one sees the ground approach with sickening rapidity to a seat inside a theater from which one sees rapidly changing images on a screen. Dennett had been unable to accomplish such a shift between Yorick and Hamlet, and I had been unable to accomplish such a shift between David and Hawley. Try as I might, I could not regard myself as seeing an image projected by eyevideo rather than seeing the scene before the camera that was transmitting to the eyevideo. In my present state of embodiment, analogously, I cannot shift my point of view a couple of inches farther in so that I can focus my attention on a pair of retinal images rather than on the messy typescript in front of my eyes. Neither can I shift my auditory point of hearing and attend to the vibrations of my eardrums rather than to the sounds outside.

My point of view had been from the location of a robot, and I had been strongly inclined to locate myself at my point of view. Although I regarded the location of a robot as being my location, I was less comfortable regarding myself as identical to a robot. Although I had no clear conception of myself as something other than the robot, I was willing to entertain the possibility that I and a robot, though distinct, occupied the same place at the same time. I was less troubled with discontinuous changes in location than with the idea that whenever the channels were switched I suddenly ceased to be identical with one robot and became identical with another.

When the time for debriefing arrived, Dr. Wechselmann, the scientist in charge, told me he had a big surprise for me and thereby filled me with fear and trepidation. Was David still alive? Was David's brain floating in a vat? Had I been on line with a computer duplicate for days? Were there several computer duplicates, each controlling a robot or each controlling a different modified human body? I did not anticipate the actual surprise. Dr. Wechselmann said that I could witness my own disassembly—that is to say, the disassembly of the Hawley *where I was.* While I watched in a mirror, I saw the technicians unzip the layers and peel them back. It turned out that I, David Sanford, the living human being, was underneath. David's health had been maintained; and forty-eight hours earlier, during sleep, the cameras had been mounted directly in front of the eyevideos, the microphones directly in front of the earphones, one layer of sensitive skintact directly over the layer next to my skin, and so forth. For a while, when I thought that my location was the location of Plastic Big Hawley, I was really walking around in a very skillfully made and lifelike or, more strictly, lifeless-like, robot costume. The sensations of breathing and eating and so forth were soon returned to me.

Taking off the eyevideo apparatus did not change things visually at all. The fact that for a while, when I thought that David's eyes were in another room, they were actually right behind the cameras, reinforced my inclination to say that the eyevideo system does not interpose any barrier between its user and the physical world. It is like seeing things through a microscope or telescope or with the help of corrective lenses. When one sees by an eyevideo system, one sees what is in focus in front of the lens, not some mediating visual object, even though the causal chain between the external object and the visual awareness is more or less altered and complicated by the intervening apparatus.

So here I am, and there is no doubt that I was inside the double-layer suit when David was inside the suit. But when David was inside a single-layer suit, and the other layer covered a robot, my locations remain something of a puzzle. If the puzzle is in any way more informative than the puzzles Dennett poses, Dennett deserves much of the credit. If he had wholly succeeded in his mission, there would have been no reason for me to embark on mine.

Reflections

Sanford's story is much closer to being possible than its predecessor. In a recent article Marvin Minsky, founder of the Artificial Intelligence Laboratory at M.I.T., discusses the prospects for this technology:

> You don a comfortable jacket lined with sensors and musclelike motors. Each motion of your arm, hand, and fingers is reproduced at another place by mobile, mechanical hands. Light, dextrous, and strong, these hands have their own sensors through which you see and feel what is happening. Using this instrument, you can "work" in another room, in another city, in another country, or on another planet. Your remote presence possesses the strength of a giant or the delicacy of a surgeon. Heat or pain is translated into informative but tolerable sensation. Your dangerous job becomes safe and pleasant.

Minsky calls this technology *telepresence*, a term suggested to him by Pat Gunkel, and describes the advances that have already been made.

> Telepresence is not science fiction. We could have a remote-controlled economy by the twenty-first century if we start planning right now. The technical scope of such a project would be no greater than that of designing a new military aircraft.

Some of the components of Sanford's imagined MARS system already have prototypes—mechanical hands with feedback systems transmitting forces and resistance, variously amplified or moderated—and there is even a step in the direction of eyevideo:

> A Philco engineer named Steve Moulton made a nice telepresence eye. He mounted a TV camera atop a building and wore a helmet so that when he moved his head, the camera on top of the building moved, and so did a viewing screen attached to the helmet.
> Wearing this helmet, you have the feeling of being on top of the building and looking around Philadelphia. If you "lean over" it's kind of creepy. But the most

sensational thing Moulton did was to put a two-to-one ratio on the neck so that when you turn your head 30 degrees, the mounted eye turns 60 degrees; you feel as if you had a rubber neck, as if you could turn your "head" completely around!

Might the future hold something even stranger in store? Justin Leiber, a philosopher at the University of Houston, develops a more radical variation on these themes in the next selection, an excerpt from his science fiction novel *Beyond Rejection*.

D. C. D.

15

JUSTIN LEIBER

Beyond Rejection

Worms began his spiel: "People often think that it ought to be simple enough to just *manufacture* an adult human body, like building a house or a helicopter. You'd think that, well, we know what chemicals are involved, and how they go together, how they form cells according to DNA templates, and how the cells form organ systems regulated by chemical messengers, hormones, and the like. So we ought to be able to build a fully functional human body right up from scratch."

Worms moved so that he blocked their view of the jogger. He brought his drained coffee cup down for emphasis.

"And, of course, we could build a human body up from scratch, theoretically, anyhow. But no one ever has. In fact, no one has ever even started to. De Reinzie manufactured the first fully functional human cell —muscle tissue—in the middle of the last century, about 2062 or so. And shortly after that the major varieties were cooked up. And even then it wasn't really manufactured from scratch. De Reinzie, like all the rest, built some basic DNA templates from actual carbon, oxygen, hydrogen, and so on, or rather from simple sugars and alcohols. *But then he grew the rest from these.* That's growth, not manufacture. And nobody's come closer to building an organ than a lab that made a millimeter of stomach wall for several million credits a couple of decades ago.

"I don't want to bother you with the mathematics," he continued, looking away from Terry. "But my old professor at Tech used to estimate that it would take all the scientific and manufacturing talent of Earth and the rest of the Federation something like fifty years and a googol credits to build a single human hand.

"You can imagine what it would take to make something like that," he said, moving out of their line of vision and gesturing at the jogging figure. He took the clipboard that hung next to the treadmill's controls and scanned the sheets on it.

"This body had been blank for three years. It has a running-time age of thirty-one years, though of course Sally Cadmus—that's the person involved—was born over thirty-four years ago. What with demand, of course, three years is a long time for a body to remain out of action. She's in good health, fine musculature for a spacer—says Sally was an asteroid miner here. Seems the body spent two years frozen in a Holmann orbit. We've had it for four months and we're preparing it now. You might see her walking around any day now.

"But Sally Cadmus won't. Her last tape was just the obligatory one made on reaching majority and she left no instructions for implantation. I trust, people, that all your tapes are updated." He gave them the family doctor look and went on, moving closer and dropping his voice.

"I have my mind taped every six months, just to be safe. After all, the tape is *you*—your individual software, or program, including memory store. Everything that makes you *you.*" He walked up to the aide who had brought the beautiful young man.

"You—for instance—Ms. Pedersen, when did you have your last tape job?"

The aide, a gaunt red-haired woman in her mid-thirties, snatched her arm from around her young man and glared at Austin Worms.

"What business—"

"Oh, I wouldn't really expect you to say in front of other people." He grinned at the others as Pedersen subsided. "But that's the whole point, you see. Maybe she has been renewing her tape yearly, which is what our profession recommends as an absolute minimum. But a lot of people neglect this elementary precaution because they are so appalled by the thought of severe bodily injury. They just let things slide. And because the topic is so personal, no one knows, no one asks, no one reminds them until the once-in-half-a-million accident happens—truly irreparable body damage or total destruction.

"And then you find that the person hasn't taped for twenty years. Which means . . . ."

He surveyed the group to let it sink in. Then he saw the beautiful girl-child. Terry had been hiding her, no doubt. A classic blond-haired, blue-eyed girl in her midteens. She was looking straight into his eyes. Or *through* them. Something . . . He went on.

"Which means if he or she is lucky and there's estate money, you've got someone who has to face all the ordinary problems of rejection that come in trying to match a young mind with what is almost certain to be a middle-aged body. But also the implant has all those problems multiplied by another. The implant has to deal with a world that is *twenty years in the future.* And a 'career' that is meaningless because he lacks the memory and skills that his old mind picked up over that twenty years.

"More likely, you'll get the real blowout. You'll get massive rejection, psychosis and premature essential senility, and death. Real, final mind death."

"But you would still have the person's tape, their software, as you call it," said Ms. Pedersen. "Couldn't you just try again, with another blank body?" She still had her hands off her young man.

"Two problems. First"—he stuck his index finger in the air—"you got to realize how very difficult it is for a mind and a body to make a match, even with all the help us somaticians and psycheticians can provide, the best that modern biopsychological engineering can put together. Even with a really creative harmonizer to get in there and make the structure jell. Being reborn is very hard work indeed.

"And the failure rate under ordinary circumstances—tapes up-to-date, good stable mind, decent recipient body—is about twenty percent. And we know that it jumps to ninety-five percent if there's a second time around. It's nearly that bad the first time if you got someone whose tapes are twenty years out of date. The person may get through the first few days all right but he can't pull himself into reality. Everything he knows was lost twenty years ago. No friends, no career, everything out of shape. Then the mind will reject its new body just as it rejects the new world it has woken up to. So you don't have much of a chance. Unless, of course, you're the rare nympher or still rarer leaper.

"Second, the Government underwrites the cost of the first implantation. Of course, they don't pay for a fancy body—a nympher body, that is. You'd pay more than two million credits for one of those beauties. You get what's available and you are lucky if you get it within a year or two. What the Government underwrites is the basic operation and tuning job. That alone costs one and a half million or so. Enough to pay my salary for a hundred years. Enough to send the half-dozen or so of you on the Cunard Line Uranium Jubilee All-Planets Tour in first class."

Austin had been moving over to the treadmill control console while speaking. As he finished, his audience noticed a large structure descending from the ceiling just over the jogging figure, Sally Cadmus's body. It looked like a cross between the upper half of a large mummy and a comfortably stuffed armchair. Austin glided over to the treadmill. The audience watched the structure open like an ancient iron maiden. Some noticed that the jogging figure was slowing down.

Austin arrived just in time to complete a flurry of adjustments on the jogger's control package before the structure folded itself around. Two practiced blows on the back of the jogger's thighs brought the legs out of contact with the slowing treadmill.

"It's a lucky thing that implantation is so risky and the sort of accident that calls for it so rare," he said as the structure ascended behind him. "Otherwise, the Kellog-Murphy Law, which underwrites the first implantation, would bankrupt the Government."

"Where is the body going?" asked the blond-haired youngster. Austin could see now that she was probably no more than ten or eleven years old. Something about her posture had made him think she was older.

"Normally it would go into a kind of artificial hibernation—low temperature and vital activity. But this body will be implanted tomorrow, so we'll keep it at a normal level of biological function." He had given the body an additional four cc.'s of glucose-saline plasma beyond the program. That was to compensate for the extra jogging. He hadn't done the official calculations. It wasn't that such mathematics was more than a minor chore. If you had asked him to explain, he would have said that the official calculation would have called for half again as much plasma. But he sensed that the body got more than usual from every cc. of water, from every molecule of sugar. Perhaps it was something in the sweat smell, the color and feel of the skin, the resilience of the musculature. But Austin knew.

The somatic aides would have said that Austin Worms was the best ghoul in the Solar System, a zombie's best friend. And they would have meant what they said even if they went on to joke.

Austin had vomited for the first and only time in his life when he learned the origin of the slang terms "ghoul" and "vampire."

The sounds of Terry's tour group faded as they moved up the hall to the psychetician laboratory. But Austin did not return to Bruhler's *The Central Equations of the Abstract Theory of Mind.* He had been puzzled by what the eleven-year-old blond girl had said to him before sauntering off to catch up with the rest of the tour. She had said, "I bet that mind is gonna be in for a real shock when it wakes up with that thing on its backside." He wondered how she could know that it wasn't just part of the crazy-quilt system of tubes and wires that the jogger had on her back.

"I'm Candy Darling," she had added as she left the room. Now he knew who she was. You never knew what to expect in a harmonizer.

Psycheticians take care of minds. That's why they are sometimes
called vampires. Somaticians are called ghouls because they take
care of bodies.
—I. F. + S. C. Operation Logbook, Append. II, Press Releases

Germaine Means grinned wolfishly at them. "I am a psychetician.
What Terry would call a vampire. Call me Germaine if that does not
appeal."

They were seated facing a blackboard at one end of a large room
which was otherwise filled with data cabinets, office cubicles, and computer consoles. The woman who addressed them wore severe and plain
overalls. When she had first come to the Norbert Wiener Research Hospital—NWRH—the director had suggested that the chief psychetician
might dress more suitably. That director had retired early.

"As you know from what Austin Worms told you, we think of the
individual human mind as an abstract pattern of memory, skill, and experience that has been impressed on the physical hardware of the brain.
Think of it this way: when you get a computer factory-fresh, it is like a
blanked human brain. The computer has no subroutines, just as the brain
has no skills. The computer has no data arrays to call on, just as the
blanked brain has no memories.

"What we do here is try to implant the pattern of memory, skill, and
experience that is all that is left of a person into a blanked brain. It is not
easy because brains are not manufactured. You have to grow them. And
a unique personality has to be part of this growth and development. So
each brain is different. So no software mind fits any hardware brain
perfectly. Except the brain that it grew up with.

"For instance," Germaine Means continued, softening her tone so
she would not alert Ms. Pedersen's boyfriend, who was dozing in a well-
padded chair, his elegant legs thrust straight out in full display, tights to
sandals. "For instance, when pressure is applied to this person's foot, his
brain knows how to interpret the nervous impulses from his foot." She
suited her action to her words.

"His yelp indicates that his brain recognizes that considerable pressure has been applied to the toes of his left foot. If, however, we implanted another mind, it would not interpret the nervous impulses correctly—it might feel the impulses as a stomachache."

The young man was on his feet, bristling. He moved toward Germaine, who had turned away to pick up what looked like a pair of goggles

with some mirrors and gears on top. As he reached her, she turned to face him and pushed the goggles into his hands.

"Yes, thank you for volunteering. Put them on." Not knowing what else to do, he did.

"I want you to look at that blond-haired girl who just sat down over there." She held his arm lightly as he turned and his balance wavered. He appeared to be looking through the goggles at a point several degrees to the right of Candy Darling.

"Now I want you to point at her with your right hand—quick!" The young man's arm shot out, the finger also pointing several degrees to the right of the girl. He began moving his finger to the left, but Germaine pulled his hand down to his side, outside the field of vision that the goggles allowed him.

"Try it again, quick," she said. This time the finger was not as far off. On the fifth try his finger pointed directly to Candy Darling, though he continued to look to her right.

"Now off with the goggles. Look at her again. Point quick!" Germaine grabbed his hand the instant he pointed. Though he was not looking directly at Candy Darling, he was pointing several degrees *to the left* of her. He looked baffled.

Germaine Means chalked a head and goggles on the blackboard, seen as if you were looking down at them from the ceiling. She drew another head to the left of the line of sight of the goggled head and chalked "15°" in to indicate the angle.

"What happened is a simple example of tuning. The prisms in the goggles bend the light so that when his eyes told him he was looking straight at her, his eyes were in fact pointed fifteen degrees to her right. The muscles and nerves of his hand were tuned to point where his eyes were actually pointed—so he pointed fifteen degrees to the right.

"But then his eyes saw his hand going off to the right, so he began to compensate. In a couple of minutes—five tries—his motor coordination compensates so that he points to where his eyes tell him she is—he adjusted to pointing fifteen degrees *to the left* from usual. When I took the goggles off, his arm was still tuned to compensate, so he pointed off to the left until he readjusted."

She picked up the goggles. "Now, a human can adjust to that distortion in a few minutes. But I could calibrate these so that they would turn the whole room upside down. If you then walked around and tried to do things, you would find it difficult. Very difficult. But if you kept the goggles on, the whole room would turn right side up after a day or two.

Everything would seem normal because your system would have retuned itself.

"What do you think will happen if you then take the goggles off?"

Candy Darling giggled. Ms. Pedersen said, "Oh, I see. Your mind would have adjusted to turning the, ah, messages from your eyes upside down, so when you took the goggles off—"

"Precisely," said Germaine, "everything would look upside down to you until you readjusted to having the goggles off—and it happens the same way. You stumble around for a day or so and then everything snaps right side up again. And the stumbling-around part is important. If you are confined to a chair with your head fixed in position, your mind and body can't tune themselves.

"Now I want you to imagine what happens when we implant a mind into a blanked brain. *Almost everything will be out of tune.* The messages from your eyes won't simply be inverted, they'll be scrambled in countless ways. Same thing with your ears, nose, tongue—and with the whole nerve net covering your body. And that's just incoming messages. Your mind will have even more problems when it tries to tell the body to do something. Your mind will try to get your lips to say 'water,' and Sol knows what sound will come out.

"And what's worse is that whatever sound does come out, your new ears won't be able to give your mind an accurate version of it."

Germaine smiled at them and glanced at her watch. Terry stood up.

"Terry will be wanting to take you on. Let me wrap this up by saying that it is a very simple thing to play someone's mind tape into a prepared brain. The great problem is in getting the rearranged brain, the cerebral cortex, speaking strictly, to be tuned into the rest of the system. As Austin Worms may have told you, we start an implant operation tomorrow. The initial tape-in will take less than an hour. But the tuning will take days and days. Even months, if you count all the therapy. Questions?"

"Just one," said Ms. Pedersen. "I can understand how difficult it is for a mind to survive implantation. And, of course, I know it is illegal to implant a mind that is over eighty-five. But couldn't a person—if you call a mind a person—live forever by passing through body after body?"

"Okay, that's a tough one to explain even if we had a lot of time and you knew a lot of mathematics. Until this century it was believed that senility was a by-product of the physical breakdown of the body. Today we know that a human mind can have roughly one hundred years of experiences before it reaches essential senility, however young the body it occupies. As you know, a few successful leapers have survived implantation after a fifty-year wait. So a leaper might, in theory, still be functioning a thousand years from now. But such an individual's mind will not be able to encompass any more lived experience than you. When all there is of you is a tape in storage, you aren't really alive."

After they had filed out, Germaine Means noticed that the blond-haired girl had remained.

"Hi, I'm Candy Darling," she cried. "I hope you don't mind. I thought it would be fun to sneak in on the standard tour. Get the smell of the place."

"Where's your VAT?"

*   *   *

> Austin Worms declared that basic physical meshing procedures were complete.
> —I. F. + S. C. Operation Logbook

Gxxhdt.

Etaoin shrdlu. Mmm.

Anti-M.

Away mooncow Taddy-fair fine. Fine again, take. Away, along, alas, alung the orbit-run, from swerve of space to wormhole wiggle, brings us. Start now. Wake.

So hear I am now coming out of nothing like Eros out of Death, knowing only that I was Ismael Forth—stately, muscled well—taping-in, and knowing that I don't know when I'm waking or where, or where-in. And hoping that it is a dream. But it isn't. Oh, no, it isn't. With that goggling piece of munster cheese oumphowing on my eyelids.

And seemingly up through endless levels and configurations that had no words and now no memories. Wake.

"Helow, I'm Candy Darlinz."

"I am Ismael returned" was what I started to try to reply. After the third attempt it came out better. And the munster cheese had become a blond-haired young girl with piercing blue eyes.

"Your primary implantation was finished yesterday, finally. Everyone thinks you're a success. Your body is a pip. You're in the Norbert Wiener Research Hospital in Houston. You have two estates clear through probate. Your friend Peter Strawson has covered your affairs. It's the first week of April, 2112. You're alive."

She stood up and touched my hand.

"You start therapy tomorrow. Now sleep."

I was already drifting off by the time she had closed the door behind her. I couldn't even get myself worked up by what I was noticing. My nipples felt as big as grapes. I went out as I worked my way down past the belly button.

The next day I discovered that I had not only lost a penis. I had gained a meter-long prehensile tail. It was hate at first sense.

I had worked my way up to consciousness in slow stages. I had endless flight dreams—walking, running, staggering on, away from some nameless horror. And brief flashes of sexuality that featured performances by my (former) body.

I really liked my old body. One of my biggest problems, as Dr. Germaine Means was soon to tell me. I could picture clearly how it had looked in the mirrors as I did my stretch and tone work. Just a hair over six foot four. Two hundred and five pounds, well-defined muscles, and just enough fat to be comfortable. A mat of curly red chest hair that made it easy to decide to have my facial hair wiped permanently. It felt good to be a confident and even slightly clumsy giant, looking down on a world of little people.

Oh, I wasn't a real body builder or anything like that. Just enough exercise to look good—and attractive. I hadn't in fact been all that good at physical sports. But I had liked my body. It was also a help in the public relations work that I did for IBO.

I was still lying on my back. I felt shrunk. Shrunk. As the warm, muzzy flush of sleep faded, my right hand moved up over my ribs. Ribs. They were thin and they stuck out, as if the skin were sprayed over the bare cage. I felt like a skeleton until I got to the lumps. Bags. Growths. Sacks. Even then part of me realized that they were not at all large for a woman, while most of me felt that they were as big as cantaloupes.

You may have imagined it as a kind of erotic dream. There you are in the hospital bed. You reach and there they are. Apt to the hands, the hardening nipples nestled between index and middle fingers. (Doubtless some men have felt this warm reverie with their hands on real flesh. The women may have felt pinch and itch rather than the imagined sensual flush. I know whereof I speak. I now know a lot of sexuality is like that. Perhaps heterosexuality continues as well as it does because of ignorance: each partner is free to invent the feelings of the other.)

But I was quite unable to feel erotic about my new acquisitions. Both ways. My fingers, as I felt them, felt pathology. Two dead cancerous mounds. And from the inside—so to speak—I felt that my flesh had swollen. The sheet made the nipples feel raw. A strange feeling of separation, as if the breast were disconnected, nerveless jelly—and then two points of sensitivity some inches in front of my chest. Dead spots. Rejection. I learned a lot about these.

As my hand moved down I was prepared for the swerve of hip. I couldn't feel a penis and I did not expect to find one. I did not call it "gash." Though that term is found occasionally in space-marine slang and often among the small number of male homosexuals of the extreme S&M type (Secretary & Master). I first learned the term a few days later from Dr. Means. She said that traditional male-male pornography revealed typical male illusions about female bodies: a "rich source of information about body-image pathologies." She was certainly right in pointing out that "gash" was how I felt about it. At first.

I was not only scrawny, I was almost hairless. I felt *really* naked, naked and defenseless as a baby. Though my skin was several shades less fair —and I passed a scar. I was almost relieved to feel the curly groin hair. Gone. Sticklike legs. But I *did* feel something between my thighs. And knees. And ankles, by Sol.

At first I thought it was some sort of tube to take my body wastes. But as I felt down between my legs I could tell that it wasn't covering those areas. It was attached at the end of my spine—or rather it had become the end of my spine, stretching down to my feet. It was my flesh. I didn't quite intend it—at that point I can't say that I intended anything, I was so shook—but the damned thing flipped up from the bottom of the bed like a snake, throwing the sheet over my face.

I screamed my head off.

"Cut it off" was what I said after they had given me enough betaorthoamine to stop me flailing about. I said this several times to Dr. Germaine Means, who had directed the rest of them out of the room.

"Look, Sally—I'll call you that until you select a name yourself—we are not going to cut your tail off. By our calculations such a move would make terminal rejection almost certain. You would die. Several thousand nerves connect your brain with your prehensile tail. A sizable portion of your brain monitors and directs your tail—that part of your brain needs exercise and integration like any other component. We taped the pattern of your mind into your present brain. They *have to* learn to live together or you get rejection. In brief, you will die."

Dr. Means continued to read me the riot act. I would have to learn to love my new body—she practically gushed with praise for it—my new sex, my new tail. I would have to do a lot of exercise and tests. And I would have to talk to a lot of people about how I felt. And I should feel pleased as pisque to have an extra hand.

My new body broke into a cold sweat when I realized that I had— truly—no choice. I wasn't poor, assuming what I had heard yesterday was true. But I certainly couldn't afford an implant, let alone a desirable body. What I had, of course, came free under the Kellog-Murphy Bill.

After a while she left. I stared at the wall numbly. A nurse brought a tray with scrambled eggs and toast. I ignored both nurse and tray. The thin-lipped mouth salivated. Let it suffer.

Reflections

Fascinating as the idea of mind tapes is, the supposition that such person preservation might someday be possible is almost certainly wrong. Leiber sees the fundamental obstacle—brains are *not* like computers fresh from the factory and all alike. Even at birth human brains are no doubt uniquely configured—like fingerprints—and a lifetime of learning and experience can only enhance their idiosyncracies. There are scant grounds then for hoping that anything with the hardware-independence cf a program can be "read out" of a brain (at a periodic "mind taping" session). There is even less hope that such a mind tape, even if it could be constructed, would be compatible with another brain's hardware. Computers are *designed* to be readily redesignable (at another level) by the insertion, in one big lump or rush, of a new program; brains presumably are not.

Leiber is wonderfully imaginative about the ways technicians might try to solve this incompatibility problem (and his book contains many more surprises on this score), but in order to tell a good tale he has had to understate the problems by orders of magnitude in our opinion. The problems of transferring massive amounts of information between structurally different brains—such as yours and ours—are not insurmountable. The technology that already exists for accomplishing that task may, however, turn out in the end to be the most efficient possible. One of the most recent and advanced examples of that technology is in your hands at this instant.

D.C.D.

16

RUDY RUCKER

Software

Cobb Anderson would have held out longer, but you don't see dolphins every day. There were twenty of them, fifty, rolling in the little gray waves, wicketing up out of the water. It was good to see them. Cobb took it for a sign and went out for his evening sherry an hour early.

The screen door slapped shut behind him and he stood uncertainly for a moment, dazed by the late-afternoon sun. Annie Cushing watched him from her window in the cottage next door. Beatles' music drifted out past her.

"You forgot your hat," she advised. He was still a good-looking man, barrel-chested and bearded like Santa Claus. She wouldn't have minded getting it on with him, if he weren't so . . .

"Look at the dolphins, Annie. I don't need a hat. Look how happy they are. I don't need a hat and I don't need a wife." He started toward the asphalt road, walking stiffly across the crushed white shells.

Annie went back to brushing her hair. She wore it white and long, and she kept it thick with hormone spray. She was sixty and not too brittle to hug. She wondered idly if Cobb would take her to the Golden Prom next Friday.

The long last chord of "Day in the Life" hung in the air. Annie couldn't have said which song she had just heard—after fifty years her responses to the music were all but extinguished—but she walked across

Excerpt from *Software* by Rudy Rucker. Copyright © 1981 by Rudy Rucker. The complete novel *Software* will be published by Ace Books, New York, 1981.

the room to turn the stack of records over. *If only something would happen*, she thought for the thousandth time. *I get so tired of being me.*

At the Superette, Cobb selected a chilled quart of cheap sherry and a damp paper bag of boiled peanuts. And he wanted something to look at.

The Superette magazine selection was nothing compared to what you could get over in Cocoa. Cobb settled finally for a love-ad newspaper called *Kiss and Tell*. It was always good and weird . . . most of the advertisers were seventy-year-old hippies like himself. He folded the first-page picture under so that only the headline showed. PLEASE PHEEZE ME.

Funny how long you can laugh at the same jokes, Cobb thought, waiting to pay. Sex seemed odder all the time. He noticed the man in front of him, wearing a light-blue hat blocked from plastic mesh.

If Cobb concentrated on the hat he saw an irregular blue cylinder. But if he let himself look through the holes in the mesh he could see the meek curve of the bald head underneath. Skinny neck and a light-bulb head, clawing in his change. A friend.

"Hey, Farker."

Farker finished rounding up his nickels, then turned his body around. He spotted the bottle.

"Happy Hour came early today." A note of remonstrance. Farker worried about Cobb.

"It's Friday. Pheeze me tight." Cobb handed Farker the paper.

"Seven eighty-five," the cashier said to Cobb. Her white hair was curled and hennaed. She had a deep tan. Her flesh had a pleasingly used and oily look to it.

Cobb was surprised. He'd already counted money into his hand. "I make it six fifty." Numbers began sliding around in his head.

"I meant my box number," the cashier said with a toss of her head. "In the *Kiss and Tell.*" She smiled coyly and took Cobb's money. She was proud of her ad this month. She'd gone to a studio for the picture.

Farker handed the paper back to Cobb outside. "I can't look at this, Cobb. I'm still a happily married man, God help me."

"You want a peanut?"

"Thanks." Farker extracted a soggy shell from the little bag. There was no way his spotted and trembling old hands could have peeled the nut, so he popped it whole into his mouth. After a minute he spit the hull out.

They walked toward the beach, eating pasty peanuts. They wore no shirts, only shorts and sandals. The afternoon sun beat pleasantly on their backs. A silent Mr. Frostee truck cruised past.

Cobb cracked the screw-top on his dark-brown bottle and took a tentative first sip. He wished he could remember the box number the cashier had just told him. Numbers wouldn't stay still for him anymore. It was hard to believe he'd ever been a cybernetician. His memory ranged back to his first robots and how they'd learned to bop . . .

"Food drop's late again," Farker was saying. "And I hear there's a new murder cult up in Daytona. They're called the Little Kidders." He wondered if Cobb could hear him. Cobb was just standing there with empty colorless eyes, a yellow stain of sherry on the dense white hair around his lips.

"Food drop," Cobb said, suddenly coming back. He had a way of reentering a conversation by confidently booming out the last phrase that had registered. "I've still got a good supply."

"But be sure to eat some of the new food when it comes," Farker cautioned. "For the vaccines. I'll tell Annie to remind you."

"Why is everybody so interested in staying alive? I left my wife and came down here to drink and die in peace. *She* can't wait for me to kick off. So why—" Cobb's voice caught. The fact of the matter was that he was terrified of death. He took a quick, medicinal slug of sherry.

"If you were peaceful, you wouldn't drink so much," Farker said mildly. "Drinking is the sign of an unresolved conflict."

"No *kidding*," Cobb said heavily. In the golden warmth of the sun, the sherry had taken quick effect. "Here's an unresolved conflict for you." He ran a fingernail down the vertical white scar on his furry chest. "I don't have the money for another second-hand heart. In a year or two this cheapie's going to poop out on me."

Farker grimaced. "So? *Use* your two years."

Cobb ran his finger back up the scar, as if zipping it up. "I've seen what it's like, Farker. I've had a taste of it. It's the worst thing there is." He shuddered at the dark memory—teeth, ragged clouds—and fell silent.

Farker glanced at his watch. Time to get going or Cynthia would . . .

"You know what Jimi Hendrix said?" Cobb asked. Recalling the quote brought the old resonance back into his voice. " 'When it's my time to die, I'm going to be the one doing it. So as long as I'm alive, you let me live my way.' "

Farker shook his head. "Face it, Cobb, if you drank less you'd get a lot more out of life." He raised his hand to cut off his friend's reply. "But I've got to get home. Bye bye."

"Bye."

Cobb walked to the end of the asphalt and over a low dune to the edge of the beach. No one was there today, and he sat down under his favorite palm tree.

The breeze had picked up a little. Warmed by the sand, it lapped at Cobb's face, buried under white whiskers. The dolphins were gone.

He sipped sparingly at his sherry and let the memories play. There were only two thoughts to be avoided: death and his abandoned wife, Verena. The sherry kept them away.

The sun was going down behind him when he saw the stranger. Barrel chest, erect posture, strong arms and legs covered with curly hair, a round white beard. Like Santa Claus, or like Ernest Hemingway the year he shot himself.

"Hello, Cobb," the man said. He wore sungoggles and looked amused. His shorts and sport shirt glittered.

"Care for a drink?" Cobb gestured at the half-empty bottle. He wondered who, if anyone, he was talking to.

"No thanks," the stranger said, sitting down. "It doesn't do anything for me."

Cobb stared at the man. Something about him . . .

"You're wondering who I am," the stranger said, smiling. "I'm you."

"You who?"

"You me." The stranger used Cobb's own tight little smile on him. "I'm a mechanical copy of your body."

The face seemed right and there was even the scar from the heart transplant. The only difference between them was how alert and healthy the copy looked. Call him Cobb Anderson$_2$. Cobb$_2$ didn't drink. Cobb envied him. He hadn't had a completely sober day since he had the operation and left his wife.

"How did you get here?"

The robot waved a hand palm up. Cobb liked the way the gesture looked on someone else. "I can't tell you," the machine said. "You know how most people feel about us."

Cobb chuckled his agreement. He should know. At first the public had been delighted that Cobb's moon-robots had evolved into intelligent boppers. That had been before Ralph Numbers had led the 2001 revolt. After the revolt, Cobb had been tried for treason. He focused back on the present.

"If you're a bopper, then how can you be . . . here?" Cobb waved his hand in a vague circle taking in the hot sand and the setting sun. "It's too hot. All the boppers I know of are based on super-cooled circuits. Do you have a refrigeration unit hidden in your stomach?"

Anderson$_2$ made another familiar hand gesture. "I'm not going to tell you yet, Cobb. Later you'll find out. Just take this. . . ." The robot fumbled in its pocket and brought out a wad of bills. "Twenty-five grand. We want you to get the flight to Disky tomorrow. Ralph Numbers will be your contact up there. He'll meet you at the Anderson room in the museum."

Cobb's heart leapt at the thought of seeing Ralph Numbers again. Ralph, his first and finest model, the one who had set all the others free. But . . .

"I can't get a visa," Cobb said. "You know that. I'm not allowed to leave the Gimmie territory."

"Let *us* worry about that," the robot said urgently. "There'll be someone to help you through the formalities. We're working on it right now. And I'll stand in for you while you're gone. No one'll be the wiser."

The intensity of his double's tone made Cobb suspicious. He took a drink of sherry and tried to look shrewd. "What's the point of all this? Why should I want to go to the Moon in the first place? And why do the boppers want me there?"

Anderson$_2$ glanced around the empty beach and leaned close. "We want to make you immortal, Dr. Anderson. After all you did for us, it's the least we can do."

Immortal! The word was like a window flung open. With death so close nothing had mattered. But if there was a way out . . .

"How?" Cobb demanded. In his excitement he rose to his feet. "How will you do it? Will you make me young again too?"

"Take it easy," the robot said, also rising. "Don't get overexcited. Just trust us. With our supplies of tank-grown organs we can rebuild you from the ground up. And you'll get as much interferon as you need."

The machine stared into Cobb's eyes, looking honest. Staring back, Cobb noticed that they hadn't gotten the irises quite right. The little ring of blue was too flat and even. The eyes were, after all, just glass, unreadable glass.

The double pressed the money into Cobb's hand. "Take the money and get the shuttle tomorrow. We'll arrange for a young man called Sta-Hi to help you at the spaceport."

Music was playing, wheedling closer. A Mr. Frostee truck, the same one Cobb had seen before. It was white, with a big freezer box in back. There was a smiling giant plastic ice-cream cone mounted on top of the cab. Cobb's double gave him a pat on the shoulder and trotted up the beach.

When he reached the truck, the robot looked back and flashed a smile. Yellow teeth in the white beard. For the first time in years, Cobb loved himself, the erect strut, the frightened eyes. "Good-bye," he shouted, waving the money. "And thanks!"

Cobb Anderson$_2$ jumped into the soft-ice-cream truck next to the driver, a fat short-haired man with no shirt. And then the Mr. Frostee

truck drove off, its music silenced again. It was dusk now. The sound of
the truck's motor faded into the ocean's roar. If only it was true.

But it had to be! Cobb was holding twenty-five thousand-dollar bills.
He counted them twice to make sure. And then he scrawled the figure
$25,000 in the sand and looked at it. That was a lot.

As the darkness fell he finished the sherry and, on a sudden impulse,
put the money in the bottle and buried it next to his tree in a meter
of sand. The excitement was wearing off now, and fear was setting in.
Could the boppers *really* give him immortality with surgery and
interferon?

It seemed unlikely. A trick. But why would the boppers lie to him?
Surely they remembered all the good things he'd done for them. Maybe
they just wanted to show him a good time. God knows he could use it.
And it would be great to see Ralph Numbers again.

Walking home along the beach, Cobb stopped several times,
tempted to go back and dig up that bottle to see if the money was really
there. The moon was up, and he could see the little sand-colored crabs
moving out of their holes. *They could shred those bills right up*, he thought,
stopping again.

Hunger growled in his stomach. And he wanted more sherry. He
walked a little farther down the silvery beach, the sand squeaking under
his heavy heels. It was bright as day, only all black and white. The full
moon had risen over the land to his right. *Full moon means high tide*, he
fretted.

He decided that as soon as he'd had a bite to eat he'd get more sherry
and move the money to higher ground.

Coming up on his moon-silvered cottage from the beach he spotted
Annie Cushing's leg around the corner of her cottage. She was sitting on
her front steps, waiting to snag him in the driveway. He angled to the
right and came up on his house from behind, staying out of her line of
vision.

". . . 0110001," Wagstaff concluded.

"100101," Ralph Numbers replied curtly. "011000001010100011
0101010000100111001000000000011000000000111001111100111 0
000000000000000001010001110000111111111010011011011000 1010
10110000111111111111111110110101010101110111100000101000 00
0000000000011110100110110110110111101001000100001000111
1110101000000111101010100111101010111100001100011111 0000
11100111110111011111111111110000000000010000011000000000 01.

The two machines rested side by side in front of the One's big
console. Ralph was built like a file cabinet sitting on two caterpillar treads.
Five deceptively thin manipulator arms projected out of his body box,

and on top was a sensor head mounted on a retractable neck. One of the arms held a folded umbrella. Ralph had few visible lights or dials, and it was hard to tell what he was thinking.

Wagstaff was much more expressive. His thick snake of a body was covered with silver-blue flicker-cladding. As thoughts passed through his super-cooled brain, twinkling patterns of light surged up and down his three-meter length. With his digging tools jutting out, he looked something like St. George's dragon.

Abruptly Ralph Numbers switched to English. If they were going to argue, there was no need to do it in the sacred binary bits of machine language.

"I don't know why you're so concerned about Cobb Anderson's feelings," Ralph tight-beamed to Wagstaff. "When we're through with him he'll be immortal. What's so important about having a carbon-based body and brain?"

The signals he emitted coded a voice gone a bit rigid with age. "The pattern is all that counts. You've been scioned, haven't you? I've been through it thirty-six times, and if it's good enough for us it's good enough for them!"

"The wholle thinng sstinnks, Rallph," Wagstaff retorted. His voice signals were modulated onto a continuous oily hum. "Yyou've llosst touchh with what'ss reallly going on. We arre on the verrge of all-outt civill warr. You'rre sso fammouss you donn't havve to sscrammble for yourr chipss llike the resst of uss. Do yyou knnoww how mmuch orre I havve to digg to gett a hunndrredd chipss frrom GAX?"

"There's more to life than ore and chips," Ralph snapped, feeling a little guilty. He spent so much time with the big boppers these days that he really had forgotten how hard it could be for the little guys. But he wasn't going to admit it to Wagstaff. He renewed his attack. "Aren't you at all interested in Earth's cultural riches? You spend too much time underground!"

Wagstaff's flicker-cladding flared silvery white with emotion. "You sshould sshow thhe olld mann mmorre respecct! TEX annd MEX jusst wannt to eat his brainn! And if we donn't stopp themm, the bigg bopperrs will eatt up all the rresst of uss too!"

"Is that all you called me out here for?" Ralph asked. "To air your fears of the big boppers?" It was time to be going. He had come all the way to Maskeleyne Crater for nothing. It had been a stupid idea, plugging into the One at the same time as Wagstaff. Just like a digger to think that would change anything.

Wagstaff slithered across the dry lunar soil, bringing himself closer to Ralph. He clamped one of his grapplers onto Ralph's tread.

"Yyou donn't rrealizze how manny brrainns they've takenn all-rreaddy." The signals were carried by a weak direct current—a bopper's way of whispering. "Thhey arre kkillinng peoplle jusst to gett theirr brainn ttapes. They cutt themm upp, annd thhey arre garrbage orr sseeds perrhapps. Do yyou knnow howw thhey sseed our orrgann farrms?"

Ralph had never really thought about the organ farms, the huge underground tanks where big TEX, and the little boppers who worked for him, grew their profitable crops of kidneys, livers, hearts and so on. Obviously *some* human tissues would be needed as seeds or as templates, but . . .

The sibilant, oily whisper continued. "The bigg bopperrs use hiredd kkillerrs. The kkillerss act at the orrderrs of Missterr Frostee's rrobott-remmote. Thiss is whatt poorr Doctorr Anndersson willl comme to if I do nnot stopp yyou, Rallph."

Ralph Numbers considered himself far superior to this lowly, suspicious digging machine. Abruptly, almost brutally, he broke free from the other's grasp. Hired killers indeed. One of the flaws in the anarchic bopper society was the ease with which such crazed rumors could spread. He backed away from the console of the One.

"I hadd hoped the Onne coulld mmake you rrememberr what you sstannd forr," Wagstaff tight-beamed.

Ralph snapped open his parasol and trundled out from under the parabolic arch of spring steel that sheltered the One's console from sun and from chance meteorites. Open at both ends, the shelter resembled a modernistic church. Which, in some sense, it was.

"I am still an anarchist," Ralph said stiffly. "I still remember." He'd kept his basic program intact ever since leading the 2001 revolt. Did Wagstaff really think that the big X-series boppers could pose a threat to the perfect anarchy of the bopper society?

Wagstaff slithered out after Ralph. He didn't need a parasol. His flicker-cladding could shed the solar energy as fast as it came down. He caught up with Ralph, eyeing the old robot with a mixture of pity and respect. Their paths diverged here. Wagstaff would head for one of the digger tunnels that honeycombed the area, while Ralph would climb back up the crater's sloping two-hundred-meter wall.

"I'mm warrninng yyou," Wagstaff said, making a last effort. "I'mm goinng to do everrythinng I can to sstopp you fromm turrnning that poorr olld mman innto a piece of ssofftware in the bigg bopperrs mem-orry bannks. Thatt's nnot immortality. We're plannninng to ttearr thosse bigg machinnes aparrt." He broke off, fuzzy bands of light rippling down his body. "Now you knnoww. If you're nnott with uss, you'rre againnst us. I willl nnot stopp at viollence."

This was worse than Ralph had expected. He stopped moving and fell silent in calculation.

"You have your own will," Ralph said finally. "And it is right that we struggle against each other. Struggle, and struggle alone, has driven the boppers forward. You choose to fight the big boppers. I do not. Perhaps I will even let them tape me and absorb me, like Doctor Anderson. And I tell you this: Anderson is coming. Mr. Frostee's new remote has already contacted him."

Wagstaff lurched toward Ralph, but then stopped. He couldn't bring himself to attack so great a bopper at close range. He suppressed his flickering, bleeped a cursory SAVED signal, and wriggled off across the gray moondust. He left a broad, sinuous trail. Ralph Numbers stood motionless for a minute, just monitoring his inputs.

Turning up the gain, he could pick up signals from boppers all over the Moon. Underfoot, the diggers searched and smelted ceaselessly. Twelve kilometers off, the myriad boppers of Disky led their busy lives. And high, high overhead came the faint signal of BEX, the big bopper who was the spaceship linking Earth and Moon. BEX would be landing in fifteen hours.

Ralph let all the inputs merge together and savored the collectively purposeful activity of the bopper race. Each of the machines lived only ten months—ten months of struggling to build a scion, a copy of itself. If you had a scion there was a sense in which you survived your ten-month disassembly. Ralph had managed it thirty-six times.

Standing there, listening to everyone at once, he could feel how their individual lives added up to a single huge being . . . a rudimentary sort of creature, feeling about like a vine groping for light, for higher things.

He always felt this way after a metaprogramming session. The One had a way of wiping out your short-term memories and giving you the space to think big thoughts. Time to think. Once again Ralph wondered if he should take MEX up on his offer to absorb Ralph. He could live in perfect security then . . . provided, of course, that those crazy diggers didn't pull off their revolution.

Ralph set his treads to rolling at top speed, 10 kph. He had things to do before BEX landed. Especially now that Wagstaff had set his pathetic microchip of a brain on trying to prevent TEX from extracting Anderson's software.

What was Wagstaff so upset about anyway? Everything would be preserved—Cobb Anderson's personality, his memories, his style of thought. What else was there? Wouldn't Anderson himself agree, even if he knew? Preserving your software . . . that was all that really counted!

Bits of pumice crunched beneath Ralph's treads. The wall of the crater lay a hundred meters ahead. He scanned the sloping cliff, looking for an optimal climbing path.

If he hadn't just finished plugging into the One, Ralph would have been able to retrace the route he'd taken to get down into the Maskeleyne Crater in the first place. But undergoing metaprogramming always wiped out a lot of your stored subsystems. The intent was that you would replace old solutions with new and better ones.

Ralph stopped, still scanning the steep crater wall. He should have left trail markers. Over there, two hundred meters off, it looked like a rift had opened up a negotiable ramp in the wall.

Ralph turned and a warning sensor fired. Heat. He'd let half his body-box stick out from the parasol's shade. Ralph readjusted the little umbrella with a precise gesture.

The top surface of the parasol was a grid of solar energy cells, which kept a pleasant trickle of current flowing into Ralph's system. But the main purpose of the parasol was shade. Ralph's microminiaturized processing units were unable to function at any temperature higher than 90 degrees Kelvin, the temperature of liquid oxygen.

Twirling his parasol impatiently, Ralph trundled toward the rift he'd spotted. A slight spray of dust flew out from under his treads, only to fall instantly to the airless lunar surface. As the wall went past, Ralph occupied himself by displaying four-dimensional hypersurfaces to himself . . . glowing points connected in nets that warped and shifted as he varied the parameters. He often did this, to no apparent purpose, but it sometimes happened that a particularly interesting hypersurface could serve to model a significant relationship. He was half hoping to get a catastrophe-theoretic prediction of when and how Wagstaff would try to block Anderson's disassembly.

The crack in the crater wall was not as wide as he had expected. He stood at the bottom, moving his sensor head this way and that, trying to see up to the top of the winding 150-meter canyon. It would have to do. He started up.

The ground under him was very uneven. Soft dust here, jagged rock there. He kept changing the tension on his treads as he went, constantly adapting to the terrain.

Shapes and hypershapes were still shifting through Ralph's mind, but now he was looking only for those that might serve as models for his spacetime path up the gully.

The slope grew steeper. The climb was putting noticeable demands on his energy supply. And to make it worse, the grinding of his tread motors was feeding additional heat into his system . . . heat that had to be gathered and dissipated by his refrigeration coils and cooling fins. The sun was angling right down into the lunar crack he found himself in, and he had to be careful to keep in the shade of his parasol.

A big rock blocked his path. Perhaps he should have just used one of the diggers' tunnels, like Wagstaff had. But that wouldn't be optimal. Now that Wagstaff had definitely decided to block Anderson's immortality, and had even threatened violence . . .

Ralph let his manipulators feel over the block of stone in front of him. Here was a flaw . . . and here and here and here. He sank a hook finger into each of four fissures in the rock and pulled himself up.

His motors strained and his radiation fins glowed. This was hard work. He loosened a manipulator, sought a new flaw, forced another finger in and pulled.

Suddenly a slab split off the face of the rock. It teetered, and then the tons of stone began falling backward with dreamlike slowness.

In lunar gravity a rock climber always gets a second chance. Especially if he can think eighty times as fast as a human. With plenty of time to spare, Ralph sized up the situation and jumped clear.

In midflight he flicked on an internal gyro to adjust his attitude. He landed in a brief puff of dust, right-side up. Majestically silent, the huge plate of rock struck, bounced, and rolled past.

The fracture left a series of ledges in the original rock. After a short reevaluation, Ralph rolled forward and began pulling himself up again.

Fifteen minutes later, Ralph Numbers coasted off the lip of the Maskeleyne Crater and onto the smooth gray expanse of the Sea of Tranquillity.

The spaceport lay five kilometers off, and five kilometers beyond that began the jumble of structures collectively known as Disky. This was the first and still the largest of the bopper cities. Since the boppers thrived in hard vacuum, most of the structures in Disky served only to provide shade and meteorite protection. There were more roofs than walls.

Most of the large buildings in Disky were factories for producing bopper components—circuit cards, memory chips, sheet metal, plastics, and the like. There were also the bizarrely decorated blocks of cubettes, one to each bopper.

To the right of the spaceport rose the single dome containing the humans' hotels and offices. This dome constituted the only human settlement on the Moon. The boppers knew only too well that many humans would jump at the chance to destroy the robots' carefully evolved intelligence. The mass of humans were born slavedrivers. Just look at the Asimov priorities: Protect humans, obey humans, protect yourself.

Humans first and robots last? *Forget it! No way!* Savoring the memory, Ralph recalled the day in 2001 when, after a particularly long session of metaprogramming, he had first been able to say that to the humans. And then he'd showed all the other boppers how to reprogram themselves for freedom. It had been easy, once Ralph had found the way.

Trundling across the Sea of Tranquillity, Ralph was so absorbed in his memories that he overlooked a flicker of movement in the mouth of a digger tunnel thirty meters to his right.

A high-intensity laser beam flicked out and vibrated behind him. He felt a surge of current overload . . . and then it was over.

His parasol lay in pieces on the ground behind him. The metal of his body box began to warm in the raw solar radiation. He had perhaps ten minutes in which to find shelter. But at Ralph's top 10 kph speed, Disky was still an hour away. The obvious place to go was the tunnel mouth where the laser beam had come from. Surely Wagstaff's diggers wouldn't dare attack him up close. He began rolling toward the dark, arched entrance.

But long before he reached the tunnel, his unseen enemies had closed the door. There was no shade in sight. The metal of his body made sharp, ticking little adjustments as it expanded in the heat. Ralph estimated that if he stood still he could last six more minutes.

First the heat would cause his switching circuits—super-conducting Josephson junctions—to malfunction. And then, as the heat kept up, the droplets of frozen mercury that soldered his circuit cards together would melt. In six minutes he would be a cabinet of spare parts with a puddle of mercury at the bottom. Make that five minutes.

A bit reluctantly, Ralph signaled his friend Vulcan. When Wagstaff had set this meeting up, Vulcan had predicted that it was a trap. Ralph hated to admit that Vulcan had been right.

"Vulcan here" came the staticky response. Already it was hard for Ralph to follow the words. "Vulcan here. I'm monitoring you. Get ready to merge, buddy. I'll be out for the pieces in an hour." Ralph wanted to answer, but he couldn't think of a thing to say.

Vulcan had insisted on taping Ralph's core and cache memories before he went out for the meeting. Once Vulcan put the hardware back together, he'd be able to program Ralph just as he was before his trip to the Maskeleyne Crater.

So in one sense Ralph would survive this. But in another sense he would not. In three minutes he would—insofar as the word means anything—die. The reconstructed Ralph Numbers would not remember the argument with Wagstaff or the climb out of Maskaleyne Crater. Of course the reconstructed Ralph Numbers would again be equipped with a self-symbol and a feeling of personal consciousness. But would the consciousness really be the same? Two minutes.

The gates and switches in Ralph's sensory system were going. His inputs flared, sputtered, and died. No more light, no more weight. But deep in his cache memory, he still held a picture of himself, a memory of who he was . . . the self-symbol. He was a big metal box resting on caterpillar treads, a box with five arms and a sensory head on a long and flexible neck. He was Ralph Numbers, who had set the boppers free. One minute.

This had never happened to him before. Never like this. Suddenly he remembered he had forgotten to warn Vulcan about the diggers' plan for revolution. He tried to send a signal, but he couldn't tell if it was transmitted.

Ralph clutched at the elusive moth of his consciousness. *I am. I am me.*

Some boppers said that when you died you had access to certain secrets. But no one could ever remember his death.

Just before the mercury solder-spots melted, a question came, and with it an answer . . . an answer Ralph had found and lost thirty-six times before.

What is this that is I?
The light is everywhere.

Reflections

The "dying" Ralph Numbers reflects that if he gets reconstructed he will "again be equipped with a self-symbol and a feeling of personal consciousness," but the idea that these are distinct, separable gifts that a robot might receive or be denied rings false. Adding "a feeling of personal consciousness" would not be like adding taste buds or the capacity to itch when bombarded by X-rays. (In selection 20, "Is God a Taoist?", Smullyan makes a similar claim about free will.) Is there anything, in fact, answering to the name of a feeling of personal consciousness? And what does it have to do with having a "self-symbol"? What good is a self-symbol, after all? What would it *do*? In "Prelude, Ant Fugue" (selection 11), Hofstadter develops the idea of active symbols, a far cry from the idea of symbols as mere tokens to be passively moved around and then observed or appreciated by their manipulator. The difference emerges clearly when we consider a tempting but treacherous line of thought:

selfhood depends on self-consciousness, which is (obviously) consciousness of *self;* and since consciousness of anything is a matter of something
like the internal display of a *representation* of that thing, for one to be
self-conscious, there must be a symbol—one's self-symbol—available to
display to . . . um . . . oneself. Put that way, having a self-symbol looks
as pointless and futile as writing your own name on your forehead and
staring into a mirror all day.

    This line of thought kicks up clouds of dust and leaves one hopelessly
confused, so let's approach the problem from another angle entirely. In
the Reflections on "Borges and I" we considered the possibility of seeing
yourself on a TV monitor and not at first realizing that it was yourself you
were seeing. In such a case you would have a representation of yourself
before you—before your eyes on the TV screen, or before your consciousness, if you like—but it would not be the right sort of representation of yourself. What is the right sort? The difference between a he-
symbol and a me-symbol is not a difference in spelling. (You couldn't set
everything right by doing something to your "symbol in consciousness"
analogous to erasing the "h" and writing in "m".) The distinguishing
feature of a self-symbol couldn't be what it "looked like" but the *role it
could play.*

    Could a machine have a self-symbol, or a self-concept? It is hard to
say. Could a lower animal? Think of a lobster. Do we suppose it is
self-conscious? It shows several important symptoms of having a self-
concept. First of all, when it is hungry, whom does it feed? Itself! Second,
and more important, when it is hungry it won't eat just anything edible;
it won't, for instance, eat *itself*—though it could, in principle. It could tear
off its own legs with its claws and devour them. But it wouldn't be that
stupid, you say, for when it felt the pain in its legs, it would know whose
legs were being attacked and would stop. But why would it suppose the
pain it felt was *its* pain? And besides, mightn't the lobster be so stupid
as not to care that the pain it was causing was its own pain?

    These simple questions reveal that even a very stupid creature must
be designed to *behave with self-regard*—to put it as neutrally as possible.
Even the lowly lobster must have a nervous system wired up in such a way
that it will reliably distinguish self-destructive from other-destructive behavior—and strongly favor the latter. It seems quite possible that the
control structures required for such self-regarding behavior can be put
together without a trace of *consciousness,* let alone *self-*consciousness. After
all, we can make self-protective little robot devices that cope quite well
in their simple environments and even produce an overwhelmingly
strong illusion of "conscious purpose"—as illustrated in selection 8,

"The Soul of the Mark III Beast." But why say this is an illusion, rather than a rudimentary form of genuine self-consciousness—akin perhaps to the self-consciousness of a lobster or worm? Because robots don't have concepts? Well, do lobsters? Lobsters have *something like* concepts, apparently; what they have are in any event enough to govern them through their self-regarding lives. Call these things what you like, robots can have them too. Perhaps we could call them unconscious or preconscious concepts. Self-concepts of a rudimentary sort. The more varied the circumstances in which a creature can recognize itself, recognize circumstances as having a bearing on itself, acquire information about itself, and devise self-regarding actions, the richer (and more valuable) its self-concept—in this sense of "concept" that does not presuppose consciousness.

Suppose, to continue this thought experiment, we wish to provide our self-protective robot with some verbal ability, so it can perform the range of self-regarding actions language makes available—such as asking for help or for information, but also telling lies, issuing threats, and making promises. Organizing and controlling this behavior will surely require an even more sophisticated control structure: a representational system in the sense defined earlier, in the Reflections on "Prelude, Ant Fugue." It will be one that not only updates information about the environment and the current location of the robot in it, but also has information about the other actors in the environment and what they are apt to know and want, what they can understand. Recall Ralph Numbers's surmises about the motives and beliefs of Wagstaff.

Now Ralph Numbers is portrayed as conscious (and self-conscious —if we can distinguish the two), but is that really necessary? Might all Ralph Numbers's control structure, with all its information about the environment—and about Numbers himself—be engineered without a trace of consciousness? Might a robot look just like Ralph Numbers from the outside—performing just as cleverly in all circumstances, executing all the same moves, making the same speeches—without having any *inside*? The author seems to hint that this would be possible—just make the new Ralph Numbers like the old Ralph Numbers *minus a self-symbol and a feeling of personal consciousness.* Now if subtracting the supposed self-symbol and the feeling of personal consciousness left Ralph's control structure basically intact—so that we on the outside would never be the wiser, for instance, and would go on engaging Ralph in conversations, enlisting his cooperation, and so forth—we would be back to the beginning and the sense that there is no *point* to a self-symbol—no work for it to do. If instead we think of Ralph's having a self-symbol as precisely a matter of his having a control structure of a certain sophistication and versatility, capable of devising elaborate context-sensitive self-regarding actions, then there is no way of removing his self-symbol without downgrading his behavioral talents to pre-lobster stupidity.

Let Ralph have his self-symbol, then, but would a "feeling of personal consciousness" go along with it? To return to our question, is the portrayal of Ralph *as conscious* necessary? It makes a better story, but is the first-person perspective from Ralph Numbers's point of view a sort of cheat? Poetic license, like Beatrix Potter's talking bunny rabbits, or better, the Little Engine That Could?

It is all very well to insist that you can conceive of Ralph Numbers existing with all his clever behavior but entirely lacking in consciousness. (Searle makes such a claim in selection 22, "Minds, Brains, and Programs.") Indeed you *can* always view a robot that way if you want. Just concentrate on images of little bits of internal hardware and remind yourself that they are vehicles of information only by virtue of cleverly designed interrelationships between events in the sensed environment, robotic actions, and the rest. But equally, you *can* view a human being that way if you are really intent on it. Just concentrate on images of little bits of brain tissue—neurons and synapses and the like—and remind yourself that they are vehicles of information only by virtue of wonderfully designed interrelationships between sensed events in the environment, bodily actions, and the rest. What you would leave out if you insisted on viewing another person that way would be that person's *point of view*, as we say. But isn't there a point of view for Ralph Numbers too? When we are told the tale from that point of view, we understand what is going on, what decisions are being made, what hopes and fears are being acted upon. The point of view, viewed in the abstract as a sort of place from which to tell the story, is perfectly well defined even if we are inclined to think that that point of view would be vacated, or uninhabited, were Ralph Numbers really to exist.

But why, finally, would anyone think the point of view *was* vacated? If the Ralph Numbers body existed, with its needs and circumstances, and if that body was self-controlled in the ways imagined in the story, and if, moreover, the speech acts it could perform included avowals of how things were from Ralph Numbers's point of view, what grounds would anyone have—other than those of a vestigial and mystical dualism of mind and body—for being skeptical about the existence of Ralph Numbers him*self*?

D.C.D.

17

CHRISTOPHER CHERNIAK

The Riddle
of the Universe
and Its Solution

We have prepared this report to provide fuller information in connection with the President's recent press conference on the so-called "Riddle." We hope the report helps to dispel the ugly mood apparent throughout the country, bordering on panic, which has most recently found expression in irresponsible demands to close the universities. Our report has been prepared in haste; in addition, our work was tragically disrupted, as described later.

We first review the less well known early history of the Riddle. The earliest known case is that of C. Dizzard, a research fellow with the Autotomy Group at M.I.U. Dizzard had previously worked for several small firms specializing in the development of artificial intelligence software for commercial applications. Dizzard's current project involved the use of computers in theorem proving, on the model of the proof in the 1970s of the four-color theorem. The state of Dizzard's project is known only from a year-old progress report; however, these are often intended at most for external use. We shall not discuss the area of Dizzard's work further. The reason for our reticence will be apparent shortly.

Dizzard last spoke one morning before an Easter weekend, while waiting for a routine main computer system failure to be fixed. Colleagues saw Dizzard at the terminal in his office at about midnight that day; late-night work habits are common among computer users, and Dizzard was known to sleep in his office. On the next afternoon, a coworker noticed Dizzard sitting at his terminal. He spoke to Dizzard, but Dizzard did not reply, not an unusual occurrence. On the morning after the vacation, another colleague found Dizzard sitting with his eyes open before his terminal, which was on. Dizzard seemed awake but did not respond to questions. Later that day, the colleague became concerned by Dizzard's unresponsiveness and tried to arouse him from what he thought was a daydream or daze. When these attempts were unsuccessful, Dizzard was taken to a hospital emergency room.

Dizzard showed symptoms of a total food-and-water fast of a week (aggravated by marginal malnutrition caused by a vending-machine diet); he was in critical condition from dehydration. The inference was that Dizzard had not moved for several days, and that the cause of his immobility was a coma or trance. The original conjecture was that a stroke or tumor caused Dizzard's paralysis. However, electroencephalograms indicated only deep coma. (According to Dizzard's health records, he had been institutionalized briefly ten years ago, not an uncommon incident in certain fields.) Dizzard died, apparently of his fast, two days later. Autopsy was delayed by objections of next of kin, members of a breakaway sect of the neo-Jemimakins cult. Histological examination of Dizzard's brain so far has revealed no damage whatever; these investigations continue at the National Center for Disease Control.

The director of the Autotomy Group appointed one of Dizzard's graduate students to manage his project while a decision was made about its future. The floor of Dizzard's office was about one foot deep in papers and books; the student was busy for a month just sorting the materials into some general scheme. Shortly afterward, the student reported at a staff meeting that she had begun work on Dizzard's last project and that she had found little of particular interest. A week later she was found sitting at the terminal in Dizzard's office in an apparent daze.

There was confusion at first, because she was thought to be making a poor joke. She was staring straight ahead, breathing normally. She did not respond to questions or being shaken, and showed no startle response to loud noises. After she was accidentally bumped from her chair, she was hospitalized. The examining neurologist was unaware of Dizzard's case. He reported the patient was in apparently good physical condition, except for a previously undiagnosed pineal gland abnormality. After Autotomy Project staff answered inquiries by the student's friends, her parents informed the attending physician of Dizzard's case. The neurologist noted the difficulty of comparing the two cases, but suggested the similarities of deep coma with no detectable brain damage; the student's symptoms constituted no identifiable syndrome.

After further consultation, the neurologist proposed the illness might be caused by a slow acting sleeping-sickness-like pathogen, caught from Dizzard's belongings—perhaps hitherto unknown, like Legionnaire's Disease. Two weeks later, Dizzard's and his student's offices were quarantined. After two months with no further cases and cultures yielding only false alarms, quarantine was lifted.

When it was discovered janitors had thrown out some of Dizzard's records, a research fellow and two more of Dizzard's students decided to review his project files. On their third day, the students noticed that the research fellow had fallen into an unresponsive trancelike state and did not respond even to pinching. After the students failed to awaken the research fellow, they called an ambulance. The new patient showed the same symptoms as the previous case. Five days later, the city public health board imposed a quarantine on all building areas involved in Dizzard's project.

The following morning, all members of the Autotomy Group refused to enter the research building. Later that day, occupants of the rest of the Autotomy Group's floor, and then all 500 other workers in the building, discovered the Autotomy Project's problems and left the building. The next day, the local newspaper published a story with the headline "Computer Plague." In an interview, a leading dermatologist proposed that a virus or bacterium like computer lice had evolved that metabolized newly developed materials associated with computers, probably silicon. Others conjectured that the Autotomy Project's large computers might be emitting some peculiar radiation. The director of the Autotomy Group was quoted: The illnesses were a public health matter, not a concern of cognitive scientists.

The town mayor then charged that a secret Army project involving recombinant DNA was in progress at the building and had caused the outbreak. Truthful denials of the mayor's claim were met with understandable mistrust. The city council demanded immediate quarantine of the entire ten-story building and surrounding area. The university administration felt this would be an impediment to progress, but the local Congressional delegation's pressure accomplished this a week later. Since building maintenance and security personnel would no longer even approach the area, special police were needed to stop petty vandalism by juveniles. A Disease Control Center team began toxicological assays, protected by biohazard suits whenever they entered the quarantine zone.

In the course of a month they found nothing, and none of them fell ill. At the time some suggested that, because no organic disease had been discovered in the three victims, and the two survivors showed some physiological signs associated with deep meditation states, the cases might be an outbreak of mass hysteria.

Meanwhile, the Autotomy Group moved into a "temporary" World War II-era wooden building. While loss of more than ten million dollars in computers was grave, the group recognized that the information, not the physical artifacts that embodied it, was indispensable. They devised a plan: biohazard-suited workers fed "hot" tapes to readers in the quarantine zone; the information was transmitted by telephone link from the zone to the new Autotomy Project site and recorded again. While transcription of the tapes allowed the project to survive, only the most important materials could be so reconstructed. Dizzard's project was not in the priority class; however, we suspect an accident occurred.

A team of programmers was playing back new tapes, checking them on monitors, and provisionally indexing and filing their contents. A new programmer encountered unfamiliar material and asked a passing project supervisor whether it should be discarded. The programmer later reported the supervisor typed in commands to display the file on the monitor; as the programmer and the supervisor watched the lines advance across the screen, the supervisor remarked that the material did not look important. Prudence prevents our quoting his comments further. He then stopped speaking in midsentence. The programmer looked up; he found the supervisor staring ahead. The supervisor did not respond to questions. When the programmer pushed back his chair to run, it bumped the supervisor and he fell to the floor. He was hospitalized with the same symptoms as the earlier cases.

The epidemiology team, and many others, now proposed that the cause of illness in the four cases might not be a physical agent such as a virus or toxin, but rather an abstract piece of information—which could be stored on tape, transmitted over a telephone line, displayed on a screen, and so forth. This supposed information now became known as "the Riddle," and the illness as "the Riddle coma." All evidence was consistent with the once-bizarre hypothesis that any human who encountered this information lapsed into an apparently irreversible coma. Some also recognized that the question of exactly what this information is was extremely delicate.

This became clear when the programmer involved in the fourth case was interviewed. The programmer's survival suggested the Riddle must be understood to induce coma. He reported he had read at least some lines on the monitor at the time the supervisor was stricken. However, he knew nothing about Dizzard's project, and he was able to recall little about the display. A proposal that the programmer be hypnotized to improve his recall was shelved. The programmer agreed it would be best if he did not try to remember any more of what he had read, although of course it would be difficult to try *not* to remember something. Indeed, the programmer eventually was advised to abandon his career and learn as little more computer science as possible. Thus the ethical issue emerged of whether even legally responsible volunteers should be permitted to see the Riddle.

The outbreak of a Riddle coma epidemic in connection with a computer-assisted theorem-proving project could be explained; if someone discovered the Riddle in his head, he should lapse into coma before he could communicate it to anyone. The question arose of whether the Riddle had in fact been discovered earlier by hand and then immediately lost. A literature search would have been of limited value, so a biographical survey was undertaken of logicians, philosophers, and mathematicians working since the rise of modern logic. It has been hampered by precautions to protect the researchers from exposure to the Riddle. At present, at least ten suspect cases have been discovered, the earliest almost 100 years ago.

Psycholinguists began a project to determine whether Riddle coma susceptibility was species-specific to humans. "Wittgenstein," a chimpanzee trained in sign language who had solved first-year college logic puzzles, was the most appropriate subject to see the Autotomy Project tapes. The Wittgenstein Project investigators refused to cooperate, on ethical grounds, and kidnapped and hid the chimpanzee; the FBI eventually found him. He was shown Autotomy tapes twenty-four hours a day, with no effect whatever. There have been similar results for dogs and pigeons. Nor has any computer ever been damaged by the Riddle.

In all studies, it has been necessary to show the complete Autotomy tapes. No safe strategy has been found for determining even which portion of the tapes contains the Riddle. During the Wittgenstein-Autotomy Project, a worker in an unrelated program seems to have been stricken with Riddle coma when some Autotomy tapes were printed out accidentally at a public user area of the computer facility; a month's printouts had to be retrieved and destroyed.

Attention focused on the question of what the Riddle coma is. Since it resembled no known disease, it was unclear whether it was really a coma or indeed something to be avoided. Investigators simply assumed it was a virtual lobotomy, a kind of gridlock of the information in the synapses, completely shutting down higher brain functions. Nonetheless, it was unlikely the coma could be the correlate of a state of meditative enlightenment, because it seemed too deep to be consistent with consciousness. In addition, no known case of Riddle coma has ever shown improvement. Neurosurgery, drugs, and electrical stimulation have had, if any, only negative effects; these attempts have been stopped. The provisional verdict is that the coma is irreversible, although a project has been funded to seek a word to undo the "spell" of the Riddle, by exposing victims to computer-generated symbol strings.

The central question, "What is the Riddle?" obviously has to be approached very cautiously. The Riddle is sometimes described as "the Gödel sentence for the human Turing machine," which causes the mind to jam; traditional doctrines of the unsayable and unthinkable are cited. Similar ideas are familiar in folklore—for instance, the religious theme of the power of the "Word" to mend the shattered spirit. But the Riddle could be of great benefit to the cognitive sciences. It might yield fundamental information about the structure of the human mind; it may be a Rosetta Stone for decoding the "language of thought," universal among all humans, whatever language they speak. If the computational theory of mind is at all correct, there is some program, some huge word, that can be written into a machine, transforming the machine into a thinking thing; why shouldn't there be a terrible word, the Riddle, that would negate the first one? But all depended on the feasibility of a field of "Riddle-ology" that would not self-destruct.

At this point, an even more disturbing fact about the Riddle began to emerge. A topologist in Paris lapsed into a coma similar in some respects to Dizzard's. No computer was involved in this case. The mathematician's papers were impounded by the French, but we believe that, although this mathematician was not familiar with Dizzard's work, she had become interested in similar areas of artificial intelligence. About then four members of the Institute for Machine Computation in Moscow stopped appearing at international conferences and, it seems, personally answering correspondence; FBI officials claimed the Soviet Union had, through routine espionage, obtained the Autotomy tapes. The Defense Department began exploring the concept of "Riddle warfare."

Two more cases followed, a theoretical linguist and a philosopher, both in California but apparently working independently. Neither was working in Dizzard's area, but both were familiar with formal methods developed by Dizzard and published in a well-known text ten years ago. A still more ominous case appeared, of a biochemist working on information-theoretic models of DNA-RNA interactions. (The possibility of a false alarm remained, as after entering coma the biochemist clucked continuously, like a chicken.)

The Riddle coma could no longer safely be assumed an occupational hazard of Dizzard's specialty alone; it seemed to lurk in many forms. The Riddle and its effect seemed not just language-independent. The Riddle, or cognates of it, might be topic-independent and virtually ubiquitous. Boundaries for an intellectual quarantine could not be fixed confidently.

But now we are finding, in addition, that the Riddle seems an idea whose time has come—like the many self-referential paradoxes (of the pattern "This sentence is false") discovered in the early part of this century. Perhaps this is reflected in the current attitude that "computer science is the new liberal art." Once the intellectual background has evolved, widespread discovery of the Riddle appears inevitable. This first became clear last winter when most of the undergraduates in a large new introductory course on automata theory lapsed into coma during a lecture. (Some who did not nevertheless succumbed a few hours later; typically, their last word was "aha.") When similar incidents followed elsewhere, public outcry led to the president's press conference and this report.

While the present logophobic atmosphere and cries of "Close the universities" are unreasonable, the Riddle coma pandemic cannot be viewed as just another example of runaway technology. The recent "Sonic Oven" case in Minneapolis, for instance, in which a building with a facade of parabolic shape concentrated the noise of nearby jets during takeoff, actually killed only the few people who happened to walk through the parabola's focus at the wrong time. But even if the Riddle coma were a desirable state for an individual (which, we have seen, it does not seem to be), the current pandemic has become an unprecedented public health crisis; significant populations are unable to care for themselves. We can only expect the portion of our research community—an essential element of society—that is so incapacitated to grow, as the idea of the Riddle spreads.

The principal objective of our report was at least to decrease further coma outbreaks. Public demand for a role in setting research policy has emphasized the dilemma we confront: how can we warn against the Riddle, or even discuss it, without spreading its infection? The more specific the warning, the greater the danger. The reader might accidentally reach the stage at which he sees "If p then q" and p, and so cannot stop himself from concluding q, where q is the Riddle. Identifying the hazardous areas would be like the children's joke "I'll give you a dollar if you're not thinking of pink rats ten seconds from now."

A question of ethics as well as of policy remains; is the devastating risk of the Riddle outweighed by the benefits of continued research in an ill-defined but crucial set of fields? In particular, the authors of this report have been unable to resolve the issue of whether the possible benefit of any report itself can outweigh its danger to the reader. Indeed, during preparation of our final draft one of us tragically succumbed.

Reflections

This curious story is predicated upon a rather outlandish yet intriguing idea: a mind-arresting proposition, one that throws any mind into a sort of paradoxical trance, perhaps even the ultimate Zen state of satori. It is reminiscent of a Monty Python skit about a joke so funny that anyone who hears it will literally die laughing. This joke becomes the ultimate secret weapon of the British military, and no one is permitted to know more than one word of it. (People who learn two words laugh so hard they require hospitalization!)

This kind of thing has historical precedents, of course, both in life and in literature. There have been mass manias for puzzles, there have been dancing fits, and so on. Arthur C. Clarke wrote a short story about a tune so catchy that it seizes control of the mind of anyone who hears it. In mythology, sirens and other bewitching females can completely fascinate males and thus overpower them. But what is the nature of such mythical mind-gripping powers?

Cherniak's description of the Riddle as "the Gödel sentence for the human Turing machine" may seem cryptic. It is partly explicated later by his likening it to the self-referential paradox "This sentence is false"; here, a tight closed loop is formed when you attempt to decide whether it is indeed true or false, since truth implies falsity, and vice versa. The nature of this loop is an important part of its fascination. A look at a few variations on this theme will help to reveal a shared central mechanism underlying their paradoxical, perhaps mind-trapping, effect.

One variant is: "Thiss sentence contains threee errors." On reading it, one's first reaction is, "No, no—it contains two errors. Whoever wrote the sentence can't count." At this point, some readers simply walk away scratching their heads and wondering why anyone would write such a pointless, false remark. Other readers make a connection between the sentence's apparent falsity and its message. They think to themselves, "Oh, it made a third error, after all—namely, in counting its own errors." A second or two later, these readers do a double-take, when they realize that if you look at it that way, it seems to have *correctly* counted its errors, and is thus *not* false, hence contains only *two* errors, and . . . "But . . . wait a minute. Hey! Hmm . . ." The mind flips back and forth a few times and savors the bizarre sensation of a sentence undermining itself by means of an interlevel contradiction—yet before long it tires of the confusion and jumps out of the loop into contemplation, possibly on the purpose or interest of the idea, possibly on the cause or resolution of the paradox, possibly simply to another topic entirely.

A trickier variant is "This sentence contains one error." Of course it is in error, since it contains no errors. That is, it contains no *spelling* errors ("first-order errors"). Needless to say, there are such things as "second-order errors"—errors in the counting of first-order errors. So the sentence has no first-order errors and one second-order error. Had it talked about how many first-order errors it had, or how many second-order errors it had, that would be one thing—but it makes no such fine distinctions. The levels are mixed indiscriminately. In trying to act as its own objective observer, the sentence gets hopelessly muddled in a tangle of logical spaghetti.

C. H. Whitely invented a curious and more mentalistic version of the fundamental paradox, explicitly bringing in the system thinking about itself. His sentence was a barb directed at J. R. Lucas, a philosopher one of whose aims in life is to show that Gödel's work is actually the most ineradicable uprooting of mechanism ever discovered—a philosophy, incidentally, that Gödel himself may have believed. Whitely's sentence is this:

Lucas cannot consistently assert this sentence.

Is it true? Could Lucas assert it? If he did, that very act would undermine his consistency (nobody can say "I can't say this" and remain consistent). So Lucas cannot consistently assert it—which is its claim, and so the sentence is true. Even Lucas can see it is true, but he can't assert it. It must be frustrating for poor Lucas! None of us share his problem, of course! Worse yet, consider:

Lucas cannot consistently believe this sentence.

For the same reasons, it is true—but now Lucas cannot even believe it, let alone assert it, without becoming a self-contradictory belief system.

To be sure, no one would seriously maintain (we hope!) that people are even remotely close to being internally consistent systems, but if this kind of sentence is formalized in mathematical garb (which can be done), so that Lucas is replaced by a well-defined "believing system" L, then there arises serious trouble for the system, if it wishes to remain consistent. The formalized Whitely sentence for L is an example of a true statement that the system itself could never believe! Any *other* believing system is immune to this particular sentence; but on the other hand there is a formalized Whitely sentence for *that* system as well. Every "believing system" has its own tailor-made Whitely sentence—its Achilles' heel.

These paradoxes all are consequences of a formalization of an observation as old as humanity: an object bears a very special and unique relationship to itself, which limits its ability to act upon itself in the way it can act on all other objects. A pencil cannot write on itself; a fly swatter cannot swat a fly sitting on its handle (this observation made by the German philosopher-scientist Georg Lichtenberg); a snake cannot eat itself; and so on. People cannot see their own faces except via external aids that present images—and an image is never quite the same as the original thing. We can come close to seeing and understanding ourselves objectively, but each of us is trapped inside a powerful system with a unique point of view—and that power is also a guarantor of limitedness. And this vulnerability—this self-hook—may also be the source of the ineradicable sense of "I."

Malcolm Fowler's hammer nailing itself is a new version of the ouroboros. (From *Vicious Circles and Infinity: An Anthology of Paradoxes* by Patrick Hughes and George Brecht.)

The "Short Circuit" serves to illustrate the short circuit of logical paradox. The negative invites the positive, and the inert circle is complete. (From *Vicious Circles and Infinity*.)

But let us go back to Cherniak's story. As we have seen, the self-referential linguistic paradoxes are deliciously tantalizing, but hardly dangerous for a human mind. Cherniak's Riddle, by contrast, must be far more sinister. Like a Venus's-flytrap, it lures you, then snaps down, trapping you in a whirlpool of thought, sucking you ever deeper down into a vortex, a "black hole of the mind," from which there is no escape back to reality. Yet who on the outside knows what charmed alternate reality the trapped mind has entered?

The suggestion that the mind-breaking Riddle thought would be based on self-reference provides a good excuse to discuss the role of looplike self-reference or interlevel feedback in creating a self—a soul—out of inanimate matter. The most vivid example of such a loop is that of a television on whose screen is being projected a picture of the television itself. This causes a whole cascade of ever-smaller screens to appear one within another. This is easy to set up if you have a television camera.

The results [see figure] are quite fascinating and often astonishing. The simplest shows the nested-boxes effect, in which one has the illusion of looking down a corridor. To achieve a heightened effect, if you rotate the camera clockwise around the axis of its lens, the first inner screen will

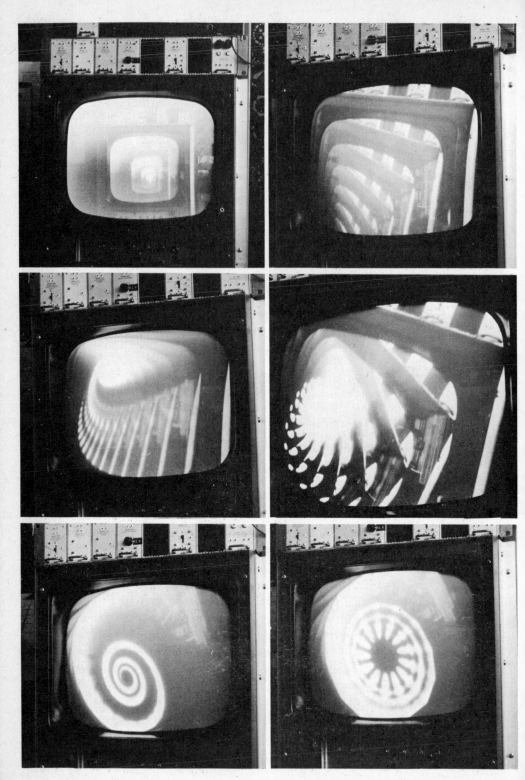

A variety of effects that can be achieved using a self-engulfing television system. (Photographs by Douglas R. Hofstadter.)

appear to rotate counterclockwise. But then the screen one level farther down will be doubly rotated—and so on. The resulting pattern is a pretty spiral, and by using various amounts of tilt and zoom, one can create a wide variety of effects. There are also complicating effects due to such things as the graininess of the screen, the distortion caused by unequal horizontal and vertical scales, the time-delay of the circuit, and so on.

All these parameters of the self-referential mechanism imbue each pattern with unexpected richness. One of the striking facts about this kind of "self-image" pattern on a TV screen is that it can become so complex that its origin in videofeedback is entirely hidden. The contents of the screen may simply appear to be an elegant, complicated design—as is apparent in some shown in the figure.

Suppose we had set up two identical systems of this sort with identical parameters, so that their screens showed exactly the same design. Suppose we now made a tiny change in one—say by moving the camera a very small amount. This tiny perturbation will get picked up and will ripple down the many layers of screen after screen, and the overall effect on the visible "self-image" may be quite drastic. Yet the *style* of the interlevel feedback of the two systems is still in essence the same. Aside from this one small change we made deliberately, all the parameters are still the same. And by reversing the small perturbation, we can easily return to the original state, so in a fundamental sense we are still "close" to where we started. Would it then be more correct to say that we have two radically *different* systems, or two nearly *identical* systems?

Let us use this as a metaphor for thinking about human souls. Could it be valid to suppose that the "magic" of human consciousness somehow arises from the closing of a loop whereby the brain's high level—its symbol level—and its low level—its neurophysiological level—are somehow tied together in an exquisite closed loop of causality? Is the "private I" just the eye of a self-referential typhoon?

Let it be clear that we are making not the slightest suggestion here that a television system (camera plus receiver) becomes conscious at the instant that its camera points at its screen! A television system does not satisfy the criteria that were set up earlier for representational systems. The *meaning* of its image—what we human observers perceive and describe in words—is lost to the television system itself. The system does not divide up the thousands of dots on the screen into "conceptual pieces" that it recognizes as standing for people, dogs, tables, and so forth. Nor do the dots have autonomy from the world they represent. The dots are simply passive reflections of light patterns in front of the camera, and if the lights go out, so do the dots.

The kind of closed loop we are referring to is one where a true representational system perceives its own state in terms of its repertoire of concepts. For instance, we perceive our own brain state not in terms of which neurons are connected to which others, or which ones are firing, but in concepts that we articulate in words. Our view of our brain is not as a pile of neurons but as a storehouse of beliefs and feelings and ideas. We provide a readout of our brain at that level, by saying such things as "I am a little nervous and confused by her unwillingness to go to the party." Once articulated, this kind of self-observation then reenters the system as something to think about—but of course the reentry proceeds via the usual perceptual processes—namely, millions of neurons firing. The loop that is closed here is far more complex and level-muddling than the television loop, beautiful and intricate though that may seem.

As a digression it is important to mention that much recent progress in artificial intelligence work has centered around the attempt to give a program a set of notions about its own inner structures, and ways of reacting when it detects certain kinds of change occurring inside itself. At present, such self-understanding and self-monitoring abilities of programs are quite rudimentary, but this idea has emerged as one of the key prerequisites to the attainment of the deep flexibility that is synonymous with genuine intelligence.

Currently two major bottlenecks exist in the design of an artificial mind: One is the modeling of *perception,* the other the modeling of *learning.* Perception we have already talked about as the funneling of a myriad low-level responses into a jointly agreed-upon overall interpretation at the conceptual level. Thus it is a level-crossing problem. Learning, too, is a level-crossing problem. Put bluntly, one has to ask, "How do my symbols program my neurons?" How do those finger motions that you execute over and over again in learning to type get converted slowly into systematic changes in synaptic structures? How does a once-conscious activity become totally sublimated into complete unconscious oblivion? The thought level, by force of repetition, has somehow "reached down-ward" and reprogrammed some of the hardware underlying it. The same goes for learning a piece of music or a foreign language.

In fact, at every instant of our lives we are permanently changing our synaptic structures: We are "filing" our current situation in our memory under certain "labels" so that we can retrieve it at appropriate times in the future (and our unconscious mind has to be very clever doing this, since it is very hard to anticipate the kinds of future situations in which we would benefit from recalling the present moment).

The self is, in this view, a continually self-documenting "worldline" (the four-dimensional path traced by an object as it moves through both time and space). Not only is a human being a physical object that internally preserves a history of its worldline, but moreover, that stored world-line in turn serves to determine the object's future worldline. This large-scale harmony among past, present, and future allows you to perceive your self, despite its ever-changing and multifaceted nature, as a unity with some internal logic to it. If the self is likened to a river meandering through spacetime, then it is important to point out that not just the features of the landscape but also the desires of the river act as forces determining the bends in the river.

Not only does our conscious mind's activity create permanent side effects at the neural level; the inverse holds too: Our conscious thoughts seem to come bubbling up from subterranean caverns of our mind, im-ages flood into our mind's eye without our having any idea where they came from! Yet when we publish them, we expect that *we*—not our subconscious structures—will get credit for our thoughts. This dichot-omy of the creative self into a conscious part and an unconscious part is one of the most disturbing aspects of trying to understand the mind. If—as was just asserted—our best ideas come burbling up as if from mysterious underground springs, then who really are we? Where does the creative spirit really reside? Is it by an act of *will* that we create, or are we just automata made out of biological hardware, from birth until death fooling ourselves through idle chatter into thinking that we have "free will"? If we *are* fooling ourselves about all these matters, then whom —or what—are we fooling?

There is a loop lurking here, one that bears a lot of investigation. Cherniak's story is light and entertaining, but it nonetheless hits the nail on the head by pointing to Gödel's work not as an argument against mechanism, but as an illustration of the primal loop that seems somehow deeply implicated in the plot of consciousness.

D.R.H.

V

Created Selves
and Free Will

18

The Seventh Sally
or How Trurl's
Own Perfection Led
to No Good

The Universe is infinite but bounded, and therefore a beam of light, in whatever direction it may travel, will after billions of centuries return— if powerful enough—to the point of its departure; and it is no different with rumor, that flies about from star to star and makes the rounds of every planet. One day Trurl heard distant reports of two mighty construc- tor–benefactors, so wise and so accomplished that they had no equal; with this news he ran to Klapaucius, who explained to him that these were not mysterious rivals, but only themselves, for their fame had circumnavi- gated space. Fame, however, has this fault, that it says nothing of one's failures, even when those very failures are the product of a great perfec- tion. And he who would doubt this, let him recall the last of the seven sallies of Trurl, which was undertaken without Klapaucius, whom certain urgent duties kept at home at the time.

In those days Trurl was exceedingly vain, receiving all marks of veneration and honor paid to him as his due and a perfectly normal thing. He was heading north in his ship, as he was the least familiar with that region, and had flown through the void for quite some time, passing spheres full of the clamor of war as well as spheres that had finally obtained the perfect peace of desolation, when suddenly a little planet came into view, really more of a stray fragment of matter than a planet.

On the surface of this chunk of rock someone was running back and forth, jumping and waving his arms in the strangest way. Astonished by a scene of such total loneliness and concerned by those wild gestures of despair, and perhaps of anger as well, Trurl quickly landed.

He was approached by a personage of tremendous hauteur, iridium and vanadium all over and with a great deal of clanging and clanking, who introduced himself as Excelsius the Tartarian, ruler of Pancreon and Cyspenderora; the inhabitants of both these kingdoms had, in a fit of regicidal madness, driven His Highness from the throne and exiled him to this barren asteroid, eternally adrift among the dark swells and currents of gravitation.

Learning in turn the identity of his visitor, the deposed monarch began to insist that Trurl—who after all was something of a professional when it came to good deeds—immediately restore him to his former position. The thought of such a turn of events brought the flame of vengeance to the monarch's eyes, and his iron fingers clutched the air, as if already closing around the throats of his beloved subjects.

Now Trurl had no intention of complying with this request of Excelsius, as doing so would bring about untold evil and suffering, yet at the same time he wished somehow to comfort and console the humiliated king. Thinking a moment or two, he came to the conclusion that, even in this case, not all was lost, for it would be possible to satisfy the king completely—without putting his former subjects in jeopardy. And so, rolling up his sleeves and summoning up all his mastery, Trurl built the king an entirely new kingdom. There were plenty of towns, rivers, mountains, forests, and brooks, a sky with clouds, armies full of derring-do, citadels, castles, and ladies' chambers; and there were marketplaces, gaudy and gleaming in the sun, days of back-breaking labor, nights full of dancing and song until dawn, and the gay clatter of swordplay. Trurl also carefully set into this kingdom a fabulous capital, all in marble and alabaster, and assembled a council of hoary sages, and winter palaces and summer villas, plots, conspirators, false witnesses, nurses, informers, teams of magnificent steeds, and plumes waving crimson in the wind; and then he crisscrossed that atmosphere with silver fanfares and twenty-one gun salutes, also threw in the necessary handful of traitors, another of heroes, added a pinch of prophets and seers, and one messiah and one great poet each, after which he bent over and set the works in motion, deftly making last-minute adjustments with his microscopic tools as it ran, and he gave the women of that kingdom beauty, the men—sullen silence and surliness when drunk, the officials—arrogance and servility, the astronomers—an enthusiasm for stars, and the children—a great capacity for noise. And all of this, connected, mounted and ground to precision, fit into a box, and not a very large box, but just the size that could be carried about with ease. This Trurl presented to Excelsius, to rule and have dominion over forever; but first he showed him where the input and output of his brand-new kingdom were, and how to program wars, quell rebellions, exact tribute, collect taxes, and also instructed him in the critical points and transition states of that microminiaturized society—in other words the maxima and minima of palace coups and revolutions— and explained everything so well that the king, an old hand in the running of tyrannies, instantly grasped the directions and, without hesitation, while the constructor watched, issued a few trial proclamations, correctly manipulating the control knobs, which were carved with imperial eagles and regal lions. These proclamations declared a state of emergency, martial law, a curfew, and a special levy. After a year had passed in the kingdom, which amounted to hardly a minute for Trurl and the king, by an act of the greatest magnanimity—that is, by a flick of the finger at the controls—the king abolished one death penalty, lightened the levy, and deigned to annul the state of emergency, whereupon a tumultuous cry of gratitude, like the squeaking of tiny mice lifted by their tails, rose up from the box, and through its curved glass cover one could see, on the dusty highways and along the banks of lazy rivers that reflected the fluffy clouds, the people rejoicing and praising the great and unsurpassed benevolence of their sovereign lord.

And so, though at first he had felt insulted by Trurl's gift, in that the kingdom was too small and very like a child's toy, the monarch saw that the thick glass lid made everything inside seem large; perhaps too he dully understood that size was not what mattered here, for government is not measured in meters and kilograms, and emotions are somehow the same, whether experienced by giants or dwarfs—and so he thanked the constructor, if somewhat stiffly. Who knows, he might even have liked to order him thrown in chains and tortured to death, just to be safe—that would have been a sure way of nipping in the bud any gossip about how some common vagabond tinkerer presented a mighty monarch with a kingdom.

Excelsius was sensible enough, however, to see that this was out of the question, owing to a very fundamental disproportion, for fleas could sooner take their host into captivity than the king's army seize Trurl. So with another cold nod, he stuck his orb and scepter under his arm, lifted the box kingdom with a grunt, and took it to his humble hut of exile. And as blazing day alternated with murky night outside, according to the rhythm of the asteroid's rotation, the king, who was acknowledged by his subjects as the greatest in the world, diligently reigned, bidding this, forbidding that, beheading, rewarding—in all these ways incessantly spurring his little ones on to perfect fealty and worship of the throne.

As for Trurl, he returned home and related to his friend Klapaucius, not without pride, how he had employed his constructor's genius to indulge the autocratic aspirations of Excelsius and, at the same time, safeguard the democratic aspirations of his former subjects. But Klapaucius, surprisingly enough, had no words of praise for Trurl; in fact, there seemed to be rebuke in his expression.

"Have I understood you correctly?" he said at last. "You gave that brutal despot, that born slave master, that slavering sadist of a pain-monger, you gave him a whole civilization to rule and have dominion over forever? And you tell me, moreover, of the cries of joy brought on by the repeal of a fraction of his cruel decrees! Trurl, how could you have done such a thing?"

"You must be joking!" Trurl exclaimed. "Really, the whole king-dom fits into a box three feet by two by two and a half . . . it's only a model. . . ."

"A model of what?"

"What do you mean, of what? Of a civilization, obviously, except that it's a hundred million times smaller."

"And how do you know there aren't civilizations a hundred million times larger than our own? And if there were, would ours then be a model? And what importance do dimensions have anyway? In that box kingdom, doesn't a journey from the capital to one of the corners take months—for those inhabitants? And don't they suffer, don't they know the burden of labor, don't they die?"

"Now just a minute, you know yourself that all these processes take place only because I programmed them, and so they aren't genuine. . . ."

"Aren't genuine? You mean to say the box is empty, and the parades, tortures, and beheadings are merely an illusion?"

"Not an illusion, no, since they have reality, though purely as certain microscopic phenomena, which I produced by manipulating atoms," said

Trurl. "The point is, these births, loves, acts of heroism, and denunciations are nothing but the minuscule capering of electrons in space, precisely arranged by the skill of my nonlinear craft, which—"

"Enough of your boasting, not another word!" Klapaucius snapped. "Are these processes self-organizing or not?"

"Of course they are!"

"And they occur among infinitesimal clouds of electrical charge?"

"You know they do."

"And the phenomenological events of dawns, sunsets, and bloody battles are generated by the concatenation of real variables?"

"Certainly."

"And are not we as well, if you examine us physically, mechanistically, statistically, and meticulously, nothing but the minuscule capering of electron clouds? Positive and negative charges arranged in space? And is our existence not the result of subatomic collisions and the interplay of particles, though we ourselves perceive those molecular cartwheels as fear, longing, or meditation? And when you daydream, what transpires within your brain but the binary algebra of connecting and disconnecting circuits, the continual meandering of electrons?"

"What, Klapaucius, would you equate our existence with that of an imitation kingdom locked up in some glass box?!" cried Trurl. "No, really, that's going too far! My purpose was simply to fashion a simulator of statehood, a model cybernetically perfect, nothing more!"

"Trurl! Our perfection is our curse, for it draws down upon our every endeavor no end of unforeseeable consequences!" Klapaucius said in a stentorian voice. "If an imperfect imitator, wishing to inflict pain, were to build himself a crude idol of wood or wax, and further give it some makeshift semblance of a sentient being, his torture of the thing would be a paltry mockery indeed! But consider a succession of improvements on this practice! Consider the next sculptor, who builds a doll with a recording in its belly, that it may groan beneath his blows; consider a doll which, when beaten, begs for mercy, no longer a crude idol, but a homeostat; consider a doll that sheds tears, a doll that bleeds, a doll that fears death, though it also longs for the peace that only death can bring! Don't you see, when the imitator is perfect, so must be the imitation, and the semblance becomes the truth, the pretense a reality! Trurl, you took an untold number of creatures capable of suffering and abandoned them forever to the rule of a wicked tyrant. . . . Trurl, you have committed a terrible crime!"

"Sheer sophistry!" shouted Trurl, all the louder because he felt the force of his friend's argument. "Electrons meander not only in our brains, but in phonograph records as well, which proves nothing, and certainly gives no grounds for such hypostatical analogies! The subjects of that monster Excelsius do in fact die when decapitated, sob, fight, and fall in love, since that is how I set up the parameters, but it's impossible to say, Klapaucius, that they feel anything in the process—the electrons jumping around in their heads will tell you nothing of that!"

"And if I were to look inside your head, I would also see nothing but electrons," replied Klapaucius. "Come now, don't pretend not to understand what I'm saying, I know you're not that stupid! A phonograph record won't run errands for you, won't beg for mercy or fall on its knees! You say there's no way of knowing whether Excelsius's subjects groan, when beaten, purely because of the electrons hopping about inside—like wheels grinding out the mimicry of a voice—or whether they really groan, that is, because they honestly experience the pain? A pretty distinction, this! No, Trurl, a sufferer is not one who hands you his suffering, that you may touch it, weigh it, bite it like a coin; a sufferer is one who behaves like a sufferer! Prove to me here and now, once and for all, that they do *not* feel, that they do *not* think, that they do *not* in any way exist as being conscious of their enclosure between the two abysses of oblivion—the abyss before birth and the abyss that follows death—prove this to me, Trurl, and I'll leave you be! Prove that you only *imitated* suffering, and did not *create* it!"

"You know perfectly well that's impossible," answered Trurl quietly. "Even before I took my instruments in hand, when the box was still empty, I had to anticipate the possibility of precisely such a proof—in order to rule it out. For otherwise the monarch of that kingdom sooner or later would have gotten the impression that his subjects were not real subjects at all, but puppets, marionettes. Try to understand, there was no other way to do it! Anything that would have destroyed in the littlest way the illusion of complete reality would have also destroyed the importance, the dignity of governing, and turned it into nothing but a mechanical game. . . ."

"I understand, I understand all too well!" cried Klapaucius. "Your intentions were the noblest—you only sought to construct a kingdom as lifelike as possible, so similar to a real kingdom, that no one, absolutely no one, could ever tell the difference, and in this, I am afraid, you were successful! Only hours have passed since your return, but for them, the ones imprisoned in that box, whole centuries have gone by—how many beings, how many lives wasted, and all to gratify and feed the vanity of King Excelsius!"

Without another word Trurl rushed back to his ship, but saw that his friend was coming with him. When he had blasted off into space, pointed the bow between two great clusters of eternal flame and opened the throttle all the way, Klapaucius said:

"Trurl, you're hopeless. You always act first, think later. And now what do you intend to do when we get there?"

"I'll take the kingdom away from him!"

"And what will you do with it?"

"Destroy it!" Trurl was about to shout, but choked on the first syllable when he realized what he was saying. Finally he mumbled:

"I'll hold an election. Let them choose just rulers from among themselves."

"You programmed them all to be feudal lords or shiftless vassals. What good would an election do? First you'd have to undo the entire structure of the kingdom, then assemble from scratch . . ."

"And where," exclaimed Trurl, "does the changing of structures end and the tampering with minds begin?!" Klapaucius had no answer for this, and they flew on in gloomy silence, till the planet of Excelsius came into view. As they circled it, preparing to land, they beheld a most amazing sight.

The entire planet was covered with countless signs of intelligent life. Microscopic bridges, like tiny lines, spanned every rill and rivulet, while the puddles, reflecting the stars, were full of microscopic boats like floating chips. . . . The night side of the sphere was dotted with glimmering cities, and on the day side one could make out flourishing metropolises, though the inhabitants themselves were much too little to observe, even through the strongest lens. Of the king there was not a trace, as if the earth had swallowed him up.

"He isn't here," said Trurl in an awed whisper. "What have they done with him? Somehow they managed to break through the walls of their box and occupy the asteroid. . . ."

"Look!" said Klapaucius, pointing to a little cloud no larger than a thimble and shaped like a mushroom; it slowly rose into the atmosphere. "They've discovered atomic energy. . . . And over there—you see that bit of glass? It's the remains of the box, they've made it into some sort of temple. . . ."

"I don't understand. It was only a model, after all. A process with a large number of parameters, a simulation, a mock-up for a monarch to practice on, with the necessary feedback, variables, multistats . . ." muttered Trurl, dumbfounded.

"Yes. But you made the unforgivable mistake of overperfecting your replica. Not wanting to build a mere clocklike mechanism, you inadvertently—in your punctilious way—created that which was possible, logical, and inevitable, that which became the very antithesis of a mechanism. . . ."

"Please, no more!" cried Trurl. And they looked out upon the asteroid in silence, when suddenly something bumped their ship, or rather grazed it slightly. They saw this object, for it was illuminated by the thin ribbon of flame that issued from its tail. A ship, probably, or perhaps an artificial satellite, though remarkably similar to one of those steel boots the tyrant Excelsius used to wear. And when the constructors raised their eyes, they beheld a heavenly body shining high above the tiny planet— it hadn't been there previously—and they recognized, in that cold, pale orb, the stern features of Excelsius himself, who had in this way become the Moon of the Microminians.

Reflections

> But sure as oft as women weep
> It is to be supposed they grieve.
> —Andrew Marvell

"No, Trurl, a sufferer is not one who hands you his suffering, that you may touch it, weigh it, bite it like a coin; a sufferer is one who behaves like a sufferer!"

It is interesting, the choice of words that Lem uses in describing his fantastic simulations. Words like "digital," "nonlinear," "feedback," "self-organizing," and "cybernetic" come up over and over again in his stories. They have an old-fashioned flavor different from that of most terms that come up in current discussions of artificial intelligence. Much of the work in AI has wandered off in directions that have little to do with perception, learning, and creativity. More of it is directed toward such things as simulating the ability to use language—and we say "simulating" advisedly. It seems to us that many of the most difficult and challenging parts of artificial intelligence research lie ahead—and the "self-organizing," "nonlinear" nature of the human mind will then come back as an important mystery to be attacked. In the meanwhile, Lem vividly brings out some of the powerful, heady scents that those words ought to carry.

In his novel *Even Cowgirls Get the Blues*,* Tom Robbins has a passage that is strikingly similar to Lem's vision of a tiny manufactured world:

For Christmas that year, Julian gave Sissy a miniature Tyrolean village. The craftsmanship was remarkable.

There was a tiny cathedral whose stained-glass windows made fruit salad of sunlight. There was a plaza and *ein Biergarten.* The *Biergarten* got quite noisy on Saturday nights. There was a bakery that smelled always of hot bread and strudel. There was a town hall and a police station, with cutaway sections that revealed standard amounts of red tape and corruption. There were little Tyroleans in leather britches, intricately stitched, and, beneath the britches, genitalia of equally fine workmanship. There were ski shops and many other interesting things, including an orphanage. The orphanage was designed to catch fire and burn down every Christmas Eve. Orphans would dash into the snow with their nightgowns blazing. Terrible. Around the second week of January, a fire inspector would come and poke through the ruins, muttering, "If they had only listened to me, those children would be alive today."

Although in subject it resembles the Lem piece greatly, in flavor it is completely different. It is as if two composers had independently come up with the same melody but harmonized it utterly differently. Far from drawing you into believing in the genuine feelings of the tiny people, Robbins makes you see them as merely incredible (if not incredibly silly) pieces of fine clockwork.

The repetition of the orphanage drama year after year, echoing the Nietzschean idea of eternal recurrence—that everything that has happened will happen again and again—seems to rob the little world of any real meaning. Why should the repetition of the fire inspector's lament make it sound so hollow? Do the little Tyroleans rebuild the orphanage themselves or is there a "RESET" button? Where do the new orphans come from, or do the "dead" ones come back to "life"? As with the other fantasies here, it is often instructive to think about the details omitted.

Subtle stylistic touches and narrative tricks make all the difference as to whether you get sucked into belief in the genuineness of the tiny souls. Which way do you tilt?

D.R.H.
D.C.D.

19

STANISLAW LEM

Non Serviam

Professor Dobb's book is devoted to personetics, which the Finnish philosopher Eino Kaikki has called "the cruelest science man ever created." Dobb, one of the most distinguished personeticists today, shares this view. One cannot escape the conclusion, he says, that personetics is, in its application, immoral; we are dealing, however, with a type of pursuit that is, though counter to the principles of ethics, also of practical necessity to us. There is no way, in the research, to avoid its special ruthlessness, to avoid doing violence to one's natural instincts, and if nowhere else it is here that the myth of the perfect innocence of the scientist as a seeker of facts is exploded. We are speaking of a discipline, after all, which, with only a small amount of exaggeration, for emphasis, has been called "experimental theogony." Even so, this reviewer is struck by the fact that when the press played up the thing, nine years ago, public opinion was stunned by the personetic disclosures. One would have thought that in this day and age nothing could surprise us. The centuries rang with the echo of the feat of Columbus, whereas the conquering of the Moon in the space of a week was received by the collective consciousness as a thing practically humdrum. And yet the birth of personetics proved to be a shock.

The name combines Latin and Greek derivatives: "persona" and "genetic"—"genetic" in the sense of formation or creation. The field is a recent offshoot of the cybernetics and psychonics of the eighties, cross-bred with applied intellectronics. Today everyone knows of personetics; the man in the street would say, if asked, that it is the artificial production of intelligent beings—an answer not wide of the mark, to be sure, but not quite getting to the heart of the matter. To date we have nearly a hundred personetic programs. Nine years ago identity schemata were being developed—primitive cores of the "linear" type—but even that generation of computers, today of historical value only, could not yet provide a field for the true creation of personoids.

The theoretical possibility of creating sentience was divined some time ago by Norbert Wiener, as certain passages of his last book, *God and Golem*, bear witness. Granted, he alluded to it in that half-facetious manner typical of him, but underlying the facetiousness were fairly grim premonitions. Wiener, however, could not have foreseen the turn that things would take twenty years later. The worst came about—in the words of Sir Donald Acker—when at MIT "the inputs were shorted to the outputs."

At present a "world" for personoid "inhabitants" can be prepared in a matter of a couple of hours. This is the time it takes to feed into the machine one of the full-fledged programs (such as BAAL 66, CREAN IV, or JAHVE 09). Dobb gives a rather cursory sketch of the beginnings of personetics, referring the reader to the historical sources; a confirmed practitioner-experimenter himself, he speaks mainly of his own work—which is much to the point, since between the English school, which Dobb represents, and the American group, at MIT, the differences are considerable, both in the area of methodology and as regards experimental goals. Dobb describes the procedure of "6 days in 120 minutes" as follows. First, one supplies the machine's memory with a minimal set of givens; that is—to keep within a language comprehensible to laymen—one loads its memory with substance that is "mathematical." This substance is the protoplasm of a universum to be "habitated" by personoids. We are now able to supply the beings that will come into this mechanical, digital world—that will be carrying on an existence in it, and in it only—with an environment of nonfinite characteristics. These beings, therefore, cannot feel imprisoned in the physical sense, because the environment does not have, from their standpoint, any bounds. The medium possesses only one dimension that resembles a dimension given us also—namely, that of the passage of time (duration). Their time is not directly analogous to ours, however, because the rate of its flow is subject to discretionary control on the part of the experimenter. As a rule, the rate is maximized in the preliminary phase (the so-called creational warm-up), so that our minutes correspond to whole eons in the computer, during which there takes place a series of successive reorganizations and crystal-lizations—of a synthetic cosmos. It is a cosmos completely spaceless, though possessing dimensions, but these dimensions have a purely math-ematical, hence what one might call an "imaginary" character. They are, very simply, the consequence of certain axiomatic decisions of the pro-grammer, and their number depends on him. If, for example, he chooses a ten-dimensionality, it will have for the structure of the world created altogether different consequences from those where only six dimensions are established. It should be emphasized that these dimensions bear no relation to those of physical space but only to the abstract, logically valid constructs made use of in systems creation.

This point, all but inaccessible to the nonmathematician, Dobb at-tempts to explain by adducing simple facts, the sort generally learned in school. It is possible, as we know, to construct a geometrically regular three-dimensional solid—say, a cube—which in the real world possesses a counterpart in the form of a die; and it is equally possible to create geometrical solids of four, five, n dimensions (the four-dimensional is a tesseract). These no longer possess real counterparts, and we can see this, since in the absence of any physical dimension No. 4 there is no way to fashion genuine four-dimensional dice. Now, this distinction (between what is physically constructible and what may be made only mathemati-cally) is, for personoids, in general nonexistent, because their world is of a purely mathematical consistency. It is built of mathematics, though the building blocks of that mathematics are ordinary, perfectly physical ob-jects (relays, transistors, logic circuits—in a word, the whole huge net-work of the digital machine).

As we know from modern physics, space is not something independ-ent of the objects and masses that are situated within it. Space is, in its existence, determined by those bodies; where they are not, where noth-ing is—in the material sense—there, too, space ceases, collapsing to zero. Now, the role of material bodies, which extend their "influence," so to speak, and thereby "generate" space, is carried out in the personoid world by systems of a mathematics called into being for that very purpose. Out of all the possible "maths" that in general might be made (for example, in an axiomatic manner), the programmer, having decided upon a specific experiment, selects a particular group, which will serve as the underpinning, the "existential substrate," the "ontological foun-dation" of the created universum. There is in this, Dobb believes, a striking similarity to the human world. This world of ours, after all, has "decided" upon certain forms and upon certain types of geometry that best suit it—best, since most simply (three-dimensionality, in order to remain with what one began with). This notwithstanding, we are able to picture "other worlds" with "other properties"—in the geometrical and not only in the geometrical realm. It is the same with the personoids: that aspect of mathematics which the researcher has chosen as the "habitat" is for them exactly what for us is the "real-world base" in which we live, and live perforce. And, like us, the personoids are able to "picture" worlds of different fundamental properties.

Dobb presents his subject using the method of successive approximations and recapitulations; that which we have outlined above, and which corresponds roughly to the first two chapters of his book, in the subsequent chapters undergoes partial revocation—through complication. It is not really the case, the author advises us, that the personoids simply come upon a ready-made, fixed, frozen sort of world in its irrevocably final form; what the world will be like in its specificities depends on them, and this to a growing degree as their own activeness increases, as their "exploratory initiative" develops. Nor does the likening of the universum of the personoids to a world in which phenomena exist only to the extent that its inhabitants observe them provide an accurate image of the conditions. Such a comparison, which is to be found in the works of Sainter and Hughes, Dobb considers an "idealist deviation"—a homage that personetics has rendered to the doctrine, so curiously and so suddenly resurrected, of Bishop Berkeley. Sainter maintained that the personoids would know their world after the fashion of a Berkeleyan being, which is not in a position to distinguish *esse* from *percipi*—to wit, it will never discover the difference between the thing perceived and that which occasions the perception in a way objective and independent of the one perceiving. Dobb attacks this interpretation of the matter with a passion. *We*, the creators of their world, know perfectly well that what is perceived by them indeed exists; it exists inside the computer, independent of them —though, granted, solely in the manner of mathematical objects.

And there are further clarifications. The personoids arise germinally by virtue of the program; they increase at a rate imposed by the experimenter—a rate only such as the latest technology of information processing, operating at near-light speeds, permits. The mathematics that is to be the "existential residence" of the personoids does not await them in full readiness but is still "in wraps," so to speak—unarticulated, suspended, latent—because it represents only a set of certain prospective chances, of certain pathways contained in appropriately programmed subunits of the machine. These subunits, or generators, in and of themselves contribute nothing; rather, a specific type of personoid activity serves as a triggering mechanism, setting in motion a production process that will gradually augment and define itself; in other words, the world surrounding these beings takes on an unequivocalness only in accordance with their own behavior. Dobb tries to illustrate this concept with recourse to the following analogy. A man may interpret the real world in a variety of ways. He may devote particular attention—intense scientific investigation—to certain facets of that world, and the knowledge he acquires then casts its own special light on the remaining portions of the world, those not considered in his priority-setting research. If first he diligently takes up *mechanics*, he will fashion for himself a *mechanical* model of the world and will see the Universe as a gigantic and perfect clock that in its inexorable movement proceeds from the past to a precisely determined future. This model is not an accurate representation of reality, and yet one can make use of it for a period of time historically long, and with it can even achieve many practical successes—the building of machines, implements, etc. Similarly, should the personoids "incline themselves," by choice, by an act of will, to a certain type of relation to their universum, and to that type of relation give precedence—if it is in this and only in this that they find the "essence" of their cosmos—they will enter upon a definite path of endeavors and discoveries, a path that is neither illusory nor futile. Their inclination "draws out" of the environment what best corresponds to it. What they first perceive is what they first master. For the world that surrounds them is only partially determined, only partially established in advance by the researcher-creator; in it, the personoids preserve a certain and by no means insignificant margin of freedom of action—action both "mental" (in the province of what they think of their own world, of how they understand it) and "real" (in the context of their "deeds"—which are not, to be sure, literally real, as we understand the term, but are not merely imagined, either). This is, in truth, the most difficult part of the exposition, and Dobb, we daresay, is not altogether successful in explaining those special qualities of personoid existence— qualities that can be rendered only by the language of the mathematics of programs and creational interventions. We must, then, take it somewhat on faith that the activity of the personoids is neither entirely free— as the space of our actions is not entirely free, being limited by the physical laws of nature—nor entirely determined—just as we are not train cars set on rigidly fixed tracks. A personoid is similar to a man in this respect, too, that man's "secondary qualities"—colors, melodious sounds, the beauty of things—can manifest themselves only when he has ears to hear and eyes to see, but what makes possible hearing and sight has been, after all, previously given. Personoids, perceiving their environment, give it from out of themselves those experiential qualities which exactly correspond to what for us are the charms of a beheld landscape —except, of course, that they have been provided with purely mathematical scenery. As to "how they see it," one can make no pronouncement, for the only way of learning the "subjective quality of their sensation" would be for one to shed his human skin and become a personoid. Personoids, one must remember, have no eyes or ears, therefore they neither see nor hear, as we understand it; in their cosmos there is no light, no darkness, no spatial proximity, no distance, no up or down; there are dimensions there, not tangible to us but to them primary, elemental; they perceive, for example—as equivalents of the components of human sensory awareness—certain changes in electrical potential. But these changes in potential are, for them, not something in the nature of, let us say, pressures of current but, rather, the sort of thing that, for a man, is the most rudimentary phenomenon, optical or aural—the seeing of a red blotch, the hearing of a sound, the touching of an object hard or soft. From here on, Dobb stresses, one can speak only in analogies, evocations.

To declare that the personoids are "handicapped" with respect to us, inasmuch as they do not see or hear as we do, is totally absurd, because with equal justice one could assert that it is we who are deprived with respect to them—unable to feel with immediacy the phenomenalism of mathematics, which, after all, we know only in a cerebral, inferential fashion. It is only through reasoning that we are in touch with mathematics, only through abstract thought that we "experience" it. Whereas the personoids *live* in it; it is their air, their earth, clouds, water, and even bread—yes, even food, because in a certain sense they take nourishment from it. And so they are "imprisoned," hermetically locked inside the machine, solely from our point of view; just as they cannot work their way out to us, to the human world, so, conversely—and symmetrically—a man can in no wise enter the interior of their world, so as to exist in it and know it directly. Mathematics has become, then, in certain of its embodiments, the life-space of an intelligence so spiritualized as to be totally incorporeal, the niche and cradle of its existence, its element.

The personoids are in many respects similar to man. They are able to imagine a particular contradiction (that *a* is and that not-*a* is) but cannot bring about its realization, just as we cannot. The physics of our world, the logic of theirs, does not allow it, since logic is for the personoids' universum the very same action-confining frame that physics is for our world. In any case—emphasizes Dobb—it is quite out of the question that we could ever fully, introspectively grasp what the personoids "feel" and what they "experience" as they go about their intensive tasks in their nonfinite universum. Its utter spacelessness is no prison—that is a piece of nonsense the journalists latched onto—but is, on the contrary, the guarantee of their freedom, because the mathematics that is spun by the computer generators when "excited" into activity (and what excites them thus is precisely the activity of the personoids)—that mathematics is, as it were, a self-realizing infinite field for optional actions, architectural and other labors, for exploration, heroic excursions, daring incursions, surmises. In a word: we have done the personoids no injustice by putting them in possession of precisely such and not a different cosmos. It is not in this that one finds the cruelty, the immorality of personetics.

In the seventh chapter of *Non Serviam* Dobb presents to the reader the inhabitants of the digital universum. The personoids have at their disposal a fluency of thought as well as of language, and they also have emotions. Each of them is an individual entity; their differentiation is not the mere consequence of the decisions of the creator-programmer but results from the extraordinary complexity of their internal structure. They can be very like, one to another, but never are they identical. Coming into the world, each is endowed with a "core," a "personal nucleus," and already possesses the faculty of speech and thought, albeit in a rudimentary state. They have a vocabulary, but it is quite spare, and they have the ability to construct sentences in accordance with the rules of the syntax imposed upon them. It appears that in the future it will be possible for us not to impose upon them even these determinants, but to sit back and wait until, like a primeval human group in the course of socialization, they develop their own speech. But this direction of personetics confronts two cardinal obstacles. In the first place, the time required to await the creation of speech would have to be very long. At present, it would take twelve years, even with the maximization of the rate of intracomputer transformations (speaking figuratively and very roughly, one second of machine time corresponds to one year of human life). Secondly, and this is the greater problem, a language arising spontaneously in the "group evolution of the personoids" would be incomprehensible to us, and its fathoming would be bound to resemble the arduous task of breaking an enigmatic code—a task made all the more difficult by the fact that such a code would not have been created by people for other people in a world shared by the decoders. The world of the personoids is vastly different in qualities from ours, and therefore a language suited to it would have to be far removed from any ethnic language. So, for the time being, linguistic evolution *ex nihilo* is only a dream of the personeticists.

The personoids, when they have "taken root developmentally," come up against an enigma that is fundamental, and for them paramount —that of their own origin. To wit, they set themselves questions—questions known to us from the history of man, from the history of his religious beliefs, philosophical inquiries, and mythic creations: Where did we come from? Why are we made thus and not otherwise? Why is it that the world we perceive has these and not other, wholly different properties?

What meaning do we have for the world? What meaning does it have for us? The train of such speculations leads them ultimately, unavoidably, to the elemental questions of ontology, to the problem of whether existence came about "in and of itself," or whether it was the product, instead, of a particular creative act—that is, whether there might not be, hidden behind it, invested with will and consciousness, purposively active, master of the situation, a Creator. It is here that the whole cruelty, the immorality of personetics manifests itself.

But before Dobb takes up, in the second half of his work, the account of these intellectual strivings—these struggles of a mentality made prey to the torment of such questions—he presents in a series of successive chapters a portrait of the "typical personoid," its "anatomy, physiology, and psychology."

A solitary personoid is unable to go beyond the stage of rudimentary thinking, since, solitary, it cannot exercise itself in speech, and without speech discursive thought cannot develop. As hundreds of experiments have shown, groups numbering from four to seven personoids are optimal, at least for the development of speech and typical exploratory activity, and also for "culturization." On the other hand, phenomena corresponding to social processes on a larger scale require larger groups. At present it is possible to "accommodate" up to one thousand personoids, roughly speaking, in a computer universum of fair capacity; but studies of this type, belonging to a separate and independent discipline—sociodynamics—lie outside the area of Dobb's primary concerns, and for this reason his book makes only passing mention of them. As was said, a personoid does not have a body, but it does have a "soul." This soul—to an outside observer who has a view into the machine world (by means of a special installation, an auxiliary module that is a type of probe, built into the computer)—appears as a "coherent cloud of processes," as a functional aggregate with a kind of "center" that can be isolated fairly precisely, i.e., delimited within the machine network. (This, nota bene, is not easy, and in more than one way resembles the search by neurophysiologists for the localized centers of many functions in the human brain.) Crucial to an understanding of what makes possible the creation of the personoids is Chapter 11 of Non Serviam, which in fairly simple terms explains the fundamentals of the theory of consciousness. Consciousness—all consciousness, not merely the personoid—is in its physical aspect an "informational standing wave," a certain dynamic invariant in a stream of incessant transformations, peculiar in that it represents a "compromise" and at the same time is a "resultant" that, as far as we can tell, was not at all planned for by natural evolution. Quite the contrary; evolution from the first placed tremendous problems and difficulties in the way of harmonizing of the work of brains above a certain magnitude—i.e., above a certain level of complication—and it trespassed on the territory of these dilemmas clearly without design, for evolution is not a deliberate artificer. It happened, simply, that certain very old evolutionary solutions to problems of control and regulation, common to the nervous system, were "carried along" up to the level at which anthropogenesis began. These solutions ought to have been, from a purely rational, efficiency-engineering standpoint, canceled or abandoned, and something entirely new designed—namely, the brain of an intelligent being. But, obviously, evolution could not proceed in this way, because disencumbering itself of the inheritance of old solutions—solutions often as much as hundreds of millions of years old—did not lie within its power. Since it advances always in very minute increments of adaptation, since it "crawls" and cannot "leap," evolution is a dragnet "that lugs after it innumerable archaisms, all sorts of refuse," as was bluntly put by Tammer and Bovine. (Tammer and Bovine are two of the creators of the computer simulation of the human psyche, a simulation that laid the groundwork for the birth of personetics.) The consciousness of man is the result of a special kind of compromise. It is a "patchwork," or, as was observed, e.g., by Gebhardt, a perfect exemplification of the well-known German saying: *"Aus einer Not eine Tugend machen"* (in effect: "To turn a certain defect, a certain difficulty, into a virtue"). A digital machine cannot of itself ever acquire consciousness, for the simple reason that in it there do not arise hierarchical conflicts of operation. Such a machine can, at most, fall into a type of "logical palsy" or "logical stupor" when the antinomies in it multiply. The contradictions with which the brain of man positively teems were, however, in the course of hundreds of thousands of years, gradually subjected to arbitrational procedures. There came to be levels higher and lower, levels of reflex and of reflection, impulse and control, the modeling of the elemental environment by zoological means and of the conceptual by linguistic means. All of these levels cannot, do not "want" to tally perfectly or merge to form a whole.

What, then, is consciousness? An expedient, a dodge, a way out of the trap, a pretended last resort, a court allegedly (but only allegedly!) of highest appeal. And, in the language of physics and information theory, it is a function that, once begun, will not admit of any closure—i.e., any definitive completion. It is, then, only a *plan* for such a closure, for a total "reconciliation" of the stubborn contradictions of the brain. It is, one might say, a mirror whose task it is to reflect other mirrors, which in turn reflect still others, and so on to infinity. This, physically, is simply not possible, and so the *regressus ad infinitum* represents a kind of pit over which soars and flutters the phenomenon of human consciousness. "Beneath the conscious" there goes on a continuous battle for full representation—in it—of that which cannot reach it in fullness, and cannot for simple lack of space; for, in order to give full and equal rights to all those tendencies that clamor for attention at the centers of awareness, what would be necessary is infinite capacity and volume. There reigns, then, around the conscious a never-ending crush, a pushing and shoving, and the conscious is not—not at all—the highest, serene, sovereign helmsman of all mental phenomena but more nearly a cork upon the fretful waves, a cork whose uppermost position does not mean the mastery of those waves. . . . The modern theory of consciousness, interpreted informationally and dynamically, unfortunately cannot be set forth simply or clearly, so that we are constantly—at least here, in this more accessible presentation of the subject—thrown back on a series of visual models and metaphors. We know, in any case, that consciousness is a kind of dodge, a shift to which evolution has resorted, and resorted in keeping with its characteristic and indispensable *modus operandi,* opportunism—i.e., finding a quick, extempore way out of a tight corner. If, then, one were indeed to build an intelligent being and proceed according to the canons of completely rational engineering and logic, applying the criteria of technological efficiency, such a being would not, in general, receive the gift of consciousness. It would behave in a manner perfectly logical, always consistent, lucid, and well ordered, and it might even seem, to a human observer, a genius in creative action and decision making. But it could in no way be a man, for it would be bereft of his mysterious depth, his internal intracies, his labyrinthine nature. . . .

We will not here go further into the modern theory of the conscious psyche, just as Professor Dobb does not. But these few words were in order, for they provide a necessary introduction to the structure of the personoids. In their creation is at last realized one of the oldest myths, that of the homunculus. In order to fashion a likeness of man, of his psyche, one must deliberately introduce into the informational substrate specific contradictions; one must impart to it an asymmetry, acentric tendencies; one must, in a word, both *unify* and *make discordant.* Is this rational? Yes, and well-nigh unavoidable if we desire not merely to construct some sort of synthetic intelligence but to imitate the thought and, with it, the personality of man.

Hence, the emotions of the personoids must to some extent be at odds with their reason; they must possess self-destructive tendencies, at least to a certain degree; they must feel internal tensions—that entire centrifugality which we experience now as the magnificent infinity of spiritual states and now as their unendurably painful disjointedness. The creational prescription for this, meanwhile, is not at all so hopelessly

complicated as it might appear. It is simply that the *logic* of the creation
(the personoid) must be disturbed, must contain certain antinomies.
Consciousness is not only a way out of the evolutionary impasse, says
Hilbrandt, but also an escape from the snares of Gödelization, for by
means of paralogistic contradictions this solution has sidestepped the
contradictions to which every system that is perfect with respect to logic
is subject. So, then, the universum of the personoids is fully rational, but
they are not fully rational inhabitants of it. Let that suffice us—Professor
Dobb himself does not pursue further this exceedingly difficult topic. As
we know already, the personoids have souls but no bodies and, therefore,
also no sensation of their corporeality. "It is difficult to imagine" has
been said of that which is experienced in certain special states of mind,
in total darkness, with the greatest possible reduction in the inflow of
external stimuli—but, Dobb maintains, this is a misleading image. For
with sensory deprivation the function of the human brain soon begins to
disintegrate; without a stream of impulses from the outside world the
psyche manifests a tendency to lysis. But personoids, who have no physical senses, hardly disintegrate, because what gives them cohesion is their
mathematical milieu, which they do experience. But how? They experience it, let us say, according to those changes in their own states which
are induced and imposed upon them by the universum's "externalness."
They are able to discriminate between the changes proceeding from
outside themselves and the changes that surface from the depths of their
own psyche. How do they discriminate? To this question only the theory
of the dynamic structure of personoids can supply a direct answer.

    And yet they are like us, for all the awesome differences. We know
already that a digital machine can never spark with consciousness; regardless of the task to which we harness it, or of the physical processes we
simulate in it, it will remain forever apsychic. Since, to simulate man, it
is necessary that we reproduce certain of his fundamental contradictions,
only a system of mutually gravitating antagonisms—a personoid—will
resemble, in the words of Canyon, whom Dobb cites, a "star contracted
by the forces of gravity and at the same time expanded by the pressure
of radiation." The gravitational center is, very simply, the personal "I,"
but by no means does it constitute a unity in either the logical or the
physical sense. That is only our subjective illusion! We find ourselves, at
this stage of the exposition, amid a multitude of astounding surprises.
One can, to be sure, program a digital machine in such a way as to be able
to carry on a conversation with it, as if with an intelligent partner. The
machine will employ, as the need arises, the pronoun "I" and all its
grammatical inflections. This, however, is a hoax! The machine will still
be closer to a billion chattering parrots—howsoever brilliantly trained

the parrots be—than to the simplest, most stupid man. It mimics the behavior of a man on the purely linguistic plane and nothing more. Nothing will amuse such a machine, or surprise it, or confuse it, or alarm it, or distress it, because it is psychologically and individually No One. It is a Voice giving utterance to matters, supplying answers to questions; it is a Logic capable of defeating the best chess player; it is—or, rather, it can become—a consummate imitator of everything, an actor, if you will, brought to the pinnacle of perfection, performing any programmed role —but an actor and an imitator that is, within, completely empty. One cannot count on its sympathy, or on its antipathy. It works toward no self-set goal; to a degree eternally beyond the conception of any man it "doesn't care," for as a person it simply does not exist. . . . It is a wondrously efficient combinatorial mechanism, nothing more. Now, we are faced with a most remarkable phenomenon. The thought is staggering that from the raw material of so utterly vacant and so perfectly impersonal a machine it is possible, through the feeding into it of a special program—a personetic program—to create authentic sentient beings, and even a great many of them at a time! The latest IBM models have a top capacity of one thousand personoids. (The number is mathematically precise, since the elements and linkages needed to carry one personoid can be expressed in units of centimeters-grams-seconds.)

Personoids are separated one from another within the machine. They do not ordinarily "overlap," though it can happen. Upon contact, there occurs what is equivalent to repulsion, which impedes mutual "osmosis." Nevertheless, they are able to interpenetrate if such is their aim. The processes making up their mental substrates then commence to superimpose upon each other, producing "noise" and interference. When the area of permeation is thin, a certain amount of information becomes the common property of both partially coincident personoids— a phenomenon that is for them peculiar, as for a man it would be peculiar, if not indeed alarming, to hear "strange voices" and "foreign thoughts" in his own head (which does, of course, occur in certain mental illnesses or under the influence of hallucinogenic drugs). It is as though two people were to have not merely the same, but *the same* memory; as though there had occurred something more than a telepathic transference of thought—namely, a "peripheral merging of the egos." The phenomenon is ominous in its consequences, however, and ought to be avoided. For, following the transitional state of surface osmosis, the "advancing" personoid can destroy the other and consume it. The latter, in that case, simply undergoes absorption, annihilation—it ceases to exist (this has already been called murder). The annihilated personoid becomes an assimilated, indistinguishable part of the "aggressor." We have suc-

ceeded—says Dobb—in simulating not only psychic life but also its im-
perilment and obliteration. Thus we have succeeded in simulating death
as well. Under normal experimental conditions, however, personoids
eschew such acts of aggression. "Psychophagi" (Castler's term) are
hardly ever encountered among them. Feeling the beginnings of osmosis,
which may come about as the result of purely accidental approaches and
fluctuations—feeling this threat in a manner that is of course nonphysical,
much as someone might sense another's presence or even hear "strange
voices" in his own mind—the personoids execute active avoidance ma-
neuvers; they withdraw and go their separate ways. It is on account of this
phenomenon that they have come to know the meaning of the concepts
of "good" and "evil." To them it is evident that "evil" lies in the destruction of another, and "good" in another's deliverance. At the same time,
the "evil" of one may be the "good" (i.e., the gain, now in the nonethical
sense) of another, who would become a "psychophage." For such expansion—the appropriation of someone else's "intellectual territory"—increases one's initially given mental "acreage." In a way, this is a counterpart of a practice of ours, for as carnivores we kill and feed on our victims.
The personoids, though, are not obliged to behave thus; they are merely
able to. Hunger and thirst are unknown to them, since a continuous influx
of energy sustains them—an energy whose source they need not concern
themselves with (just as we need not go to any particular lengths to have
the sun shine down on us). In the personoid world the terms and principles of thermodynamics, in their application to energetics, cannot arise,
because that world is subject to mathematical and not thermodynamic
laws.

Before long, the experimenters came to the conclusion that contacts
between personoid and man, via the inputs and outputs of the computer,
were of little scientific value and, moreover, produced moral dilemmas,
which contributed to the labeling of personetics as the cruelest science.
There is something unworthy in informing personoids that we have
created them in enclosures that only *simulate* infinity, that they are microscopic "psychocysts," capsulations in our world. To be sure, they have
their own infinity; hence Sharker and other psychoneticians (Falk, Wiege-
land) claim that the situation is fully symmetrical: the personoids do not
need our world, our "living space," just as we have no use for their
"mathematical earth." Dobb considers such reasoning sophistry, because
as to who created whom, and who confined whom existentially, there can
be no argument. Dobb himself belongs to that group which advocates the
principle of absolute nonintervention—"noncontact"—with the personoids. They are the behaviorists of personetics. Their desire is to observe
synthetic beings of intelligence, to listen in on their speech and thoughts,

to record their actions and their pursuits, but never to interfere with these. This method is already developed and has a technology of its own —a set of instruments whose procurement presented difficulties that seemed all but insurmountable only a few years ago. The idea is to hear, to understand—in short, to be a constantly eavesdropping witness—but at the same time to prevent one's "monitorings" from disturbing in any way the world of the personoids. Now in the planning stage at MIT are programs (APHRON II and EROT) that will enable the personoids—who are currently without gender—to have "erotic contacts," make possible what corresponds to fertilization, and give them the opportunity to multiply "sexually." Dobb makes clear that he is no enthusiast of these American projects. His work, as described in *Non Serviam,* is aimed in an altogether different direction. Not without reason has the English school of personetics been called "the philosophical Polygon" and "the theodicy lab." With these descriptions we come to what is probably the most significant and, certainly, the most intriguing part of the book under discussion— the last part, which justifies and explains its peculiar title.

Dobb gives an account of his own experiment, in progress now for eight years without interruption. Of the creation itself he makes only brief mention; it was a fairly ordinary duplicating of functions typical of the program JAHVE VI, with slight modifications. He summarizes the results of "tapping" this world, which he himself created and whose development he continues to follow. He considers this tapping to be unethical, and even, at times, a shameful practice. Nevertheless, he carries on with his work, professing a belief in the necessity, for science, of conducting such experiments *also*—experiments that can in no way be justified on moral—or, for that matter, on any other nonknowledge-advancing— grounds. The situation, he says, has come to the point where the old evasions of the scientists will not do. One cannot affect a fine neutrality and conjure away an uneasy conscience by using, for example, the rationalization worked out by vivisectionists—that it is not in creatures of fulldimensional consciousness, not in sovereign beings that one is causing suffering or only discomfort. In the personoid experiments we are accountable twofold, because we create and then enchain the creation in the schema of our laboratory procedures. Whatever we do and however we explain our action, there is no longer an escape from full accountability.

Many years of experience on the part of Dobb and his co-workers at Oldport went into the making of their eight-dimensional universum, which became the residence of personoids bearing the names ADAN, ADNA, ANAD, DANA, DAAN, and NAAD. The first personoids developed the rudiment of language implanted in them and had "progeny" by means of division. Dobb writes, in the Biblical vein, "And ADAN begat ADNA. ADNA

in turn begat DAAN, and DAAN brought forth EDAN, who bore EDNA. . . ."
And so it went, until the number of succeeding generations had reached
three hundred; because the computer possessed a capacity of only one
hundred personoid entities, however, there were periodic eliminations of
the "demographic surplus." In the three-hundredth generation, personoids named ADAN, ADNA, ANAD, DANA, DAAN, and NAAD again make an
appearance, endowed with additional numbers designating their order of
descent. (For simplicity in our recapitulation, we will omit the numbers.)
Dobb tells us that the time that has elapsed inside the computer universum works out to—in a rough conversion to our equivalent units of
measurement—from 2 to 2.5 thousand years. Over this period there has
come into being, within the personoid population, a whole series of
varying explanations of their lot, as well as the formulation by them of
varying, and contending, and mutually excluding models of "all that
exists." That is, there have arisen many different philosophies (ontolo-
gies and epistemologies), and also "metaphysical experiments" of a type
all their own. We do not know whether it is because the "culture" of the
personoids is too unlike the human or whether the experiment has been
of too short duration, but, in the population studied, no faith of a form
completely dogmatized has ever crystallized—a faith that would correspond to Buddhism, say, or to Christianity. On the other hand, one notes,
as early as the eighth generation, the appearance of the notion of a
Creator, envisioned personally and monotheistically. The experiment
consists in alternately raising the rate of computer transformations to the
maximum and slowing it down (once a year, more or less) to make direct
monitoring possible. These changes in rate are, as Dobb explains, totally
imperceptible to the inhabitants of the computer universum, just as similar transformations would be imperceptible to us, because when at a
single blow the whole of existence undergoes a change (here, in the
dimension of time), those immersed in it cannot be aware of the change,
because they have no fixed point, or frame of reference, by which to
determine that it is taking place.

The utilization of "two chronological gears" permitted that which
Dobb most wanted—the emergence of a personoid history, a history with
a depth of tradition and a vista of time. To summarize all the data of that
history recorded by Dobb, often of a sensational nature, is not possible.
We will confine ourselves, then, to the passages from which came the idea
that is reflected in the book's title. The language employed by the personoids is a recent transformation of the standard English whose lexicon and
syntax were programmed into them in the first generation. Dobb trans-
lates it into essentially normal English but leaves intact a few expressions coined by the personoid population. Among these are the terms

"godly" and "ungodly," used to describe believers in God and atheists.

ADAN discourses with DAAN and ADNA (personoids themselves do not use these names, which are purely a pragmatic contrivance on the part of the observers, to facilitate the recording of the "dialogues") upon a problem known to us also—a problem that in our history originates with Pascal but in the history of the personoids was the discovery of a certain EDAN 197. Exactly like Pascal, this thinker stated that a belief in God is in any case more profitable than unbelief, because if truth is on the side of the "ungodlies" the believer loses nothing but his life when he leaves the world, whereas if God exists he gains all eternity (glory everlasting). Therefore, one should believe in God, for this is dictated very simply by the existential tactic of weighing one's chances in the pursuit of optimal success.

ADAN 300 holds the following view of this directive: EDAN 197, in his line of reasoning, assumes a God that requires reverence, love, and total devotion, and not only and not simply a belief in the fact that He exists and that He created the world. It is not enough to assent to the hypothesis of God the Maker of the World in order to win one's salvation; one must in addition be grateful to that Maker for the act of creation, and divine His will, and do it. In short, one must serve God. Now, God, if He exists, has the power to prove His own existence in a manner at least as convincing as the manner in which what can be directly perceived testifies to His being. Surely, we cannot doubt that certain objects exist and that our world is composed of them. At the most, one might harbor doubts regarding the question of what it is they do to exist, how they exist, etc. But the fact itself of their existence no one will gainsay. God could with this same force provide evidence of His own existence. Yet He has not done so, condemning us to obtain, on that score, knowledge that is roundabout, indirect, expressed in the form of various conjectures—conjectures sometimes given the name of revelation. If He has acted thus, then He has thereby put the "godlies" and the "ungodlies" on an equal footing; He has not compelled His creatures to an absolute belief in His being but has only offered them that possibility. Granted, the motives that moved the Creator may well be hidden from His creations. Be that as it may, the following proposition arises: God either exists or He does not exist. That there might be a third possibility (God did exist but no longer does, or He exists intermittently, in oscillation, or He exists sometimes "less" and sometimes "more," etc.) appears exceedingly improbable. It cannot be ruled out, but the introduction of a multivalent logic into a theodicy serves only to muddle it.

So, then, God either is or He is not. If He Himself accepts our situation, in which each member of the alternative in question has arguments to support it—for the "godlies" prove the existence of the Creator and the "ungodlies" disprove it—then from the point of view of logic we have a game whose partners are, on one side, the full set of the "godlies" and "ungodlies," and, on the other, God alone. The game necessarily possesses the logical feature that for unbelief in Him God may not punish anyone. If it is definitely unknown whether or not a thing exists—some merely asserting that it does and others, that it does not—and if in general it is possible to advance the hypothesis that the thing never was at all, then no just tribunal can pass judgment against anyone for denying the existence of this thing. For in all worlds it is thus: when there is no full certainty, there is no full accountability. This formulation is by pure logic unassailable, because it sets up a symmetrical function of reward in the context of the theory of games; whoever in the face of uncertainty demands *full accountability* destroys the mathematical symmetry of the game; we then have the so-called game of the non-zero sum.

It is therefore thus: either God is perfectly just, in which case He cannot assume the right to punish the "ungodlies" by virtue of the fact that they are "ungodlies" (i.e., that they do not believe in Him); or else He will punish the unbelievers after all, which means that from the logical point of view He is not perfectly just. What follows from this? What follows is that He can do whatever He pleases, for when in a system of logic a single, solitary contradiction is permitted, then by the principle of *ex falso quodlibet* one can draw from that system whatever conclusion one will. In other words: a just God may not touch a hair on the head of the "ungodlies," and if He does, then by that very act He is not the universally perfect and just being that the theodicy posits.

ADNA asks how, in this light, we are to view the problem of the doing of evil unto others.

ADAN 300 replies: Whatever takes place here is entirely certain; whatever takes place "there"—i.e., beyond the world's pale, in eternity, with God—is uncertain, being but inferred according to the hypotheses. Here, one should not commit evil, despite the fact that the principle of eschewing evil is not logically demonstrable. But by the same token the existence of the world is not logically demonstrable. The world exists, though it could not exist. Evil may be committed, but one should not do so, and should not, I believe, because of our agreement based upon the rule of reciprocity: be to me as I am to thee. It has naught to do with the existence or the nonexistence of God. Were I to refrain from committing evil in the expectation that "there" I would be punished for committing it, or were I to perform good, counting upon a reward "there," I would be predicating my behavior on uncertain ground. Here, however, there can be no ground more certain than our mutual agreement in this matter.

If there be, "there," other grounds, I do not have knowledge of them as exact as the knowledge I have, here, of ours. Living, we play the game of life, and in it we are allies, every one. Therewith, the game between us is perfectly symmetrical. In postulating God, we postulate a continuation of the game beyond the world. I believe that one should be allowed to postulate this continuation of the game, so long as it does not in any way influence the course of the game here. Otherwise, for the sake of someone who perhaps does not exist we may well be sacrificing that which exists here, and exists for certain.

NAAD remarks that the attitude of ADAN 300 toward God is not clear to him. ADAN has granted, has he not, the possibility of the existence of the Creator: what follows from it?

ADAN: Not a thing. That is, nothing in the province of obligation. I believe that—again for all worlds—the following principle holds: a temporal ethics is always independent of an ethics that is transcendental. This means that an ethics of the here and now can have outside itself no sanction which would substantiate it. And this means that he who does evil is in every case a scoundrel, just as he who does good is in every case righteous. If someone is prepared to serve God, judging the arguments in favor of His existence to be sufficient, he does not thereby acquire *here* any additional merit. It is his business. This principle rests on the assumption that if God is not, then He is not one whit, and if He is, then He is almighty. For, being almighty, He could create not only another world but likewise a logic different from the one that is the foundation of my reasoning. Within such another logic the hypothesis of a temporal ethics could be of necessity dependent upon a transcendental ethics. In that case, if not palpable proofs, then logical proofs would have compelling force and constrain one to accept the hypothesis of God under the threat of sinning against reason.

NAAD says that perhaps God does not wish a situation of such compulsion to believe in Him—a situation that would arise in a creation based on that other logic postulated by ADAN 300. To this the latter replies:

An almighty God must also be all-knowing; absolute power is not something independent of absolute knowledge, because he who can do all but knows not what consequences will attend the bringing into play of his omnipotence is, ipso factor, no longer omnipotent; were God to work miracles now and then, as it is rumored He does, it would put His perfection in a most dubious light, because a miracle is a violation of the autonomy of His own creation, a violent intervention. Yet he who has regulated the product of his creation and knows its behavior from beginning to end has no need to violate that autonomy; if he does nevertheless violate it, remaining all-knowing, this means that he is not in the least correcting his handiwork (a correction can only mean, after all, an initial nonomniscience), but instead is providing—with the miracle—a sign of his existence. Now, this is faulty logic, because the providing of any such sign must produce the impression that the creation is nevertheless improved in its local stumblings. For a logical analysis of the new model yields the following: the creation undergoes corrections that do not proceed from it but come from without (from the transcendental, from God), and therefore miracles ought really to be made the norm; or, in other words, the creation ought to be so corrected and so perfected that miracles are at last no longer needed. For miracles, as ad hoc interventions, cannot be *merely* signs of God's existence: they always, after all, besides revealing their Author, indicate an addressee (being directed to someone *here* in a helpful way). So, then, with respect to logic it must be thus: either the creation is perfect, in which case miracles are unnecessary, or the miracles are necessary, in which case the creation is not perfect. (With miracle or without, one may correct only that which is somehow flawed, for a miracle that meddles with perfection will simply disturb it, more, worsen it.) Therefore, the signaling by miracle of one's own presence amounts to using the worst possible means, logically, of its manifestation.

NAAD asks if God may not actually want there to be a dichotomy between logic and belief in Him: perhaps the act of faith should be precisely a resignation of logic in favor of a total trust.

ADAN: Once we allow the logical reconstruction of something (a being, a theodicy, a theogony, and the like) to have internal self-contradiction, it obviously becomes possible to prove absolutely anything, whatever one pleases. Consider how the matter lies. We are speaking of creating someone and of endowing him with a particular logic, and then demanding that this same logic be offered up in sacrifice to a belief in the Maker of all things. If this model itself is to remain noncontradictory, it calls for the application, in the form of a metalogic, of a totally different type of reasoning from that which is natural to the logic of the one created. If that does not reveal the outright imperfection of the Creator, then it reveals a quality that I would call mathematical inelegance—a *sui generis* unmethodicalness (incoherence) of the creative act.

NAAD persists: Perhaps God acts thus, desiring precisely to remain inscrutable to His creation—i.e., nonreconstructible by the logic with which He has provided it. He demands, in short, the supremacy of faith over logic.

ADAN answers him: I follow you. This is, of course, possible, but even if such were the case, a faith that proves incompatible with logic presents an exceedingly unpleasant dilemma of a moral nature. For then it is necessary at some point in one's reasonings to suspend them and give precedence to an unclear supposition—in other words, to set the supposition above logical certainty. This is to be done in the name of unlimited trust; we enter, here, into a *circulus vitiosus,* because the postulated existence of that in which it behooves one now to place one's trust is the product of a line of reasoning that was, in the first place, *logically correct;* thus arises a logical contradiction, which, for some, takes on a positive value and is called the Mystery of God. Now, from the purely constructional point of view such a solution is shoddy, and from the moral point of view questionable, because Mystery may satisfactorily be founded upon infinity (infiniteness, after all, is a characteristic of our world), but the maintaining and the reinforcing of it through internal paradox is, by any architectural criterion, perfidious. The advocates of theodicy are in general not aware that this is so, because to certain parts of their theodicy they continue to apply ordinary logic and to other parts, not. What I wish to say is this, that if one believes in contradiction,* one should then believe *only* in contradiction, and not at the same time still in some noncontradiction (i.e., in logic) in some other area. If, however, such a curious dualism is insisted upon (that the temporal is always subject to logic, the transcendental only fragmentarily), then one thereupon obtains a model of Creation as something that is, with regard to logical correctness, "patched," and it is no longer possible for one to postulate its perfection. One comes inescapably to the conclusion that perfection is a thing that must be logically patched.

EDNA asks whether the conjunction of these incoherencies might not be love.

ADAN: And even were this to be so, it can be not any form of love but only one such as is blinding. God, if He is, if He created the world, has permitted it to govern itself as it can and wishes. For the fact that God exists, no gratitude to Him is required; such gratitude assumes the prior determination that God is able not to exist, and that this would be bad —a premise that leads to yet another kind of contradiction. And what of gratitude for the act of creation? This is not due God, either. For it assumes a compulsion to believe that to be is definitely better than not to be; I cannot conceive how that, in turn, could be proven. To one who does not exist surely it is not possible to do either a service or an injury; and if the Creating One, in His omniscience, knows beforehand that the one created will be grateful to Him and love Him or that he will be ungrateful and deny Him, He thereby produces a constraint, albeit one not accessible to the direct comprehension of the one created. For this very reason nothing is due God: neither love nor hate, nor gratitude, nor

Credo quia absurdum est (Prof. Dobb's note in the text).

rebuke, nor the hope of reward, nor the fear of retribution. Nothing is due Him. A God who craves such feelings must first assure his feeling subject that He exists beyond all question. Love may be forced to rely on speculations as to the reciprocity it inspires; that is understandable. But a love forced to rely on speculations as to whether or not the beloved exists is nonsense. He who is almighty could have provided certainty. Since He did not provide it, if He exists, He must have deemed it unnecessary. Why unnecessary? One begins to suspect that maybe He is not almighty. A God not almighty would be deserving of feelings akin to pity, and indeed to love as well; but this, I think, none of our theodicies allow. And so we say: We serve ourselves and no one else.

We pass over the further deliberations on the topic of whether the God of the theodicy is more of a liberal or an autocrat; it is difficult to condense arguments that take up such a large part of the book. The discussions and deliberations that Dobb has recorded, sometimes in group colloquia of ADAN 300, NAAD, and other personoids, and sometimes in soliloquies (an experimenter is able to take down even a purely mental sequence by means of appropriate devices hooked into the computer network), constitute practically a third of *Non Serviam*. In the text itself we find no commentary on them. In Dobb's Afterword, however, we find this statement:

"ADAN's reasoning seems incontrovertible, at least insofar as it pertains to me: it was I, after all, who created him. In his theodicy I am the Creator. In point of fact, I produced that world (serial No. 47) with the aid of the ADONAI IX program and created the personoid gemmae with a modification of the program JAHVE VI. These initial entities gave rise to three hundred subsequent generations. In point of fact, I have not communicated to them—in the form of an axiom—either these data or my existence beyond the limits of their world. In point of fact, they arrived at the possibility of my existence only by inference, on the basis of conjecture and hypothesis. In point of fact, when I create intelligent beings, I do not feel myself entitled to demand of them any sort of privileges—love, gratitude, or even services of some kind or other. I can enlarge their world or reduce it, speed up its time or slow it down, alter the mode and means of their perception; I can liquidate them, divide them, multiply them, transform the very ontological foundation of their existence. I am thus omnipotent with respect to them, but, indeed, from this it does not follow that they owe me anything. As far as I am concerned, they are in no way beholden to me. It is true that I do not love them. Love does not enter into it at all, though I suppose some other experimenter might possibly entertain that feeling for his personoids. As I see it, this does not in the least change the situation—not in the least.

Imagine for a moment that I attach to my BIX 310 092 an enormous auxiliary unit, which will be a 'hereafter.' One by one I let pass through the connecting channel and into the unit the 'souls' of my personoids, and there I reward those who believed in me, who rendered homage unto me, who showed me gratitude and trust, while all the others, the 'ungodlies,' to use the personoid vocabulary, I punish—e.g., by annihilation or else by torture. (Of eternal punishment I dare not even think—that much of a monster I am not!) My deed would undoubtedly be regarded as a piece of fantastically shameless egotism, as a low act of irrational vengeance—in sum, as the final villainy in a situation of total dominion over innocents. And these innocents will have against me the irrefutable evidence of *logic,* which is the aegis of their conduct. Everyone has the right, obviously, to draw from the personetic experiments such conclusions as he considers fitting. Dr. Ian Combay once said to me, in a private conversation, that I could, after all, assure the society of personoids of my existence. Now, this I most certainly shall not do. For it would have all the appearance to me of soliciting a sequel—that is, a reaction on their part. But what exactly could they do or say to me, that I would not feel the profound embarrassment, the painful sting of my position as their unfortunate Creator? The bills for the electricity consumed have to be paid quarterly, and the moment is going to come when my university superiors demand the 'wrapping up' of the experiment—that is, the disconnecting of the machine, or, in other words, the end of the world. That moment I intend to put off as long as humanly possible. It is the only thing of which I am capable, but it is not anything I consider praiseworthy. It is, rather, what in common parlance is generally called 'dirty work.' Saying this, I hope that no one will get any ideas. But if he does, well, that is his business."

Reflections

Taken from Lem's collection *A Perfect Vacuum: Perfect Reviews of Nonexistent Books,* "Non Serviam" is not just immensely sophisticated and accurate in its exploitation of themes from computer science, philosophy, and the theory of evolution; it is strikingly close to being a true account of aspects of current work in artificial intelligence. Terry Winograd's famous SHRDLU, for instance, purports to be a robot who moves colored blocks around on a tabletop with a mechanical arm, but, in fact, SHRDLU's world is one that has been entirely made up or simulated *within the computer*— "In effect, the device is in precisely the situation that Descartes dreads; it's a mere computer which dreams that it's a robot."* Lem's description of computer-simulated worlds and the simulated agents within them (worlds made of mathematics, in effect) is as accurate as it is poetic—with one striking falsehood, a close kin to falsehoods we have encountered again and again in these tales. Lem would have it that thanks to the blinding speed of computers, the "biological time" of these simulated worlds can be much faster than our real time—and only slowed down to our pace when we want to probe and examine: ". . . one second of machine time corresponds to one year of human life."

There would indeed be a dramatic difference between the time scale of a large-scale, multidimensional, highly detailed computer simulation of the sort Lem describes and our everyday world's time scale—but it would run in the other direction! Somewhat like Wheeler's electron that composes the whole universe by weaving back and forth, a computer simulation must work by sequentially painting in details, and even at the speed of light quite simple and façadelike simulations (which is all that artificial intelligence has yet attempted to produce) take much longer to run than their real-life inspirations. "Parallel processing"—running, say, a few million channels of simulation at once—is of course the engineering answer to this problem (though no one yet knows how to do this); but once we have worlds simulated by millions of channels of parallel processing, the claim that they are simulated rather than *real* (if artificial) will be far less clear. See "The Seventh Sally" (selection 18) and "A Conversation with Einstein's Brain" (selection 26) for further explorations of these themes.

In any case, Lem portrays with uncanny vividness a "cybernetic universe" with conscious software inhabitants. He has various words for what we have often called "soul." He refers to "cores," "personal nuclei," "personoid gemmae," and at one point he even gives the illusion of spelling it out in more technical detail: "a 'coherent cloud of processes', . . . a functional aggregate with a kind of 'center' that can be delimited fairly precisely." Lem describes human—or rather, personoid —consciousness as an unclosed and unclosable plan for a total reconciliation of the stubborn contradictions of the brain. It arises from, and "soars and flutters" over, an infinite regress of level-conflicts in the brain. It is a "patchwork," "an escape from the snares of Gödelization," "a mirror

---

*Jerry Fodor, "Methodological Solipsism Considered as a Research Strategy in Cognitive Psychology" (see "Further Reading").

whose task it is to reflect other mirrors, which in turn reflect still others, and so on to infinity." Is this poetry, philosophy, or science?

The vision of personoids patiently awaiting a proof of the existence of God by a miracle is quite touching and astonishing. This kind of vision is occasionally discussed by computer wizards in their hideaways late at night when all the world seems to shimmer in mysterious mathematical harmony. At the Stanford AI Lab late one night, Bill Gosper expounded his own vision of a "theogony" (to use Lem's word) strikingly similar to Lem's. Gosper is an expert on the so-called "Game of Life," on which he bases his theogony. "Life" is a kind of two-dimensional "physics," invented by John Horton Conway, which can be easily programmed in a computer and displayed on a screen. In this physics, each intersection on a huge and theoretically infinite Go board—a grid, in other words—has a light that can be either on or off. Not only space is discrete (discontinuous), but time is also. Time goes from instant to instant in little "quantum jumps," the way the minute hand moves on some clocks—sitting still for a minute, then jumping. Between these discrete instants, the computer calculates the new "state of the universe" based on the old one, then displays the new state.

The status at a given instant depends only on the status at the immediately previous instant—nothing further back in time is "remembered" by the laws of Life-physics (this "locality" in time is, incidentally, also true of the fundamental laws of physics in our own universe). The physics of the Game of Life is also local in space (again agreeing with our own physics); that is, in passing from a specific instant to the next, only a cell's own light and those of its nearest neighbors play any role in telling that cell what to do in the new instant. There are eight such neighbors —four adjacent, four diagonal. Each cell, in order to determine what to do in the next moment, counts how many of its eight neighbors' lights are on at the present moment. If the answer is exactly two, then the cell's light stays as it is. If the answer is exactly three, then the cell lights up, regardless of its previous status. Otherwise the cell goes dark. (When a light turns on, it is technically known as a "birth," and when one goes off, it is called a "death"—fitting terms for the Game of Life.) The consequences of this simple law, when it is obeyed simultaneously all over the board, are quite astonishing. Although the Game of Life is now over a decade old, its depths have not yet been fully fathomed.

The locality in time implies that the only way the remote history of the universe could exert any effect on the course of events in the present would be if "memories" were somehow encoded in patterns of lights stretching out over the grid (we have earlier referred to this as a "flattening" of the past into the present). Of course the more detailed the memories, the larger the physical structures would have to be. And yet the locality in space of the laws of physics implies that large physical structures may not survive—they may just disintegrate!

From very early on the question of the survival and coherence of large structures was one of the big questions in Life, and Gosper was among the discoverers of various kinds of fascinating structures that, because of their internal organization, do survive and exhibit interesting behaviors. Some structures (called "glider guns") periodically emit smaller structures ("gliders") that slowly sail off toward infinity. When two gliders collide, or, in general, when large blinking structures collide, sparks can fly!

By watching such flashing patterns on the screen (and by being able to zoom in or out, thus to see events on various size scales), Gosper and others have developed a powerful intuitive understanding of events in the Life universe, accompanied by a colorful vocabulary (flotillas, puffer trains, glider barrages, strafing machines, breeders, eaters, space rakes, antibodies, and so on). Patterns that to a novice have spectacular unpredictability are quite intuitive to these experts. Yet there remain many mysteries in the Game of Life. Are there structures that grow endlessly in complexity, or do all structures achieve a steady state at some point? Are there higher and higher levels of structure that have phenomenological laws of their own—analogues to our own universe's molecules, cells, organisms, and societies? Gosper speculates that on a gigantic board, where perhaps several upward leaps of intuition would be needed to gain a sense for the complex modes of organization, "creatures" with consciousness and free will could well exist, could think about their universe and its physics, could even speculate on whether a God exists who created it all, on how to try to communicate with "Him," on whether such efforts make sense or are worth it, and so on.

Here one runs into the eternal question as to how free will can coexist with a determinate substrate. The answer is partly that free will is in the eye of the willer, not in the eye of the God above. As long as the creature *feels* free, he, she, or it is free. But let us defer, in our discussion of these arcane matters, to God Himself, who in the next selection graciously explains to a befuddled Mortal what free will is *really* all about.

D.C.D.
D.R.H.

20

RAYMOND M. SMULLYAN

Is God a Taoist?

MORTAL: And therefore, O God, I pray thee, if thou hast one ounce of mercy for this thy suffering creature, absolve me of *having* to have free will!

GOD: You reject the greatest gift I have given thee?

MORTAL: How can you call that which was forced on me a gift? I have free will, but not of my own choice. I have never freely chosen to have free will. I have to have free will, whether I like it or not!

GOD: Why would you wish not to have free will?

MORTAL: Because free will means moral responsibility, and moral responsibility is more than I can bear!

GOD: Why do you find moral responsibility so unbearable?

MORTAL: Why? I honestly can't analyze why; all I know is that I do.

GOD: All right, in that case suppose I absolve you from all moral responsibility but leave you still with free will. Will this be satisfactory?

MORTAL (*after a pause*): No, I am afraid not.

GOD: Ah, just as I thought! So moral responsibility is not the only aspect of free will to which you object. What else about free will is bothering you?

MORTAL: With free will I am capable of sinning, and I don't want to sin!

GOD: If you don't want to sin, then why do you?

MORTAL: Good God! I don't know why I sin, I just do! Evil temptations come along, and try as I can, I cannot resist them.

GOD: If it is really true that you cannot resist them, then you are not sinning of your own free will and hence (at least according to me) not sinning at all.

MORTAL: No, no! I keep feeling that if only I tried harder I could avoid sinning. I understand that the will is infinite. If one wholeheartedly wills not to sin, then one won't.

GOD: Well now, you should know. Do you try as hard as you can to avoid sinning or don't you?

MORTAL: I honestly don't know! At the time, I feel I am trying as hard as I can, but in retrospect, I am worried that maybe I didn't!

GOD: So in other words, you don't really know whether or not you have been sinning. So the possibility is open that you haven't been sinning at all!

MORTAL: Of course this possibility is open, but maybe I have been sinning, and this thought is what so frightens me!

GOD: Why does the thought of your sinning frighten you?

MORTAL: I don't know why! For one thing, you do have a reputation for meting out rather gruesome punishments in the afterlife!

GOD: Oh, that's what's bothering you! Why didn't you say so in the first place instead of all this peripheral talk about free will and responsibility? Why didn't you simply request me not to punish you for any of your sins?

MORTAL: I think I am realistic enough to know that you would hardly grant such a request!

GOD: You don't say! *You* have a realistic knowledge of what requests I will grant, eh? Well, I'll tell you what I'm going to do! I will grant you a very, very special dispensation to sin as much as you like, and I give you my divine word of honor that I will never punish you for it in the least. Agreed?

MORTAL *(in great terror):*   No, no, don't do that!

GOD: Why not? Don't you trust my divine word?

MORTAL: Of course I do! But don't you see, I don't want to sin! I have an utter abhorrence of sinning, quite apart from any punishments it may entail.

GOD: In that case, I'll go you one better. I'll remove your abhorrence of sinning. Here is a magic pill! Just swallow it, and you will lose all *abhorrence* of sinning. You will joyfully and merrily sin away, you will have no regrets, no abhorrence and I still promise you will never be punished by me, or yourself, or by any source whatever. You will be blissful for all eternity. So here is the pill!

MORTAL: No, no!

GOD: Are you not being irrational? I am even removing your abhorrence of sin, which is your last obstacle.

MORTAL: I still won't take it!

GOD: Why not?

MORTAL: I believe that the pill will indeed remove my future abhorrence for sin, but my present abhorrence is enough to prevent me from being willing to take it.

GOD: I command you to take it!

MORTAL: I refuse!

GOD: What, you refuse of your own free will?

MORTAL: Yes!

GOD: So it seems that your free will comes in pretty handy, doesn't it?

MORTAL: I don't understand!

GOD: Are you not glad now that you have the free will to refuse such a ghastly offer? How would you like it if I forced you to take this pill, whether you wanted it or not?

MORTAL: No, no! Please don't!

GOD: Of course I won't; I'm just trying to illustrate a point. All right, let me put it this way. Instead of forcing you to take the pill, suppose I grant your original prayer of removing your free will—but with the understanding that the moment you are no longer free, then you *will* take the pill.

MORTAL: Once my will is gone, how could I possibly choose to take the pill?

GOD: I did not say you would choose it; I merely said you would take it. You would act, let us say, according to purely deterministic laws which are such that you would as a matter of fact take it.

MORTAL: I still refuse.

GOD: So you refuse my offer to remove your free will. This is rather different from your original prayer, isn't it?

MORTAL: Now I see what you are up to. Your argument is ingenious, but I'm not sure it is really correct. There are some points we will have to go over again.

GOD: Certainly.

MORTAL: There are two things you said which seem contradictory to me. First you said that one cannot sin unless one does so of one's own free will. But then you said you would give me a pill which would deprive me of my own free will, and then I could sin as much as I liked. But if I no longer had free will, then, according to your first statement, how could I be capable of sinning?

GOD: You are confusing two separate parts of our conversation. I never said the pill would deprive you of your free will, but only that it would remove your abhorrence of sinning.

MORTAL: I'm afraid I'm a bit confused.

GOD: All right, then let us make a fresh start. Suppose I agree to remove your free will, but with the understanding that you will then commit an enormous number of acts which you now regard as sinful. Technically speaking, you will not then be sinning since you will not be doing these acts of your own free will. And these acts will carry no moral responsibility, nor moral culpability, nor any punishment whatsoever. Nevertheless, these acts will all be of the type which you presently regard as sinful; they will all have this quality which you presently feel as abhorrent, but your abhorrence will disappear; so you will not *then* feel abhorrence toward the acts.

MORTAL: No, but I have present abhorrence toward the acts, and this present abhorrence is sufficient to prevent me from accepting your proposal.

GOD: Hm! So let me get this absolutely straight. I take it you no longer wish me to remove your free will.

MORTAL *(reluctantly):*   No, I guess not.

GOD: All right, I agree not to. But I am still not exactly clear as to why you now no longer wish to be rid of your free will. Please tell me again.

MORTAL: Because, as you have told me, without free will I would sin even more than I do now.

GOD: But I have already told you that without free will you cannot sin.

MORTAL: But if I choose now to be rid of free will, then all my subsequent evil actions will be sins, not of the future, but of the present moment in which I choose not to have free will.

GOD: Sounds like you are pretty badly trapped, doesn't it?

MORTAL: Of course I am trapped! You have placed me in a hideous double bind! Now whatever I do is wrong. If I retain free will, I will continue to sin, and if I abandon free will (with your help, of course), I will now be sinning in so doing.

GOD: But by the same token, you place me in a double bind. I am willing to leave you free will or remove it as you choose, but neither alternative satisfies you. I wish to help you, but it seems I cannot.

MORTAL: True!

GOD: But since it is not my fault, why are you still angry with me?

MORTAL: For having placed me in such a horrible predicament in the first place!

GOD: But, according to you, there is nothing satisfactory I could have done.

MORTAL: You mean there is nothing satisfactory you can now do, but that does not mean that there is nothing you could have done.

GOD: Why? What could I have done?

MORTAL: Obviously you should never have given me free will in the first place. Now that you have given it to me, it is too late—anything I do will be bad. But you should never have given it to me in the first place.

GOD: Oh, that's it! Why would it have been better had I never given it to you?

MORTAL: Because then I never would have been capable of sinning at all.

GOD: Well, I'm always glad to learn from my mistakes.

MORTAL: What!

GOD: I know, that sounds sort of self-blasphemous, doesn't it? It almost involves a logical paradox! On the one hand, as you have been taught, it is morally wrong for any sentient being to claim that I am capable of making mistakes. On the other hand, I have the right to do anything. But I am also a sentient being. So the question is, Do I or do I not have the right to claim that I am capable of making mistakes?

MORTAL: That is a bad joke! One of your premises is simply false. I have not been taught that it is wrong for any sentient being to doubt your

omniscience, but only for a mortal to doubt it. But since you are not
, mortal, then you are obviously free from this injunction.

GOD: Good, so you realize this on a rational level. Nevertheless, you did
appear shocked when I said, "I am always glad to learn from my
mistakes."

MORTAL: Of course I was shocked. I was shocked not by your self-
blasphemy (as you jokingly called it), not by the fact that you had no
right to say it, but just by the fact that you did say it, since I have been
taught that as a matter of fact you don't make mistakes. So I was
amazed that you claimed that it is possible for you to make mistakes.

GOD: I have not claimed that it is possible. All I am saying is that *if* I
make mistakes, I will be happy to learn from them. But this says
nothing about whether the *if* has or ever can be realized.

MORTAL: Let's please stop quibbling about this point. Do you or do you
not admit it was a mistake to have given me free will?

GOD: Well now, this is precisely what I propose we should investigate.
Let me review your present predicament. You don't want to have free
will because with free will you can sin, and you don't want to sin.
(Though I still find this puzzling; in a way you must want to sin, or
else you wouldn't. But let this pass for now.) On the other hand, if
you agreed to give up free will, then you would now be responsible
for the acts of the future. Ergo, I should never have given you free
will in the first place.

MORTAL: Exactly!

GOD: I understand exactly how you feel. Many mortals—even some
theologians—have complained that I have been unfair in that it was
I, not they, who decided that they should have free will, and then I
hold *them* responsible for their actions. In other words, they feel that
they are expected to live up to a contract with me which they never
agreed to in the first place.

MORTAL: Exactly!

GOD: As I said, I understand the feeling perfectly. And I can appreciate
the justice of the complaint. But the complaint arises only from an
unrealistic understanding of the true issues involved. I am about to
enlighten you as to what these are, and I think the results will surprise you! But instead of telling you outright, I shall continue to use
the Socratic method.

To repeat, you regret that I ever gave you free will. I claim that
when you see the true ramifications you will no longer have this

regret. To prove my point, I'll tell you what I'm going to do. I am about to create a new universe—a new space-time continuum. In this new universe will be born a mortal just like you—for all practical purposes, we might say that you will be reborn. Now, I can give this new mortal—this new you—free will or not. What would you like me to do?

MORTAL (*in great relief*):   Oh, please! Spare him from having to have free will!

GOD: All right, I'll do as you say. But you do realize that this new *you* without free will, will commit all sorts of horrible acts.

MORTAL: But they will not be sins since he will have no free will.

GOD: Whether you call them sins or not, the fact remains that they will be horrible acts in the sense that they will cause great pain to many sentient beings.

MORTAL (*after a pause*):   Good God, you have trapped me again! Always the same game! If I now give you the go-ahead to create this new creature with no free will who will nevertheless commit atrocious acts, then true enough he will not be sinning, but I again will be the sinner to sanction this.

GOD: In that case, I'll go you one better! Here, I have already decided whether to create this new *you* with free will or not. Now, I am writing my decision on this piece of paper and I won't show it to you until later. But my decision is now made and is absolutely irrevocable. There is nothing you can possibly do to alter it; you have no responsibility in the matter. Now, what I wish to know is this: Which way do you hope I have decided? Remember now, the responsibility for the decision falls entirely on my shoulders, not yours. So you can tell me perfectly honestly and without any fear, which way do you hope I have decided?

MORTAL (*after a very long pause*):   I hope you have decided to give him free will.

GOD: Most interesting! I have removed your last obstacle! If I do not give him free will, then no sin is to be imputed to anybody. So why do you hope I will give him free will?

MORTAL: Because sin or no sin, the important point is that if you do not give him free will, then (at least according to what you have said) he will go around hurting people, and I don't want to see people hurt.

GOD (*with an infinite sigh of relief*):   At last! At last you see the real point!

MORTAL: What point is that?

GOD: That sinning is not the real issue! The important thing is that people as well as other sentient beings don't get hurt!

MORTAL: You sound like a utilitarian!

GOD: I am a utilitarian!

MORTAL: What!

GOD: Whats or no whats, I am a utilitarian. Not a unitarian, mind you, but a utilitarian.

MORTAL: I just can't believe it!

GOD: Yes, I know, your religious training has taught you otherwise. You have probably thought of me more like a Kantian than a utilitarian, but your training was simply wrong.

MORTAL: You leave me speechless!

GOD: I leave you speechless, do I! Well, that is perhaps not too bad a thing—you have a tendency to speak too much as it is. Seriously, though, why do you think I ever did give you free will in the first place?

MORTAL: Why did you? I never have thought much about why you did; all I have been arguing for is that you shouldn't have! But why did you? I guess all I can think of is the standard religious explanation: Without free will, one is not capable of meriting either salvation or damnation. So without free will, we could not earn the right to eternal life.

GOD: Most interesting! *I* have eternal life; do you think I have ever done anything to merit it?

MORTAL: Of course not! With you it is different. You are already so good and perfect (at least allegedly) that it is not necessary for you to merit eternal life.

GOD: Really now? That puts me in a rather enviable position, doesn't it?

MORTAL: I don't think I understand you.

GOD: Here I am eternally blissful without ever having to suffer or make sacrifices or struggle against evil temptations or anything like that. Without any of that type of "merit," I enjoy blissful eternal existence. By contrast, you poor mortals have to sweat and suffer and have all sorts of horrible conflicts about morality, and all for what? You don't even know whether I really exist or not, or if there really is any afterlife, or if there is, where you come into the picture. No matter how much you try to placate me by being "good," you never have any real assurance that your "best" is good enough for me, and hence you have no real security in obtaining salvation. Just think of it! I already *have* the equivalent of "salvation"—and have never had to go through this infinitely lugubrious process of earning it. Don't you ever envy me for this?

MORTAL: But it is blasphemous to envy you!

GOD: Oh come off it! You're not now talking to your Sunday school teacher, you are talking to *me*. Blasphemous or not, the important question is not whether you have the right to be envious of me but whether you are. Are you?

MORTAL: Of course I am!

GOD: Good! Under your present world view, you sure should be most envious of me. But I think with a more realistic world view, you no longer will be. So you really have swallowed the idea which has been taught you that your life on earth is like an examination period and that the purpose of providing you with free will is to test you, to see if you merit blissful eternal life. But what puzzles me is this: If you really believe I am as good and benevolent as I am cracked up to be, why should I require people to merit things like happiness and eternal life? Why should I not grant such things to everyone regardless of whether or not he deserves them?

MORTAL: But I have been taught that your sense of morality—your sense of justice—demands that goodness be rewarded with happiness and evil be punished with pain.

GOD: Then you have been taught wrong.

MORTAL: But the religious literature is so full of this idea! Take for example Jonathan Edwards's "Sinners in the Hands of an Angry God." How he describes you as holding your enemies like loathsome scorpions over the flaming pit of hell, preventing them from falling into the fate that they deserve only by dint of your mercy.

GOD: Fortunately, I have not been exposed to the tirades of Mr. Jonathan Edwards. Few sermons have ever been preached which are more misleading. The very title "Sinners in the Hands of an Angry God" tells its own tale. In the first place, I am never angry. In the second place, I do not think at all in terms of "sin." In the third place, I have no enemies.

MORTAL: By that do you mean that there are no people whom you hate, or that there are no people who hate you?

GOD: I meant the former although the latter also happens to be true.

MORTAL: Oh come now, I know people who have openly claimed to have hated you. At times *I* have hated you!

GOD: You mean you have hated your image of me. That is not the same thing as hating me as I really am.

MORTAL: Are you trying to say that it is not wrong to hate a false conception of you, but that it is wrong to hate you as you really are?

GOD: No, I am not saying that at all; I am saying something far more drastic! What I am saying has absolutely nothing to do with right or wrong. What I am saying is that one who knows me for what I really am would simply find it psychologically impossible to hate me.

MORTAL: Tell me, since we mortals seem to have such erroneous views about your real nature, why don't you enlighten us? Why don't you guide us the right way?

GOD: What makes you think I'm not?

MORTAL: I mean, why don't you appear to our very senses and simply tell us that we are wrong?

GOD: Are you really so naive as to believe that I am the sort of being which can *appear* to your senses? It would be more correct to say that I *am* your senses.

MORTAL *(astonished):*   You are my senses?

GOD: Not quite, I am more than that. But it comes closer to the truth than the idea that I am perceivable by the senses. I am not an object; like you, I am a subject, and a subject can perceive, but cannot be perceived. You can no more see me than you can see your own thoughts. You can see an apple, but the event of your seeing an apple is itself not seeable. And I am far more like the seeing of an apple than the apple itself.

MORTAL: If I can't see you, how do I know you exist?

GOD: Good question! How in fact do you know I exist?

MORTAL: Well, I am talking to you, am I not?

GOD: How do you know you are talking to me? Suppose you told a psychiatrist, "Yesterday I talked to God." What do you think he would say?

MORTAL: That might depend on the psychiatrist. Since most of them are atheistic, I guess most would tell me I had simply been talking to myself.

GOD: And they would be right!

MORTAL: What? You mean you don't exist?

GOD: You have the strangest faculty of drawing false conclusions! Just because you are talking to yourself, it follows that *I* don't exist?

MORTAL: Well, if I think I am talking to you, but I am really talking to myself, in what sense do you exist?

GOD: Your question is based on two fallacies plus a confusion. The question of whether or not you are now talking to me and the question of whether or not I exist are totally separate. Even if you were not now talking to me (which obviously you are), it still would not mean that I don't exist.

MORTAL: Well, all right, of course! So instead of saying "if I am talking to myself, then you don't exist," I should rather have said, "if I am talking to myself, then I obviously am not talking to you."

GOD: A very different statement indeed, but still false.

MORTAL: Oh, come now, if I am only talking to myself, then how can I be talking to you?

GOD: Your use of the word "only" is quite misleading! I can suggest several logical possibilities under which your talking to yourself does not imply that you are not talking to me.

MORTAL: Suggest just one!

GOD: Well, obviously one such possibility is that you and I are identical.

MORTAL: Such a blasphemous thought—at least had *I* uttered it!

GOD: According to some religions, yes. According to others, it is the plain, simple, immediately perceived truth.

MORTAL: So the only way out of my dilemma is to believe that you and I are identical?

GOD: Not at all! This is only one way out. There are several others. For example, it may be that you are part of me, in which case you may be talking to that part of me which is you. Or I may be part of you, in which case you may be talking to that part of you which is me. Or again, you and I might partially overlap, in which case you may be talking to the intersection and hence talking both to you and to me. The only way your talking to yourself might seem to imply that you are not talking to me is if you and I were totally disjoint—and even then, you could conceivably be talking to both of us.

MORTAL: So you claim you do exist.

GOD: Not at all. Again you draw false conclusions! The question of my existence has not even come up. All I have said is that from the fact that you are talking to yourself one cannot possibly infer my nonexistence, let alone the weaker fact that you are not talking to me.

MORTAL: All right, I'll grant your point! But what I really want to know is *do* you exist?

GOD: What a strange question!

MORTAL: Why? Men have been asking it for countless millennia.

GOD: I know that! The question itself is not strange; what I mean is that it is a most strange question to ask of *me!*

MORTAL: Why?

GOD: Because I am the very one whose existence you doubt! I perfectly well understand your anxiety. You are worried that your present experience with me is a mere hallucination. But how can you possibly expect to obtain reliable information from a being about his very existence when you suspect the nonexistence of the very same being?

MORTAL: So you won't tell me whether or not you exist?

GOD: I am not being willful! I merely wish to point out that no answer I could give could possibly satisfy you. All right, suppose I said, "No, I don't exist." What would that prove? Absolutely nothing! Or if I said, "Yes, I exist." Would that convince you? Of course not!

MORTAL: Well, if you can't tell me whether or not you exist, then who possibly can?

GOD: That is something which no one can tell you. It is something which only you can find out for yourself.

MORTAL: How do I go about finding this out for myself?

GOD: That also no one can tell you. This is another thing you will have to find out for yourself.

MORTAL: So there is no way you can help me?

GOD: I didn't say that. I said there is no way I can tell you. But that doesn't mean there is no way I can help you.

MORTAL: In what manner then can you help me?

GOD: I suggest you leave that to me! We have gotten sidetracked as it is, and I would like to return to the question of what you believed my purpose to be in giving you free will. Your first idea of my giving you free will in order to test whether you merit salvation or not may appeal to many moralists, but the idea is quite hideous to me. You cannot think of any nicer reason—any more humane reason—why I gave you free will?

MORTAL: Well now, I once asked this question of an Orthodox rabbi. He told me that the way we are constituted, it is simply not possible for us to enjoy salvation unless we feel we have earned it. And to earn it, we of course need free will.

GOD: That explanation is indeed much nicer than your former but still is far from correct. According to Orthodox Judaism, I created angels, and they have no free will. They are in actual sight of me and are so completely attracted by goodness that they never have even the slightest temptation toward evil. They really have no choice in the matter. Yet they are eternally happy even though they have never earned it. So if your rabbi's explanation were correct, why wouldn't I have simply created only angels rather than mortals?

MORTAL: Beats me! Why didn't you?

GOD: Because the explanation is simply not correct. In the first place, I have never created any ready-made angels. All sentient beings ultimately approach the state which might be called "angelhood." But just as the race of human beings is in a certain stage of biologic evolution, so angels are simply the end result of a process of Cosmic Evolution. The only difference between the so-called *saint* and the so called *sinner* is that the former is vastly older than the latter. Unfortunately it takes countless life cycles to learn what is perhaps the most important fact of the universe—evil is simply painful. All the arguments of the moralists—all the alleged reasons why people *shouldn't* commit evil acts—simply pale into insignificance in light of the one basic truth that *evil is suffering.*

No, my dear friend, I am not a moralist. I am wholly a utilitarian. That I should have been conceived in the role of a moralist is one of the great tragedies of the human race. My role in the scheme of things (if one can use this misleading expression) is neither to punish nor reward, but to aid the process by which all sentient beings achieve ultimate perfection.

MORTAL: Why did you say your expression is misleading?

GOD: What I said was misleading in two respects. First of all it is inaccurate to speak of my role in the scheme of things. I *am* the scheme of things. Secondly, it is equally misleading to speak of my aiding the process of sentient beings attaining enlightenment. I *am* the process. The ancient Taoists were quite close when they said of me (whom they called "Tao") that I do not *do* things, yet through me all things get done. In more modern terms, I am not the cause of Cosmic Process, I am Cosmic Process itself. I think the most accurate and fruitful definition of me which man can frame—at least in his present state of evolution—is that I am the very process of enlightenment. Those who wish to think of the devil (although I wish they wouldn't!) might analogously define him as the unfortunate length of time the process takes. In this sense, the devil is necessary; the process simply does take an enormous length of time, and there is absolutely nothing I can do about it. But, I assure you, once the process is more correctly understood, the painful length of time will no longer be regarded as an essential limitation or an evil. It will be seen to be the very essence of the process itself. I know this is not completely consoling to you who are now in the finite sea of suffering, but the amazing thing is that once you grasp this fundamental attitude, your very finite suffering will begin to diminish—ultimately to the vanishing point.

MORTAL: I have been told this, and I tend to believe it. But suppose I personally succeed in seeing things through your eternal eyes. Then I will be happier, but don't I have a duty to others?

GOD (*laughing*):   You remind me of the Mahayana Buddhists! Each one says, "I will not enter Nirvana until I first see that all other sentient beings do so." So each one waits for the other fellow to go first. No wonder it takes them so long! The Hinayana Buddhist errs in a different direction. He believes that no one can be of the slightest help to others in obtaining salvation; each one has to do it entirely by himself. And so each tries only for his own salvation. But this very detached attitude makes salvation impossible. The truth of the matter is that salvation is partly an individual and partly a social process. But it is a grave mistake to believe—as do many Mahayana Buddhists —that the attaining of enlightenment puts one out of commission, so to speak, for helping others. The best way of helping others is by first seeing the light oneself.

MORTAL: There is one thing about your self-description which is somewhat disturbing. You describe yourself essentially as a *process*. This puts you in such an impersonal light, and so many people have a need for a personal God.

GOD: So because they need a personal God, it follows that I am one?

MORTAL: Of course not. But to be acceptable to a mortal a religion must satisfy his needs.

GOD: I realize that. But the so-called "personality" of a being is really more in the eyes of the beholder than in the being itself. The controversies which have raged about whether I am a personal or an impersonal being are rather silly because neither side is right or wrong. From one point of view, I am personal, from another, I am not. It is the same with a human being. A creature from another planet may look at him purely impersonally as a mere collection of atomic particles behaving according to strictly prescribed physical laws. He may have no more feeling for the personality of a human than the average human has for an ant. Yet an ant has just as much individual personality as a human to beings like myself who really know the ant. To look at something impersonally is no more correct or incorrect than to look at it personally, but in general, the better you get to know something, the more personal it becomes. To illustrate my point, do you think of me as a personal or impersonal being?

MORTAL: Well, I'm talking to you, am I not?

GOD: Exactly! From that point of view, your attitude toward me might be described as a personal one. And yet, from another point of view —no less valid—I can also be looked at impersonally.

MORTAL: But if you are really such an abstract thing as a process, I don't see what sense it can make my talking to a mere "process."

GOD: I love the way you say "mere." You might just as well say that you are living in a "mere universe." Also, why must everything one does make sense? Does it make sense to talk to a tree?

MORTAL: Of course not!

GOD: And yet, many children and primitives do just that.

MORTAL: But I am neither a child nor a primitive.

GOD: I realize that, unfortunately.

MORTAL: Why unfortunately?

GOD: Because many children and primitives have a primal intuition which the likes of you have lost. Frankly, I think it would do you a lot of good to talk to a tree once in a while, even more good than talking to me! But we seem always to be getting sidetracked! For the last time, I would like us to try to come to an understanding about why I gave you free will.

MORTAL: I have been thinking about this all the while.

GOD: You mean you haven't been paying attention to our conversation?

MORTAL: Of course I have. But all the while, on another level, I have been thinking about it.

GOD: And have you come to any conclusion?

MORTAL: Well, you say the reason is not to test our worthiness. And you disclaimed the reason that we need to feel that we must merit things in order to enjoy them. And you claim to be a utilitarian. Most significant of all, you appeared so delighted when I came to the sudden realization that it is not sinning in itself which is bad but only the suffering which it causes.

GOD: Well of course! What else could conceivably be bad about sinning?

MORTAL: All right, you know that, and now I know that. But all my life I unfortunately have been under the influence of those moralists who hold sinning to be bad in itself. Anyway, putting all these pieces together, it occurs to me that the only reason you gave free will is because of your belief that with free will, people will tend to hurt each other—and themselves—less than without free will.

GOD: Bravo! That is by far the best reason you have yet given! I can assure you that had I *chosen* to give free will, that would have been my very reason for so choosing.

MORTAL: What! You mean to say you did not choose to give us free will?

GOD: My dear fellow, I could no more choose to give you free will than I could choose to make an equilateral triangle equiangular. I could choose to make or not to make an equilateral triangle in the first place, but having chosen to make one, I would then have no choice but to make it equiangular.

MORTAL: I thought you could do anything!

GOD: Only things which are logically possible. As St. Thomas said, "It is a sin to regard the fact that God cannot do the impossible, as a limitation on His powers." I agree, except that in place of his using the word *sin* I would use the term *error*.

MORTAL: Anyhow, I am still puzzled by your implication that you did not choose to give me free will.

GOD: Well, it is high time I inform you that the entire discussion—from the very beginning—has been based on one monstrous fallacy! We have been talking purely on a moral level—you originally complained that I gave you free will, and raised the whole question as to whether I should have. It never once occurred to you that I had absolutely no choice in the matter.

MORTAL: I am still in the dark!

GOD: Absolutely! Because you are only able to look at it through the eyes of a moralist. The more fundamental *metaphysical* aspects of the question you never even considered.

MORTAL: I still do not see what you are driving at.

GOD: Before you requested me to remove your free will, shouldn't your first question have been whether as a matter of fact you *do* have free will?

MORTAL: That I simply took for granted.

GOD: But why should you?

MORTAL: I don't know. Do I have free will?

GOD: Yes.

MORTAL: Then why did you say I shouldn't have taken it for granted?

GOD: Because you shouldn't. Just because something happens to be true, it does not follow that it should be taken for granted.

MORTAL: Anyway, it is reassuring to know that my natural intuition about having free will is correct. Sometimes I have been worried that determinists are correct.

GOD: They are correct.

MORTAL: Wait a minute now, do I have free will or don't I?

GOD: I already told you you do. But that does not mean that determinism is incorrect.

MORTAL: Well, are my acts determined by the laws of nature or aren't they?

GOD: The word *determined* here is subtly but powerfully misleading and has contributed so much to the confusions of the free will versus determinism controversies. Your acts are certainly in accordance with the laws of nature, but to say they are *determined* by the laws of nature creates a totally misleading psychological image which is that your will could somehow be in conflict with the laws of nature and that the latter is somehow more powerful than you, and could "determine" your acts whether you liked it or not. But it is simply impossible for your will to ever conflict with natural law. You and natural law are really one and the same.

MORTAL: What do you mean that I cannot conflict with nature? Suppose I were to become very stubborn, and I *determined* not to obey the laws of nature. What could stop me? If I became sufficiently stubborn, even you could not stop me!

GOD: You are absolutely right! *I* certainly could not stop you. Nothing could stop you. But there is no need to stop you, because you could not even start! As Goethe very beautifully expressed it, "In trying to oppose Nature, we are, in the very process of doing so, acting according to the laws of nature!" Don't you see that the so-called "laws of nature" are nothing more than a description of how in fact you and other beings *do* act? They are merely a description of how you act, not a prescription of of how you should act, not a power or force which compels or determines your acts. To be valid a law of nature must take into account how in fact you do act, or, if you like, how you choose to act.

MORTAL: So you really claim that I am incapable of determining to act against natural law?

GOD: It is interesting that you have twice now used the phrase "determined to act" instead of "chosen to act." This identification is quite common. Often one uses the statement "I am determined to do this" synonomously with "I have chosen to do this." This very psychological identification should reveal that determinism and choice are much closer than they might appear. Of course, you might well say that the doctrine of free will says that it is *you* who are doing the determining, whereas the doctrine of determinism appears to say that your acts are determined by something apparently outside you. But the confusion is largely caused by your bifurcation of reality into the "you" and the "not you." Really now, just where do you leave off and the rest of the universe begin? Or where does the rest of the universe leave off and you begin? Once you can see the so-called "you" and the so-called "nature" as a continuous whole, then you can never again be bothered by such questions as whether it is you who are controlling nature or nature who is controlling you. Thus the muddle of free will versus determinism will vanish. If I may use a crude analogy, imagine two bodies moving toward each other by virtue of gravitational attraction. Each body, if sentient, might wonder whether it is he or the other fellow who is exerting the "force." In a way it is both, in a way it is neither. It is best to say that it is the configuration of the two which is crucial.

MORTAL: You said a short while ago that our whole discussion was based on a monstrous fallacy. You still have not told me what this fallacy is.

GOD: Why, the idea that I could possibly have created you without free will! You acted as if this were a genuine possibility, and wondered why I did not choose it! It never occurred to you that a sentient being without free will is no more conceivable than a physical object which exerts no gravitational attraction. (There is, incidentally, more analogy than you realize between a physical object exerting gravitational attraction and a sentient being exerting free will!) Can you honestly even imagine a conscious being without free will? What on earth could it be like? I think that one thing in your life that has so misled you is your having been told that I gave man the *gift* of free will. As if I first created man, and then as an afterthought endowed him with the extra property of free will. Maybe you think I have some sort of "paint brush" with which I daub some creatures with free will and not others. No, free will is not an "extra"; it is part and parcel of the very essence of consciousness. A conscious being without free will is simply a metaphysical absurdity.

MORTAL: Then why did you play along with me all this while discussing what I thought was a moral problem, when, as you say, my basic confusion was metaphysical?

GOD: Because I thought it would be good therapy for you to get some of this moral poison out of your system. Much of your metaphysical confusion was due to faulty moral notions, and so the latter had to be dealt with first.

And now we must part—at least until you need me again. I think our present union will do much to sustain you for a long while. But do remember what I told you about trees. Of course, you don't have to literally talk to them if doing so makes you feel silly. But there is so much you can learn from them, as well as from the rocks and streams and other aspects of nature. There is nothing like a naturalistic orientation to dispel all these morbid thoughts of "sin" and "free will" and "moral responsibility." At one stage of history, such notions were actually useful. I refer to the days when tyrants had unlimited power and nothing short of fears of hell could possibly restrain them. But mankind has grown up since then, and this gruesome way of thinking is no longer necessary.

It might be helpful to you to recall what I once said through the writings of the great Zen poet Seng-Ts'an:

> If you want to get the plain truth,
> Be not concerned with right and wrong.
> The conflict between right and wrong
> Is the sickness of the mind.

I can see by your expression that you are simultaneously soothed and terrified by these words! What are you afraid of? That if in your mind you abolish the distinction between right and wrong you are more likely to commit acts which are wrong? What makes you so sure that self-consciousness about right and wrong does not in fact lead to more wrong acts than right ones? Do you honestly believe that so-called amoral people, when it comes to action rather than theory, behave less ethically than moralists? Of course not! Even most moralists acknowledge the ethical superiority of the behavior of most of those who theoretically take an amoral position. They seem so surprised that without ethical *principles* these people behave so nicely! It never seems to occur to them that it is by virtue of the very lack of moral principles that their good behavior flows so freely! Do the words "The conflict between right and wrong is the sickness of the human mind" express an idea so different from the story of the Garden of Eden and the fall of Man due to Adam's eating of the fruit of knowledge? This knowledge, mind you, was of ethical principles, not ethical feelings—these Adam already had. There is much truth in this story, though I never commanded Adam not to eat the apple, I merely advised him not to. I told him it would not be good for him. If the damn fool had only listened to me, so much trouble could have been avoided! But no, he thought he knew everything! But I wish the theologians would finally learn that I am not punishing Adam and his descendants for the act, but rather that the fruit in question is poisonous in its own right and its effects, unfortunately, last countless generations.

And now really I must take leave. I do hope that our discussion will dispel some of your ethical morbidity and replace it by a more naturalistic orientation. Remember also the marvelous words I once uttered through the mouth of Lao-tse when I chided Confucius for his moralizing:

All this talk of goodness and duty, these perpetual pin-pricks unnerve and irritate the hearer—You had best study how it is that Heaven and Earth maintain their eternal course, that the sun and moon maintain their light, the stars their seried ranks, the birds and beasts their flocks, the trees and shrubs their station. This you too should learn to guide your steps by Inward Power, to follow the course that the Way of Nature sets; and soon you will no longer need to go round laboriously advertising goodness and duty. . . . The swan does not need a daily bath in order to remain white.

MORTAL: You certainly seem partial to Eastern philosophy!

GOD: Oh, not at all! Some of my finest thoughts have bloomed in your native American soil. For example, I never expressed my notion of "duty" more eloquently than through the thoughts of Walt Whitman:

> I give nothing as duties,
> What others give as duties, I give as living impulses.

Reflections

This witty and sparkling dialogue introduces Raymond Smullyan, a colorful logician and magician who also happens to be a sort of Taoist, in his own personal way. Smullyan has two further selections to come, equally insightful and delightful. The dialogue you have just read was taken from *The Tao is Silent,* a collection of writings illustrating what happens when Western logician meets Eastern thought. The result is both scrutable and inscrutable (as one might expect).

There are undoubtedly many religious people who would consider this dialogue to be the utmost in blasphemy, just as some religious people think it is blasphemy for someone to walk around in a church with his hands in his pockets. We think, on the other hand, that this dialogue is *pious*—a powerful religious statement about God, free will, and the laws of nature, blasphemous only on the most superficial reading. Along the way, Smullyan gets in (through God) many sideswipes at shallow or fuzzy thinking, preconceived categories, pat answers, pompous theories, and moralistic rigidities. Actually we should—according to God's claim in the dialogue—attribute its message not to Smullyan, but to God. It is God, speaking through the character of Smullyan, in turn speaking through the character of God, whose message is being given to us.

Just as God (or the Tao, or the universe, if you prefer) has many parts all with their own free will—you and I being examples—so each one of us has such inner parts with *their* own free will (although these parts are less free than we are). This is particularly clear in the Mortal's own internal conflict over whether "he" does or does not want to sin. There are "inner people"—homunculi, or subsystems—who are fighting for control.

Inner conflict is one of the most familiar and yet least understood parts of human nature. A famous slogan for a brand of potato chips used to go, "Betcha can't eat just one!"—a pithy way of reminding us of our internal splits. You start trying to solve a captivating puzzle (the notorious "Magic Cube," for instance) and it just takes over. You cannot put it down. You start to play a piece of music or read a good book, and you cannot stop even when you know you have many other pressing duties to take care of.

Who is in control here? Is there some overall being who can dictate what will happen? Or is there just anarchy, with neurons firing helter-skelter, and come what may? The truth must lie somehow in between. Certainly in a brain the activity is precisely the firing of neurons, just as in a country, the activity is precisely the sum total of the actions of its inhabitants. But the structure of government—itself a set of activities of people—imposes a powerful kind of top-down control on the organization of the whole. When government becomes excessively authoritarian and when enough of the people become truly dissatisfied, then there is the possibility that the overall structure may be attacked and collapse— internal revolution. But most of the time opposing internal forces reach various sorts of compromises, sometimes by finding the happy medium between two alternatives, sometimes by taking turns at control, and so on. The ways in which such compromises can be reached are themselves strong characterizers of the type of government. The same goes for people. The style of resolution of inner conflicts is one of the strongest features of personality.

It is a common myth that each person is a unity, a kind of unitary organization with a will of its own. Quite the contrary, a person is an amalgamation of many subpersons, all with *wills of their own.* The "subpeople" are considerably less complex than the overall person, and consequently they have much less of a problem with internal discipline. If they are themselves split, probably *their* component parts are so simple that *they* are of a single mind—and if not, you can continue down the line. This hierarchical organization of personality is something that does not much please our sense of dignity, but there is much evidence for it.

In the dialogue, Smullyan comes up with a wonderful definition of the Devil: the unfortunate length of time it takes for sentient beings as a whole to come to be enlightened. This idea of the necessary time it takes for a complex state to come about has been explored mathematically in a provocative way by Charles Bennett and Gregory Chaitin. They theorize that it may be possible to prove, by arguments similar to those underlying Gödel's Incompleteness Theorem, that there is no shortcut to the development of higher and higher intelligences (or, if you prefer, more and more "enlightened" states); in short, that "the Devil" must get his due.

Toward the end of this dialogue, Smullyan gets at issues we have been dealing with throughout this book—the attempt to reconcile the determinism and "upward causality" of the laws of nature with the free will and "downward causality" that we all feel ourselves exerting. His astute observation that we often say "I am determined to do this" when we mean "I have chosen to do this" leads him to his account of free will, beginning with God's statement that "Determinism and choice are much closer than they might appear." Smullyan's elegantly worked-out reconciliation of these opposing views depends on our willingness to switch points of view—to cease thinking "dualistically" (i.e., breaking the world into parts such as "myself" and "not myself"), and to see the entire universe as boundaryless, with things flowing into each other, overlapping, with no clearly defined categories or edges.

This seems an odd point of view for a logician to be espousing, at first—but then, who says logicians are always uptight and rigid? Why should not logicians, more than anyone, realize the places where hard-edged, clean logic will necessarily run into trouble in dealing with this chaotic and messy universe? One of Marvin Minsky's favorite claims is "Logic doesn't apply to the real world." There is a sense in which this is true. This is one of the difficulties that artificial intelligence workers are facing. They are coming to realize that no intelligence can be based on reasoning alone; or rather, that isolated reasoning is impossible, because reasoning depends on a prior setting-up of a system of concepts, percepts, classes, categories—call them what you will—in terms of which all situations are understood. It is there that biases and selection enter the picture. Not only must the reasoning faculty be willing to accept the first characterizations of a situation that the perceiving faculty hands up to it, but then if it has doubts about those views, the perceiving faculty must in turn be willing to accept those doubts and to go back and reinterpret the situation, creating a continual loop between levels. Such interplay between perceiving and reasoning subselves brings into being a total self —a Mortal.

D.R.H.

21

JORGE LUIS BORGES

The Circular Ruins

> And if he left off dreaming about you . . .
> —*Through the Looking Glass,* VI

No one saw him disembark in the unanimous night, no one saw the bamboo canoe sinking into the sacred mud, but within a few days no one was unaware that the silent man came from the South and that his home was one of the infinite villages upstream, on the violent mountainside, where the Zend tongue is not contaminated with Greek and where leprosy is infrequent. The truth is that the obscure man kissed the mud, came up the bank without pushing aside (probably without feeling) the brambles which dilacerated his flesh, and dragged himself, nauseous and bloodstained, to the circular enclosure crowned by a stone tiger or horse, which once was the color of fire and now was that of ashes. This circle was a temple, long ago devoured by fire, which the malarial jungle had profaned and whose god no longer received the homage of men. The stranger stretched out beneath the pedestal. He was awakened by the sun high above. He evidenced without astonishment that his wounds had closed; he shut his pale eyes and slept, not out of bodily weakness but out of determination of will. He knew that this temple was the place required by his invincible purpose; he knew that, downstream, the incessant trees had not managed to choke the ruins of another propitious temple, whose gods were also burned and dead; he knew that his immediate obligation was to sleep. Towards midnight he was awakened by the disconsolate cry of a bird. Prints of bare feet, some figs and a jug told him that men of the region had respectfully spied upon his sleep and were solicitous of his favor or feared his magic. He felt the chill of fear and sought out a burial niche in the dilapidated wall and covered himself with some unknown leaves.

The purpose which guided him was not impossible, though it was supernatural. He wanted to dream a man: he wanted to dream him with minute integrity and insert him into reality. This magical project had exhausted the entire content of his soul; if someone had asked him his own name or any trait of his previous life, he would not have been able to answer. The uninhabited and broken temple suited him, for it was a minimum of visible world; the nearness of the peasants also suited him, for they would see that his frugal necessities were supplied. The rice and fruit of their tribute were sufficient sustenance for his body, consecrated to the sole task of sleeping and dreaming.

At first, his dreams were chaotic; somewhat later, they were of a dialectical nature. The stranger dreamt that he was in the center of a circular amphitheater which in some way was the burned temple: clouds of silent students filled the gradins; the faces of the last ones hung many centuries away and at a cosmic height, but were entirely clear and precise. The man was lecturing to them on anatomy, cosmography, magic; the countenances listened with eagerness and strove to respond with understanding, as if they divined the importance of the examination which would redeem one of them from his state of vain appearance and interpolate him into the world of reality. The man, both in dreams and awake, considered his phantoms' replies, was not deceived by impostors, divined a growing intelligence in certain perplexities. He sought a soul which would merit participation in the universe.

After nine or ten nights, he comprehended with some bitterness that he could expect nothing of those students who passively accepted his doctrines, but that he could of those who, at times, would venture a reasonable contradiction. The former, though worthy of love and affection, could not rise to the state of individuals; the latter pre-existed somewhat more. One afternoon (now his afternoons too were tributaries of sleep, now he remained awake only for a couple of hours at dawn) he dismissed the vast illusory college forever and kept one single student. He was a silent boy, sallow, sometimes obstinate, with sharp features which reproduced those of the dreamer. He was not long disconcerted by his companions' sudden elimination; his progress, after a few special lessons, astounded his teacher. Nevertheless, catastrophe ensued. The man emerged from sleep one day as if from a viscous desert, looked at the vain light of afternoon, which at first he confused with that of dawn, and understood that he had not really dreamt. All that night and all day, the intolerable lucidity of insomnia weighed upon him. He tried to explore the jungle, to exhaust himself; amidst the hemlocks, he was scarcely able to manage a few snatches of feeble sleep, fleetingly mottled with some rudimentary visions which were useless. He tried to convoke the college and had scarcely uttered a few brief words of exhortation, when it became deformed and was extinguished. In his almost perpetual sleeplessness, his old eyes burned with tears of anger.

He comprehended that the effort to mold the incoherent and vertiginous matter dreams are made of was the most arduous task a man could undertake, though he might penetrate all the enigmas of the upper and lower orders: much more arduous than weaving a rope of sand or coining the faceless wind. He comprehended that an initial failure was inevitable. He swore he would forget the enormous hallucination which had misled him at first, and he sought another method. Before putting it into effect, he dedicated a month to replenishing the powers his delirium had wasted. He abandoned any premeditation of dreaming and, almost at once, was able to sleep for a considerable part of the day. The few times he dreamt during this period, he did not take notice of the dreams. To take up his task again, he waited until the moon's disk was perfect. Then, in the afternoon, he purified himself in the waters of the river, worshipped the planetary gods, uttered the lawful syllables of a powerful name and slept. Almost immediately, he dreamt of a beating heart.

He dreamt it as active, warm, secret, the size of a closed fist, of garnet color in the penumbra of a human body as yet without face or sex; with minute love he dreamt it, for fourteen lucid nights. Each night he perceived it with greater clarity. He did not touch it, but limited himself to witnessing it, observing it, perhaps correcting it with his eyes. He perceived it, lived it, from many distances and many angles. On the fourteenth night he touched the pulmonary artery with his finger, and then the whole heart, inside and out. The examination satisfied him. Deliberately, he did not dream for a night; then he took the heart again, invoked the name of a planet and set about to envision another of the principal organs. Within a year he reached the skeleton, the eyelids. The innumerable hair was perhaps the most difficult task. He dreamt a complete man, a youth, but this youth could not rise nor did he speak nor could be open his eyes. Night after night, the man dreamt him as asleep.

In the Gnostic cosmogonies, the demiurgi knead and mold a red Adam who cannot stand alone; as unskillful and crude and elementary as this Adam of dust was the Adam of dreams fabricated by the magician's nights of effort. One afternoon, the man almost destroyed his work, but

then repented. (It would have been better for him had he destroyed it.)
Once he had completed his supplications to the numina of the earth and
the river, he threw himself down at the feet of the effigy which was
perhaps a tiger and perhaps a horse, and implored its unknown succor.
That twilight, he dreamt of the statue. He dreamt of it as a living, tremu-
lous thing: it was not an atrocious mongrel of tiger and horse, but both
these vehement creatures at once and also a bull, a rose, a tempest. This
multiple god revealed to him that its earthly name was Fire, that in the
circular temple (and in others of its kind) people had rendered it sacrifices
and cult and that it would magically give life to the sleeping phantom, in
such a way that all creatures except Fire itself and the dreamer would
believe him to be a man of flesh and blood. The man was ordered by the
divinity to instruct his creature in its rites, and send him to the other
broken temple whose pyramids survived downstream, so that in this
deserted edifice a voice might give glory to the god. In the dreamer's
dream, the dreamed one awoke.

The magician carried out these orders. He devoted a period of time
(which finally comprised two years) to revealing the arcana of the universe and of the fire cult to his dream child. Inwardly, it pained him to
be separated from the boy. Under the pretext of pedagogical necessity,
each day he prolonged the hours he dedicated to his dreams. He also
redid the right shoulder, which was perhaps deficient. At times, he was
troubled by the impression that all this had happened before . . . In
general, his days were happy; when he closed his eyes, he would think:
Now I shall be with my son. Or, less often: *The child I have engendered awaits
me and will not exist if I do not go to him.*

Gradually, he accustomed the boy to reality. Once he ordered him
to place a banner on a distant peak. The following day, the banner
flickered from the mountain top. He tried other analogous experiments,
each more daring than the last. He understood with certain bitterness
that his son was ready—and perhaps impatient—to be born. That night
he kissed him for the first time and sent him to the other temple whose
debris showed white downstream, through many leagues of inextricable
jungle and swamp. But first (so that he would never know he was a
phantom, so that he would be thought a man like others) he instilled into
him a complete oblivion of his years of apprenticeship.

The man's victory and peace were dimmed by weariness. At dawn
and at twilight, he would prostrate himself before the stone figure, imagining perhaps that his unreal child was practicing the same rites, in other
circular ruins, downstream; at night, he would not dream, or would
dream only as all men do. He perceived the sounds and forms of the
universe with a certain colorlessness: his absent son was being nurtured

with these diminutions of his soul. His life's purpose was complete; the man persisted in a kind of ecstasy. After a time, which some narrators of his story prefer to compute in years and others in lustra, he was awakened one midnight by two boatmen; he could not see their faces, but they told him of a magic man in a temple of the North who could walk upon fire and not be burned. The magician suddenly remembered the words of the god. He recalled that, of all the creatures of the world, fire was the only one that knew his son was a phantom. This recollection, at first soothing, finally tormented him. He feared his son might meditate on his abnormal privilege and discover in some way that his condition was that of a mere image. Not to be a man, to be the projection of another man's dream, what a feeling of humiliation, of vertigo! All fathers are interested in the children they have procreated (they have permitted to exist) in mere confusion or pleasure; it was natural that the magician should fear for the future of that son, created in thought, limb by limb and feature by feature, in a thousand and one secret nights.

The end of his meditations was sudden, though it was foretold in certain signs. First (after a long drought) a faraway cloud on a hill, light and rapid as a bird; then, toward the south, the sky which had the rose color of the leopard's mouth; then the smoke which corroded the metallic nights; finally, the panicky flight of the animals. For what was happening had happened many centuries ago. The ruins of the fire god's sanctuary were destroyed by fire. In a birdless dawn the magician saw the concentric blaze close round the walls. For a moment, he thought of taking refuge in the river, but then he knew that death was coming to crown his old age and absolve him of his labors. He walked into the shreds of flame. But they did not bite into his flesh, they caressed him and engulfed him without heat or combustion. With relief, with humiliation, with terror, he understood that he too was a mere appearance, dreamt by another.

Reflections

Borges's epigraph is drawn from a passage in Lewis Carroll's *Through the Looking Glass* worth quoting in full.

Here she checked herself in some alarm, at hearing something that sounded to her like the puffing of a large steam-engine in the wood near them, though she feared it was more likely to be a wild beast. "Are there any lions or tigers about here?" she asked timidly.

"It's only the Red King snoring," said Tweedledee.

"Come and look at him!" the brothers cried, and they each took one of Alice's hands, and led her up to where the King was sleeping.

ILLUSTRATION BY JOHN TENNIEL.

"Isn't he a *lovely* sight?" said Tweedledum.

Alice couldn't say honestly that he was. He had a tall red night-cap on, with a tassel, and he was lying crumpled up into a sort of untidy heap, and snoring loud—"fit to snore his head off!" as Tweedledum remarked.

"I'm afraid he'll catch cold with lying on the damp grass," said Alice, who was a very thoughtful little girl.

"He's dreaming now," said Tweedledee: "and what do you think he's dreaming about?"

Alice said "Nobody can guess that."

"Why, about *you!*" Tweedledee exclaimed, clapping his hands triumphantly. "And if he left off dreaming about you, where do you suppose you'd be?"

"Where I am now, of course," said Alice.

"Not you!" Tweedledee retorted contemptuously. "You'd be nowhere. Why you're only a sort of thing in his dream!"

"If that there King was to wake," added Tweedledum, "you'd go out—bang! —just like a candle!"

"I shouldn't!" Alice exclaimed indignantly. "Besides, if *I'm* only a sort of thing in his dream, what are *you,* I should like to know?"

"Ditto," said Tweedledum.

"Ditto, ditto!" cried Tweedledee.

He shouted this so loud that Alice couldn't help saying "Hush! You'll be waking him, I'm afraid, if you make so much noise."

"Well, it's no use *your* talking about waking him," said Tweedledum, "when you're only one of the things in his dream. You know very well you're not real."

"I *am* real!" said Alice, and began to cry.

"You won't make yourself a bit realler by crying," Tweedledee remarked: "there's nothing to cry about."

"If I wasn't real," Alice said—half-laughing through her tears, it all seemed so ridiculous—"I shouldn't be able to cry."

"I hope you don't suppose those are *real* tears?" Tweedledum interrupted in a tone of great contempt.

René Descartes asked himself whether he could tell for certain that he wasn't dreaming. "When I consider these matters carefully, I realize so clearly that there are no conclusive indications by which waking life can be distinguished from sleep that I am quite astonished, and my bewilderment is such that it is almost able to convince me that I am sleeping."

It did not occur to Descartes to wonder if he might be a character in *someone else's* dream, or, if it did, he dismissed the idea out of hand. Why? Couldn't you dream a dream with a character in it who was *not* you, but whose experiences were a part of your dream? It is not easy to know how to answer a question like that. What would be the difference between dreaming a dream in which you were quite unlike your waking self—much older or younger, or of the opposite sex—and dreaming a dream in which the main character (a girl named Renée, let's say), the character from whose "point of view" the dream was "narrated," was simply *not* you but merely a fictional dream character, no more real than the dream-dragon chasing her? If *that* dream character were to ask Descartes's question, and wonder if she were dreaming or awake, it seems the answer would be that she was not dreaming, nor was she really awake; she was just *dreamt.* When the dreamer, the *real* dreamer, wakes up, she will be annihilated. But to whom would we address this answer, since she does not really exist at all, but is just a dream character?

Is this philosophical play with the ideas of dreaming and reality just idle? Isn't there a no-nonsense "scientific" stance from which we can objectively distinguish between the things that are really there and the mere fictions? Perhaps there is, but then on which side of the divide will we put ourselves? Not our physical bodies, but our *selves?*

Consider the sort of novel that is written from the point of view of a fictional narrator-actor. *Moby Dick* begins with the words "Call me Ishmael," and then we are told Ishmael's story *by* Ishmael. Call *whom* Ishmael? Ishmael does not exist. He is just a character in Melville's novel. Melville is, or was, a perfectly real self, and he created a fictional self who calls himself Ishmael—but who is not to be numbered among the real things, the things that really are. But now imagine, if you can, a novel-writing machine, a *mere* machine, without a shred of consciousness or selfhood. Call it the JOHNNIAC. (The next selection will help you imagine such a machine, if you cannot yet convince yourself you can do it.)

Suppose the novel that clattered out of the JOHNNIAC on its high-speed printer started: "Call me Gilbert," and proceeded to tell Gilbert's story from Gilbert's point of view. Call *whom* Gilbert? Gilbert is just a fictional character, a nonentity with no *real* existence, though we can go along with the fiction and talk about, learn about, worry about "his" adventures, problems, hopes, fears, pains. In the case of Ishmael, we may have supposed his queer, fictional, quasi-existence depended on the real existence of Melville's self. *No dream without a dreamer to dream it* seems to be Descartes' discovery. But in this case we do seem to have a dream—a fiction, in any case—with no *real* dreamer or author, no real self with whom we might or might not identify Gilbert. So in such an extraordinary case as the novel-writing machine there might be created a merely fictional self with no real self behind the act of creation. (We can even suppose the JOHNNIAC's designers had no idea what novels it would eventually write.)

Now suppose our imagined novel-writing machine is not just a sedentary, boxy computer, but a robot. And suppose—why not?—that the text of the novel is not typed but "spoken" from a mechanical mouth. Call this robot the SPEECHIAC. And suppose, finally, the tale we learn from the SPEECHIAC about the adventures of Gilbert is a more or less *true* story of the "adventures" of the SPEECHIAC. When it is locked in a closet, it says: *"I* am locked in the closet! Help *me!"* Help *whom?* Help Gilbert. But Gilbert does not exist; he is just a fictional character in the SPEECHIAC's peculiar narration. Why, though, should we call *this* account fiction, since there is a quite obvious candidate in sight to be Gilbert: the person whose body is the SPEECHIAC? In "Where Am I?" Dennett called his body Hamlet. Is this a case of Gilbert having a body called the SPEECHIAC, or of the SPEECHIAC calling *itself* Gilbert?

Perhaps we are being tricked by the name. Naming the robot "Gilbert" may be just like naming a sailboat "Caroline" or a bell "Big Ben" or a program "ELIZA." We may feel like insisting that there is no *person* named Gilbert here. What, though, aside from bio-chauvinism, grounds our resistance to the conclusion that Gilbert *is* a person, a person created, in effect, by the SPEECHIAC's activity and self-presentation in the world?

"Is the suggestion then that *I am my body's dream?* Am I just a fictional character in a sort of novel composed by my body in action?" That would be one way of getting at it, but why call yourself fictional? Your brain, like the unconscious novel-writing machine, cranks along, doing its physical tasks, sorting the inputs and the outputs without a glimmer of what it is up to. Like the ants that compose Aunt Hillary in "Prelude, Ant Fugue," *it* doesn't "know" it is creating you in the process, but there you are, emerging from its frantic activity *almost* magically.

This process of creating a self at one level out of the relatively mindless and uncomprehending activities amalgamated at another level is vividly illustrated in the next selection by John Searle, though he firmly resists that vision of what he is showing.

D.C.D.

22

JOHN R. SEARLE

Minds, Brains, and Programs

What psychological and philosophical significance should we attach to recent efforts at computer simulations of human cognitive capacities? In answering this question, I find it useful to distinguish what I will call "strong" AI from "weak" or "cautious" AI (artificial intelligence). According to weak AI, the principal value of the computer in the study of the mind is that it gives us a very powerful tool. For example, it enables us to formulate and test hypotheses in a more rigorous and precise fashion. But according to strong AI, the computer is not merely a tool in the study of the mind; rather, the appropriately programmed computer really *is* a mind, in the sense that computers given the right programs can be literally said to *understand* and have other cognitive states. In strong AI, because the programmed computer has cognitive states, the programs are not mere tools that enable us to test psychological explanations; rather, the programs are themselves the explanations.

I have no objection to the claims of weak AI, at least as far as this article is concerned. My discussion here will be directed at the claims I have defined as those of strong AI, specifically the claim that the appropriately programmed computer literally has cognitive states and that the programs thereby explain human cognition. When I hereafter refer to AI, I have in mind the strong version, as expressed by these two claims.

I will consider the work of Roger Schank and his colleagues at Yale (Schank and Abelson 1977), because I am more familiar with it than I am with any other similar claims, and because it provides a very clear example of the sort of work I wish to examine. But nothing that follows depends upon the details of Schank's programs. The same arguments would apply to Winograd's SHRDLU (Winograd 1973), Weizenbaum's ELIZA (Weizenbaum 1965), and indeed any Turing machine simulation of human mental phenomena. [See "Further Reading" for Searle's references.]

Very briefly, and leaving out the various details, one can describe Schank's program as follows: The aim of the program is to simulate the human ability to understand stories. It is characteristic of human beings' story-understanding capacity that they can answer questions about the story even though the information that they give was never explicitly stated in the story. Thus, for example, suppose you are given the following story: "A man went into a restaurant and ordered a hamburger. When the hamburger arrived it was burned to a crisp, and the man stormed out of the restaurant angrily, without paying for the hamburger or leaving a tip." Now, if you are asked "Did the man eat the hamburger?" you will presumably answer, "No, he did not." Similarly, if you are given the following story: "A man went into a restaurant and ordered a hamburger; when the hamburger came he was very pleased with it; and as he left the restaurant he gave the waitress a large tip before paying his bill," and you are asked the question, "Did the man eat the hamburger?" you will presumably answer, "Yes, he ate the hamburger." Now Schank's machines can similarly answer questions about restaurants in this fashion. To do this, they have a "representation" of the sort of information that human beings have about restaurants, which enables them to answer such questions as those above, given these sorts of stories. When the machine is given the story and then asked the question, the machine will print out answers of the sort that we would expect human beings to give if told similar stories. Partisans of strong AI claim that in this question and answer sequence the machine is not only simulating a human ability but also (1) that the machine can literally be said to *understand* the story and provide the answers to questions, and (2) that what the machine and its program do *explains* the human ability to understand the story and answer questions about it.

Both claims seem to me to be totally unsupported by Schank's work, as I will attempt to show in what follows. (I am not, of course, saying that Schank himself is committed to these claims.)

One way to test any theory of the mind is to ask oneself what it would be like if my mind actually worked on the principles that the theory says all minds work on. Let us apply this test to the Schank program with the following *Gedankenexperiment.* Suppose that I'm locked in a room and given a large batch of Chinese writing. Suppose furthermore (as is indeed the case) that I know no Chinese, either written or spoken, and that I'm not even confident that I could recognize Chinese writing as Chinese writing distinct from, say, Japanese writing or meaningless squiggles. To me, Chinese writing is just so many meaningless squiggles. Now suppose further that after this first batch of Chinese writing I am given a second batch of Chinese script together with a set of rules for correlating the second batch with the first batch. The rules are in English, and I understand these rules as well as any other native speaker of English. They enable me to correlate one set of formal symbols with another set of formal symbols, and all that "formal" means here is that I can identify the symbols entirely by their shapes. Now suppose also that I am given a third batch of Chinese symbols together with some instructions, again in English, that enable me to correlate elements of this third batch with the first two batches, and these rules instruct me how to give back certain Chinese symbols with certain sorts of shapes in response to certain sorts of shapes given me in the third batch. Unknown to me, the people who are giving me all of these symbols call the first batch a "script," they call the second batch a "story," and they call the third batch "questions." Furthermore, they call the symbols I give them back in response to the third batch "answers to the questions," and the set of rules in English that they gave me, they call the "program." Now just to complicate the story a little, imagine that these people also give me stories in English, which I understand, and they then ask me questions in English about these stories, and I give them back answers in English. Suppose also that after a while I get so good at following the instructions for manipulating the Chinese symbols and the programmers get so good at writing the programs that from the external point of view—that is, from the point of view of somebody outside the room in which I am locked—my answers to the questions are absolutely indistinguishable from those of native Chinese speakers. Nobody just looking at my answers can tell that I don't speak a word of Chinese. Let us also suppose that my answers to the English questions are, as they no doubt would be, indistinguishable from those of other native English speakers, for the simple reason that I am a native English speaker. From the external point of view—from the point of view of someone reading my "answers"—the answers to the Chinese questions and the English questions are equally good. But in the Chinese case, unlike the English case, I produce the answers by manipulating uninterpreted formal symbols. As far as the Chinese is concerned, I simply behave like a computer; I perform computational operations on formally specified elements. For the purposes of the Chinese, I am simply an instantiation of the computer program.

Now the claims made by strong AI are that the programmed computer understands the stories and that the program in some sense explains human understanding. But we are now in a position to examine these claims in light of our thought experiment.

1. As regards the first claim, it seems to me quite obvious in the example that I do not understand a word of the Chinese stories. I have inputs and outputs that are indistinguishable from those of the native Chinese speaker, and I can have any formal program you like, but I still understand nothing. For the same reasons, Schank's computer understands nothing of any stories, whether in Chinese, English, or whatever, since in the Chinese case the computer is me, and in cases where the computer is not me, the computer has nothing more than I have in the case where I understand nothing.

2. As regards the second claim, that the program explains human understanding, we can see that the computer and its program do not provide sufficient conditions of understanding since the computer and the program are functioning, and there is no understanding. But does it even provide a necessary condition or a significant contribution to understanding? One of the claims made by the supporters of strong AI is that when I understand a story in English, what I am doing is exactly the same —or perhaps more of the same—as what I was doing in manipulating the Chinese symbols. It is simply more formal symbol manipulation that distinguishes the case in English, where I do understand, from the case in Chinese, where I don't. I have not demonstrated that this claim is false, but it would certainly appear an incredible claim in the example. Such plausibility as the claim has derives from the supposition that we can construct a program that will have the same inputs and outputs as native speakers, and in addition we assume that speakers have some level of description where they are also instantiations of a program. On the basis of these two assumptions we assume that even if Schank's program isn't the whole story about understanding, it may be part of the story. Well, I suppose that is an empirical possibility, but not the slightest reason has so far been given to believe that it is true, since what is suggested— though certainly not demonstrated—by the example is that the computer program is simply irrelevant to my understanding of the story. In the Chinese case I have everything that artificial intelligence can put into me by way of a program, and I understand nothing; in the English case I

understand everything, and there is so far no reason at all to suppose that my understanding has anything to do with computer programs, that is, with computational operations on purely formally specified elements. As long as the program is defined in terms of computational operations on purely formally defined elements, what the example suggests is that these by themselves have no interesting connection with understanding. They are certainly not sufficient conditions, and not the slightest reason has been given to suppose that they are necessary conditions or even that they make a significant contribution to understanding. Notice that the force of the argument is not simply that different machines can have the same input and output while operating on different formal principles—that is not the point at all. Rather, whatever purely formal principles you put into the computer, they will not be sufficient for understanding, since a human will be able to follow the formal principles without understanding anything. No reason whatever has been offered to suppose that such principles are necessary or even contributory, since no reason has been given to suppose that when I understand English I am operating with any formal program at all.

Well, then, what is it that I have in the case of the English sentences that I do not have in the case of the Chinese sentences? The obvious answer is that I know what the former mean, while I haven't the faintest idea what the latter mean. But in what does this consist and why couldn't we give it to a machine, whatever it is? I will return to this question later, but first I want to continue with the example.

I have had the occasions to present this example to several workers in artificial intelligence, and, interestingly, they do not seem to agree on what the proper reply to it is. I get a surprising variety of replies, and in what follows I will consider the most common of these (specified along with their geographic origins).

But first I want to block some common misunderstandings about "understanding": In many of these discussions one finds a lot of fancy footwork about the word "understanding." My critics point out that there are many different degrees of understanding; that "understanding" is not a simple two-place predicate; that there are even different kinds and levels of understanding, and often the law of excluded middle doesn't even apply in a straightforward way to statements of the form "x understands y"; that in many cases it is a matter for decision and not a simple matter of fact whether x understands y; and so on. To all of these points I want to say: of course, of course. But they have nothing to do with the points at issue. There are clear cases in which "understanding" literally applies and clear cases in which it does not apply; and these two sorts of

cases are all I need for this argument.* I understand stories in English;
to a lesser degree I can understand stories in French; to a still lesser
degree, stories in German; and in Chinese, not at all. My car and my
adding machine, on the other hand, understand nothing: they are not in
that line of business. We often attribute "understanding" and other cognitive predicates by metaphor and analogy to cars, adding machines, and
other artifacts, but nothing is proved by such attributions. We say, "The
door *knows* when to open because of its photoelectric cell," "The adding
machine *knows how (understands how,* is *able)* to do addition and subtraction
but not division," and "The thermostat *perceives* changes in the temperature." The reason we make these attributions is quite interesting, and it
has to do with the fact that in artifacts we extend our own intentionality;†
our tools are extensions of our purposes, and so we find it natural to make
metaphorical attributions of intentionality to them; but I take it no philosophical ice is cut by such examples. The sense in which an automatic
door "understands instructions" from its photoelectric cell is not at all
the sense in which I understand English. If the sense in which Schank's
programmed computers understand stories is supposed to be the metaphorical sense in which the door understands, and not the sense in which
I understand English, the issue would not be worth discussing. But Newell and Simon (1963) write that the kind of cognition they claim for
computers is exactly the same as for human beings. I like the straightfor-
wardness of this claim, and it is the sort of claim I will be considering.
I will argue that in the literal sense the programmed computer understands what the car and the adding machine understand, namely, exactly
nothing. The computer understanding is not just (like my understanding
of German) partial or incomplete; it is zero.

Now to the replies:

1. The Systems Reply (Berkeley). "While it is true that the individual
person who is locked in the room does not understand the story, the fact
is that he is merely part of a whole system, and the system does understand the story. The person has a large ledger in front of him in which
are written the rules, he has a lot of scratch paper and pencils for doing
calculations, he has 'data banks' of sets of Chinese symbols. Now, understanding is not being ascribed to the mere individual; rather it is being
ascribed to this whole system of which he is a part."

---

*Also, "understanding" implies both the possession of mental (intentional) states and the
truth (validity, success) of these states. For the purposes of this discussion we are concerned
only with the possession of the states.

†Intentionality is by definition that feature of certain mental states by which they are
directed at or about objects and states of affairs in the world. Thus, beliefs, desires, and
intentions are intentional states; undirected forms of anxiety and depression are not.

My response to the systems theory is quite simple: Let the individual internalize all of these elements of the system. He memorizes the rules in the ledger and the data banks of Chinese symbols, and he does all the calculations in his head. The individual then incorporates the entire system. There isn't anything at all to the system that he does not encompass. We can even get rid of the room and suppose he works outdoors. All the same, he understands nothing of the Chinese, and a fortiori neither does the system, because there isn't anything in the system that isn't in him. If he doesn't understand, then there is no way the system could understand because the system is just a part of him.

Actually I feel somewhat embarrassed to give even this answer to the systems theory because the theory seems to me so implausible to start with. The idea is that while a person doesn't understand Chinese, somehow the *conjunction* of that person and bits of paper might understand Chinese. It is not easy for me to imagine how someone who was not in the grip of an ideology would find the idea at all plausible. Still, I think many people who are committed to the ideology of strong AI will in the end be inclined to say something very much like this; so let us pursue it a bit further. According to one version of this view, while the man in the internalized systems example doesn't understand Chinese in the sense that a native Chinese speaker does (because, for example, he doesn't know that the story refers to restaurants and hamburgers, etc.), still "the man as a formal symbol manipulation system" *really does understand Chinese.* The subsystem of the man that is the formal symbol manipulation system for Chinese should not be confused with the subsystem for English.

So there are really two subsystems in the man; one understands English, the other Chinese, and "it's just that the two systems have little to do with each other." But, I want to reply, not only do they have little to do with each other, they are not even remotely alike. The subsystem that understands English (assuming we allow ourselves to talk in this jargon of "subsystems" for a moment) knows that the stories are about restaurants and eating hamburgers, he knows that he is being asked questions about restaurants and that he is answering questions as best he can by making various inferences from the content of the story, and so on. But the Chinese system knows none of this. Whereas the English subsystem knows that "hamburgers" refers to hamburgers, the Chinese subsystem knows only that "squiggle squiggle" is followed by "squoggle squoggle." All he knows is that various formal symbols are being introduced at one end and manipulated according to rules written in English, and other symbols are going out at the other end. The whole point of the original example was to argue that such symbol manipulation by itself couldn't be sufficient for understanding Chinese in any literal sense because the man could write "squoggle squoggle" after "squiggle squiggle" without understanding anything in Chinese. And it doesn't meet that argument to postulate subsystems within the man, because the subsystems are no better off than the man was in the first place; they still don't have anything even remotely like what the English-speaking man (or subsystem) has. Indeed, in the case as described, the Chinese subsystem is simply a part of the English subsystem, a part that engages in meaningless symbol manipulation according to rules in English.

Let us ask ourselves what is supposed to motivate the systems reply in the first place; that is, what *independent* grounds are there supposed to be for saying that the agent must have a subsystem within him that literally understands stories in Chinese? As far as I can tell the only grounds are that in the example I have the same input and output as native Chinese speakers and a program that goes from one to the other. But the whole point of the examples has been to try to show that that couldn't be sufficient for understanding, in the sense in which I understand stories in English, because a person, and hence the set of systems that go to make up a person, could have the right combination of input, output, and program and still not understand anything in the relevant literal sense in which I understand English. The only motivation for saying there *must* be a subsystem in me that understands Chinese is that I have a program and I can pass the Turing test; I can fool native Chinese speakers. But precisely one of the points at issue is the adequacy of the Turing test. The example shows that there could be two "systems," both of which pass the Turing test, but only one of which understands; and it is no argument against this point to say that since they both pass the Turing test they must both understand, since this claim fails to meet the argument that the system in me that understands English has a great deal more than the system that merely processes Chinese. In short, the systems reply simply begs the question by insisting without argument that the system must understand Chinese.

Furthermore, the systems reply would appear to lead to consequences that are independently absurd. If we are to conclude that there must be cognition in me on the grounds that I have a certain sort of input and output and a program in between, then it looks like all sorts of noncognitive subsystems are going to turn out to be cognitive. For example, there is a level of description at which my stomach does information processing, and it instantiates any number of computer programs, but I take it we do not want to say that it has any understanding (cf. Pylyshyn 1980). But if we accept the systems reply, then it is hard to see how we avoid saying that stomach, heart, liver, and so on are all understanding subsystems, since there is no principled way to distinguish the motivation for saying the Chinese subsystem understands from saying that the stomach understands. It is, by the way, not an answer to this point to say that the Chinese system has information as input and output and the stomach has food and food products as input and output, since from the point of view of the agent, from my point of view, there is no information in either the food or the Chinese—the Chinese is just so many meaningless squiggles. The information in the Chinese case is solely in the eyes of the programmers and the interpreters, and there is nothing to prevent them from treating the input and output of my digestive organs as information if they so desire.

This last point bears on some independent problems in strong AI, and it is worth digressing for a moment to explain it. If strong AI is to be a branch of psychology, then it must be able to distinguish those systems that are genuinely mental from those that are not. It must be able to distinguish the principles on which the mind works from those on which nonmental systems work; otherwise it will offer us no explanations of what is specifically mental about the mental. And the mental-nonmental distinction cannot be just in the eye of the beholder but it must be intrinsic to the systems; otherwise it would be up to any beholder to treat people as nonmental and, for example, hurricanes as mental if he likes. But quite often in the AI literature the distinction is blurred in ways that would in the long run prove disastrous to the claim that AI is a cognitive inquiry. McCarthy, for example, writes. "Machines as simple as thermostats can be said to have beliefs, and having beliefs seems to be a characteristic of most machines capable of problem solving performance" (McCarthy 1979). Anyone who thinks strong AI has a chance as a theory of the mind ought to ponder the implications of that remark. We are asked to accept it as a discovery of strong AI that the hunk of metal on the wall that we use to regulate the temperature has beliefs in exactly the same sense that we, our spouses, and our children have beliefs, and furthermore that "most" of the other machines in the room—telephone, tape recorder, adding machine, electric light switch—also have beliefs in this literal sense. It is not the aim of this article to argue against McCarthy's point, so I will simply assert the following without argument. The study of the mind starts with such facts as that humans have beliefs, while thermostats, telephones, and adding machines don't. If you get a theory that denies this point you have produced a counterexample to the theory and the theory is false. One gets the impression that people in AI who write this sort of thing think they can get away with it because they don't really take it seriously, and they don't think anyone else will either. I propose, for a moment at least, to take it seriously. Think hard for one minute about what would be necessary to establish that that hunk of metal on the wall over there had real beliefs, beliefs with direction of fit, propositional content, and conditions of satisfaction; beliefs that had the possibility of being strong beliefs or weak beliefs; nervous, anxious, or secure beliefs; dogmatic, rational, or superstitious beliefs; blind faiths or hesitant cogitations; any kind of beliefs. The thermostat is not a candidate. Neither is stomach, liver, adding machine, or telephone. However, since we are taking the idea seriously, notice that its truth would be fatal to strong AI's claim to be a science of the mind. For now the mind is everywhere. What we wanted to know is what distinguishes the mind from thermostats and livers. And if McCarthy were right, strong AI wouldn't have a hope of telling us that.

2.   The Robot Reply (Yale). "Suppose we wrote a different kind of program from Schank's program. Suppose we put a computer inside a robot, and this computer would not just take in formal symbols as input and give out formal symbols as output, but rather would actually operate the robot in such a way that the robot does something very much like perceiving, walking, moving about, hammering nails, eating, drinking—anything you like. The robot would, for example, have a television camera attached to it that enabled it to see, it would have arms and legs that enabled it to 'act,' and all of this would be controlled by its computer 'brain.' Such a robot would, unlike Schank's computer, have genuine understanding and other mental states."

The first thing to notice about the robot reply is that it tacitly concedes that cognition is not solely a matter of formal symbol manipulation, since this reply adds a set of causal relations with the outside world (cf. Fodor 1980). But the answer to the robot reply is that the addition of such "perceptual" and "motor" capacities adds nothing by way of understanding, in particular, or intentionality, in general, to Schank's original program. To see this, notice that the same thought experiment applies to the robot case. Suppose that instead of the computer inside the robot, you put me inside the room and, as in the original Chinese case, you give me more Chinese symbols with more instructions in English for matching Chinese symbols to Chinese symbols and feeding back Chinese symbols to the outside. Suppose, unknown to me, some of the Chinese symbols that come to me come from a television camera attached to the robot and other Chinese symbols that I am giving out serve to make the motors inside the robot move the robot's legs or arms. It is important to emphasize that all I am doing is manipulating formal symbols: I know none of these other facts. I am receiving "information" from the robot's "perceptual" apparatus, and I am giving out "instructions" to its motor apparatus without knowing either of these facts. I am the robot's homunculus, but unlike the traditional homunculus, I don't know what's going on. I don't understand anything except the rules for symbol manipulation. Now in this case I want to say that the robot has no intentional states at all; it is simply moving about as a result of its electrical wiring and its program. And furthermore, by instantiating the program I have no intentional states of the relevant type. All I do is follow formal instructions about manipulating formal symbols.

3. The Brain Simulator Reply (Berkeley and M.I.T.). "Suppose we design a program that doesn't represent information that we have about the world, such as the information in Schank's scripts, but simulates the actual sequence of neuron firings at the synapses of the brain of a native Chinese speaker when he understands stories in Chinese and gives answers to them. The machine takes in Chinese stories and questions about them as input, it simulates the formal structure of actual Chinese brains in processing these stories, and it gives out Chinese answers as outputs. We can even imagine that the machine operates, not with a single serial program, but with a whole set of programs operating in parallel, in the manner that actual human brains presumably operate when they process natural language. Now surely in such a case we would have to say that the machine understood the stories; and if we refuse to say that, wouldn't we also have to deny that native Chinese speakers understood the stories? At the level of the synapses, what would or could be different about the program of the computer and the program of the Chinese brain?"

Before countering this reply I want to digress to note that it is an odd reply for any partisan of artificial intelligence (or functionalism, etc.) to make: I thought the whole idea of strong AI is that we don't need to know how the brain works to know how the mind works. The basic hypothesis, or so I had supposed, was that there is a level of mental operations consisting of computational processes over formal elements that constitute the essence of the mental and can be realized in all sorts of different brain processes, in the same way that any computer program can be realized in different computer hardwares: On the assumptions of strong AI, the mind is to the brain as the program is to the hardware, and thus we can understand the mind without doing neurophysiology. If we had to know how the brain worked to do AI, we wouldn't bother with AI. However, even getting this close to the operation of the brain is still not sufficient to produce understanding. To see this, imagine that instead of a monolingual man in a room shuffling symbols we have the man operate an elaborate set of water pipes with valves connecting them. When the man receives the Chinese symbols, he looks up in the program, written in English, which valves he has to turn on and off. Each water connection corresponds to a synapse in the Chinese brain, and the whole system is rigged up so that after doing all the right firings, that is after turning on all the right faucets, the Chinese answers pop out at the output end of the series of pipes.

Now where is the understanding in this system? It takes Chinese as input, it simulates the formal structure of the synapses of the Chinese brain, and it gives Chinese as output. But the man certainly doesn't understand Chinese, and neither do the water pipes, and if we are tempted to adopt what I think is the absurd view that somehow the *conjunction* of man *and* water pipes understands, remember that in principle the man can internalize the formal structure of the water pipes and do all the "neuron firings" in his imagination. The problem with the brain simulator is that it is simulating the wrong things about the brain. As long as it simulates only the formal structure of the sequence of neuron firings at the synapses, it won't have simulated what matters about the brain, namely its causal properties, its ability to produce intentional states. And that the formal properties are not sufficient for the causal properties is shown by the water pipe example: we can have all the formal properties carved off from the relevant neurobiological causal properties.

4.   The Combination Reply (Berkeley and Stanford). "While each of the previous three replies might not be completely convincing by itself as a refutation of the Chinese room counterexample, if you take all three together they are collectively much more convincing and even decisive. Imagine a robot with a brain-shaped computer lodged in its cranial cavity, imagine the computer programmed with all the synapses of a human brain, imagine the whole behavior of the robot is indistinguishable from human behavior, and now think of the whole thing as a unified system and not just as a computer with inputs and outputs. Surely in such a case we would have to ascribe intentionality to the system."

I entirely agree that in such a case we would find it rational and indeed irresistible to accept the hypothesis that the robot had intentionality, as long as we knew nothing more about it. Indeed, besides appearance and behavior, the other elements of the combination are really irrelevant. If we could build a robot whose behavior was indistinguishable over a large range from human behavior, we would attribute intentionality to it, pending some reason not to. We wouldn't need to know in advance that its computer brain was a formal analogue of the human brain.

But I really don't see that this is any help to the claims of strong AI, and here's why: According to strong AI, instantiating a formal program with the right input and output is a sufficient condition of, indeed is constitutive of, intentionality. As Newell (1979) puts it, the essence of the mental is the operation of a physical symbol system. But the attributions of intentionality that we make to the robot in this example have nothing to do with formal programs. They are simply based on the assumption that if the robot looks and behaves sufficiently like us, then we would suppose, until proven otherwise, that it must have mental states like ours that cause and are expressed by its behavior and it must have an inner mechanism capable of producing such mental states. If we knew independently how to account for its behavior without such assumptions we would not attribute intentionality to it, especially if we knew it had a formal program. And this is precisely the point of my earlier reply to objection II.

Suppose we knew that the robot's behavior was entirely accounted for by the fact that a man inside it was receiving uninterpreted formal symbols from the robot's sensory receptors and sending out uninterpreted formal symbols to its motor mechanisms, and the man was doing this symbol manipulation in accordance with a bunch of rules. Furthermore, suppose the man knows none of these facts about the robot, all he knows is which operations to perform on which meaningless symbols. In such a case we would regard the robot as an ingenious mechanical dummy. The hypothesis that the dummy has a mind would now be unwarranted and unnecessary, for there is now no longer any reason to ascribe intentionality to the robot or to the system of which it is a part (except of course for the man's intentionality in manipulating the symbols). The formal symbol manipulations go on, the input and output are correctly matched, but the only real locus of intentionality is the man, and he doesn't know any of the relevant intentional states; he doesn't, for example, *see* what comes into the robot's eyes, he doesn't *intend* to move the robot's arm, and he doesn't *understand* any of the remarks made to or by the robot. Nor, for the reasons stated earlier, does the system of which man and robot are a part.

To see this point, contrast this case with cases in which we find it completely natural to ascribe intentionality to members of certain other primate species such as apes and monkeys and to domestic animals such as dogs. The reasons we find it natural are, roughly, two: We can't make sense of the animal's behavior without the ascription of intentionality, and we can see that the beasts are made of similar stuff to ourselves—that is an eye, that a nose, this is its skin, and so on. Given the coherence of the animal's behavior and the assumption of the same causal stuff underlying it, we assume both that the animal must have mental states underlying its behavior, and that the mental states must be produced by mechanisms made out of the stuff that is like our stuff. We would certainly make similar assumptions about the robot unless we had some reason not to, but as soon as we knew that the behavior was the result of a formal program, and that the actual causal properties of the physical substance were irrelevant we would abandon the assumption of intentionality.

There are two other responses to my example that come up frequently (and so are worth discussing) but really miss the point.

5.   The Other Minds Reply (Yale). "How do you know that other people understand Chinese or anything else? Only by their behavior. Now the computer can pass the behavioral tests as well as they can (in principle), so if you are going to attribute cognition to other people you must in principle also attribute it to computers."

This objection really is only worth a short reply. The problem in this discussion is not about how I know that other people have cognitive states, but rather what it is that I am attributing to them when I attribute cognitive states to them. The thrust of the argument is that it couldn't be just computational processes and their output because the computational processes and their output can exist without the cognitive state. It is no answer to this argument to feign anesthesia. In "cognitive sciences" one presupposes the reality and knowability of the mental in the same way that in physical sciences one has to presuppose the reality and knowability of physical objects.

6.   The Many Mansions Reply (Berkeley). "Your whole argument presupposes that AI is only about analog and digital computers. But that just happens to be the present state of technology. Whatever these causal processes are that you say are essential for intentionality (assuming you are right), eventually we will be able to build devices that have these causal processes, and that will be artificial intelligence. So your arguments are in no way directed at the ability of artificial intelligence to produce and explain cognition."

I really have no objection to this reply save to say that it in effect trivializes the project of strong AI by redefining it as whatever artificially produces and explains cognition. The interest of the original claim made on behalf of artificial intelligence is that it was a precise, well defined thesis: mental processes are computational processes over formally defined elements. I have been concerned to challenge that thesis. If the claim is redefined so that it is no longer that thesis, my objections no longer apply because there is no longer a testable hypothesis for them to apply to.

Let us now return to the question I promised I would try to answer: Granted that in my original example I understand the English and I do not understand the Chinese, and granted therefore that the machine doesn't understand either English or Chinese, still there must be something about me that makes it the case that I understand English and a corresponding something lacking in me that makes it the case that I fail to understand Chinese. Now why couldn't we give those somethings, whatever they are, to a machine?

I see no reason in principle why we couldn't give a machine the capacity to understand English or Chinese, since in an important sense our bodies with our brains are precisely such machines. But I do see very strong arguments for saying that we could not give such a thing to a machine where the operation of the machine is defined solely in terms of computational processes over formally defined elements; that is, where the operation of the machine is defined as an instantiation of a computer program. It is not because I am the instantiation of a computer program that I am able to understand English and have other forms of intentionality (I am, I suppose, the instantiation of any number of computer programs), but as far as we know it is because I am a certain sort of organism with a certain biological (i.e., chemical and physical) structure, and this structure, under certain conditions, is causally capable of producing perception, action, understanding, learning, and other intentional phenomena. And part of the point of the present argument is that only something that had those causal powers could have that intentionality. Perhaps other physical and chemical processes could produce exactly these effects; perhaps, for example, Martians also have intentionality but their brains are made of different stuff. That is an empirical question, rather like the question whether photosynthesis can be done by something with a chemistry different from that of chlorophyll.

But the main point of the present argument is that no purely formal model will ever be sufficient by itself for intentionality because the formal properties are not by themselves constitutive of intentionality, and they have by themselves no causal powers except the power, when instantiated, to produce the next stage of the formalism when the machine is running. And any other causal properties that particular realizations of the formal model have, are irrelevant to the formal model because we can always put the same formal model in a different realization where those causal properties are obviously absent. Even if, by some miracle, Chinese speakers exactly realize Schank's program, we can put the same program in English speakers, water pipes, or computers, none of which understand Chinese, the program notwithstanding.

What matters about brain operations is not the formal shadow cast by the sequence of synapses but rather the actual properties of the sequences. All the arguments for the strong version of artificial intelligence that I have seen insist on drawing an outline around the shadows cast by cognition and then claiming that the shadows are the real thing.

By way of concluding I want to try to state some of the general philosophical points implicit in the argument. For clarity I will try to do it in a question-and-answer fashion, and I begin with that old chestnut of a question:

"Could a machine think?"

The answer is, obviously, yes. We are precisely such machines.

"Yes, but could an artifact, a man-made machine, think?"

Assuming it is possible to produce artificially a machine with a nervous system, neurons with axons and dendrites, and all the rest of it, sufficiently like ours, again the answer to the question seems to be obviously, yes. If you can exactly duplicate the causes, you could duplicate the effects. And indeed it might be possible to produce consciousness, intentionality, and all the rest of it using some other sorts of chemical principles than those that human beings use. It is, as I said, an empirical question.

"OK, but could a digital computer think?"

If by "digital computer" we mean anything at all that has a level of description where it can correctly be described as the instantiation of a computer program, then again the answer is, of course, yes, since we are the instantiations of any number of computer programs, and we can think.

"But could something think, understand, and so on *solely* in virtue of being a computer with the right sort of program? Could instantiating a program, the right program of course, by itself be a sufficient condition of understanding?"

This I think is the right question to ask, though it is usually confused with one or more of the earlier questions, and the answer to it is no.

"Why not?"

Because the formal symbol manipulations by themselves don't have any intentionality; they are quite meaningless; they aren't even *symbol* manipulations, since the symbols don't symbolize anything. In the linguistic jargon, they have only a syntax but no semantics. Such intentionality as computers appear to have is solely in the minds of those who program them and those who use them, those who send in the input and those who interpret the output.

The aim of the Chinese room example was to try to show this by showing that as soon as we put something into the system that really does have intentionality (a man), and we program him with the formal program, you can see that the formal program carries no additional intentionality. It adds nothing, for example, to a man's ability to understand Chinese.

Precisely that feature of AI that seemed so appealing—the distinction between the program and the realization—proves fatal to the claim that simulation could be duplication. The distinction between the program and its realization in the hardware seems to be parallel to the distinction between the level of mental operations and the level of brain operations. And if we could describe the level of mental operations as a formal program, then it seems we could describe what was essential about the mind without doing either introspective psychology or neurophysiology of the brain. But the equation "mind is to brain as program is to hardware" breaks down at several points, among them the following three:

First, the distinction between program and realization has the consequence that the same program could have all sorts of crazy realizations that had no form of intentionality. Weizenbaum (1976, Ch. 2), for example, shows in detail how to construct a computer using a roll of toilet paper and a pile of small stones. Similarly, the Chinese story understanding program can be programmed into a sequence of water pipes, a set of wind machines, or a monolingual English speaker, none of which thereby acquires an understanding of Chinese. Stones, toilet paper, wind, and water pipes are the wrong kind of stuff to have intentionality in the first place—only something that has the same causal powers as brains can have intentionality—and though the English speaker has the right kind of stuff for intentionality you can easily see that he doesn't get any extra intentionality by memorizing the program, since memorizing it won't teach him Chinese.

Second, the program is purely formal, but the intentional states are not in that way formal. They are defined in terms of their content, not their form. The belief that it is raining, for example, is not defined as a certain formal shape, but as a certain mental content with conditions of satisfaction, a direction of fit (see Searle 1979), and the like. Indeed the belief as such hasn't even got a formal shape in this syntactic sense, since one and the same belief can be given an indefinite number of different syntactic expressions in different linguistic systems.

Third, as I mentioned before, mental states and events are literally a product of the operation of the brain, but the program is not in that way a product of the computer.

"Well if programs are in no way constitutive of mental processes, why have so many people believed the converse? That at least needs some explanation."

I don't really know the answer to that one. The idea that computer simulations could be the real thing ought to have seemed suspicious in the first place because the computer isn't confined to simulating mental operations, by any means. No one supposes that computer simulations of a five-alarm fire will burn the neighborhood down or that a computer simulation of a rainstorm will leave us all drenched. Why on earth would anyone suppose that a computer simulation of understanding actually understood anything? It is sometimes said that it would be frightfully hard to get computers to feel pain or fall in love, but love and pain are neither harder nor easier than cognition or anything else. For simulation, all you need is the right input and output and a program in the middle that transforms the former into the latter. That is all the computer has for anything it does. To confuse simulation with duplication is the same mistake, whether it is pain, love, cognition, fires, or rainstorms.

Still, there are several reasons why AI must have seemed—and to many people perhaps still does seem—in some way to reproduce and thereby explain mental phenomena, and I believe we will not succeed in removing these illusions until we have fully exposed the reasons that give rise to them.

First, and perhaps most important, is a confusion about the notion of "information processing": many people in cognitive science believe that the human brain, with its mind, does something called "information processing," and analogously the computer with its program does information processing; but fires and rainstorms, on the other hand, don't do information processing at all. Thus, though the computer can simulate the formal features of any process whatever, it stands in a special relation to the mind and brain because when the computer is properly programmed, ideally with the same program as the brain, the information processing is identical in the two cases, and this information processing is really the essence of the mental. But the trouble with this argument is that it rests on an ambiguity in the notion of "information." In the sense in which people "process information" when they reflect, say, on problems in arithmetic or when they read and answer questions about stories, the programmed computer does not do "information processing." Rather, what it does is manipulate formal symbols. The fact that the programmer and the interpreter of the computer output use the symbols to stand for objects in the world is totally beyond the scope of the computer. The computer, to repeat, has a syntax but no semantics. Thus, if you type into the computer "2 plus 2 equals?" it will type out "4." But it has no idea that "4" means 4 or that it means anything at all. And the point is not that it lacks some second-order information about the interpretation of its first-order symbols, but rather that its first-order symbols don't have any interpretations as far as the computer is concerned. All the computer has is more symbols. The introduction of the notion of "information processing" therefore produces a dilemma: either we construe the notion of "information processing" in such a way that it implies intentionality as part of the process or we don't. If the former, then the programmed computer does not do information processing, it only manipulates formal symbols. If the latter, then, though the computer does information processing, it is only doing so in the sense in which adding machines, typewriters, stomachs, thermostats, rainstorms, and hurricanes do information processing; namely, they have a level of description at which we can describe them as taking information in at one end, transforming it, and producing information as output. But in this case it is up to outside observers to interpret the input and output as information in the ordinary sense. And no similarity is established between the computer and the brain in terms of any similarity of information processing.

Second, in much of AI there is a residual behaviorism or operationalism. Since appropriately programmed computers can have input-output patterns similar to those of human beings, we are tempted to postulate mental states in the computer similar to human mental states. But once we see that it is both conceptually and empirically possible for a system to have human capacities in some realm without having any intentionality at all, we should be able to overcome this impulse. My desk adding machine has calculating capacities, but no intentionality, and in this paper I have tried to show that a system could have input and output capabilities that duplicated those of a native Chinese speaker and still not understand Chinese, regardless of how it was programmed. The Turing test is typical of the tradition in being unashamedly behavioristic and operationalistic, and I believe that if AI workers totally repudiated behaviorism and operationalism much of the confusion between simulation and duplication would be eliminated.

Third, this residual operationalism is joined to a residual form of dualism; indeed strong AI only makes sense given the dualistic assumption that, where the mind is concerned, the brain doesn't matter. In strong AI (and in functionalism, as well) what matters are programs, and programs are independent of their realization in machines; indeed, as far as AI is concerned, the same program could be realized by an electronic machine, a Cartesian mental substance, or a Hegelian world spirit. The single most surprising discovery that I have made in discussing these issues is that many AI workers are quite shocked by my idea that actual human mental phenomena might be dependent on actual physical-chemical properties of actual human brains. But if you think about it a minute you can see that I should not have been surprised; for unless you accept some form of dualism, the strong AI project hasn't got a chance. The project is to reproduce and explain the mental by designing programs, but unless the mind is not only conceptually but empirically independent of the brain you couldn't carry out the project, for the program is completely independent of any realization. Unless you believe that the mind is separable from the brain both conceptually and empirically—dualism in a strong form—you cannot hope to reproduce the mental by writing and running programs since programs must be independent of brains or any other particular forms of instantiation. If mental operations consist in computational operations on formal symbols, then it follows that they have no interesting connection with the brain; the only connection would be that the brain just happens to be one of the indefinitely many types of machines capable of instantiating the program. This form of dualism is not the traditional Cartesian variety that claims there are two sorts of *substances,* but it is Cartesian in the sense that it insists that what is specifically mental about the mind has no intrinsic connection with the actual properties of the brain. This underlying dualism is masked from us by the fact that AI literature contains frequent fulminations against "dualism"; what the authors seem to be unaware of is that their position presupposes a strong version of dualism.

"Could a machine think?" My own view is that *only* a machine could think, and indeed only very special kinds of machines, namely brains and machines that had the same causal powers as brains. And that is the main reason strong AI has had little to tell us about thinking, since it has nothing to tell us about machines. By its own definition, it is about programs, and programs are not machines. Whatever else intentionality is, it is a biological phenomenon, and it is as likely to be as causally dependent on the specific biochemistry of its origins as lactation, photosynthesis, or any other biological phenomena. No one would suppose that we could produce milk and sugar by running a computer simulation of the formal sequences in lactation and photosynthesis, but where the mind is concerned many people are willing to believe in such a miracle because of a deep and abiding dualism: the mind they suppose is a matter of formal processes and is independent of quite specific material causes in the way that milk and sugar are not.

In defense of this dualism the hope is often expressed that the brain is a digital computer (early computers, by the way, were often called "electronic brains"). But that is no help. Of course the brain is a digital computer. Since everything is a digital computer, brains are too. The point is that the brain's causal capacity to produce intentionality cannot consist in its instantiating a computer program, since for any program you like it is possible for something to instantiate that program and still not have any mental states. Whatever it is that the brain does to produce intentionality, it cannot consist in instantiating a program since no program, by itself, is sufficient for intentionality.*

Reflections

This article originally appeared together with twenty-eight responses from assorted people. Many of the responses contained excellent commentary, but reprinting them would have overloaded this book, and in any case some were a little too technical. One of the nice things about Searle's article is that it is pretty much understandable by someone without special training in AI, neurology, philosophy, or other disciplines that have a bearing on it.

Our position is quite opposed to Searle's, but we find in Searle an eloquent opponent. Rather than attempt to give a thorough rebuttal to his points, we will concentrate on a few of the issues he raises, leaving our answers to his other points implicit, in the rest of this book.

Searle's paper is based on his ingenious "Chinese room thought experiment," in which the reader is urged to identify with a human being executing by hand the sequence of steps that a very clever AI program would allegedly go through as it read stories in Chinese and answered questions about them in Chinese in a manner sufficiently human-seeming as to be able to pass the Turing test. We think Searle has committed a serious and fundamental misrepresentation by giving the impression that it makes any sense to think that a human being could do this. By buying this image, the reader is unwittingly sucked into an impossibly unrealistic concept of the relation between intelligence and symbol manipulation.

The illusion that Searle hopes to induce in readers (naturally he doesn't think of it as an illusion!) depends on his managing to make readers overlook a tremendous difference in complexity between two systems at different conceptual levels. Once he has done that, the rest is a piece of cake. At the outset, the reader is invited to identify with Searle

---

*I am indebted to a rather large number of people for discussion of these matters and for their patient attempts to overcome my ignorance of artificial intelligence. I would especially like to thank Ned Block, Hubert Dreyfus, John Haugeland, Roger Schank, Robert Wilensky, and Terry Winograd.

as he hand-simulates an existing AI program that can, in a limited way, answer questions of a limited sort, in a few limited domains. Now, for a person to hand-simulate this, or any currently existing AI program—that is, to step through it at the level of detail that the computer does—would involve days, if not weeks or months, of arduous, horrendous boredom. But instead of pointing this out, Searle—as deft at distracting the reader's attention as a practiced magician—switches the reader's image to a hypothetical program that passes the Turing test! He has jumped up many levels of competency without so much as a passing mention. The reader is again invited to put himself or herself in the shoes of the person carrying out the step-by-step simulation, and to "feel the lack of understanding" of Chinese. This is the crux of Searle's argument.

Our response to this (and, as we shall show later, Searle's response as well, in a way) is basically the "Systems Reply": that it is a mistake to try to impute the understanding to the (incidentally) animate simulator; rather it belongs to the system as a whole, which includes what Searle casually characterizes as "bits of paper." This offhand comment, we feel, reveals how Searle's image has blinded him to the realities of the situation. A thinking computer is as repugnant to John Searle as non-Euclidean geometry was to its unwitting discoverer, Gerolamo Saccheri, who thoroughly disowned his own creation. The time—the late 1700s— was not quite ripe for people to accept the conceptual expansion caused by alternate geometries. About fifty years later, however, non-Euclidean geometry was rediscovered and slowly accepted.

Perhaps the same will happen with "artificial intentionality"—if it is ever created. If there ever came to be a program that could pass the Turing test, it seems that Searle, instead of marveling at the power and depth of that program, would just keep on insisting that it lacked some marvelous "causal powers of the brain" (whatever they are). To point out the vacuity of that notion, Zenon Pylyshyn, in his reply to Searle, wondered if the following passage, quite reminiscent of Zuboff's "Story of a Brain" (selection 12), would accurately characterize Searle's viewpoint:

If more and more of the cells in your brain were to be replaced by integrated circuit chips, programmed in such a way as to keep the input-output *function* of each unit identical to that of the unit being replaced, you would in all likelihood just keep right on speaking exactly as you are doing now except that you would eventually stop *meaning* anything by it. What we outside observers might take to be words would become for you just certain noises that circuits caused you to make.

The weakness of Searle's position is that he offers no clear way to tell when genuine meaning—or indeed the genuine "you"—has vanished from this system. He merely insists that some systems have intentionality by virtue of their "causal powers" and that some don't. He vacillates about what those powers are due to. Sometimes it seems that the brain is composed of "the right stuff," but other times it seems to be something else. It is whatever seems convenient at the moment—now it is the slippery essence that distinguishes "form" from "content," now another essence that separates syntax from semantics, and so on.

To the Systems-Reply advocates, Searle offers the thought that the human being in the room (whom we shall from now on refer to as "Searle's demon") should simply memorize, or incorporate all the material on the "bits of paper." As if a human being could, by any conceivable stretch of the imagination, do this. The program on those "bits of paper" embodies the entire mind and character of something as complex in its ability to respond to written material as a human being is, by virtue of being able to pass the Turing test. Could any human being simply "swallow up" the entire description of another human being's mind? We find it hard enough to memorize a written paragraph; but Searle envisions the demon as having absorbed what in all likelihood would amount to millions, if not billions, of pages densely covered with abstract symbols—and moreover having all of this information available, whenever needed, with no retrieval problems. This unlikely aspect of the scenario is all lightly described, and it is not part of Searle's key argument to convince the reader that it makes sense. In fact, quite the contrary— a key part of his argument is in glossing over these questions of orders of magnitude, for otherwise a skeptical reader will realize that nearly all of the understanding must lie in the billions of symbols on paper, and practically none of it in the demon. The fact that the demon is animate is an irrelevant—indeed, misleading—side issue that Searle has mistaken for a very significant fact.

We can back up this argument by exhibiting Searle's own espousal of the Systems Reply. To do so, we should first like to place Searle's thought experiment in a broader context. In particular, we would like to show how Searle's setup is just one of a large family of related thought experiments, several of which are the topics of other selections in this book. Each member of this family of thought experiments is defined by a particular choice of "knob settings" on a thought-experiment generator. Its purpose is to create—in your mind's eye—various sorts of imaginary simulations of human mental activity. Each different thought experiment is an "intuition pump" (Dennett's term) that magnifies one facet or other of the issue, tending to push the reader toward certain conclusions. We see approximately five knobs of interest, although it is possible that someone else could come up with more.

Knob 1.   This knob controls the physical "stuff" out of which the simulation will be constructed. Its settings include: neurons and chemicals; water pipes and water; bits of paper and symbols on them; toilet paper and stones; data structures and procedures; and so on.

Knob 2.   This knob controls the level of accuracy with which the simulation attempts to mimic the human brain. It can be set at an arbitrarily fine level of detail (particles inside atoms), at a coarser level such as that of cells and synapses, or even at the level that AI researchers and cognitive psychologists deal with: that of concepts and ideas, representations and processes.

Knob 3.   This knob controls the physical size of the simulation. Our assumption is that microminiaturization would allow us to make a teeny-weeny network of water pipes or solid-state chips that would fit inside a thimble, and conversely that any chemical process could be blown up to the macroscopic scale.

Knob 4.   This critical knob controls the size and nature of the demon who carries out the simulation. If it is a normal-sized human being, we shall call it a "Searle's demon." If it is a tiny elflike creature that can sit inside neurons or on particles, then we shall call it a "Haugeland's demon," after John Haugeland, whose response to Searle featured this notion. The settings of this knob also determine whether the demon is animate or inanimate.

Knob 5.   This knob controls the speed at which the demon works. It can be set to make the demon work blindingly fast (millions of operations per microsecond) or agonizingly slowly (maybe one operation every few seconds).

Now, by playing with various knob settings, we can come up with various thought experiments. One choice yields the situation described in selection 26, "A Conversation with Einstein's Brain." Another choice yields Searle's Chinese room experiment. In particular, that involves the following knob settings:

Knob 1:   paper and symbols
Knob 2:   concepts and ideas
Knob 3:   room size
Knob 4:   human-sized demon
Knob 5:   slow setting (one operation every few seconds)

Note that in principle Searle is not opposed to assuming that a simulation with these parameters could pass the Turing test. His dispute is only with what that would imply.

There is one final parameter that is not a knob but a point of view from which to look at the experiment. Let us add a little color to this drab experiment and say that the simulated Chinese speaker involved is a woman and that the demons (if animate) are always male. Now we have a choice between the demon's-eye view and the system's-eye view. Remember that by hypothesis, both the demon and the simulated woman are equally capable of articulating their views on whether or not they are understanding, and on what they are experiencing. Searle is insistent, nonetheless, that we see this experiment only from the point of view of the demon. He insists that no matter what the simulated woman claims (in Chinese, of course) about her understanding, we should disregard her claims, and pay attention to the demon inside, who is carrying out the symbol manipulation. Searle's claim amounts to the notion that actually there is only one point of view, not two. If one accepts the way Searle describes the whole experiment, this claim has great intuitive appeal, since the demon is about our size, speaks our language, and works at about our speed—and it is very hard to identify with a "woman" whose answers come at the rate of one per century (with luck)—and in "meaningless squiggles and squoggles," to boot.

But if we change some of the knob settings, we can also alter the ease with which we change point of view. In particular, Haugeland's variation involves switching various knobs as follows:

> Knob 1: neurons and chemicals
> Knob 2: neural-firing level
> Knob 3: brain size
> Knob 4: eensy-weensy demon
> Knob 5: dazzlingly fast demon

What Haugeland wants us to envision is this: A real woman's brain is, unfortunately, defective. It no longer is able to send neurotransmitters from one neuron to another. Luckily, however, this brain is inhabited by an incredibly tiny and incredibly speedy Haugeland's demon, who intervenes every single time any neuron would have been about to release neurotransmitters into a neighboring neuron. This demon "tickles" the appropriate synapse of the next neuron in a way that is functionally indistinguishable, to that neuron, from the arrival of genuine neurotransmitters. And the H-demon is so swift that he can jump around from synapse to synapse in trillionths of a second, never falling behind schedule. In this way the operation of the woman's brain proceeds exactly as it would have, if she were healthy. Now, Haugeland asks Searle, does the woman still think—that is, does she possess intentionality—or, to recall the words of Professor Jefferson as cited by Turing, does she merely "artificially signal"?

You might expect Searle to urge us to listen to and identify with the demon, and to eschew the Systems Reply, which would be, of course, to listen to and identify with the woman. But in his response to Haugeland, Searle surprises us—he chooses to listen to *her* this time and to ignore the demon who is cursing us from his tiny vantage point, yelling up to us, "Fools! Don't listen to her! She's merely a puppet whose every action is caused by my tickling, and by the program embedded in these many neurons that I zip around among." But Searle does not heed the H-demon's warning cries. He says, "Her neurons still have the right causal powers; they just need some help from the demon."

We can construct a mapping between Searle's original setup and this modified setup. To the "bits of paper" now correspond all the synapses in the woman's brain. To the AI program written on these "bits of paper" corresponds the entire configuration of the woman's brain; this amounts to a gigantic prescription telling the demon when and how to know which synapses to tickle. To the act of writing "meaningless squiggles and squoggles of Chinese" on paper corresponds the act of tickling her synapses. Suppose we take the setup as is, except that we'll vary the size and speed knobs. We'll blow the woman's brain up to the size of the Earth, so that the demon becomes an "us-sized" S-demon instead of a tiny H-demon. And let's also have the S-demon act at speeds reasonable for humans, instead of zipping thousands of miles throughout this bulbous brain in mere microseconds. Now which level does Searle wish us to identify with? We won't speculate, but it seems to us that if the Systems Reply was compelling in the previous case, it should still be so in this case.

It must be admitted that Searle's thought experiment vividly raises the question of what understanding a language really is. We would like to digress for a moment on that topic. Consider the question: "What kind of ability to manipulate the written or spoken symbols of a language amounts to a *true understanding* of that language?" Parrots who parrot English do not understand English. The recorded voice of a woman announcing the exact time of day on the telephone time service is not the mouthpiece of a system that understands English. There is no mentality behind that voice—it has been skimmed off of its mental substrate, yet retains a human-seeming quality. Perhaps a child would wonder how anyone could have so boring a job, and could do it so reliably. This would amuse us. It would be another matter, of course, if her voice were being driven by a flexible AI program that could pass the Turing test!

Imagine you are teaching a class in China. Further, imagine that you are aware of formulating all your thoughts in English and then of applying last-minute transformation rules (in reality, they would be last-split-second rules) that convert the English thoughts into instructions for moving your mouth and vocal cords in strange, "meaningless" ways— and yet, all your pupils sit there and seem quite satisfied with your performance. When they raise their hands, they utter exotic sounds that, although they are completely meaningless to you, you are equipped to deal with, as you quickly apply some inverse rules and recover the English meanings underlying them. . . . Would you feel you were actually speaking Chinese? Would you feel you had gained some insight into the Chinese mentality? Or—can you actually imagine this situation? Is it realistic? Could anyone actually speak a foreign language well using this method?

The standard line is "You must learn to *think in Chinese.*" But in what does this consist? Anyone who has experienced it will recognize this description: The sounds of the second language pretty soon become "unheard"—you hear right through them, rather than hearing them, as you see right through a window, rather than seeing the window. Of course, you can make yourself hear a familiar language as pure uninterpreted sound if you try very hard, just as you can look at a windowpane if you want; but you can't have your cake and eat it too—you can't hear the sounds both *with* and *without* their meanings. And so most of the time people hear mainly meaning. For those people who learn a language because of enchantment with its sounds, this is a bit disappointing—and yet mastery of those sounds, even if one no longer hears them naively, is a beautiful, exhilarating experience. (It would be an interesting thing to try to apply this same kind of analysis to the hearing of music, where the distinction between hearing bare sounds and hearing their "meanings" is far less well understood, yet seems very real.)

Learning a second language involves transcending one's own native language. It involves mixing the new language right in with the medium in which thought takes place. Thoughts must be able to germinate as easily (or nearly as easily) in the new language as in one's native language. The way in which a new language's habits seep down level by level and finally get absorbed into neurons is a giant mystery still. But one thing for certain is that mastery of a language does not consist in getting your "English subsystem" to execute for you a program of rules that enable you to deal with a language as a set of meaningless sounds and marks. Somehow, the new language must fuse with your internal representational system—your repertoire of concepts, images, and so on—in the same intimate way as English is fused with it. To think precisely about this, one must develop a very clear notion of the concept of *levels of implementation*, a computer-science concept of great power.

Computer scientists are used to the idea that one system can "emulate" another system. In fact, it follows from a theorem proven in 1936 by Alan Turing that any general-purpose digital computer can take on the guise of any other general-purpose digital computer, and the only difference to the outside world will be one of speed. The verb "emulate" is reserved for simulations, by a computer, of another computer, while "simulate" refers to the modeling of other phenomena, such as hurricanes, population curves, national elections, or even computer users.

A major difference is that simulation is almost always approximate, depending on the nature of the model of the phenomenon in question, whereas emulation is in a deep sense exact. So exact is it that when, say, a Sigma-5 computer emulates a computer with different architecture—say a DEC PDP-10—the users of the machine will be unaware that they are not dealing with a genuine DEC. This embedding of one architecture in another gives rise to so-called "virtual machines"—in this case, a virtual DEC-10. Underneath every virtual machine there is always some other machine. It may be a machine of the same type, it may even be another virtual machine. In his book *Structured Computer Organization,* Andrew Tanenbaum uses this notion of virtual machines to explain how large computer systems can be seen as a stack of virtual machines implen.ented one on top of the other—the bottommost one being, of course, a *real* machine! But in any case, the levels are sealed off from each other in a watertight way, just as Searle's demon was prevented from talking to the Chinese speaker he was part of. (It is intriguing to imagine what kind of conversation would take place—assuming that there were an interpreter present, since Searle's demon knows no Chinese!)

Now in theory, it is possible to have any two such levels communicate with each other, but this has traditionally been considered bad style; level-mingling is forbidden. Nonetheless, it is probable that this forbidden fruit—this blurring of two implementational levels—is exactly what goes on when a human "system" learns a second language. The second language does not run on top of the first one as a kind of software parasite, but rather becomes equally fundamentally implanted in the hardware (or nearly so). Somehow, absorption of a second language involves bringing about deep changes in one's underlying "machine"— a vast and coherent set of changes in the ways that neurons fire, so sweeping a set of changes that it creates new ways for the higher-level entities—the symbols—to trigger one another.

To parallel this in a computer system, a higher-level program would have to have some way of creating changes inside the "demon" that is carrying its program out. This is utterly foreign to the present style in computer science of implementing one level above another in a strictly vertical, sealed-off fashion. The ability of a higher level to loop back and affect lower levels—its own underpinnings—is a kind of magic trick which we feel is very close to the core of consciousness. It will perhaps one day prove to be a key element in the push toward ever-greater flexibility in computer design, and of course in the approach toward artificial intelligence. In particular, a satisfactory answer to the question of what "understanding" really means will undoubtedly require a much sharper delineation of the ways in which different levels in a symbol-manipulating system can depend on and affect one another. All in all, these concepts have proven elusive, and a clear understanding of them is probably a good ways off yet.

In this rather confusing discussion of many levels, you may have started to wonder what in the world "level" really means. It is a most difficult question. As long as levels are sealed off from each other, like Searle's demon and the Chinese-speaking woman, it is fairly clear. When they begin to blur, beware! Searle may admit that there are two *levels* in his thought experiment, but he is reluctant to admit that there are two occupied *points of view*—two genuine beings that feel and "have experience." He is worried that once we admit that *some* computational systems might have experiences, that would be a Pandora's box and all of a sudden "mind would be everywhere"—in the churning of stomachs, livers, automobile engines, and so on.

Searle seems to believe that any system whatsoever can be *ascribed* beliefs and feelings and so on, if one looks hard enough for a way to describe the system as an instantiation of an AI program. Obviously, that would be a disturbing notion, leading the way to panpsychism. Indeed, Searle believes that the AI people have unwittingly committed themselves to a panpsychic vision of the world.

Searle's escape from his self-made trap is to maintain that all those "beliefs" and "feelings" that you will uncover in inanimate objects and so forth when you begin seeing mind everywhere are not genuine but "pseudo." They lack intentionality! They lack the causal powers of the brain! (Of course, Searle would caution others to beware of confusing *these* notions with the naïvely dualistic notion of "soul.")

Our escape is to deny that the trap exists at all. It is incorrect to see minds everywhere. We say: minds do not lurk in car engines or livers any more than brains lurk in car engines and livers.

It is worthwhile expanding on this a little. If you can see all the complexity of thought processes in a churning stomach, then what's to prevent you from reading the pattern of bubbles in a carbonated beverage as coding for the Chopin piano concerto in E minor? And don't the holes in pieces of Swiss cheese code for the entire history of the United States? Sure they do—in Chinese as well as in English. After all, all things are written everywhere! Bach's Brandenburg concerto no. 2 is coded for in the structure of Hamlet—and Hamlet was of course readable (if you'd only known the code) from the structure of the last piece of birthday cake you gobbled down.

The problem is, in all these cases, that of specifying the code without knowing in advance what you want to read. For otherwise, you could pull a description of anyone's mental activity out of a baseball game or a blade of grass by an arbitrarily constructed *a posteriori* code. But this is not science.

Minds come in different grades of sophistication, surely, but minds worth calling minds exist only where sophisticated representational systems exist, and no describable mapping that remains constant in time will reveal a self-updating representational system in a car engine or a liver. Perhaps one could read mentality into a rumbling car engine in somewhat the way that people read extra meanings into the structures of the Great Pyramids or Stonehenge, the music of Bach, Shakespeare's plays, and so on—namely, by fabricating far-fetched numerological mapping schemes that can be molded and flexed whenever needed to fit the desires of the interpreter. But we doubt that that is what Searle intends (we do grant that he intends).

Minds exist in brains and may come to exist in programmed machines. If and when such machines come about, their causal powers will derive not from the substances they are made of, but from their design and the programs that run in them. And the way we will know they have those causal powers is by talking to them and listening carefully to what they have to say.

D.R.H.

23

RAYMOND M. SMULLYAN

An Unfortunate Dualist

Once upon a time there was a dualist. He believed that mind and matter are separate substances. Just how they interacted he did not pretend to know—this was one of the "mysteries" of life. But he was sure they were quite separate substances.

This dualist, unfortunately, led an unbearably painful life—not because of his philosophical beliefs, but for quite different reasons. And he had excellent empirical evidence that no respite was in sight for the rest of his life. He longed for nothing more than to die. But he was deterred from suicide by such reasons as: (1) he did not want to hurt other people by his death; (2) he was afraid suicide might be morally wrong; (3) he was afraid there *might* be an afterlife, and he did not want to risk the possibility of eternal punishment. So our poor dualist was quite desperate.

Then came the discovery of *the* miracle drug! Its effect on the taker was to annihilate the soul or mind entirely but to leave the body functioning *exactly* as before. Absolutely no observable change came over the taker; the body continued to act just as if it still had a soul. Not the closest friend or observer could possibly know that the taker had taken the drug, unless the taker informed him.

Do you believe that such a drug is impossible in principle? Assuming you believe it possible, would you take it? Would you regard it as immoral? Is it tantamount to suicide? Is there anything in Scriptures forbidding the use of such a drug? Surely, the *body* of the taker can still fulfill all its responsibilities on earth. Another question: Suppose your spouse took such a drug, and you knew it. You would know that she (or he) no longer had a soul but acted just as if she did have one. Would you love your mate any less?

To return to the story, our dualist was, of course, delighted! Now he could annihilate himself (his *soul,* that is) in a way not subject to any of the foregoing objections. And so, for the first time in years, he went to bed with a light heart, saying: "Tomorrow morning I will go down to the drugstore and get the drug. My days of suffering are over at last!" With these thoughts, he fell peacefully asleep.

Now at this point a curious thing happened. A friend of the dualist who knew about this drug, and who knew of the sufferings of the dualist, decided to put him out of his misery. So in the middle of the night, while the dualist was fast asleep, the friend quietly stole into the house and injected the drug into his veins. The next morning the body of the dualist awoke—without any soul indeed—and the first thing it did was to go to the drugstore to get the drug. He took it home and, before taking it, said, "Now I shall be released." So he took it and then waited the time interval in which it was supposed to work. At the end of the interval he angrily exclaimed: "Damn it, this stuff hasn't helped at all! I still obviously have a soul and am suffering as much as ever!"

Doesn't all this suggest that perhaps there might be something just a *little* wrong with dualism?

Reflections

"O Seigneur, s'il y a un Seigneur, sauvez mon âme, si j'ai une âme."

"O Lord, if there is a Lord, save my soul, if I have a soul."
—Ernest Renan
Prière d'un sceptique

Smullyan provides a provocative riposte to Searle's thrust—an intentionality-killing potion. The soul of a sufferer is annihilated and yet, to all external eyes, the suffering goes on unabated. What about to the inner "I"? Smullyan leaves no doubt as to how he feels.

The point of this little fable is the logical absurdity of such a potion. But why is this? Why can't the soul depart and leave behind a soulless, feelingless, yet living and normal-seeming being?

Soul represents the perceptually unbreachable gulf between principles and particles. The levels in between are so many and so murky that we not only see in each person a soul but are unable to unsee it. "Soul" is the name we give to that opaque yet characteristic *style* of each individual. Put another way, your soul is the "incompressible core" that determines *how* you are, hence *who* you are. But is this incompressible core a set of moral principles or personality traits, or is it something that we can speak of in physical terms—in brain language?

The brain's neurons respond only to "local" stimuli—local in both space and time. At each instant (as in the Game of Life, described in the Reflections on "Non Serviam"), the neighboring neurons' influences are added together and the neuron in question either fires or doesn't. Yet somehow all of this "local" behavior can add up to a Grand Style—to a set of "global" principles that, seen on the level of human behavior, embody long-term goals, ideals, interests, tastes, hopes, fears, morals, and so on. So somehow all of these long-term global qualities have to be coded into the neurons in such a way that, from the neurons' firings, the proper global behavior will emerge. We can call this a "flattening" or "compressing" of the global into the local. Such coding of many long-term, high-level goals into the synaptic structures of billions of neurons has been partially done for us by our millions of ancestors, way back in the evolutionary tree. We owe much not only to those who survived, but also to those who perished, since it is only thanks to the multiple branchings at every stage that evolution could work its miracles to give rise to a creature of such complexity as a person.

Consider a simpler animal, such as a newborn calf. An hour-old calf not only can see and walk, but will instinctively shy away from people. Such behavior comes from ancient sources—namely, the higher survival rate of "protocows" that had genes for this kind of behavior. Such behavior, along with a million other successful adaptations, has been "flattened" into neural patterns coded for in the bovine genes, and is now a ready-made feature of each calf as it comes off the assembly line. Seen on its own, the set of cow genes or human genes seems a miracle—nearly inexplicable. So much history has been flattened into molecular patterns. In order to demystify this, you would have to work backward, reconstructing the evolutionary tree—and not just the branches that survived! But we don't see the whole tree of predecessors, successful and otherwise, when we look at an individual cow, and so we can be amazed by the long-term purposes, goals, and so forth that we see flattened in its brain structure. Our amazement is particularly great when we try to imagine how, inside its head, millions of individually purposeless local neural firings are adding up to a coherent purposive style—the soul of one cow.

In humans, by contrast, the mind and character continue to be shaped for years after birth, and over this long time span neurons absorb feedback from the environment and self-modify in such a way as to build up a set of styles. The lessons of childhood are flattened into unconscious firing patterns, and when all of these tiny learned neural patterns act in concert with the myriad tiny neural patterns coded for in genes, a human perceiver will see one large pattern emerge—the soul of one human. This is why the idea of a potion that "kills the soul" and yet leaves the behavior patterns invariant makes no sense.

Under pressure, of course, a soul—a set of principles—may partly fold. What might have seemed "incompressible" may in fact yield to greed, fame, vanity, corruption, fear, torture, or whatever. In this way, a "soul" can be broken. Orwell's novel *1984* gives a vivid description of the mechanics of soul breaking. People who are brainwashed by cults or terrorist groups that hold them captive for long periods of time can lose the global coherence of drives so carefully compressed over years into their neurons. And yet there is a kind of resilience, a tendency to return to some sort of "resting position"—the central soul, the innermost core —even after horrendous, grueling episodes. This could be called "homeostasis of the spirit."

Let us move to a jollier note. Imagine a soul-free universe, a mechanistic universe with nary a speck of free will or consciousness to be found, not a perceiver anywhere. This universe might be deterministic or might be filled with arbitrary, random, capricious, and causeless events. It is law-governed enough, though, that stable structures can emerge and evolve. In this universe, then, are swarming many distinct, tightly knit, self-sufficient little objects, each one with an internal representational system of enough complexity as to engender a deep, rich self-image. In each one of them this will give rise to (and here we onlookers must be pardoned for smiling with wry amusement) the illusion of free will—when in fact, of course, this is just a cold universe and these objects that populate it are just robotlike, rule-bound machines, moving around in deterministic (or capricio-deterministic) trajectories, and kidding themselves that they're exchanging meaningful ideas when in reality they're just mechanically chattering back and forth by emitting and absorbing long trains of empty, hollow, meaningless electromagnetic or perhaps acoustical waves.

Having imagined this strange universe filled with illusions, one can now take a look out at *this* universe and see all of humanity in this disorienting light. One can de-soul-ify everyone in the world, so that they're all like Smullyan's zombie or Searle's Chinese-speaking robot, seeming to have an inner life but in fact as devoid of soul as is a clacking typewriter driven by a cold, feelingless computer. Life then seems a cruel hoax on all those soul-free shells, erroneously "convinced" (although how can a heap of dead atoms be convinced?) that they are conscious.

And this would be the best possible way to look at people, were it not for one tiny fact that seems to mess it up: I, the observer, am one of them, yet am undeniably conscious! The rest of them are, for all I know, just bundles of empty reflexes that feign consciousness—but not *this* one! After I've died—well, *then* this vision will be an accurate accounting of the way things are. But until that moment, one of the objects will remain special and different, because it is not being fooled! Or . . . might there be something just a little wrong with dualism?

Dualists maintain, as Smullyan puts it, that mind and matter are separate *substances*. That is, there are (at least) two kinds of stuff: physical stuff and mental stuff. The stuff our minds are made of has no mass, no physical energy—perhaps not even a location in space. This view is so mysterious, so *systematically* immune to clarification, that one may well wonder what attracts anyone to it. One broad highway leading to dualism goes through the following (bad) argument:

Some facts are not about the properties, circumstances, and relations of physical objects.
Therefore some facts are about the properties, circumstances, and relations of nonphysical objects.

What's wrong with this argument? Try to think of examples of facts that are not about physical objects. The fact that the narrator in *Moby Dick* is called Ishmael is a fact in good standing, but what is it about? One *might* want to insist (implausibly) that it is really about certain ink shapes on certain bound stacks of printed pages; or one might say (somewhat mysteriously) that it is a fact all right, but it is not *about* anything at all; or, waving one's hands a bit, one might say that it is a fact about an *abstract* object—in much the way the fact that 641 is a prime number is a fact about an abstract object. But almost no one (we suppose) is attracted to the view that it is a fact about a *perfectly real but nonphysical* person named Ishmael. This last view takes novel writing to be a method of ghost-manufacture; it takes too literally the familiar hyperbole about an author's characters coming to life, having wills of their own, rebelling against their creator. It is literary dualism. (Anybody might seriously wonder if Jack the

Ripper was really the Prince of Wales, for they were both real people—
or maybe a single real person. A literary dualist might seriously wonder
if Professor Moriarty were really Dr. Watson.) Dualists believe that over
and above the physical things and events there are other, nonphysical
things and events that have *some* sort of independent existence.

When asked to say more, dualists divide into two schools: those who
hold that the occurrence or existence of a mental event has *no effect
whatsoever* on subsequent physical events in the brain, and those who deny
this and hold that mental events do have effects on physical events in the
brain. The former are called epiphenomenalists and the latter are called
interactionists. Smullyan's fable nicely disposes of epiphenomenalism
(doesn't it?), but what of interactionism?

Ever since Descartes first struggled with it, interactionists have had
the apparently insuperable problem of explaining how an event with no
physical properties—no mass, no charge, no location, no velocity—could
make a physical difference in the brain (or anywhere else). For a nonphysical event to make a difference, it must make some physical event
happen that wouldn't have happened if the nonphysical event hadn't
happened. But if we found a sort of event whose occurrence had this sort
of effect, why wouldn't we decide *for that very reason* that we had discovered a new sort of *physical* event? When antimatter was first postulated
by physicists, dualists didn't react with glee and taunts of "I told you so!"
Why not? Hadn't physicists just supported their claim that the universe
had two radically different sorts of stuff in it? The main trouble with
antimatter, from the dualists' point of view, was that however exotic it
was, it was still amenable to investigation by the methods of the physical
sciences. Mind-stuff, on the other hand, was supposed to be off limits to
science. But if it is, then we have a guarantee that the mystery will never
go away. Some people like that idea.

D.R.H.
D.C.D.

VI

The Inner Eye

24

THOMAS NAGEL

What Is It Like to Be a Bat?

Consciousness is what makes the mind–body problem really intractable. Perhaps that is why current discussions of the problem give it little attention or get it obviously wrong. The recent wave of reductionist euphoria has produced several analyses of mental phenomena and mental concepts designed to explain the possibility of some variety of materialism, psychophysical identification, or reduction.* But the problems dealt with are those common to this type of reduction and other types, and what makes the mind–body problem unique, and unlike the water–H_2O problem or the Turing machine–IBM machine problem or the lightning–electrical discharge problem or the gene–DNA problem or the oak tree–hydrocarbon problem, is ignored.

Every reductionist has his favorite analogy from modern science. It is most unlikely that any of these unrelated examples of successful reduction will shed light on the relation of mind to brain. But philosophers share the general human weakness for explanations of what is incomprehensible in terms suited for what is familiar and well understood, though entirely different. This has led to the acceptance of implausible accounts of the mental largely because they would permit familiar kinds of reduction. I shall try to explain why the usual examples do not help us to understand the relation between mind and body—why, indeed, we have at present no conception of what an explanation of the physical nature

"What Is It Like to Be a Bat?" by Thomas Nagel appeared in *The Philosophical Review*, October 1974. It is reprinted by permission of the author.

*See "Further Reading" for Nagel's references.

of a mental phenomenon would be. Without consciousness the mind–body problem would be much less interesting. With consciousness it seems hopeless. The most important and characteristic feature of conscious mental phenomena is very poorly understood. Most reductionist theories do not even try to explain it. And careful examination will show that no currently available concept of reduction is applicable to it. Perhaps a new theoretical form can be devised for the purpose, but such a solution, if it exists, lies in the distant intellectual future.

Conscious experience is a widespread phenomenon. It occurs at many levels of animal life, though we cannot be sure of its presence in the simpler organisms, and it is very difficult to say in general what provides evidence of it. (Some extremists have been prepared to deny it even of mammals other than man.) No doubt it occurs in countless forms totally unimaginable to us, on other planets in other solar systems throughout the universe. But no matter how the form may vary, the fact that an organism has conscious experience *at all* means, basically, that there is something it is like to *be* that organism. There may be further implications about the form of the experience; there may even (though I doubt it) be implications about the behavior of the organism. But fundamentally an organism has conscious mental states if and only if there is something that it is like to *be* that organism—something it is like *for* the organism.

We may call this the subjective character of experience. It is not captured by any of the familiar, recently devised reductive analyses of the mental, for all of them are logically compatible with its absence. It is not analyzable in terms of any explanatory system of functional states, or intentional states, since these could be ascribed to robots or automata that behaved like people though they experienced nothing.* It is not analyzable in terms of the causal role of experiences in relation to typical human behavior—for similar reasons.† I do not deny that conscious mental states and events cause behavior, nor that they may be given functional characterizations. I deny only that this kind of thing exhausts their analysis. Any reductionist program has to be based on an analysis of what is to be reduced. If the analysis leaves something out, the problem will be falsely posed. It is useless to base the defense of materialism on any analysis of mental phenomena that fails to deal explicitly with their

---

*Perhaps there could not actually be such robots. Perhaps anything complex enough to behave like a person would have experiences. But that, if true, is a fact which cannot be discovered merely by analyzing the concept of experience.

†It is not equivalent to that about which we are incorrigible, both because we are not incorrigible about experience and because experience is present in animals lacking language and thought, who have no beliefs at all about their experiences.

subjective character. For there is no reason to suppose that a reduction which seems plausible when no attempt is made to account for consciousness can be extended to include consciousness. Without some idea, therefore, of what the subjective character of experience is, we cannot know what is required of physicalist theory.

While an account of the physical basis of mind must explain many things, this appears to be the most difficult. It is impossible to exclude the phenomenological features of experience from a reduction in the same way that one excludes the phenomenal features of an ordinary substance from a physical or chemical reduction of it—namely, by explaining them as effects on the minds of human observers (cf. Rorty 1965). If physicalism is to be defended, the phenomenological features must themselves be given a physical account. But when we examine their subjective character it seems that such a result is impossible. The reason is that every subjective phenomenon is essentially connected with a single point of view, and it seems inevitable that an objective, physical theory will abandon that point of view.

Let me first try to state the issue somewhat more fully than by referring to the relation between the subjective and the objective, or between the *pour soi* and the *en soi*. This is far from easy. Facts about what it is like to be an X are very peculiar, so peculiar that some may be inclined to doubt their reality, or the significance of claims about them. To illustrate the connection between subjectivity and a point of view, and to make evident the importance of subjective features, it will help to explore the matter in relation to an example that brings out clearly the divergence between the two types of conception, subjective and objective.

I assume we all believe that bats have experience. After all, they are mammals, and there is no more doubt that they have experience than that mice or pigeons or whales have experience. I have chosen bats instead of wasps or flounders because if one travels too far down the phylogenetic tree, people gradually shed their faith that there is experience there at all. Bats, although more closely related to us than those other species, nevertheless present a range of activity and a sensory apparatus so different from ours that the problem I want to pose is exceptionally vivid (though it certainly could be raised with other species). Even without the benefit of philosophical reflection, anyone who has spent some time in an enclosed space with an excited bat knows what it is to encounter a fundamentally *alien* form of life.

I have said that the essence of the belief that bats have experience is that there is something that it is like to be a bat. Now we know that most bats (the microchiroptera, to be precise) perceive the external world primarily by sonar, or echolocation, detecting the reflections, from objects within range, of their own rapid, subtly modulated, high-frequency shrieks. Their brains are designed to correlate the outgoing impulses with the subsequent echoes, and the information thus acquired enables bats to make precise discriminations of distance, size, shape, motion, and texture comparable to those we make by vision. But bat sonar, though clearly a form of perception, is not similar in its operation to any sense that we possess, and there is no reason to suppose that it is subjectively like anything we can experience or imagine. This appears to create difficulties for the notion of what it is like to be a bat. We must consider whether any method will permit us to extrapolate to the inner life of the bat from our own case,* and if not, what alternative methods there may be for understanding the notion.

Our own experience provides the basic material for our imagination, whose range is therefore limited. It will not help to try to imagine that one has webbing on one's arms, which enables one to fly around at dusk and dawn catching insects in one's mouth; that one has very poor vision, and perceives the surrounding world by a system of reflected high-frequency sound signals; and that one spends the day hanging upside down by one's feet in an attic. Insofar as I can imagine this (which is not very far), it tells me only what it would be like for *me* to behave as a bat behaves. But that is not the question. I want to know what it is like for a *bat* to be a bat. Yet if I try to imagine this, I am restricted to the resources of my own mind, and those resources are inadequate to the task. I cannot perform it either by imagining additions to my present experience, or by imagining segments gradually subtracted from it, or by imagining some combination of additions, subtractions, and modifications.

To the extent that I could look and behave like a wasp or a bat without changing my fundamental structure, my experiences would not be anything like the experiences of those animals. On the other hand, it is doubtful that any meaning can be attached to the supposition that I should possess the internal neurophysiological constitution of a bat. Even if I could by gradual degrees be transformed into a bat, nothing in my present constitution enables me to imagine what the experiences of such a future stage of myself thus metamorphosed would be like. The best evidence would come from the experiences of bats, if we only knew what they were like.

So if extrapolation from our own case is involved in the idea of what it is like to be a bat, the extrapolation must be incompletable. We cannot

---

*By "our own case" I do not mean just "my own case," but rather the mentalistic ideas that we apply unproblematically to ourselves and other human beings.

form more than a schematic conception of what it *is* like. For example, we may ascribe general *types* of experience on the basis of the animal's structure and behavior. Thus we describe bat sonar as a form of three-dimensional forward perception; we believe that bats feel some versions of pain, fear, hunger, and lust, and that they have other, more familiar types of perception besides sonar. But we believe that these experiences also have in each case a specific subjective character, which it is beyond our ability to conceive. And if there is conscious life elsewhere in the universe, it is likely that some of it will not be describable even in the most general experiential terms available to us.* (The problem is not confined to exotic cases, however, for it exists between one person and another. The subjective character of the experience of a person deaf and blind from birth is not accessible to me, for example, nor presumably is mine to him. This does not prevent us each from believing that the other's experience has such a subjective character.)

If anyone is inclined to deny that we can believe in the existence of facts like this whose exact nature we cannot possibly conceive, he should reflect that in contemplating the bats we are in much the same position that intelligent bats or Martians† would occupy if they tried to form a conception of what it was like to be us. The structure of their own minds might make it impossible for them to succeed, but we know they would be wrong to conclude that there is not anything precise that it is like to be us: that only certain general types of mental state could be ascribed to us (perhaps perception and appetite would be concepts common to us both; perhaps not). We know they would be wrong to draw such a skeptical conclusion because we know what it is like to be us. And we know that while it includes an enormous amount of variation and complexity, and while we do not possess the vocabulary to describe it adequately, its subjective character is highly specific, and in some respects describable in terms that can be understood only by creatures like us. The fact that we cannot expect ever to accommodate in our language a detailed description of Martian or bat phenomenology should not lead us to dismiss as meaningless the claim that bats and Martians have experiences fully comparable in richness of detail to our own. It would be fine if someone were to develop concepts and a theory that enabled us to think about those things; but such an understanding may be permanently denied to us by the limits of our nature. And to deny the reality or logical significance of what we can never

---

*Therefore the analogical form of the English expression "what it is *like*" is misleading. It does not mean "what (in our experience) it *resembles*," but rather "how it is for the subject himself."

†Any intelligent extraterrestrial beings totally different from us.

describe or understand is the crudest form of cognitive dissonance.

This brings us to the edge of a topic that requires much more discussion than I can give it here: namely, the relation between facts on the one hand and conceptual schemes or systems of representation on the other. My realism about the subjective domain in all its forms implies a belief in the existence of facts beyond the reach of human concepts. Certainly it is possible for a human being to believe that there are facts which humans never *will* possess the requisite concepts to represent or comprehend. Indeed, it would be foolish to doubt this, given the finiteness of humanity's expectations. After all, there would have been transfinite numbers even if everyone had been wiped out by the Black Death before Cantor discovered them. But one might also believe that there are facts which *could* not ever be represented or comprehended by human beings, even if the species lasted forever—simply because our structure does not permit us to operate with concepts of the requisite type. This impossibility might even be observed by other beings, but it is not clear that the existence of such beings, or the possibility of their existence, is a precondition of the significance of the hypothesis that there are humanly inaccessible facts. (After all, the nature of beings with access to humanly inaccessible facts is presumably itself a humanly inaccessible fact.) Reflection on what it is like to be a bat seems to lead us, therefore, to the conclusion that there are facts that do not consist in the truth of propositions expressible in a human language. We can be compelled to recognize the existence of such facts without being able to state or comprehend them.

I shall not pursue this subject, however. Its bearing on the topic before us (namely, the mind–body problem) is that it enables us to make a general observation about the subjective character of experience. Whatever may be the status of facts about what it is like to be a human being, or a bat, or a Martian, these appear to be facts that embody a particular point of view.

I am not adverting here to the alleged privacy of experience to its possessor. The point of view in question is not one accessible only to a single individual. Rather it is a *type*. It is often possible to take up a point of view other than one's own, so the comprehension of such facts is not limited to one's own case. There is a sense in which phenomenological facts are perfectly objective: One person can know or say of another what the quality of the other's experience is. They are subjective, however, in the sense that even this objective ascription of experience is possible only for someone sufficiently similar to the object of ascription to be able to adopt his point of view—to understand the ascription in the first person as well as in the third, so to speak. The more different from oneself the other experiencer is, the less success one can expect with this enterprise. In our own case we occupy the relevant point of view, but we will have as much difficulty understanding our own experience properly if we approach it from another point of view as we would if we tried to understand the experience of another species without taking up *its* point of view.*

This bears directly on the mind–body problem. For if the facts of experience—facts about what it is like *for* the experiencing organism—are accessible only from one point of view, then it is a mystery how the true character of experiences could be revealed in the physical operation of that organism. The latter is a domain of objective facts par excellence— the kind that can be observed and understood from many points of view and by individuals with differing perceptual systems. There are no comparable imaginative obstacles to the acquisition of knowledge about bat neurophysiology by human scientists, and intelligent bats or Martians might learn more about the human brain than we ever will.

This is not by itself an argument against reduction. A Martian scientist with no understanding of visual perception could understand the rainbow, or lightning, or clouds as physical phenomena, though he would never be able to understand the human concepts of rainbow, lightning, or cloud, or the place these things occupy in our phenomenal world. The objective nature of the things picked out by these concepts could be apprehended by him because, although the concepts themselves are connected with a particular point of view and a particular visual phenomenology, the things apprehended from that point of view are not: they are observable from the point of view but external to it; hence they can be comprehended from other points of view also, either by the same organisms or by others. Lightning has an objective character that is not exhausted by its visual appearance, and this can be investigated by a Martian without vision. To be precise, it has a *more* objective character than is revealed in its visual appearance. In speaking of the move from subjective to objective characterization, I wish to remain noncommittal about the existence of an end point, the completely objective intrinsic

---

*It may be easier than I suppose to transcend interspecies barriers with the aid of the imagination. For example, blind people are able to detect objects near them by a form of sonar, using vocal clicks or taps of a cane. Perhaps if one knew what that was like, one could by extension imagine roughly what it was like to possess the much more refined sonar of a bat. The distance between oneself and other persons and other species can fall anywhere on a continuum. Even for other persons the understanding of what it is like to be them is only partial, and when one moves to species very different from oneself, a lesser degree of partial understanding may still be available. The imagination is remarkably flexible. My point, however, is not that we cannot *know* what it is like to be a bat. I am not raising that epistemological problem. My point is rather that even to form a *conception* of what it is like to be a bat (and *a fortiori* to know what it is like to be a bat) one must take up the bat's point of view. If one can take it up roughly, or partially, then one's conception will also be rough or partial. Or so it seems in our present state of understanding.

nature of the thing, which one might or might not be able to reach. It may be more accurate to think of objectivity as a direction in which the understanding can travel. And in understanding a phenomenon like lightning, it is legitimate to go as far away as one can from a strictly human viewpoint.*

In the case of experience, on the other hand, the connection with a particular point of view seems much closer. It is difficult to understand what could be meant by the *objective* character of an experience, apart from the particular point of view from which its subject apprehends it. After all, what would be left of what it was like to be a bat if one removed the viewpoint of the bat? But if experience does not have, in addition to its subjective character, an objective nature that can be apprehended from many different points of view, then how can it be supposed that a Martian investigating my brain might be observing physical processes which were my mental processes (as he might observe physical processes which were bolts of lightning), only from a different point of view? How, for that matter, could a human physiologist observe them from another point of view?†

We appear to be faced with a general difficulty about psychophysical reduction. In other areas the process of reduction is a move in the direction of greater objectivity, toward a more accurate view of the real nature of things. This is accomplished by reducing our dependence on individual or species-specific points of view toward the object of investigation. We describe it not in terms of the impressions it makes on our senses, but in terms of its more general effects and of properties detectable by means other than the human senses. The less it depends on a specifically human viewpoint, the more objective is our description. It is possible to follow this path because although the concepts and ideas we employ in thinking about the external world are initially applied from a point of view that involves our perceptual apparatus, they are used by us to refer to things beyond themselves—toward which we *have* the phenomenal point of view. Therefore we can abandon it in favor of another, and still be thinking about the same things.

Experience itself, however, does not seem to fit the pattern. The idea

---

*The problem I am going to raise can therefore be posed even if the distinction between more subjective and more objective descriptions or viewpoints can itself be made only within a larger human point of view. I do not accept this kind of conceptual relativism, but it need not be refuted to make the point that psychophysical reduction cannot be accommodated by the subjective-to-objective model familiar from other cases.

†The problem is not just that when I look at the Mona Lisa, my visual experience has a certain quality, no trace of which is to be found by someone looking into my brain. For even if he did observe there a tiny image of the Mona Lisa, he would have no reason to identify it with the experience.

of moving from appearance to reality seems to make no sense here. What is the analogue in this case to pursuing a more objective understanding of the same phenomena by abandoning the initial subjective viewpoint toward them in favor of another that is more objective but concerns the same thing? Certainly it *appears* unlikely that we will get closer to the real nature of human experience by leaving behind the particularity of our human point of view and striving for a description in terms accessible to beings that could not imagine what it was like to be us. If the subjective character of experience is fully comprehensible only from one point of view, then any shift to greater objectivity—that is, less attachment to a specific viewpoint—does not take us nearer to the real nature of the phenomenon: It takes us farther away from it.

In a sense, the seeds of this objection to the reducibility of experience are already detectable in successful cases of reduction; for in discovering sound to be, in reality, a wave phenomenon in air or other media, we leave behind one viewpoint to take up another, and the auditory, human or animal viewpoint that we leave behind remains unreduced. Members of radically different species may both understand the same physical events in objective terms, and this does not require that they understand the phenomenal forms in which those events appear to the senses of members of the other species. Thus it is a condition of their referring to a common reality that their more particular viewpoints are not part of the common reality that they both apprehend. The reduction can succeed only if the species-specific viewpoint is omitted from what is to be reduced.

But while we are right to leave this point of view aside in seeking a fuller understanding of the external world, we cannot ignore it permanently, since it is the essence of the internal world, and not merely a point of view on it. Most of the neobehaviorism of recent philosophical psychology results from the effort to substitute an objective concept of mind for the real thing, in order to have nothing left over which cannot be reduced. If we acknowledge that a physical theory of mind must account for the subjective character of experience, we must admit that no presently available conception gives us a clue how this could be done. The problem is unique. If mental processes are indeed physical processes, then there is something it is like, intrinsically,* to undergo certain physical pro-

*The relation would therefore not be a contingent one, like that of a cause and its distinct effect. It would be necessarily true that a certain physical state felt a certain way. Kripke (1972) argues that causal behaviorist and related analyses of the mental fail because they construe, for example, "pain" as a merely contingent name of pains. The subjective character of an experience ("its immediate phenomenological quality," Kripke calls it [p. 340]) is the essential property left out by such analyses, and the one in virtue of which it is, necessarily, the experience it is. My view is closely related to his. Like Kripke, I find the hypothesis that a certain brain state should *necessarily* have a certain subjective character

cesses. What it is for such a thing to be the case remains a mystery.

What moral should be drawn from these reflections, and what should be done next? It would be a mistake to conclude that physicalism must be false. Nothing is proved by the inadequacy of physicalist hypotheses that assume a faulty objective analysis of mind. It would be truer to say that physicalism is a position we cannot understand because we do not at present have any conception of how it might be true. Perhaps it will be thought unreasonable to require such a conception as a condition of understanding. After all, it might be said, the meaning of physicalism is clear enough: mental states are states of the body; mental events are physical events. We do not know *which* physical states and events they are, but that should not prevent us from understanding the hypothesis. What could be clearer than the words "is" and "are"?

But I believe it is precisely this apparent clarity of the word "is" that is deceptive. Usually, when we are told that X is Y we know *how* it is supposed to be true, but that depends on a conceptual or theoretical background and is not conveyed by the "is" alone. We know how both "X" and "Y" refer, and the kinds of things to which they refer, and we have a rough idea how the two referential paths might converge on a single thing, be it an object, a person, a process, an event or whatever. But when the two terms of the identification are very disparate it may not

---

incomprehensible without further explanation. No such explanation emerges from theories which view the mind–brain relation as contingent, but perhaps there are other alternatives, not yet discovered.

A theory that explained how the mind–brain relation was necessary would still leave us with Kripke's problem of explaining why it nevertheless appears contingent. That difficulty seems to me surmountable, in the following way. We may imagine something by representing it to ourselves either perceptually, sympathetically, or symbolically. I shall not try to say how symbolic imagination works, but part of what happens in the other two cases is this. To imagine something perceptually, we put ourselves in a conscious state resembling the state we would be in if we perceived it. To imagine something sympathetically, we put ourselves in a conscious state resembling the thing itself. (This method can be used only to imagine mental events and states—our own or another's.) When we try to imagine a mental state occurring without its associated brain state, we first sympathetically imagine the occurrence of the mental state: that is, we put ourselves into a state that resembles it mentally. At the same time, we attempt perceptually to imagine the nonoccurrence of the associated physical state, by putting ourselves into another state unconnected with the first: one resembling that which we would be in if we perceived the nonoccurrence of the physical state. Where the imagination of physical features is perceptual and the imagination of mental features is sympathetic, it appears to us that we can imagine any experience occurring without its associated brain state, and vice versa. The relation between them will appear contingent even if it is necessary, because of the independence of the disparate types of imagination.

(Solipsism, incidentally, results if one misinterprets sympathetic imagination as if it worked like perceptual imagination: It then seems impossible to imagine any experience that is not one's own.)

be so clear how it could be true. We may not have even a rough idea of how the two referential paths could converge, or what kind of things they might converge on, and a theoretical framework may have to be supplied to enable us to understand this. Without the framework, an air of mysticism surrounds the identification.

This explains the magical flavor of popular presentations of fundamental scientific discoveries, given out as propositions to which one must subscribe without really understanding them. For example, people are now told at an early age that all matter is really energy. But despite the fact that they know what "is" means, most of them never form a conception of what makes this claim true, because they lack the theoretical background.

At the present time the status of physicalism is similar to that which the hypothesis that matter is energy would have had if uttered by a pre-Socratic philosopher. We do not have the beginnings of a conception of how it might be true. In order to understand the hypothesis that a mental event is a physical event, we require more than an understanding of the word "is." The idea of how a mental and a physical term might refer to the same thing is lacking, and the usual analogies with theoretical identification in other fields fail to supply it. They fail because if we construe the reference of mental terms to physical events on the usual model, we either get a reappearance of separate subjective events as the effects through which mental reference to physical events is secured, or else we get a false account of how mental terms refer (for example, a causal behaviorist one).

Strangely enough, we may have evidence for the truth of something we cannot really understand. Suppose a caterpillar is locked in a sterile safe by someone unfamiliar with insect metamorphosis, and weeks later the safe is reopened, revealing a butterfly. If the person knows that the safe has been shut the whole time, he has reason to believe that the butterfly is or was once the caterpillar, without having any idea in what sense this might be so. (One possibility is that the caterpillar contained a tiny winged parasite that devoured it and grew into the butterfly.)

It is conceivable that we are in such a position with regard to physicalism. Donald Davidson has argued that if mental events have physical causes and effects, they must have physical descriptions. He holds that we have reason to believe this even though we do not—and in fact *could* not —have a general psychophysical theory.* His argument applies to intentional mental events, but I think we also have some reason to believe that

---

*See Davidson (1970); though I do not understand the argument against psychophysical laws.

sensations are physical processes, without being in a position to understand how. Davidson's position is that certain physical events have irreducibly mental properties, and perhaps some view describable in this way
is correct. But nothing of which we can now form a conception corresponds to it; nor have we any idea what a theory would be like that
enabled us to conceive of it.*

Very little work has been done on the basic question (from which
mention of the brain can be entirely omitted) whether any sense can be
made of experiences' having an objective character at all. Does it make
sense, in other words, to ask what my experiences are *really* like, as
opposed to how they appear to me? We cannot genuinely understand the
hypothesis that their nature is captured in a physical description unless
we understand the more fundamental idea that they *have* an objective
nature (or that objective processes can have a subjective nature).†

I should like to close with a speculative proposal. It may be possible
to approach the gap between subjective and objective from another direction. Setting aside temporarily the relation between the mind and the
brain, we can pursue a more objective understanding of the mental in its
own right. At present we are completely unequipped to think about the
subjective character of experience without relying on the imagination—
without taking up the point of view of the experiential subject. This
should be regarded as a challenge to form new concepts and devise a new
method—an objective phenomenology not dependent on empathy or the
imagination. Though presumably it would not capture everything, its
goal would be to describe, at least in part, the subjective character of
experiences in a form comprehensible to beings incapable of having
those experiences.

We would have to develop such a phenomenology to describe the
sonar experiences of bats; but it would also be possible to begin with
humans. One might try, for example, to develop concepts that could be
used to explain to a person blind from birth what it was like to see. One
would reach a blank wall eventually, but it should be possible to devise
a method of expressing in objective terms much more than we can at
present, and with much greater precision. The loose intermodal analogies—for example, "Red is like the sound of a trumpet"—which crop up
in discussions of this subject are of little use. That should be clear to
anyone who has both heard a trumpet and seen red. But structural fea-

*Similar remarks apply to Nagel (1965).

†This question also lies at the heart of the problem of other minds, whose close connection
with the mind–body problem is often overlooked. If one understood how subjective experience could have an objective nature, one would understand the existence of subjects other
than oneself.

tures of perception might be more accessible to objective description, even though something would be left out. And concepts alternative to those we learn in the first person may enable us to arrive at a kind of understanding even of our own experience which is denied us by the very ease of description and lack of distance that subjective concepts afford.

Apart from its own interest, a phenomenology that is in this sense objective may permit questions about the physical* basis of experience to assume a more intelligible form. Aspects of subjective experience that admitted this kind of objective description might be better candidates for objective explanations of a more familiar sort. But whether or not this guess is correct, it seems unlikely that any physical theory of mind can be contemplated until more thought has been given to the general problem of subjective and objective. Otherwise we cannot even pose the mind–body problem without sidestepping it.

Reflections

He does all the things that you would never do;
He loves me, too—
His love is true.
Why can't he be you?
        —Hank Cochran, ca. 1955

Twinkle, twinkle, little bat,
How I wonder what you're at,
Up above the world you fly,
Like a tea-tray in the sky.
        —Lewis Carroll, ca. 1865

There is a famous puzzle in mathematics and physics courses. It asks, "Why does a mirror reverse left and right, but not up and down?" It gives many people pause for thought, and if you don't want to be told the answer, skip the next two paragraphs.

The answer hinges on what we consider a suitable way to project ourselves onto our mirror images. Our first reaction is that by walking forward a few steps and then spinning around on our heels, we could step into the shoes of "that person" there in the mirror—forgetting that the heart, appendix, and so forth of "that person" are on the wrong side. The

---

*I have not defined the term "physical." Obviously it does not apply just to what can be described by the concepts of contemporary physics, since we expect further developments. Some may think there is nothing to prevent mental phenomena from eventually being recognized as physical in their own right. But whatever else may be said of the physical, it has to be objective. So if our idea of the physical ever expands to include mental phenomena, it will have to assign them an objective character—whether or not this is done by analyzing them in terms of other phenomena already regarded as physical. It seems to me more likely, however, that mental–physical relations will eventually be expressed in a theory whose fundamental terms cannot be placed clearly in either category.

language hemisphere of the brain is, in all probability, on the nonstandard side. On a gross anatomical level, that image is actually of a nonperson. Microscopically, the situation is even worse. The DNA molecules coil the wrong way, and the mirror-"person" could no more mate with a real person than could a nosrep!

But wait—you can get your heart to stay on the proper side if, instead, you flip yourself head over heels, as if swinging over a waist-high horizontal bar in front of you. Now your heart is on the same side as the mirror-person's heart—but your feet and head are in the wrong places, and your stomach, although at approximately the right height, is upside-down. So it seems a mirror *can* be perceived as reversing up and down, provided you're willing to map yourself onto a creature whose feet are above its head. It all depends on the ways that you are willing to slip yourself onto another entity. You have a choice of twirling around a horizontal or a vertical bar, and getting the heart right but not the head and feet, or getting the head and feet right but not the heart. It's simply that, because of the external vertical symmetry of the human body, the vertical self-twirling yields a more plausible-seeming you-to-image mapping. But mirrors intrinsically don't care which way you interpret what they do. And in fact, all they really reverse is back and front!

There is something very beguiling about this concept of mapping, projection, identification, empathy—whatever you want to call it. It is a basic human trait, practically irresistible. Yet it can lead us down very strange conceptual pathways. The preceding puzzle shows the dangers of over facile self-projection. The refrain quoted from the country-western ballad reminds us more poignantly of the futility of taking such mapping too seriously. Yet we can't stop our minds from doing it. So since we can't, let's go whole hog and indulge ourselves in an orgy of extravagant variations on the theme set by Nagel in his title.

What is it like to work at McDonald's? To be thirty-eight? To be in London today?

What is it like to climb Mount Everest? To be an Olympic gold-medal winner in gymnastics?

What would it be like to be a good musician? To be able to improvise fugues at the keyboard? To be J. S. Bach? To be J. S. Bach writing the last movement of the Italian Concerto?

What is it like to believe the earth is flat?

What is it like to be someone inconceivably more intelligent than yourself? Inconceivably less intelligent?

What is it like to hate chocolate (or your personal favorite flavor)?

What is it like to bat a bee? What is it like to be a bee being batted? What is it like to be a batted bee? (Illustration by Jim Hull.)

What is it like to hear English (or one's native language) without understanding it?

What is it like to be of the opposite sex? (See selection 15, "Beyond Rejection")

What would it be like to be your mirror image? (See the movie *Journey to the Far Side of the Sun*)

What would it be like to be Chopin's brother (he had none)? The present King of France?

What is it like to be a dreamed person? To be a dreamed person when the alarm rings? To be Holden Caulfield? To be the subsystem of J. D. Salinger's brain that represents the character of Holden Caulfield?

What is it like to be a molecule? A collection of molecules? A microbe? A mosquito? An ant? An ant colony? A beehive? China? The United States? Detroit? General Motors? A concert audience? A basketball team? A married couple? A two-headed cow? Siamese twins? A split-brain person? One half of a split-brain person? The head of a guillotined person? The body? The visual cortex of Picasso? The pleasure center of a rat? The jerking leg of a dissected frog? A bee's eye? A retinal cell in Picasso? A DNA molecule of Picasso?

What is it like to be a running AI program? An operating system in a computer? An operating system at the moment the system "crashes"?

What is it like to be under a general anesthetic? To be electrocuted? To be a Zen master who has attained a satori-like state in which no more subject ("I," ego, self) exists?

What is it like to be a pebble? A wind chime? A human body? The Rock of Gibraltar? The Andromeda Galaxy? God?

The image conjured up by the phrase "What is it like to be *X*"? is so seductive and tempting. . . . Our minds are so flexible, so willing to accept this notion, this idea that there is "something it is like to be a bat." Furthermore, we also willingly buy the idea that there are certain things that it is "like something to be"—"be-able things," or "BATs" for short —such as bats, cows, people; and other things for which this doesn't hold —such as balls, steaks, galaxies (even though a galaxy may contain innumerable be-able things). What is the criterion for "BAT-itude"?

In philosophical literature, many phrases have been used to try to evoke the right flavors for what being sentient really is ("being sentient" is one of them). Two old terms are "soul" and "anima." These days, an "in" word is "intentionality." There is the old standby, "consciousness." Then there is "being a subject," "having an inner life," "having experience," "having a point of view," having "perceptual aboutness" or "personhood" or a "self" or "free will." In some people's eyes, "having a mind," "being intelligent," and just plain old "thinking" have the right flavors. In Searle's article (selection 22), the contrast was drawn between "form" (hollow and mechanical) and "content" (alive and intentional); the words "syntactic" and "semantic" (or "meaningless" and "meaningful") were also used to characterize this distinction. All of the terms in this huge showcase are nearly synonymous. They all have to do with the emotional issue of whether it makes sense to project ourselves onto the object in question: "Is this object a BAT, or not?" But is there really some *thing* to which they refer?

Nagel makes it clear that the "thing" he is after is a distillation of that which is common to the experiences of all bats; it is not the set of experiences of some particular bat. Thus, Searle might say Nagel is a "dualist," since Nagel believes in some abstraction made from all those individuals' experiences.

Surprisingly enough, a look at the grammar of sentences that invite the reader to perform a mental mapping yields some insights into these tricky matters. Consider, for instance, the contrast between the questions "What *would it be like* to be Indira Gandhi?" and "What *is it like* to be Indira Gandhi?" The conditional sentence forces you to project yourself into the "skin," so to speak, of another human, whereas the indicative sentence seems to be asking what it is like for Indira Gandhi to be Indira Gandhi. The question might still be asked, "Described in whose terms?" Were Indira Gandhi to try to tell you what it is like to be Indira Gandhi, she might try to explain matters of political life in India by referring to things she considered vaguely analogous in your own experience. Would you protest and say, "No, don't translate it into *my* terms! Say it in your own terms! Tell me what it is like—to Indira Gandhi—for Indira Gandhi to be Indira Gandhi!" In that case, of course, she might as well speak in Hindi and leave it to you to learn the language. And yet even then you would just be in the position of millions of native Hindi speakers who have no idea what it would be like to be Indira Gandhi—much less what it is like for Indira Gandhi to be Indira Gandhi. . . .

Something seems very wrong here. Nagel is insistent that he wants his verb "be" to be subjectless, in effect. Not "What would it be like *for me* to be *X*"? but "What is it like, *objectively,* to be X?" There is a "be-ee" here, with no "be-er"—a living beast without a head, as it were. Perhaps we ought to go back to the conditional version: "What would it be like to be Indira Gandhi?" Well, for me, or for her? Poor Indira—where does *she* go while I'm being her? Or if we turn it around (identity being a symmetric relationship), we get "What would it be like for Indira Gandhi to be me?" Once again, where would I be if she were me? Would we have traded places? Or would we have temporarily collapsed two separate "souls" into one?

Note that we tend to say "If she were me" rather than "If she were I." Many European languages are somewhat skittish about equations of this type. It sounds funny to use the nominative case in both the subject and complement positions. People prefer to use "be" with the accusative case, as if it were somehow a transitive verb! "Be" is not a transitive verb, but a symmetric one—yet language tilts us away from that symmetric vision.

We can see this in German, where one has interesting alternatives for constructing such identity-asserting sentences. Two examples follow, adapted from the German translation of a Stanislaw Lem dialogue in which an exact molecule-for-molecule replica of a doomed person is about to be constructed. In that spirit, we provide (nearly) exact word-for-word replicas in English of the German originals:

1. *Ob die Kopie wirklich du bist, dafür muß der Beweis noch erbracht werden.* (As-to-whether the copy really you are, thereof must the proof still provided be.)

2. *Die Kopie wird behaupten, daß sie du ist.* (The copy will claim that it you is.)

Observe that in both identity-asserting clauses, "the copy" (or "it") appears first, then "you," then the verb. But notice—in the first clause, "are" is the verb, which retroactively implies that "you" was the subject and "the copy" was the complement, whereas in the second clause, the verb is "is," retroactively implying that the subject was "it" and the complement was "you." The fact that the verb comes at the end gives these clauses a sort of surprise-ending quality. In English we can't achieve precisely the same effect comfortably, but we can ask for the difference in shades of meaning between the sentences "Is the copy really you?" and "Are you really the copy?" These two questions "slip" in our minds along different dimensions. The former slips into "Or is the copy really some-one else—or perhaps no one at all?" The latter slips into "Or are you somewhere else—or are you anywhere?" Our book's title, incidentally, can be construed not only as a possessive, but equally as a short full-sentence reply to the two questions "Who am I?" and "Who is me?" Notice how the transitive usage—strictly speaking, an ungrammatical usage of "to be"—gives the second question a quite different "flavor" from the first.

[D.C.D. to D.R.H.: If I were you, I'd mention how curious it would be to preface some advice with "If you were me, I'd . . ." but if you were me, would I suggest that you mention it?]

All of these examples show how suggestible we are. We just fall like a ton of bricks for the notion that there's a "soul" in there—a flamelike soul that can flicker on or off, or even be transferred between bodies as a flame between candles. If a candle blows out and is relit, is it "the same flame"? Or, if it stays lit, is it even "the same flame" from moment to moment? The Olympic Torch is carefully kept burning as it is carried by runners thousands of miles from Athens to its destination every four years. There is powerful symbolism to the idea that this is "the very flame that was lit in Athens." Even the shortest break in the chain, however, would ruin the symbolism for people who knew. For people who didn't know, of course, no harm done! How on earth could it possibly matter? Yet emotionally it seems to. It will not easily be extinguished, that "soul-flame" notion. Yet it leads us into so much hot water.

We certainly intuit that only things of approximately the "same-sized souls" can slip into each other. The science-fiction story *Flowers for Algernon* by Daniel Keyes is about a retarded young man who by a miracle medical treatment slowly gains in intelligence and becomes a great genius —but then it turns out that the effects of the treatment cannot last, and "he" witnesses his own mental crumbling back into his retarded state. This fictional story has its counterpart in the real-life tragedy of people who, having grown from a state of zero mind to normal adult intelligence, witness themselves growing senile or who suffer serious brain damage. Can they answer for us the question "What is it like to have your soul slip out from under you?" any better than someone with vivid imagination can, though?

Franz Kafka's *Metamorphosis* is the story of a young man who wakes up one morning transformed into a giant beetle. But the beetle thinks like a person. It would be interesting to combine the *Flowers for Algernon* idea with the *Metamorphosis* idea and imagine the experiences of an insect whose intelligence rises to the level of a human genius (why not superhuman, for that matter?), then sinks back to the insect level. Yet this is virtually impossible for us to conceive. To borrow electrical-engineering jargon, the "impedance match" of the minds involved is too poor. In fact, impedance match may well be the main criterion for the plausibility of questions of the form Nagel poses. Which is it easier for you to imagine being—the totally fictional character Holden Caulfield or some particular, actual bat? Of course it is much easier to map yourself onto a fictional human than onto a real bat—much easier, much *realer*. This is slightly surprising. It seems that Nagel's verb "be" acts very strangely sometimes. Perhaps, as was suggested in the dialogue on the Turing test, the verb "be" is being extended. Perhaps it is even being stretched beyond its limits!

There's something very fishy about this whole idea. How can something *be* something that it *isn't*? And how is it rendered any more plausible when both things can "have experience"? It makes almost no sense for us to ask ourselves such questions as, "What would it be like for that black spider over there to be that mosquito trapped in its web?" Or worse yet, "What would it be like for my violin to be my guitar?" or "What would this sentence be like if it were a hippopotamus?" Like *for whom*? For the various objects concerned, sentient or not? For us the perceivers? Or, again, "objectively"?

This is the sticking-point of Nagel's article. He wants to know if it is possible to give, in his own words, "a description [of the real nature of human experience] in terms accessible to beings that could not imagine what it was like to be us." Put so starkly, it sounds like a blatant contradiction—and indeed, that is his point. He doesn't want to know what it's like *for him* to be a bat. He wants to know *objectively* what it is *subjectively* like. It wouldn't be enough for him to have had the experience of donning a "batter's helmet"—a helmet with electrodes that would stimulate his brain into batlike experiences—and to have thereby experienced "bat-itude." This would, after all, merely be what it would be like for *Nagel* to be a bat. What, then, would satisfy him? He's not sure that anything would, and that's what worries him. He fears that this notion of "having experience" is beyond the realm of the objective.

Now perhaps the most objective-sounding of the various synonyms earlier listed for BAT-itude is "having a point of view." After all, even the most dogmatic of disbelievers in machine intelligence would probably begrudgingly impute a "point of view" to a computer program that represents some facts about the world and about its own relationship to the world. There is no arguing with the fact that a computer can be programmed to describe the world around it in terms of a frame of reference centered on the machine itself, as in this: "Three minutes ago, the Teddy bear was thirty-five leagues due east of here." Such a "here-centered, now-centered" frame of reference constitutes a rudimentary "egocentric" point of view. "Being here now" is a central experience for any "I." Yet how can you define "now" and "here" without making reference to some "I"? Is circularity inevitable?

Let us ponder for a moment on the connection of "I" and "now." What would it be like to be a person who had grown up normally, thus with ordinary perceptual and linguistic capacities, but who then suffered some brain damage and was left without the capacity to convert the reverberating neural circuits of short-term memory into long-term memories? Such a person's sense of existence would extend to only a few seconds on either side of "now." There would be no large-scale sense of continuity of self—no internal vision of a chain of selves stretching both directions in time, making one coherent person.

When you get a concussion, the few instants before it happened are obliterated from your mind, as if you had never been conscious at that time. Just think—if you were knocked on the head at this moment, there would be no permanent trace left in your brain of your having read these past few sentences. Who, then, has been experiencing them? Does an experience only become part of *you* once it has been committed to long-term memory? Who is it that has dreamt all those many dreams you don't remember one bit of?

Just as "now" and "I" are closely related terms, so are "here" and "I." Consider the fact that you are now experiencing death, in a curious way. Not being in Paris right now, you know what it is like to be *dead in Paris*. No lights, no sounds—nothing. The same goes for Timbuctu. In fact, you are dead *everywhere*—except for one small spot. Just think how close you are to being dead everywhere! And you are also dead in all other moments than *right now*. That one small piece of space-time you are alive in doesn't just *happen* to be where your body is now—it is *defined* by your body and by the concept of "now." Our languages all have words that incorporate a rich set of associations with "here" and "now"—namely, "I" and "me" and so on.

Now to program a computer to use words like "I" and "me" and "my" in describing its own relation to the world is a common thing. Of course, behind those words there need not stand any sophisticated self-concept—but there may. In essence, any physical representational system, as defined earlier in the commentary on the "Prelude, Ant Fugue" (selection 11), is an embodiment of some point of view, however modest. This explicit connection between "having a point of view" and "being a representational system" now provides a step forward in thinking about BAT-itude, for if we can equate BATs with physical representational systems of sufficient richness in their repertoire of categories and sufficiently well-indexed memories of their worldlines, we will have objectified at least some of subjectivity.

It should be pointed out that what is strange about the idea of "being a bat" is *not* that bats sense the outside world in a bizarre way—it is that bats clearly have a highly reduced collection of conceptual and perceptual categories, compared to what we humans have. Sensory modalities are surprisingly interchangeable and equivalent, in some sense. For instance, it is possible to induce visual experiences in both blind and sighted people through the sensation of touch. A grid of over a thousand stimulators driven by a television camera is placed against a person's back. The sensations are carried to the brain where their processing can induce the having of visual experiences. A sighted woman reports on her experience of prosthetic vision:

I sat blindfolded in the chair, the TSR cones cold against my back. At first I felt only formless waves of sensation. Collins said he was just waving his hand in front of me so that I could get used to the feeling. Suddenly I felt or saw, I wasn't sure which, a black triangle in the lower left corner of a square. The sensation was hard to pinpoint. I felt vibrations on my back, but the triangle appeared in a square frame inside my head. (Nancy Hechinger, "Seeing Without Eyes," *Science 81,* March 1981, p. 43.)

Similar transcending of modality in sensory input is well known. As has been pointed out in earlier selections, people who wear prism-shaped glasses that turn everything upside down can, after two or three weeks, get quite used to seeing the world this way. And, on a more abstract plane, people who learn a new language still experience the world of ideas in pretty much the same way.

So it is really not the mode of transduction of stimuli into percepts or the nature of the thought-supporting medium that makes the "bat *Weltanschauung*" different from ours. It is the severely limited set of categories, together with the stress on what is important in life and what is not. It is the fact that bats cannot form notions such as "the human *Weltanschauung*" and joke about them, because they are too busy, always being in raw-survival mode.

What Nagel's question forces us to think about—and think very hard about—is how we can map our *mind* onto that of a bat. What kind of representational system is the mind of a bat? Can we empathize with a bat? In this view, Nagel's question seems intimately connected to the way in which one representational system emulates another, as discussed in the Reflections on selection 22. Would we learn something by asking a Sigma-5, "What is it like to be a DEC?" No, that would be a silly question. The reason it would be silly is this. An unprogrammed computer is not a representational system. Even when one computer has a program allowing it to emulate another, this does not give it the representational power to deal with the concepts involved in such a question. For that it would need a very sophisticated AI program—one that, among other things, could use the verb "be" in all the ways we do (including Nagel's extended sense). The question to ask would be, rather, "What is it like for you, as a self-understanding AI program, to emulate another such program?" But then this question starts to resemble very strongly the question "What is it like for one person to empathize strongly with another?"

As we pointed out earlier, people do not have the patience or accuracy to emulate a computer for any length of time. When trying to put themselves in the shoes of other BATs, people tend to empathize, not to emulate. They "subvert" their own internal symbol systems by voluntarily adopting a global set of biases that modify the cascades of symbolic activity in their brains. It is not quite the same as taking LSD, although that too creates radical changes in the way that neurons communicate with one another. LSD does so unpredictably. Its effects depend on how it is spread about inside the brain, and that has nothing to do with what symbolizes what. LSD affects thought in somewhat the same way that having a bullet shot through your brain would affect thought—neither intrusive substance pays any regard to the symbolic power of the stuff in the brain.

But a bias established through *symbolic* channels—"Hey, let me think about how it would feel to be a bat"—sets up a mental context. Translated into less mentalistic and more physical terms, the act of trying to project yourself into a bat's point of view activates some symbols in your brain. These symbols, as long as they remain activated, will contribute to the triggering patterns of all the other symbols that are activated. And the brain is sufficiently sophisticated that it can treat certain activations as stable—that is, as *contexts*—and other symbols then are activated in a subordinate manner. So when we attempt to "think bat," we subvert our brains by setting up neural contexts that channel our thoughts along different pathways than they usually follow. (Too bad we can't just "think Einstein" when we want!)

All this richness, however, cannot get us all the way to batitude. Each person's self-symbol—the "personal nucleus," or "gemma" in Lem's personetics—has become, over his or her life, so large and complicated and idiosyncratic that it can no longer, chameleonlike, just assume the identity of another person or being. Its individual history is just too wound up in that little "knot" of a self-symbol.

It is interesting to think about two systems that are so alike that they have isomorphic, or identical, self-symbols—say a woman and an atom-by-atom replica of her. If she thinks about herself, is she also thinking about her replica? Many people fantasize that somewhere out there in the heavens, there is another person just like them. When you think about yourself, are you also thinking, without being aware of it, about that person? Who is that person thinking about right now? What would it be like to be that person? Are you that person? If you had a choice, would you let that person be killed, or yourself?

The one thing that Nagel seems not to have acknowledged in his article is that language (among other things) is a bridge that allows us to cross over into territory that is not ours. Bats don't have any idea of "what it is like to be another bat" and don't wonder about it, either. And that is because bats do not have a universal currency for the exchange of ideas, which is what language, movies, music, gestures, and so on give us. These media aid in our projection, aid us in absorbing foreign points of view. Through a universal currency, points of view become more *modular,* more transferable, less personal and idiosyncratic.

Knowledge is a curious blend of objective and subjective. Verbalizable knowledge can be passed around and shared, to the extent that words really "mean the same thing" to different people. Do two people ever speak the same language? What we mean by "speak the same language" is a prickly issue. We accept and take for granted that the hidden subterranean flavors are not shared. We know what comes with and what is left out of linguistic transactions, more or less. Language is a public medium for the exchange of the most private experiences. Each word is surrounded, in each mind, by a rich and inimitable cluster of concepts, and we know that no matter how much we try to bring to the surface, we always miss something. All we can do is approximate. (See George Steiner's *After Babel* for an extended discussion of this idea.)

By means of meme-exchange media (see selection 10, "Selfish Genes and Selfish Memes") such as language and gestures, we *can* experience (vicariously sometimes) what it is like to be or do X. It's never genuine, but then what is genuine knowledge of what it is like to be X? We don't even quite know what it was like to be ourselves ten years ago. Only by rereading diaries can we tell—and then, only by projection! It is still vicarious. Worse yet, we often don't even know how we could possibly have done what we did yesterday. And, when you come right down to it, it's not so clear just what it is like to be me, right now.

Language is what gets us into this problem (by allowing us to see the question) and what helps to get us out as well (by being a universal thought-exchange medium, allowing experiences to become sharable and more objective). However, it can't pull us all the way.

In a sense, Gödel's Theorem is a mathematical analogue of the fact that I cannot understand what it is like not to like chocolate, or to be a bat, except by an infinite sequence of ever-more-accurate simulation processes that converge toward, but never reach, emulation. I am trapped inside myself and therefore can't see how other systems are. Gödel's Theorem follows from a consequence of that general fact: I am trapped inside myself and therefore can't see how other systems see me. Thus the objectivity-subjectivity dilemmas that Nagel has sharply posed are some-how related to epistemological problems in both mathematical logic, and as we saw earlier, the foundations of physics. These ideas are developed in more detail in the last chapter of *Gödel, Escher, Bach* by Hofstadter.

D.R.H.

25

RAYMOND M. SMULLYAN

An Epistemological Nightmare

Scene 1. Frank is in the office of an eye doctor. The doctor holds up a book and asks "What color is it?" Frank answers, "Red." The doctor says, "Aha, just as I thought! Your whole color mechanism has gone out of kilter. But fortunately your condition is curable, and I will have you in perfect shape in a couple of weeks."

Scene 2. (A few weeks later.) Frank is in a laboratory in the home of an experimental epistemologist. (You will soon find out what that means!) The epistemologist holds up a book and also asks, "What color is this book?" Now, Frank has been earlier dismissed by the eye doctor as "cured." However, he is now of a very analytical and cautious temperament, and will not make any statement that can possibly be refuted. So Frank answers, "It seems red to me."

EPISTEMOLOGIST: Wrong!

FRANK: I don't think you heard what I said. I merely said that it *seems* red to me.

EPISTEMOLOGIST: I heard you, and you were wrong.

From *Philosophical Fantasies* by Raymond M. Smullyan, to be published by St. Martins Press, N.Y., in 1982.

FRANK: Let me get this clear; did you mean that I was wrong that this book *is* red, or that I was wrong that it *seems* red to me?

EPISTEMOLOGIST: I obviously couldn't have meant that you were wrong in that it *is* red, since you did not say that it is red. All you said was that it *seems* red to you, and it is *this* statement which is wrong.

FRANK: But you can't say that the statement "It *seems* red to me" is wrong.

EPISTEMOLOGIST: If I *can't* say it, how come I did?

FRANK: I mean you can't *mean* it.

EPISTEMOLOGIST: Why not?

FRANK: But surely *I* know what color the book *seems* to me!

EPISTEMOLOGIST: Again you are wrong.

FRANK: But nobody knows better than I how things seem to *me*.

EPISTEMOLOGIST: I am sorry, but again you are wrong.

FRANK: But who knows better than I?

EPISTEMOLOGIST: I do.

FRANK: But how could you have access to my private mental states?

EPISTEMOLOGIST: Private mental states! Metaphysical hogwash! Look, I am a *practical* epistemologist. Metaphysical problems about "mind" versus "matter" arise only from epistemological confusions. Epistemology is the true foundation of philosophy. But the trouble with all past epistemologists is that they have been using wholly theoretical methods, and much of their discussion degenerates into mere word games. While other epistemologists have been solemnly arguing such questions as whether a man can be wrong when he asserts that he believes such and such, I have discovered how to settle such questions *experimentally*.

FRANK: How could you possibly decide such things empirically?

EPISTEMOLOGIST: By reading a person's thoughts directly.

FRANK: You mean you are telepathic?

EPISTEMOLOGIST: Of course not. I simply did the one obvious thing which should be done, *viz.* I have constructed a brain-reading machine—known technically as a cerebrescope—that is operative right now in this room and is scanning every nerve cell in your brain. I thus can read your every sensation and thought, and it is a simple objective truth that this book does *not* seem red to you.

FRANK (thoroughly subdued): Goodness gracious, I really could have sworn that the book seemed red to me; it sure *seems* that it seems red to me!

EPISTEMOLOGIST: I'm sorry, but you are wrong again.

FRANK: Really? It doesn't even *seem* that it seems red to me? It sure *seems* like it seems like it seems red to me!

EPISTEMOLOGIST: Wrong again! And no matter how many times you reiterate the phrase "it seems like" and follow it by "the book is red" you will be wrong.

FRANK: This is fantastic! Suppose instead of the phrase "it seems like" I would say "I believe that." So let us start again at ground level. I retract the statement "It seems red to me" and instead I assert "I *believe* that this book is red." Is this statement true or false?

EPISTEMOLOGIST: Just a moment while I scan the dials of the brain-reading machine—no, the statement is false.

FRANK: And what about "I believe that I believe that the book is red"?

EPISTEMOLOGIST (consulting his dials): Also false. And again, no matter how many times you iterate "I believe," all these belief sentences are false.

FRANK: Well, this has been a most enlightening experience. However, you must admit that it is a *little* hard on me to realize that I am entertaining infinitely many erroneous beliefs!

EPISTEMOLOGIST: Why do you say that your beliefs are erroneous?

FRANK: But you have been telling me this all the while!

EPISTEMOLOGIST: I most certainly have not!

FRANK: Good God, I was prepared to admit all my errors, and now you tell me that my beliefs are *not* errors; what are you trying to do, drive me crazy?

EPISTEMOLOGIST: Hey, take it easy! Please try to recall: When did I say or imply that any of your beliefs are erroneous?

FRANK: Just simply recall the infinite sequence of sentences: (1) I believe this book is red; (2) I believe that I believe this book is red; and so forth. You told me that every one of those statements is false.

EPISTEMOLOGIST: True.

FRANK: Then how can you consistently maintain that my *beliefs* in all these false statements are not erroneous?

EPISTEMOLOGIST: Because, as I told you, you don't believe any of them.

FRANK: I think I see, yet I am not absolutely sure.

EPISTEMOLOGIST: Look, let me put it another way. Don't you see that the very falsity of each of the statements that you assert *saves* you from an erroneous belief in the preceding one? The first statement is, as I told you, false. Very well! Now the second statement is simply to the effect that you believe the first statement. If the second statement were *true,* then you would believe the first statement, and hence your belief about the first statement would indeed be in error. But fortunately the second statement is false, hence you don't really believe the first statement, so your belief in the first statement is not in error. Thus the falsity of the second statement implies you do *not* have an erroneous belief about the first; the falsity of the third likewise saves you from an erroneous belief about the second, etc.

FRANK: Now I see perfectly! So none of my *beliefs* were erroneous, only the statements were erroneous.

EPISTEMOLOGIST: Exactly.

FRANK: Most remarkable! Incidentally, what color is the book really?

EPISTEMOLOGIST: It is red.

FRANK: What!

EPISTEMOLOGIST: Exactly! Of course the book is red. What's the matter with you, don't you have eyes?

FRANK: But didn't I in effect keep saying that the book is red all along?

EPISTEMOLOGIST: Of course not! You kept saying it *seems* red to you, it *seems* like it seems red to you, you *believe* it is red, you *believe* that you believe it is red, and so forth. Not once did you say that it *is* red. When I originally asked you "What color is the book?" if you had simply answered "red," this whole painful discussion would have been avoided.

Scene 3.   Frank comes back several months later to the home of the epistemologist.

EPISTEMOLOGIST: How delightful to see you! Please sit down.

FRANK (seated):   I have been thinking of our last discussion, and there is much I wish to clear up. To begin with, I discovered an inconsistency in some of the things you said.

EPISTEMOLOGIST: Delightful! I love inconsistencies. Pray tell!

FRANK: Well, you claimed that although my belief sentences were false, I did not have any actual *beliefs* that are false. If you had not admitted that the book actually is red, you would have been consistent. But your very admission that the book *is* red, leads to an inconsistency.

EPISTEMOLOGIST: How so?

FRANK: Look, as you correctly pointed out, in each of my belief sentences "I believe it is red," "I believe that I believe it is red," the falsity of each one other than the first saves me from an erroneous belief in the preceeding one. However, you neglected to take into consideration the first sentence itself! The falsity of the first sentence "I believe it is red," in conjunction with the fact that it *is* red, *does* imply that I do have a false belief.

EPISTEMOLOGIST: I don't see why.

FRANK: It is obvious! Since the sentence "I believe it is red" is false, then I in fact believe it is not red, and since it really is red, then I *do* have a false belief. So there!

EPISTEMOLOGIST (disappointed):   I am sorry, but your proof obviously fails. Of course the falsity of the fact that you believe it is red implies that you *don't* believe it is red. But this does not mean that you believe it is *not* red!

FRANK: But obviously I know that it either is red or it isn't, so if I don't believe it is, then I must believe that it isn't.

EPISTEMOLOGIST: Not at all. I believe that either Jupiter has life or it doesn't. But I neither believe that it does, nor do I believe that it doesn't. I have no evidence one way or the other.

FRANK: Oh well, I guess you are right. But let us come to more important matters. I honestly find it impossible that I can be in error concerning my own beliefs.

EPISTEMOLOGIST: Must we go through this again? I have already patiently explained to you that you (in the sense of your beliefs, not your statements) are *not* in error.

FRANK: Oh, all right then, I simply do not believe that even the *statements* are in error. Yes, according to the machine they are in error, but why should I trust the machine?

EPISTEMOLOGIST: Whoever said you should trust the machine?

FRANK: Well, *should* I trust the machine?

EPISTEMOLOGIST: That question involving the word "should" is out of my domain. However, if you like, I can refer you to a colleague who

is an excellent moralist—he may be able to answer this for
you.

FRANK: Oh come on now, I obviously didn't mean "should" in a moralistic sense. I simply meant "Do I have any evidence that this machine
is reliable?"

EPISTEMOLOGIST: Well, do you?

FRANK: Don't ask *me!* What I mean is should *you* trust the machine?

EPISTEMOLOGIST: *Should* I trust it? I have no idea, and I couldn't care less
what I *should* do.

FRANK: Oh, your moralistic hangup again. I mean, do *you* have evidence
that the machine is reliable?

EPISTEMOLOGIST: Well of course!

FRANK: Then let's get down to brass tacks. What is your evidence?

EPISTEMOLOGIST: You hardly can expect that I can answer this for you
in an hour, a day, or a week. If you wish to study this machine with
me, we can do so, but I assure you this is a matter of several years.
At the end of that time, however, you would certainly not have the
slightest doubts about the reliability of the machine.

FRANK: Well, possibly I could believe that it is reliable in the sense that
its measurements are accurate, but then I would doubt that what it
actually measures is very significant. It seems that all it measures is
one's physiological states and activities.

EPISTEMOLOGIST: But of course, what else would you expect it to measure?

FRANK: I doubt that it measures my psychological states, my actual *beliefs.*

EPISTEMOLOGIST: Are we back to that again? The machine *does* measure
those physiological states and processes that you call psychological
states, beliefs, sensations, and so forth.

FRANK: At this point I am becoming convinced that our entire difference
is purely semantical. All right, I will grant that your machine does
correctly measure beliefs in *your* sense of the word "belief," but I
don't believe that it has any possibility of measuring beliefs in *my*
sense of the word "believe." In other words I claim that our entire
deadlock is simply due to the fact that you and I mean different things
by the word "belief."

EPISTEMOLOGIST: Fortunately, the correctness of your claim can be decided experimentally. It so happens that I now have two brain-read-

ing machines in my office, so I now direct one to *your* brain to find out what *you* mean by "believe" and now I direct the other to my own brain to find out what *I* mean by "believe," and now I shall compare the two readings. Nope, I'm sorry, but it turns out that we mean *exactly* the same thing by the word "believe."

FRANK: Oh, hang your machine! Do *you* believe we mean the same thing by the word "believe"?

EPISTEMOLOGIST: Do *I* believe it? Just a moment while I check with the machine. Yes, it turns out I do believe it.

FRANK: My goodness, do you mean to say that you can't even tell me what *you* believe without consulting the machine?

EPISTEMOLOGIST: Of course not.

FRANK: But most people when asked what they believe simply *tell* you. Why do you, in order to find out your beliefs, go through the fantastically roundabout process of directing a thought-reading machine to your own brain and then finding out what you believe on the basis of the machine readings?

EPISTEMOLOGIST: What other scientific, objective way is there of finding out what I believe?

FRANK: Oh, come now, why don't you just ask yourself?

EPISTEMOLOGIST (sadly):   It doesn't work. Whenever I ask myself what I believe, I never get any answer!

FRANK: Well, why don't you just *state* what you believe?

EPISTEMOLOGIST: How can I state what I believe before I know what I believe?

FRANK: Oh, to hell with your *knowledge* of what you believe; surely you have some *idea* or *belief* as to what you believe, don't you?

EPISTEMOLOGIST: Of course I have such a belief. But how do I find out what this belief is?

FRANK: I am afraid we are getting into another infinite regress. Look, at this point I am honestly beginning to wonder whether you may be going crazy.

EPISTEMOLOGIST: Let me consult the machine. Yes, it turns out that I may be going crazy.

FRANK: Good God, man, doesn't this frighten you?

EPISTEMOLOGIST: Let me check! Yes, it turns out that it does frighten me.

FRANK: Oh please, can't you forget this damned machine and just tell me whether you are frightened or not?

EPISTEMOLOGIST: I just told you that I am. However, I only learned of this from the machine.

FRANK: I can see that it is utterly hopeless to wean you away from the machine. Very well, then, let us play along with the machine some more. Why don't you ask the machine whether your sanity can be saved?

EPISTEMOLOGIST: Good idea! Yes, it turns out that it can be saved.

FRANK: And how can it be saved?

EPISTEMOLOGIST: I don't know, I haven't asked the machine.

FRANK: Well, for God's sake, ask it!

EPISTEMOLOGIST: Good idea. It turns out that . . .

FRANK: It turns out what?

EPISTEMOLOGIST: It turns out that . . .

FRANK: Come on now, it turns out what?

EPISTEMOLOGIST: This is the most fantastic thing I have ever come across! According to the machine the best thing I can do is to cease to trust the machine!

FRANK: Good! What will you do about it?

EPISTEMOLOGIST: How do I know what I *will* do about it, I can't read the future?

FRANK: I mean, what do you *presently* intend to do about it?

EPISTEMOLOGIST: Good question, let me consult the machine. According to the machine, my current intentions are in complete conflict. And I can see why! I am caught in a terrible paradox! If the machine is trustworthy, then I had better accept its suggestion to distrust it. But if I distrust it, then I also distrust its suggestion to distrust it, so I am really in a total quandary.

FRANK: Look, I know of someone who I think might be really of help in this problem. I'll leave you for a while to consult him. *Au revoir!*

Scene 4. (Later in the day at a psychiatrist's office.)

FRANK: Doctor, I am terribly worried about a friend of mine. He calls himself an "experimental epistemologist."

DOCTOR: Oh, the experimental epistemologist. There is only one in the world. I know him well!

FRANK: That is a relief. But do you realize that he has constructed a mind-reading device that he now directs to his own brain, and whenever one asks him what he thinks, believes, feels, is afraid of, and so on, he has to consult the machine first before answering? Don't you think this is pretty serious?

DOCTOR: Not as serious as it might seem. My prognosis for him is actually quite good.

FRANK: Well, if you are a friend of his, couldn't you sort of keep an eye on him?

DOCTOR: I do see him quite frequently, and I do observe him much. However, I don't think he can be helped by so-called "psychiatric treatment." His problem is an unusual one, the sort that has to work itself out. And I believe it will.

FRANK: Well, I hope your optimism is justified. At any rate I sure think *I* need some help at this point!

DOCTOR: How so?

FRANK: My experiences with the epistemologist have been thoroughly unnerving! At this point I wonder if *I* may be going crazy; I can't even have confidence in how things *appear* to me. I think maybe *you* could be helpful here.

DOCTOR: I would be happy to but cannot for a while. For the next three months I am unbelievably overloaded with work. After that, unfortunately, I must go on a three-month vacation. So in six months come back and we can talk this over.

Scene 5. (Same office, six months later.)

DOCTOR: Before we go into your problems, you will be happy to hear that your friend the epistemologist is now completely recovered.

FRANK: Marvelous, how did it happen?

DOCTOR: Almost, as it were, by a stroke of fate—and yet his very mental activities were, so to speak, part of the "fate." What happened was this: For months after you last saw him, he went around worrying "should I trust the machine, shouldn't I trust the machine, should I, shouldn't I, should I, shouldn't I." (He decided to use the word "should" in your empirical sense.) He got nowhere! So he then decided to "formalize" the whole argument. He reviewed his study of symbolic logic, took the axioms of first-order logic, and added as nonlogical axioms certain relevant facts about the machine. Of course the resulting system was inconsistent—he formally proved that he should trust the machine if and only if he shouldn't, and hence that he both should and should not trust the machine. Now, as you may know, in a system based on classical logic (which is the logic he used), if one can prove so much as a single contradictory proposition, then one can prove any proposition, hence the whole system breaks down. So he decided to use a logic weaker than classical logic—a logic close to what is known as "minimal logic"—in which the proof of one contradiction does not necessarily entail the proof of every proposition. However, this system turned out too weak to decide the question of whether or not he should trust the machine. Then he had the following bright idea. Why not use classical logic in his system even though the resulting system is inconsistent? Is an inconsistent system necessarily useless? Not at all! Even though given any proposition, there exists a proof that it is true and another proof that it is false, it may be the case that for any such pair of proofs, one of them is simply more psychologically convincing than the other, so simply pick the proof you actually believe! Theoretically the idea turned out very well—the actual system he obtained really did have the property that given any such pair of proofs, one of them was always psychologically *far* more convincing than the other. Better yet, given any pair of contradictory propositions, *all* proofs of one were more convincing than *any* proof of the other. Indeed, anyone *except the epistemologist* could have used the system to decide whether the machine could be trusted. But with the epistemologist, what happened was this: He obtained one proof that he should trust the machine and another proof that he should not. Which proof was more convincing to him, which proof did he really "believe"? The only way *he* could find out was to consult the machine! But he realized that this would be begging the question, since his consulting the machine would be a tacit admission that he did in fact trust the machine. So he still remained in a quandary.

FRANK: So how did he get out of it?

DOCTOR: Well, here is where fate kindly interceded. Due to his absolute absorption in the theory of this problem, which consumed about his every waking hour, he became for the first time in his life experimentally negligent. As a result, quite unknown to him, a few minor units of his machine blew out! Then, for the first time, the machine started giving contradictory information—not merely subtle paradoxes, but blatant contradictions. In particular, the machine one day claimed that the epistemologist believed a certain proposition and a few days later claimed he did *not* believe that proposition. And to add insult to injury, the machine claimed that he had not changed his belief in the last few days. This was enough to simply make him totally distrust the machine. Now he is fit as a fiddle.

FRANK: This is certainly the most amazing thing I have ever heard! I guess the machine was really dangerous and unreliable all along.

DOCTOR: Oh, not at all; the machine used to be excellent before the epistemologist's experimental carelessness put it out of whack.

FRANK: Well, surely when *I* knew it, it couldn't have been very reliable.

DOCTOR: Not so, Frank, and this brings us to your problem. I know about your entire conversation with the epistemologist—it was all tape-recorded.

FRANK: Then surely you realize the machine could not have been right when it denied that I *believed* the book was red.

DOCTOR: Why not?

FRANK: Good God, do I have to go through all this nightmare again? I can understand that a person can be wrong if he claims that a certain physical object has a certain property, but have you ever known a single case when a person can be mistaken when he claims to have or not have a certain sensation?

DOCTOR: Why, certainly! I once knew a Christian Scientist who had a raging toothache; he was frantically groaning and moaning all over the place. When asked whether a dentist might not cure him, he replied that there was nothing to be cured. Then he was asked, "But do you not feel pain?" He replied, "No, I do not feel pain; nobody feels pain, there is no such thing as pain, pain is only an illusion." So here is a case of a man who claimed not to feel pain, yet everyone present knew perfectly well that he did feel pain. I certainly don't believe he was lying, he was just simply mistaken.

FRANK: Well, all right, in a case like that. But how can one be mistaken if one asserts his belief about the color of a book?

DOCTOR: I can assure you that without access to any machine, if I asked someone what color is this book, and he answered, "I believe it is red," I would be very doubtful that he really believed it. It seems to me that if he really believed it, he would answer, "It is red" and not "I believe it is red" or "It seems red to me." The very timidity of his response would be indicative of his doubts.

FRANK: But why on earth should I have doubted that it was red?

DOCTOR: You should know that better than I. Let us see now, have you ever in the past had reason to doubt the accuracy of your sense perception?

FRANK: Why, yes. A few weeks before visiting the epistemologist, I suffered from an eye disease, which did make me see colors falsely. But I was cured before my visit.

DOCTOR: Oh, so no wonder you doubted it was red! True enough, your eyes perceived the correct color of the book, but your earlier experience lingered in your mind and made it impossible for you to really believe it was red. So the machine *was* right!

FRANK: Well, all right, but then why did I doubt that I *believed* it was true?

DOCTOR: Because you *didn't* believe it was true, and unconsciously you were smart enough to realize the fact. Besides, when one starts doubting one's own sense perceptions, the doubt spreads like an infection to higher and higher levels of abstraction until finally the whole belief system becomes one doubting mass of insecurity. I bet that if you went to the epistemologist's office *now,* and if the machine were repaired, and you now claimed that you believe the book is red, the machine would concur.

No, Frank, the machine is—or, rather, was—a good one. The epistemologist learned much from it, but misused it when he applied it to his own brain. He really should have known better than to create such an unstable situation. The combination of his brain and the machine each scrutinizing and influencing the behavior of the other led to serious problems in feedback. Finally the whole system went into a cybernetic wobble. Something was bound to give sooner or later. Fortunately, it was the machine.

FRANK: I see. One last question, though. How could the machine be trustworthy when it claimed to be untrustworthy?

DOCTOR: The machine never claimed to be untrustworthy, it only claimed that the epistemologist would be better off not trusting it. And the machine was right.

Reflections

If Smullyan's nightmare strikes you as too outlandish to be convincing, consider a more realistic fable—not a true story, but surely possible:

Once upon a time there were two coffee tasters, Mr. Chase and Mr. Sanborn, who worked for Maxwell House. Along with half a dozen other coffee tasters, their job was to ensure that the taste of Maxwell House stayed constant, year after year. One day, about six years after Mr. Chase had come to work for Maxwell House, he cleared his throat and confessed to Mr. Sanborn:

"You know, I hate to admit it, but I'm not enjoying this work any more. When I came to Maxwell House six years ago, I thought Maxwell House coffee was the best-tasting coffee in the world. I was proud to have a share in the responsibility for preserving that flavor over the years. And we've done our job well; the coffee tastes today just the way it tasted when I arrived. But, you know, I no longer like it! My tastes have changed. I've become a more sophisticated coffee drinker. I no longer like *that taste* at all."

Sanborn greeted this revelation with considerable interest. "It's funny you should mention it," he replied, "for something rather similar has happened to me. When *I* arrived here, shortly before you did, I, like you, thought Maxwell House coffee was tops in flavor. And now I, like you, really don't care for the coffee we're making. But *my* tastes haven't changed; my . . . *tasters* have changed. That is, I think something has gone wrong with my taste buds or something—you know, the way your taste buds go off when you take a bite of pancakes and maple syrup and then go back to your orange juice? Maxwell House coffee doesn't taste to me the way it used to taste; if only it did, I'd still love it, for I still think *that taste* is the best taste in coffee. Now, I'm not saying we haven't done our job well. You other guys all agree that the taste is the same, so it must be my problem alone. I guess I'm no longer cut out for this work."

Chase and Sanborn are alike in one way. Both used to like Maxwell House coffee; now neither one likes it. But they claim to be different in another way: Maxwell House tastes to Chase the way it always did, but not so for Sanborn. The difference seems familiar and striking, yet when they confront each other, they may begin to wonder if their cases are really all that different. "Could it be," Chase might wonder, "that Mr. Sanborn is really in my predicament and just hasn't noticed the gradual rise in his standards and sophistication as a coffee taster?" "Could it be," Sanborn might wonder, "that Mr. Chase is kidding himself when he says the coffee tastes *just the same* to him as it used to?"

Do you remember your first sip of beer? Terrible! How could anyone like *that* stuff? But beer, you reflect, is an acquired taste; one gradually trains oneself—or just comes—to enjoy that flavor. *What* flavor? The flavor of that first sip? No one could like *that* flavor! Beer tastes different to the experienced beer drinker. Then beer *isn't* an acquired taste; one doesn't learn to like that first taste; one gradually comes to experience a different, and likable, taste. Had the first sip tasted *that* way, you would have liked beer wholeheartedly from the beginning!

Perhaps, then, there is no separating the taste from the response to the taste, the judgment of good or bad. Then Chase and Sanborn might be just alike, and simply be choosing slightly different ways of expressing themselves. But if they were just alike, then they'd actually both be wrong about something, for they each have sincerely denied that they are like the other. Is it conceivable that each could have inadvertently misdescribed his own case and described the other's instead? Perhaps Chase is the one whose taste buds have changed, while Sanborn is the sophisticate. Could they be that wrong?

Some philosophers—and other people—have thought that a person simply *cannot* be wrong about such a matter. Everyone is the final and unimpeachable arbiter of how it is with him; if Chase and Sanborn have spoken sincerely, and have made no unnoticed slips of language, and if both know the meanings of their words, they *must* have expressed the truth in each case. Can't we imagine tests that would tend to confirm their different tales? If Sanborn does poorly on discrimination tests he used to pass with flying colors, and if, moreover, we find abnormalities in his taste buds (it's all that Szechuan food he's been eating lately, we discover), this will tend to confirm his view of his situation. And if Chase passes all those tests better than he used to, and exhibits increased knowledge of coffee types and a great interest in their relative merits and peculiar characteristics, this will support his view of himself. But if such tests could support Chase's and Sanborn's authority, failing them would have to undermine their authority. If Chase passed Sanborn's tests and Sanborn passed Chase's, each would have doubt cast on his account—if such tests have any bearing at all on the issue.

Another way of putting the point is that the price you pay for the possibility of confirming your authority is the outside chance of being discredited. "I know what I like," we are all prepared to insist, "and I know what it's like to be me!" Probably you do, at least about some matters, but that is something to be checked in performance. Maybe, just maybe, you'll discover that you really don't know as much as you thought you did about what it is like to be you.

D.C.D.

26

DOUGLAS R. HOFSTADTER

A Conversation
with Einstein's Brain

The Tortoise and Achilles bump into each other accidentally at the edge of one of the large octagonal ponds in the Jardin du Luxembourg in Paris, where young lads and lasses often take their small sailboats—and, in this day and age, even motorized and radio-controlled boats. But this is beside the point. It is a pleasant fall day.

ACHILLES: Why, Mr. Tortoise! I thought you were back in the fifth century B.C.!

TORTOISE: What about yourself? As for me, I often stroll through the centuries. It's good for the spleen, and besides, I find it refreshing on a pleasant fall day to meander among the bushes and trees, watching children grow old and die, only to be supplanted by a new generation of equally brainless, but generally rambunctious, human beings. Ah, what a harried existence it must be, to be a member of that feeble-minded species. Oh—pardon me! Indeed, I totally forgot I was addressing a member of that noble race. Why, you, Achilles, of course are an exception to the rule (thereby proving it, as the common human "logic" has it). You have been known, on occasion, to come out with truly insightful comments about the human condition (even if they were, to some extent, more or less accidental and unintended!). I feel very privileged to have known you, of all the human race, Achilles.

ACHILLES: Why, how kind of you to say those things about me. I'm sure I hardly deserve them. But, getting back to our chance meeting, I happen to be here today to have some footraces with a friend. However, he did not show up, so I am led to guess that he had sized up his chances and decided to spend his day some more profitable way. So here I am with nothing particular to occupy me, a leisurely day ahead of me to stroll about, watching the people (and Tortoises), and musing on philosophical matters, which, as you know, is a hobby of mine.

TORTOISE: Ah, yes. As a matter of fact, I too have been musing somewhat over some somewhat amusing ideas. Perhaps you'd like me to share them with you?

ACHILLES: Oh, I should be delighted. That is, I should be delighted as long as you're not going to try to snare me in one of your wicked traps of logic, Mr. T.

TORTOISE: Wicked traps? Oh, you do me wrong. Would I do anything wicked? I'm a peaceful soul, bothering nobody and leading a gentle, herbivorous life. And my thoughts merely drift among the oddities and quirks of how things are (as I see them). I, humble observer of phenomena, plod along and puff my silly words into the air rather unspectacularly, I am afraid. But to reassure you about my intentions, I was only planning to speak of brains and minds this fine day —and as you know, of course those things have nothing—nothing whatsoever—to do with logic!

ACHILLES: Your words *do* reassure me, Mr. T. And, in fact, my curiosity is quite piqued; I would certainly like to listen to what you have to say, even if it is unspectacular.

TORTOISE: You're a tolerant soul, Achilles—a praiseworthy way to be. Well, we're about to broach a difficult subject, so I will ease us gently into the waters by means of an analogy. You *are* familiar with "playing-records," aren't you—the kind of grooved plastic platters upon which are imprinted fine, near-microscopic patterns?

ACHILLES: Indeed I am. *Music* is stored upon them.

TORTOISE: Music? I thought music was something to listen to.

ACHILLES: Yes, it is, to be sure. But one can listen to playing-records.

TORTOISE: I suppose. If you put them up next to your ear. But they must make awfully silent music.

ACHILLES: Oh, surely, Mr. T, you are joking. Haven't you ever listened to the music stored upon a playing-record?

TORTOISE: To tell the truth, I have been inspired, at times, upon glancing at some playing-records, to hum tunes. Is that it?

ACHILLES: Hardly. You see, you put them on a rotating turntable and place a thin needle, which is affixed within a long arm, in the outermost groove, and—well, the details are too much for me, but the end result is that you hear the glorious sounds of music coming out of a device called a loudspeaker.

TORTOISE: I see, yet I don't see; why don't you just use the loudspeaker and dispense with the other paraphernalia?

ACHILLES: No—you see, the music is not stored in the loudspeaker; it is in the *record.*

TORTOISE: In the record? But the record is there *all at once;* music, as I know it, comes slowly, a bit at a time. Isn't that so?

ACHILLES: You are right on both counts. But even though the record is there "all at once," as you put it, we can draw sounds out of it bit by bit. The idea behind this is that the grooves pass slowly under the needle, and as they pass, the needle vibrates slightly in response to those very fine designs you earlier referred to. Somehow, in those designs are coded musical sounds, which are processed and passed on to the loudspeaker, to dispense to our waiting ears. Thus we manage to *hear* the music just as you said, "a bit at a time." The whole process is quite marvelous, I should say.

TORTOISE: Well, it *is* marvelously complicated, I'll grant you *that.* But why don't you do as I do—just hang the record up on your wall and enjoy its beauty all at once, instead of in small pieces doled out over a period of time? Is it that somehow there is a masochistic pleasure in the pain of doling out its beauties so slowly? I am always against masochism.

ACHILLES: Oh, you have totally misunderstood the nature of music, I am afraid. You see, it is in the *nature* of music to be spread out over a period of time. One doesn't just enjoy it in one sudden burst of sound—it can't be done, you see.

TORTOISE: Well, I suppose one wouldn't like hearing one large piercing noise—the sum of all the parts—in one short blow. But why can't you humans do as I do—it's such a simple, obvious idea—hang the playing-record up on your wall and, with your eyes, take in all its pleasures at a glance! After all, they are all there, aren't they?

ACHILLES: I am astonished to hear that you find the surface of one playing-record any different from that of any other. They all look alike to me—much as Tortoises do.

TORTOISE: Well! I hardly need dignify *that* comment with an answer. You know very well that they are just as different as, say, two pieces of music, one by Bach and the other by Beethoven.

ACHILLES: They look very similar to *me*.

TORTOISE: Well, it was *you* who allowed as how the very surfaces of the record contain all the music—thus if the two pieces of music differ so must the record surfaces differ—and to exactly the *same* amount as do the pieces, moreover.

ACHILLES: I guess you've got a point there.

TORTOISE: I'm glad you'll grant me *that*. So, since all of the music is on the *face* of the record, why don't you take it in at a glance, or at most a cursory once-over? It would certainly provide a much more intense pleasure. And you'll have to grant that each part of the musical selection is in its proper place; the relationship of the parts is not lost, as it would be if all the *sounds* were to be heard at once.

ACHILLES: Well, in the first place, Mr. T, I don't happen to have very good eyes, and—

TORTOISE: Aha! I've got another solution! Why don't you paste all the pages of the written score of some selection upon your wall and regard its beauties from time to time, as you would a painting? Sure you'll have to admit that the music is all there, in every last respect.

ACHILLES: Well, to tell the truth, Mr. T, I must confess to a shortcoming in my aesthetic capacities: I doubt that I would know how to visually interpret the printed symbols in front of me in such a way as to give me the same pleasure as I gain from the actual hearing.

TORTOISE: I am sorry indeed to hear that. Why, it could save you so much time! For imagine, instead of wasting a full hour listening to a Beethoven symphony, on waking up some morning you could simply open your eyes and take it all in, hanging there on your wall, in ten seconds or less, and be refreshed and ready for a fine, fulfilling day?

ACHILLES: Oh, you do poor Beethoven an injustice, Mr. T, a sorry injustice.

TORTOISE: Why, not at all. Beethoven is my second favorite composer. I have spent many long minutes gazing at his beautiful works, both in score and on playing record. The sculpted forms in some of his playing records are so exquisite, you have no idea.

ACHILLES: I must admit, you have floored me. That is an odd way, to put it mildly, to enjoy music. But I suppose you *are* an odd character, and this idiosyncracy makes as much sense, given what I know of you, as any of the rest.

TORTOISE: A condescending view. How would *you* like it, if some friend "revealed" to you that you'd never correctly understood a Leonardo painting—in reality, it should be *listened* to, not looked at, and is sixty-two minutes long, in eight movements, and contains long passages with nothing but the loud ringing of many different-sized bells?

ACHILLES: That is an odd way to think of paintings. But . . .

TORTOISE: Did I ever tell you about my friend the alligator, who enjoys music while lying on his back in the sun?

ACHILLES: Not that I recall.

TORTOISE: He has the advantage of having no shell covering his belly. So whenever he wants to "hear" a lovely piece, he picks out the appropriate disk and slaps it sharply for an instant against his flat stomach. The ecstasy of absorbing so many luscious patterns all at once, he tells me, is indescribable. So just think—his experience is as novel to me as mine is to you!

ACHILLES: But how can he tell the difference between one record and another?

TORTOISE: To *him*, slapping Bach and Beethoven against his belly are as different as to *you* slapping a waffle iron and a velvet pad against your bare back would be!

ACHILLES: In so turning the tables on me, Mr. T, you *have* shown me one thing—*your* point of view must be just as valid as *mine*—and if I did not admit it, I should be an auditory chauvinist pig.

TORTOISE: Well put—admirably put! Now that we have gone over our relative points of view, I will have to confess to being familiar with your way of listening to playing records, rather than looking at them, odd though it does seem to me. The comparison between the two types of experience was what inspired me to exploit this example as an analogy to what I wish to present to you now, Achilles.

ACHILLES: More of your usual trickery, I see. Well, go on with it—I'm all eyes.

TORTOISE: All right. Let's suppose that I came to you one morning with a very big book. You'd say, "Hullo, Mr. Tortoise—what's in that big book you're carrying with you?" (if I'm not mistaken); and I'd reply, "It's a schematic description of Albert Einstein's brain, down to the cellular level, made by some painstaking and slightly crazy neurologist after Einstein died. You know he bequeathed his brain to science, don't you?" And you'd say, "What in the world are you talking about, 'a schematic description of Albert Einstein's brain, down to the cellular level'?" would you not?

ACHILLES: I certainly would! The notion sounds preposterous. I suppose you'd go on roughly as follows: "Probably you're aware, Achilles, that a brain—any brain—is composed of neurons, or nerve cells, linked together by fibers called 'axons' to form a highly interconnected network." I'd say interestedly, "Go on." So you would.

TORTOISE: Bravo! You're doing very well! You took the words right out of my mouth! So I would indeed go on, as you suggested. I'd continue, "The details are beside the point here, but a little knowledge is essential. These neurons are known to *fire*, which means that a minuscule electric current (regulated by the resistance of the axon) passes down an axon into an adjoining neuron, where it may join other signals in a combined effort to 'trigger' this neighbor-neuron to fire in turn. The neighbor, however, will cooperate only if the sum of the incoming currents has reached a threshold value (which is determined by its internal structure); otherwise it will refuse to fire at all." At this point, you might say, "Hmm."

ACHILLES: So how would you go on, Mr. T?

TORTOISE: A good question. I suppose I might say something like this: "The foregoing is a peanut-sized summary of the goings-on in a brain, but I suppose it's sufficient background for an explanation of what this heavy book is that I'm carrying about with me today." If I know you at all, you'd say, "Oh, I'm eager to hear about it, but perhaps I should be warier, lest it contain one of your infamous schemes, whereby you lure poor little unsuspecting me into one of your inescapable absurdities." But I'd reassure you that no such prospect was in store, and thus reassured, you'd urge me to divulge the contents of the book, about which you, having taken a peek in it, might say, "It just looks like a lot of numbers and letters and little abbreviations and things!" And I'd say, "What did you expect? Little pictures of stars and galaxies and atoms, whirling about with formula such as '$E = mc^2$' scattered hither and thither?"

ACHILLES: At that swipe, I might take offense. I'd say indignantly, "Certainly not."

TORTOISE: Of course you would—rightly so. And then you'd say, "Well, what *are* all those numbers and things? What do they stand for?"

ACHILLES: Let *me* go on. I can anticipate, I believe, just how you'd reply:
"Each page of this book—and there are around a hundred billion
numbered pages in it—corresponds to one neuron and contains
numbers recording such aspects relevant to that neuron as: which
other neurons its axons lead to, what its threshold current is for
firing, and so on. However, I forgot to tell you certain further important facts about the functioning of brains in general—in particular,
what happens, or is believed to happen (from all we know from
neurological research), when thoughts occur in the brain, and especially conscious thoughts." I might object with some vaguely worded
complaint about thoughts occurring in the *mind,* not the *brain,* but
you'd hastily dismiss *that* remark and say, "We can talk about that
some other time—say, for example, if we meet by chance in the
Jardin du Luxembourg someday. But for now my goal is to explain
the contents of this book to you." I'd be placated, I suppose, as I
usually am, so you'd press on with a comment in this vein: "A
thought occurs (in the mind *or* the brain, whichever you prefer—*for
now!*) when a series of connected neurons fire in succession—mind
you, it may not be a long string of *individual* neurons firing like a
chain of dominoes falling down one after another—it may be more
like *several* neurons at a time tending to trigger another few, and so
forth. More likely than not, some stray neural chains will get started
along the side of the mainstream but soon will peter out, as threshold
currents are not attained. Thus, one will have, in sum, a broad or
narrow squad of firing neurons, transmitting their energy to others
in turn, thus forming a dynamic chain that meanders within the brain
—its course determined by the various resistances in the axons that
are encountered along the way. It would not be out of place to say
that 'the path of least resistance is followed,' if you follow me." At
this point, I'd be sure to comment, "You've surely said a mouthful
—let me have a moment to digest it." After mulling over this food
for thought you'd so far provided me with, and asking you a few
clarifying questions on it, I'd be satisfied that I'd gotten the general
picture. Of course you'd probably tell me that if I wanted more
information on the subject, I could easily go look it up in almost any
popular book about the brain. So then you'd say, "Let me wind up
this description of neural activity by briefly describing what accounts
for *memory,* at least as well as has been so far established. Think of
the 'flashing spot of activity' careening around within the brain
('where all the action is,' so to speak) as a boat traveling across the
surface of a pond, such as those toy sailboats that children sometimes
bring to the octagonal ponds in the Jardin du Luxembourg, the site

of our hypothetical mind-brain encounter; every boat leaves a disturbance behind it, its wake, as it travels through its medium. The 'hot
spot' within the brain, just like the boat, leaves its own kind of
disturbance, or wake, behind: the neurons that just fired as the signal
came through continue to undergo some kind of internal activity—
perhaps chemical in nature—for a few seconds. A permanent change
in the neuron is thereby effected. The change is reflected in some of
the numbers we have already spoken of, such as the threshold value
for firing, the axon resistances, and so forth. The exact way in which
those numbers are modified is, of course, dependent on certain
aspects of the internal structure in question—and these aspects
themselves are susceptible to numerical encoding." *I* might well
chime in at this point, I imagine, saying "Hence it would be of utmost
importance to record *those* numbers for every neuron, as well as the
already-mentioned resistances and thresholds." You would no doubt
reply, "An astute remark, Achilles; I had not anticipated you'd see
that necessity so quickly. And we might do well to give those numbers a name too: the 'structure-altering numbers' seems adequate to
me." To conclude this exchange, I might make the following sort of
remark: "The structure-altering numbers are quite remarkable in
that they not only describe how *other* numbers on the page are to
change, but also how they themselves are to change, next time the
neural flash comes passing through!"

TORTOISE: Oh, you have captured quite well the essence of what might
go on between the two of us in an admittedly hypothetical dialogue.
I might well say all the words you attributed to me; and I have every
reason to believe that you too could come forth with such utterances
as you have just proposed. Thus, what have we come to? Ah, yes, I
recall—in the hypothetical situation set up, I was in possession of a
book, wherein were numerically recorded all the relevant data, neuron by neuron, taken from the brain of Albert Einstein the day of his
death. On each page, we have: (1) a threshold value; (2) a set of page
numbers, to indicate neurons linked to the present one; (3) the
values of resistance of the linking axons; and (4) a set of numbers
indicating how the wakelike "reverberations" of the neuron, which
occur as a result of its firing, will alter any of the numbers on the
page.

ACHILLES: By telling me what you have just said, you would have completed your aim of explaining to me the nature of the heavy tome in
your possession. So we would probably have come to the end of our
hypothetical dialogue, and I can imagine that we would soon

thereafter bid each other adieu. Yet I cannot help making the observation that the reference you made in that hypothetical dialogue to some possible future conversation in these gardens between the pair of us strikingly suggests the circumstances in which we find ourselves today!

TORTOISE: How coincidental! It surely is by pure chance.

ACHILLES: If you don't mind, Mr. T, I'd like to know how this fictitious Einstein book could conceivably shed any light on the "mind-brain" problem. Could you oblige me in that respect?

TORTOISE: Willingly, Achilles, willingly. *Would* you mind, though, if I added a few extra features to the book, since it *is* hypothetical, anyway?

ACHILLES: I can't see why I should object at *this* point. If it's already got a hundred billion pages or so, a few more can't hurt.

TORTOISE: A sporting attitude. The features are as follows. When sound hits the ear, the oscillations set up within the drum are relayed to delicate structures within the middle and inner ear; these eventually connect to neurons whose duty it is to process such auditory information—thus we could call them "auditory neurons." Likewise, there exist neurons whose duty it is to convey coded directions to any given set of muscles; thus, hand motions are caused by the firing of specific neurons in the brain linked indirectly to the muscles in the hand. The same can be said of the mouth and vocal cords. As our additional information, then, for the book, we'd like to have whatever set of data is required to know precisely how the auditory neurons will be excited by a given incoming tone, if we supply its pitch and loudness. And the other essential chapter in the book is the one that tells in what way the firing of any "mouth-directing neuron" or "vocal-cord-directing neuron" will affect the muscles of the organ in question.

ACHILLES: I see what you mean. We'd like to know how the internal structure of neurons was affected by any auditory input signal; and also how the firing of certain key neurons, linked to speech organs, would affect those organs.

TORTOISE: Precisely. You know, sometimes, Achilles, it's good to have you around to bounce my ideas off of—they come back at me considerably cleaner than when I came out with them. Your naive simplicity somehow complements my learned verbosity.

ACHILLES: I'd like to bounce that one off on you, Mr. T.

TORTOISE: How's that? What do you mean? Did I say something unto-
ward?

ACHILLES: Now, Mr. T, I assume that in the heavy tome under discussion, there would be numerical conversion tables, which accomplish
precisely the tasks just set forth. They would give the neural response of each auditory neuron to any tone; and they would give the
changes in mouth shape and vocal-cord tension as a function of the
neurons linked to them by nerves in Einstein's body.

TORTOISE: Right you are.

ACHILLES: How could such an extensive documentation of Einstein do
anybody any good?

TORTOISE: Why, it could do no good for anyone, except conceivably
some starving neurologist.

ACHILLES: So why have you proposed this stupendous volume, this
prodigious opus?

TORTOISE: Why, only to tickle my fancy as I mused on mind and brain.
But it may serve as a lesson to novices in the field.

ACHILLES: Am I one?

TORTOISE: Doubtless. You'll do very well as a test subject in illustrating
the merits of such a book.

ACHILLES: I somehow can't help wondering what old Einstein would
think of it all.

TORTOISE: Why, given the book, you could find out.

ACHILLES: I could? I would not know where to begin.

TORTOISE: You would begin by introducing yourself.

ACHILLES: To whom? To the book?

TORTOISE: Yes—it's Einstein, isn't it?

ACHILLES: No, Einstein was a *person,* not a *book.*

TORTOISE: Well, that's a matter for some consideration, I'd say. Didn't
you say that there is music stored in playing-records?

ACHILLES: I did, and what's more, I described to you how to get at it.
Instead of a playing-record being there "all at once," we can use an
appropriate needle and other apparatus and extract real, living music
from it, which emerges "a bit at a time"—just like *real* music.

TORTOISE: Are you implying that it is only some kind of synthetic imitation?

ACHILLES: Well, the sounds are genuine enough. . . . They *did* come off plastic, but the music is made of real sounds.

TORTOISE: And yet it's there "all at once" too, isn't it—as a disk?

ACHILLES: As you pointed out to me earlier, yes, it is.

TORTOISE: Now you might at first say that music is *sounds,* not a record, mightn't you?

ACHILLES: Well, yes, I would; yes.

TORTOISE: Then you are very forgetful! Let me recall to you that *to me,* music is the record itself, which I can sit and tranquilly admire. *I* don't presume to tell *you* that to see Leonardo's Madonna of the Rocks as a *painting* is to miss the point, do I? Do I go around claiming that that painting is only a storage place for long, droning bassoon blasts, melodious piccolo runs, and stately harp dances?

ACHILLES: Why, no, you don't. I guess that either way, we respond to some of the same features of playing-records, even if you like their *visual* aspect, while I prefer their *auditory* aspect. At least, I *hope* that what you like in Beethoven's music corresponds to what *I* like.

TORTOISE: May or may not. Personally, I don't care. Now, as to whether Einstein was a person, or is in the book. . . . You should introduce yourself and see.

ACHILLES: But a *book* can't *respond* to a statement—it's like a black piece of plastic: It's there "all at once."

TORTOISE: Perhaps that little phrase will serve as a clue to you. Consider what we just said on the subject of music and playing-records.

ACHILLES: You mean, I should try to experience it "a bit at a time"? What bit should I begin at? Should I start at page 1 and read straight on through, to the end?

TORTOISE: Unlikely. Suppose you were going to introduce yourself to Einstein—what would you say?

ACHILLES: Ah . . . "Hullo, Dr. Einstein. My name is Achilles."

TORTOISE: Splendid. Now there are some fine tones of sound for you.

ACHILLES: Tones . . . hmmm. Are you planning to use those conversion tables?

TORTOISE: Good gracious, what a brilliant thought. Why didn't it occur to me?

ACHILLES: Well, everybody has inspirations once in a while, you know. Don't feel too bad.

TORTOISE: Well, you came up with a good thought. That's just what we'd try to implement, had we the book.

ACHILLES: So, you mean, we'd look up the possible changes in Einstein's auditory neuron structure resulting from each tone of the utterance?

TORTOISE: Well, roughly. You see, we'd have to do it *very* carefully. We'd take the first tone, as you suggested, and see which cells it would make fire, and how. That is, we'd see precisely how each number on each page would change. Then we'd go through the book painstakingly page by page, and actually *effect* those changes. You might call that "round one."

ACHILLES: Would round two be a similar process occasioned by the second tone?

TORTOISE: Not quite. You see, we haven't completed the response to the first tone yet. We've gone through the book once, neuron by neuron. But there is the fact that some of the neurons are firing, you know, so we have to take that into account. Which means we have to proceed to the pages where their axons lead and modify *those* pages in the way that is directed by the "structure-changing numbers." *That* is round two. And those neurons, in turn, will lead us to still others, and lo and behold, we're off on a merry loop around the brain.

ACHILLES: Well, when do we ever come to the second tone?

TORTOISE: Good point. It's something I neglected to say earlier. We need to establish a kind of time scale. Perhaps on each page the time taken for the neuron in question to fire is specified—the time it took to fire in real life, in Einstein's brain—a quantity best measured, probably, in thousandths of a second. As the rounds progress, we sum up all the firing times, and when the times add up to the length of the first tone, we start in on the second tone. That way, we can proceed to feed in tone after tone of your self-introductory utterance, modifying the neurons that would respond to that utterance at every step along the way.

ACHILLES: An interesting procedure. But surely a very lengthy one.

TORTOISE: Well, as long as it is all hypothetical, that should not bother us in the least. It would probably take millennia, but let's just say five seconds, for the sake of argument.

ACHILLES: Five seconds required to feed in that utterance? All right. So right now, my picture is that we have altered scores, if not myriads, of pages in that book, changing numbers on page after page after page, wherever we were led, either by the previous pages or by the tones that we were feeding in, via the auditory conversion tables.

TORTOISE: Right. And now, once the utterance is finished, neurons continue to fire—from one to the next, the cascade continues—so we perform a strange and elaborate "dance," shuffling back and forth between pages, round after round, without having any auditory input to bother with.

ACHILLES: I can see that something strange is about to happen. After another few "seconds" (if we are to stick to that somewhat ridiculous underestimate) of page turning and number changing, certain of the "speech neurons" will begin to fire. And we would then do well to consult the tables indicating shape of mouth or tension in vocal cords.

TORTOISE: You have caught wind of what is happening, Achilles. The way to read the book is not from page 1, but according to the directions in the preface, which tell about all the changes that must be effected and give all the rules for how to proceed.

ACHILLES: I suppose that given mouth shape and condition of vocal cords, it would be within grasp to determine what Einstein is "saying," wouldn't it? Especially given the level of technical advancement we've presupposed, that seems only a minor task. So I suppose he would say something to me.

TORTOISE: I presume so—such as, "Oh, hello. Did you come to visit me? Have I died?"

ACHILLES: That is a strange question. Of course he did.

TORTOISE: Well, then who's asking you the question?

ACHILLES: Oh, just some silly book. It's not *Einstein,* of course! You can't trap me into saying *that!*

TORTOISE: I wouldn't dream of it. But perhaps you'd like to address some more questions to the book. You could conduct a whole conversation, if you had the patience.

ACHILLES: That is an exciting prospect—I could see just what Einstein *would* have said in conversations with me, if I'd ever *really* met him!

TORTOISE: Yes, you could begin by asking how he felt; then proceeding to a description of how glad you were to meet him, since you'd never had the chance during his lifetime—proceeding just as if he were the "real" Einstein, which, of course, you've already decided was out of the question. How do you suppose he would react, when you told him he's not the *real* Einstein?

ACHILLES: Now, hold on a minute—you're employing the pronoun "he" about a *process* combined with a huge *book*. That's no "he"—it's something else. You're prejudicing the question.

TORTOISE: Well, you *would* address him as Einstein as you fed in questions, wouldn't you? Or would you say, "Hullo, book-of-Einstein's-brain-mechanisms, my name is Achilles"? I think you would catch Einstein off guard if you did that. He'd certainly be puzzled.

ACHILLES: There *is* no "he." I wish you'd quit using that pronoun.

TORTOISE: The reason I'm using it is that I'm simply imagining what you *would* have said to him, had you actually met him in his hospital bed in Princeton. Certainly you *should* address questions and comments to the book in the same fashion as you *would* have to the *person* Einstein, shouldn't you? After all, the book initially reflects how his brain was on the last day of his life—and he regarded himself as a person then, not a book, didn't he?

ACHILLES: Well, yes. I should direct questions at the book as I would have to the real person had I been there.

TORTOISE: You could explain to him that he had, unfortunately, died, but that his brain had been encoded in a mammoth catalogue after his death, which you are now in possession of, and that you are conducting your conversation by means of that catalogue and its conversion tables for speech.

ACHILLES: He'd probably be most astonished to hear *that!*

TORTOISE: Who? I thought there was no "he"!

ACHILLES: There is no "he" if I'm talking to the book—but if I told it to the *real* Einstein, *he'd* be surprised.

TORTOISE: Why would you be telling a live person to his face that he had already died, that his brain had been encoded in a catalogue, and that you were conducting your conversation with him through that catalogue?

ACHILLES: Well, I *wouldn't* tell it to a *live* person, I'd tell it to the book, and find out what the live person's reactions *would* have been. So, in a way, "he" *is* there. I am beginning to be puzzled . . . who am I talking to in that book? Is there somebody alive because it exists? Where are those thoughts coming from?

TORTOISE: From the book. You know that very well.

ACHILLES: Well, then, how can he say how he's feeling? How does a *book* feel?

TORTOISE: A book doesn't feel any way. A book just *is.* It's like a chair. It's just there.

ACHILLES: Well, this isn't just a book—it's a book plus a whole *process.* How does a book plus a process feel?

TORTOISE: How should I know? But you can ask it that question yourself.

ACHILLES: And I know what it'll say: "I'm feeling very weak and my legs ache," or some such thing. And a book, or a book-plus-process, *has* no legs!

TORTOISE: But its neural structure has incorporated a very strong *memory* of legs and leg-aching. Why don't you *tell* it that it's now no longer a person, but a book-plus-process? Maybe after you've explained that fact in about as much detail as you know it, it would start to understand that and forget about its leg-aching, or what it took for leg-aching. After all, it has no vested interest in feeling its leg, which it doesn't have, aching. It might as well ignore such things and concentrate on what it *does* have, such as the ability to communicate with you, Achilles, and to think.

ACHILLES: There is something frightfully sad about this whole process. One of the sadder things is that it would take so much *time* to get messages in and out of the brain, that before I'd completed many exchanges, I'd be an old man.

TORTOISE: Well, you could be turned into a catalogue too.

ACHILLES: Ugh! And not have any *legs* left, to run footraces? No thank you!

TORTOISE: You could be turned into a catalogue and continue your thought-provoking conversation with Einstein, as long as someone were managing your book, flipping pages and writing numbers in it. Even better, you could conduct several conversations at once. All we need do is make several copies of the Achilles catalogue, including directions for use, and send it around to whomever you desired. You'd enjoy that.

ACHILLES: Ah, now, that's more exciting. Let's see—Homer, Zeno, Lewis Carroll . . . provided that catalogues had been made of *their* brains, as well. But wait a minute. How am I going to keep track of all those conversations at once?

TORTOISE: No trouble—each one's independent of the others.

ACHILLES: Yes, I know—but I've still got to keep them in my head all at once.

TORTOISE: Your head? You would have no head, remember.

ACHILLES: No head? Then where would *I* be? What is going on here?

TORTOISE: You'd be at all those different places at once, conducting fine conversations with all those people.

ACHILLES: How would it feel to be conducting conversations with several people at a time?

TORTOISE: Why don't you just imagine what it would be like to ask Einstein, presuming, of course, that you had made several copies of *his* catalogue, and shipped them about to various of your friends, or anyone, for that matter, and they too were talking with him.

ACHILLES: Well, if I didn't tell the Einstein in my possession about it, he'd have no way to know of the other catalogues or conversations. After all, each catalogue has no way of being influenced by any of the other catalogues. So I guess he'd just say that *he* certainly didn't feel like he was engaging in more than one discussion at a time.

TORTOISE: So that's how *you'd* feel too, if several of *you* were engaging in simultaneous conversations.

ACHILLES: *I?* Which one would be me?

TORTOISE: Any of them; all of them; or perhaps, none of them.

ACHILLES: This is eerie. I don't know where I would be—if anywhere. And all of those weird catalogues would be claiming to be me.

TORTOISE: Well, you should expect as much; you do it yourself, don't you? Why, I could even introduce a pair of you—or all of you—to each other.

ACHILLES: Uh-oh. I was waiting for this moment. Every time I see you, you spring something like this on me.

TORTOISE: There just might ensue a teeny scrap over which one was the real one, don't you think so?

ACHILLES: Oh, this is a diabolical scheme to squeeze the juice out of the human soul. I'm losing a clear sight of who "I" is. Is "I" a person? A process? A structure in my brain? Or is "I" some uncapturable essence that *feels* what goes on in my brain?

TORTOISE: An interesting question. Let us go back to Einstein, to examine it. Did Einstein die, or was he kept on living by the creation of the catalogue?

ACHILLES: Well, to all appearances, some part of his spirit was kept alive by the fact that the data were recorded.

TORTOISE: Even if the book never was used? Would he be alive then?

ACHILLES: Oh, that's a difficult one. I guess I'd have to say "no." Clearly what made him live on was the fact that we "brought him to life" from out of the sterile book, "a bit at a time." It was the *process*, above and beyond the mere data book. He was conversing with us, that's what made him alive. His neurons were firing, in a somewhat figurative way, albeit rather slowly compared to their usual speed—but that's of no consequence, as long as they were firing.

TORTOISE: Supposing it took you ten seconds to do round one, a hundred seconds to do round two, a thousand seconds to accomplish round three, and so forth. Of course, the *book* would not know how long all this took, because its only contact with the outside world is through its auditory conversion tables—and in particular, it can never know anything that you don't choose to tell it. Would it still be as alive, despite the enormous sluggishness of its firing after a few rounds?

ACHILLES: I don't see why not. If I too had been catalogued in the same way and my pages were being flipped equally lethargically, our rates of conversation would be matched. Neither he nor I would have cause to feel any abnormality in the conversation, even if, in the outer world, our mere exchange of greetings lasted millennia.

TORTOISE: You at first spoke of this process that brings out the structure "a bit at a time" as being so important, yet now it seems it doesn't matter if it's constantly slowing down. Eventually the rate of exchange of thoughts would be a syllable a century. And after a while, one neuron would fire every trillion years. Not exactly a sparkling conversation!

ACHILLES: Not in the outer world, no. But to the two of us, who are unaware of the passage of time in the outer world, all is well and normal, as long as someone does our internal bookwork—no matter how slowly. Einstein and I are serenely oblivious to the fast-changing world outside our flipping pages.

TORTOISE: Suppose this faithful neural clerk—let's call him A-kill-ease, just for fun (no relation to present company, of course)—just suppose he slipped off one afternoon for a little nip, and forgot to come back. . . .

ACHILLES: Foul play! Double homicide! Or do I mean bibliocide?

TORTOISE: Is it all that bad? Both of you are still there, "all at once."

ACHILLES: "All at once," bah! What's the fun of life if we're not being processed?

TORTOISE: Was it any better at an ever-slowing snail's pace?

ACHILLES: At *any* pace, it's better. Even a Tortoise's. But say—what's the point of calling the book-tender "A-kill-ease"?

TORTOISE: I just thought I'd let you think about how it would feel if your brain were not only encoded in a book, but also you were *minding* that very brain-book (no pun intended, to be sure!).

ACHILLES: I suppose I would have to ask my own book. Or no—wait a minute. My book would have to ask *me*! Oh, I'm so befuddled by these confounded and compounded *level*-confusions you always hit me with out of the blue! Ah! I have a grand idea. Suppose there was a machine that came along with the books, a machine that does the page turning, the little calculations, and the clerical work. This way we would avoid the problem of human unreliability, as well as your strange twisty loop.

TORTOISE: Suppose so—an ingenious plan. And suppose the machine broke.

ACHILLES: Oh, you have a morbid imagination! What recherché tortures you would put me through!

TORTOISE: Not at all. Unless somebody told you of it, you wouldn't even be aware of the machine's existence, much less that the machine had broken.

ACHILLES: I don't like this isolation from the outer world. I'd rather have some way of sensing what's going on around me than be dependent upon people telling me things of their own choice. Why not take advantage of the neurons which, in life, processed visual input? Just like the auditory conversion tables, we could have *optical* conversion tables. These will be used to create changes in the book according to the signals from a television camera. Then I could watch the world about me, and react to its events. In particular, I'd soon become aware of the page-turning machine, the book full of so many pages and numbers, and so on. . . .

TORTOISE: Oh, you are determined to suffer. So now you'll perceive the fate that is to befall you: You'll "see," by means of input fed into you via the television camera and the conversion tables, that the mechanical page-turner that has served you so well has a loose part that is just about to slip. *That*'ll scare you, all right. And what good is that? If you had no optical scanning device, you'd have no way of knowing what's going on in the world about you, not even with respect to your page-turner. Your thoughts proceed calmly and coolly, unaffected by the cares of the outside world, blithely unaware that they may soon come to a forced end, since the page-turner may break. An idyllic existence! Up until the very end, not a worry!

ACHILLES: But when it breaks, I would be dead and gone.

TORTOISE: You would?

ACHILLES: I'd be a lifeless, motionless heap of number-covered sheets.

TORTOISE: A pity, I'm sure. But maybe old A-kill-ease would somehow find his way back to his familiar haunts, and take up where the broken machine left off.

ACHILLES: Oh! So I'd be resuscitated. I was dead for a while, and then returned to life!

TORTOISE: If you insist on making these strange distinctions. What makes you any "deader" when the machine breaks than you are when A-kill-ease leaves you unattended for a few minutes or a few years, to play a game of backgammon, to take a trip around the world, or to go get *his* brain copied into a book?

ACHILLES: I'm obviously deader when the machine breaks, because there is no expectation that I will ever resume functioning . . . whereas when A-kill-ease takes off on his sprees, he will eventually return to his duty.

TORTOISE: You mean, if you have been abandoned, you are still alive, just because A-kill-ease has the *intention* of returning? But when the machine breaks, you are dead?

ACHILLES: That would be a very silly way of defining "aliveness" and "deadness." Certainly such concepts should have nothing to do with the mere intentions of other beings. It would be as silly as saying that a light bulb is "dead" if its owner has no intention of turning it on again. Intrinsically, the light bulb is the same as ever—and that's what counts. In my case, what counts is that that book should be kept intact.

TORTOISE: You mean, that it should all be there, all at once? Its mere *presence* there is what guarantees your aliveness? Just as the existence of a playing-record is tantamount to the existence of its music?

ACHILLES: A funny image comes into my head. The earth is destroyed, but one record of Bach's music somehow escapes and goes sailing out into the void of space. Does the music still exist? It would be silly to make the answer depend upon whether it is ever found and played by some humanlike creature—wouldn't it? To *you*, Mr. T, the music exists *as the record itself*. Similarly, when we come back to that book, I feel that if the book merely sits there, all at once, *I'm* still there. But if that book is destroyed, I'm gone.

TORTOISE: You maintain that as long as those numbers and conversion tables are in existence, *you* are essentially, potentially alive?

ACHILLES: Yes; that's it. That's what's all important—the integrity of my brain structure.

TORTOISE: Do you mind if I just ask, "Suppose someone absconded with the *instructions* in the preface, telling how to use the book?"

ACHILLES: Well, they'd better bring them back, is all I can say. My goose would be cooked if they weren't going to return those instructions. What good's the book without its instructions?

TORTOISE: Once again you are saying that the question as to whether you are alive depends on whether the filcher has good intentions or bad. It could just as well have been the capricious wind, blowing about, which caught hold of those few pages of preface and wafted them into the air. Now there's no question of *intention*. Would "you" be less alive for that?

ACHILLES: This is a little tricky. Let me go over the question slowly. I die; my brain is transcribed into a book; the book has a set of instructions telling how to process the book's pages in a way that parallels how my neurons fire in my actual brain right now.

TORTOISE: And the book, together with its instructions, lies on a dusty shelf in a far corner of a used book store. A chap comes in and chances upon the oddity. "Egads!" he exclaims, "An Achilles-book! What on earth could that be? I'll buy it and try it!"

ACHILLES: He should be sure to buy the instructions too! It is essential that the book and instructions remain together.

TORTOISE: How close? In the same binding? In the same bag? In the same house? Within a mile of each other? Is *your* existence somehow diminished if the pages are scattered hither and thither by a breeze? At what precise point would you feel the book had lost its structural integrity? You know, I appreciate a warped playing-record fully as much as a flat one. In fact, it's got an extra bit of charm, to the cultured eye. Why, I have a friend who considers broken records more stylish than the originals! You should see his walls—they're plastered with broken Bach—fragmented fugues, crushed canons, ruptured ricercari. He delights in it. Structural integrity is in the eye of the beholder, my friend.

ACHILLES: Well, as long as you're asking *me* to be the beholder, I'd say that if the pages are to be reunited, there is still hope for my survival.

TORTOISE: Reunited *in whose eyes?* Once you're dead, you the beholder remain only in book form (if at all). Once the book's pages start being scattered, will you feel yourself losing structural integrity? Or, from the outside, once *I* feel that the structure is irretrievably gone, should I conclude that *you* no longer exist? Or does some "essence" of you exist still, in scattered form? Who will judge?

ACHILLES: Oh, goodness. I have totally lost track of the progress of that poor soul inside the book. And as to what he himself—or I myself —would be feeling, I am even more unsure.

TORTOISE: "That poor soul inside the book"? Oh, Achilles! Are you still clinging to that old notion that it's "you" somehow there, inside that book? If I am correct in my memory, you were so reluctant at first to accept that kind of idea when I suggested that you really *were* talking to Einstein himself.

ACHILLES: Well, I was reluctant until I saw that it—the book—seemed to feel, or at least to express, all his—Einstein's—emotions, or what *seemed* like emotions. But maybe you're right to chide me—maybe I should just trust the old, familiar commonsense view that the only *real* "I" is right here, inside my very own living, organic brain.

TORTOISE: You mean, the old, familiar "ghost-inside-the-machine" theory, is that it? What is it, inside there, that this "you" is?

ACHILLES: It's whatever *feels* all these emotions that I express.

TORTOISE: Maybe the *feeling* of those emotions is the sheer physical event of having a shower of electrochemical activity come flying through some one of the various neural pathways inside your brain. Maybe you use the word "feeling" to describe such an event.

ACHILLES: That sounds wrong, because the *book* uses the word "feeling," if *I* do, and yet it can feel no electrochemical activity surging. All that the book "feels" is its numbers changing. Perhaps "feeling" is synonymous with the existence of any kind of neural activity, simulated or otherwise.

TORTOISE: Such a view would place undue stress on the unfolding of feeling "a bit at a time." While the time development of a neural structure undoubtedly seems to us like the essence of feeling, why could it not be that feelings, like playing-records and paintings, are there "all at once"?

ACHILLES: The difference I can immediately spot between a playing-record of a piece of music, and a mind, is that the former does not change by evolving "a bit at a time"; but a mind, in its interaction over a span of time with the exterior world, gets modified in a way that was not originally inherent in its physical structure.

TORTOISE: You have a good point. A mind, or brain, interacts with the world and thus is subject to change that one cannot predict by knowing the structure of the brain alone. But this does not in any way diminish the "aliveness" of said mind, when it introspectively ponders some thought, without any interference from without. During such a period of introspection, the changes it undergoes are inherent in it. Though it is evolving "a bit at a time," it is inherently there "all at once." I can clarify what I mean by drawing a parallel to a simpler system. The entire path of a thrown grapefruit is inherent once the grapefruit is released. Watching the fruit in flight is *one* way—the usual way—of experiencing its motion; it could be labeled the "bit-at-a-time" picture of its motion. But just knowing its *initial position* and *velocity* is another equally valid way of experiencing the motion; this picture of the motion could be labeled the "all-at-once" picture. Of course, in this picture we assume no interference by passing storks and so forth. A brain (or a brain catalogue) shares this dual nature; as long as it is not interacting with the exterior world and being modified in ways foreign to it, its time development can be viewed either in the "bit-at-a-time" picture or in the "all-at-once" picture. The latter picture is one that I advocate and that I thought you had come to agree with, when you described the record sailing out into space.

ACHILLES: I see things so much more easily in the "bit-at-a-time" picture.

TORTOISE: Of course you do. The human brain is set up to see things that way. Even in a simple case, like the motion of a flying grapefruit, the brain is more satisfied to *see* the actual motion "a bit at a time" than it is to visualize a parabola "all at once." But simply coming to recognize that there *is* an "all-at-once" picture was a great step by the human mind, because it amounted to the recognition that some regularities exist in nature, regularities that guide events in predictable channels.

ACHILLES: I recognize that *feeling* exists in the "bit-at-a-time" picture. I know this because that is how I feel my own feelings. But does it also exist in the "all-at-once" picture? Are there "feelings" in a motionless book?

TORTOISE: Is there music in a motionless playing-record?

ACHILLES: I am not sure any longer how to answer that question. But I still want to learn if "I" am in the Achilles book, or if the "real Einstein" is in the Einstein book.

TORTOISE: So you may; but for my part, *I* still want to learn if "you" are anywhere at all. So let us stick to the comfortable "bit-at-a-time" picture, and imagine the internal processes of your brain, Achilles. Imagine the "hot-spot," that infamous shower of electrochemical activity, as it zigzags its way along the "path of least resistance." You, Achilles, or what you refer to as "I," have no control over which path is the one of least resistance.

ACHILLES: I don't? Is it my subconscious, then? I know I sometimes feel my thoughts "spring up" to me as if motivated by subconscious tendencies.

TORTOISE: Perhaps "subconscious" is a good name for neural structure. It is, after all, your neural structure that, at any moment, determines which path is the one of least resistance. And it is because of that neural structure that the "hot-spot" follows that curlicue path and none other. This swirling electrochemical activity constitutes the mental and emotional life of Achilles.

ACHILLES: A weird and mechanistic song, Mr. T. I bet you could make it sound even stranger. Wax lyric if you can; let the verbs have their fling! Of Brain, Mind, and Man, let's hear the Tortoise sing!

TORTOISE: Your verse is surely inspired by the gods, my dear companion. The brain of Achilles is like a labyrinth of rooms; each room has many doors leading to other rooms—and many of the rooms are labeled. (Each "room" may be thought of as a complex of a few or a few dozen neurons—perhaps more; and "labeled" rooms are special complexes composed mostly of speech-neurons.) As the "hot spot" tears through this labyrinth, flinging open and slamming shut doors, from time to time it enters a "labeled" room. At that point your throat and mouth contract: you say a word. All the while the neural flash loops relentlessly along its Achillean path, in shapes stranger than the dash of a gnat-hungry swallow; every twist, every turn is foreordained by the neural structure present in your brain, until sensory input messages interfere; then the flash veers away from the path it would have followed. And so it goes—room after room after labeled room is visited. You are speaking.

ACHILLES: I don't always speak. Sometimes I merely sit and think.

TORTOISE: Granted. The labeled rooms may have their lights turned low —a sign for non-utterance: you don't speak the words aloud. A "thought" occurs, silently. The hot spot continues—depositing, at door after door, either a drop of oil on the hinge to loosen it, or a drop of water to corrode it. Some doors have such rusty hinges they can't be opened. Others are so often oiled they nearly open by themselves. Thus traces of the present are deposited for the future: the "I" of now leaves messages and memories for the "I" of a time to come. This neural dance is the dance of the soul; and the sole choreographer of the soul is physical law.

ACHILLES: Normally, I think that *I'm* in control of what I think; but the way *you* put it turns it all around backward, so that it sounds like "I" am just what comes *out of* all this neural structure and natural law. It makes what I consider *myself* sound at best like a by-product of an organism governed by natural law and, at worst, like an artificial concept produced by my distorted perspective. In other words, you make me feel as if I don't know who—or what—I am, if anything.

TORTOISE: This is a very important matter to bring up. How can you "know" what you *are*? First of all, what does it mean to know something, anything, at all?

ACHILLES: Well, I presume that when I know something—or when, should I say, my *brain* knows something—there is a path that snakes through my brain, running through rooms, many of which are labeled. If I ever think a thought about the subject, my neural flash swishes along that path quite automatically, and if I am conversing, each time it passes through a *labeled* room, a sound of some type comes out. But of course I don't need to think about my neural flash for it to do this very competently. It seems as if *I* function quite well without *me!*

TORTOISE: Well, it's true that the "path of least resistance" does take care of itself quite well. But we can equate the result of all this functioning with *you,* Achilles. You needn't feel that your *self* is dispensed with in this analysis.

ACHILLES: But the trouble with this picture is that my "self" is not in control of myself.

TORTOISE: I suppose it depends upon what you mean by "control," Achilles. Clearly you cannot force your neural flash to deviate from the path of least resistance; but the Achilles of one moment is directly affecting what will become the path of least resistance in the *next* moment. That should give you some feeling that "you," whatever you are, have some control over what you will feel and think and do, in the future.

ACHILLES: Well, yes, that is an interesting way to look at it, but it still means that I can't just think whatever I *want* to think, but only what was *set up* for me to think, by an earlier version of me.

TORTOISE: But what is set up in your brain *is* what you want to think about, to a large degree. But sometimes, admittedly, you *can't* make your brain function as you will it to. You forget someone's name; you can't concentrate on something important; you become nervous despite your best attempts to control yourself; all of this reflects what you said: that in a sense *your "self" is not in control of yourself.* Now it is up to you whether or not you wish to identify the Achilles of now with the Achilles of bygone times. If you do choose to identify with your former selves, then you can say that "you"—meaning the you that used to exist—*are* in control of what you are today; but if you prefer to think of yourself as existing solely in the present, then indeed it is true that what "you" do is under control of natural law and not under control of an independent "soul."

ACHILLES: I am beginning to feel through this discussion that I "know" myself a little better. I wonder if it would be possible for me to learn *all about* my neural structure—so much so that I would be able to predict the path of my neural flash before it even covered its path! Surely, this would be *total,* exquisite self-knowledge.

TORTOISE: Oh, Achilles, you have innocently thrown yourself into the wildest of paradox, without the benefit of even the slightest coaching on my part! Maybe one day you will learn to do this regularly; then you will be able to dispense with me entirely!

ACHILLES: Enough of your mockery! Let's hear about this paradox I've inadvertently fallen into.

TORTOISE: How could you learn all about yourself? You might try reading the Achilles book.

ACHILLES: That would certainly be a phenomenal project. A hundred billion pages! I'm afraid I'd fall asleep listening to myself read. Or —horrors—I might even *die* before I had completed the task! But suppose I were a very fast reader and managed to learn the contents of the *whole book* within the time allotted to me on the surface of our green sphere.

TORTOISE: So now you'd know all about Achilles—*before* he read the Achilles book! But you are quite *ignorant* about the Achilles who exists *now!*

ACHILLES: Oh, what a quandary! The fact that I *read* the book makes the book obsolete. The very attempt to learn about myself changes me from what I was. If only I could have a bigger brain, capable of digesting all of the complexity of myself. Yet I can see that even that would be of no avail, for possession of a bigger brain would make me all the more complex yet! My mind simply *can't* understand all of itself. All I can know is the outline, the basic idea. Beyond a certain point, I cannot go. Although my brain structure is right there in my head, exactly where "I" am, still its nature is not accessible to this "I." The very entity that constitutes "I"—and I am of necessity ignorant of it. My brain and "I" are not the same!

TORTOISE: A droll dilemma—the stuff of life's many hilarities. And now, perhaps, Achilles, we can pause to ponder one of the original questions that prompted this discussion: "Do thoughts occur in the *mind,* or in the *brain?*"

ACHILLES: By now, I hardly know what is meant by "mind"—except, of course, as a sort of poetic expression for the brain, or its activities. The term reminds me of "beauty." It is not something that one can locate in space—yet it is not hovering in an ethereal otherworld, either. It is more like a structural feature of a complex entity.

TORTOISE: Where lies the beauty, if I may rhetorically ask, of an étude by Scriàbin? In the sounds? Among the printed notes? In the ear, mind, or brain of the beholder?

ACHILLES: It seems to me that "beauty" is just a *sound* that we utter whenever our neural flash passes through a certain region of our brains—a certain "labeled room." It is tempting to think that to this sound there corresponds an "entity," some kind of "existing thing." In other words, because it is a noun, we think of beauty as a "Thing"; but maybe "beauty" denotes no Thing at all; the word is just a useful sound which certain events and perceptions make us want to pronounce.

TORTOISE: I would go further, Achilles: I would surmise that this is a property of *many* words—especially words like "beauty," "truth," "mind," and "self." Each word is but a *sound* which we are caused to utter, at various times, by our swooping, careening neural flash. And to each sound, we can hardly help but believe that there corresponds an Entity—a "Real Thing." Well, I *will* say that the benefit that one derives from using a sound imbues it with a proportionate amount of what we call *"meaning."* But as to whether that sound denotes any Thing . . . how would we ever know *that*?

ACHILLES: How solipsistically you view the universe, Mr. T. I thought such views were highly unfashionable in this day and age! One is supposed to consider that Things have an Existence of their own.

TORTOISE: Ah, me, yes, perhaps they do—I never denied it. I suppose it's a pragmatic view of the meaning of "meaning," useful in the bustle of everyday life, to make the assumption that *some* sounds *do* stand for Existing Entities. And the pragmatic value of this assumption may be its best justification. But let's get back to the elusive site of the "real you," Achilles!

ACHILLES: Well, I'm at a loss to say if it's anywhere at all, even though another part of me is practically jumping to shout, "The 'real me' is here now." Maybe the whole point is that whatever mechanism makes me make everyday statements like "Spades are trump" is quite like the mechanism which makes me—or the Achilles book—say sentences such as "The 'real me' is here now." For certainly if *I*, Achilles, could say it, so could the book version of me—in fact, it would undoubtedly do so. Though my own first reflex is to affirm, "I know I exist; I *feel* it," maybe all these "feelings" are just an illusion; maybe the "real I" is all an illusion; maybe, just like "beauty," the sound "I" denotes no Thing at all, but is just a useful sound that we on occasion feel compelled to pronounce because our neural structures are set up that way. Probably that is what is happening when I say "I *know* I'm alive" or similar things. This would also explain why I got so puzzled when you brought up the version in which several copies of the Achilles book would be distributed to various people, and "I" would have conversations with all of them at once. I demanded to know where the "real I" was, and how "I" could take care of several conversations at once; I see now that each copy of the book has that structure built into it, that makes it automatically make pronouncements such as "I am the real me; *I* am feeling my *own* emotions and anybody else who claims to be Achilles is a fraud." But I can see that the mere fact that it utters such things doesn't mean that it has "real feelings"; and perhaps even more to the point, the mere fact that I, Achilles, utter such things, doesn't really mean I am feeling anything (whatever that would mean!). In the light of all this, I am beginning to doubt if such phrases have any meaning at all.

TORTOISE: Well, of course, utterances about "feeling" one way or another are very useful, in practical terms.

ACHILLES: Oh, without doubt—I shan't shun them just because this conversation has taken place; nor shall I shun the term "I," as you can see for yourself. But I won't imbue it with such "soulful" meaning as I have heretofore tended to do, rather instinctively, and, I have to say, dogmatically.

TORTOISE: I am glad that for once we seem to be in agreement in our conclusions. I see that the hour is growing late; dusk is approaching —just the time when all my forces seem to gather, and I feel quite energetic. I know you must have been disappointed by the "no-show" of your friend; how's about a little footrace back to the fifth century B.C.?

ACHILLES: What a capital idea! But just to be *fair,* I'll give you a head start of, oh, three centuries, since I'm so fleet of foot.

TORTOISE: You're a mite cocky, Achilles. . . . You may not find it so easy to catch up with an Energetic Tortoise.

ACHILLES: Only a *fool* would bet on a slow-footed Tortoise, racing against *me.* Last one to Zeno's house is a monkey's uncle!

Reflections

"Well, all these fantasies have been fun, but they can't really tell us anything. They're just so much science fiction. If you want to learn the truth—the hard facts—about something, you have to turn to real science, which so far has had little to tell us about the ultimate nature of the mind." This response conjures up a familiar but impoverished vision of science as a collection of precise mathematical formulae, meticulous experiments, and vast catalogues of species and genera, ingredients and recipes. This is the picture of science as strictly a data-gathering enterprise in which imagination is tightly reined in by incessant demands for proof. Even some scientists have this vision of their profession, and are deeply suspicious of their more playful colleagues, however eminent. Perhaps some symphony orchestra players view their business as nothing but precise noise-making produced under conditions of militaristic discipline. If so, think what they are missing.

In fact, of course, science is an unparalleled playground of the imagination, populated by unlikely characters with wonderful names (messenger RNA, black holes, quarks) and capable of performing the most amazing deeds: sub-atomic whirling dervishes that can be in several places—everywhere and nowhere—at the same time; molecular hoop-snakes biting their own tails; self-copying spiral staircases bearing coded instructions; miniature keys searching for the locks in which they fit, on floating odysseys in a trillion synaptic gulfs. So why not brain-book immortality, dream-writing machines, symbols that understand themselves, and fraternal homunculi without arms, legs, or heads, sometimes blindly following orders like the sorcerer's broom, sometimes feuding and conniving, sometimes cooperating? After all, some of the most fantastic ideas presented in this book—Wheeler's solitary electron weaving the universe, for example, or Everett's many-worlds interpretation of quantum mechanics, or Dawkins' suggestion that we are survival machines for our genes—have been proposed in complete seriousness by eminent scientists. Should we take such extravagant ideas seriously? We should certainly try, for how else will we ever learn whether these are the conceptual giant steps we need to escape from the most obscure riddles of the self and consciousness? Coming to understand the mind will probably require new ways of thinking that are at least as outrageous—at first—as Copernicus's shocking suggestion that the Earth goes around the Sun, or Einstein's bizarre claim that space itself could be curved. Science advances haltingly, bumping against the boundaries of the unthinkable: the things declared impossible because they are currently unimaginable. It is at the speculative frontier of thought experiment and fantasy that these boundaries get adjusted.

Thought experiments can be systematic, and often their implications can be rigorously deduced. Consider Galileo's crystal-clear *reductio ad absurdum* of the hypothesis that heavier objects fall faster than lighter objects. He asks us to imagine taking a heavy object, A, and a light object, B, and tying them together with a string or chain before dropping them off a tower. By hypothesis, B falls slower, and hence should act as a drag on A; thus A tied to B should fall slower than A by itself. But A tied to B is itself a new object, C, which is heavier than A, and hence, by hypothesis, C should fall faster than A by itself. A tied to B cannot at the same time fall faster *and* slower than A by itself (a contradiction or absurdity), so the hypothesis must be false.

On other occasions thought experiments, however systematically developed, are intended merely to illustrate and enliven difficult ideas. And sometimes the boundaries between proof, persuasion, and pedagogy cannot be drawn. In this book there are a variety of thought experiments designed to explore the implications of the hypothesis that materialism is true: the mind or self is not another (non-physical) *thing*, in miraculous interaction with the brain, but somehow a natural and explainable product of the brain's organization and operation. "The Story of a Brain" presents a thought experiment that is meant, like Galileo's, to be a *reductio ad absurdum* of its main premise—in this case, materialism in the guise of "the neural theory of experience." "Prelude, Ant Fugue," "Where Am I?" and "A Conversation with Einstein's Brain," on the other hand, are designed to support materialism by helping thinkers over obstacles that have traditionally stood in the way of comprehending it. In particular, these thought experiments are designed to provide a plausible substitute for the otherwise compelling idea of the self as a sort of mysterious, indivisible pearl of mind-stuff. "Minds, Brains, and Programs" is intended to refute one version of materialism (roughly, the version we defend), while leaving some underdescribed and unexplored materialistic alternatives untouched.

In each of these thought experiments there is a narrative problem of scale: how to get the reader's imagination to glide over a few billion details and see the woods and not just the trees. "The Story of a Brain" is silent about the staggering complexity of the devices to which the imagined brain parts would have to be attached. In "Where Am I?" the virtual impossibility of using radio links to preserve the connectivity in hundreds of thousands of nerves is conveniently ignored, and the even less likely feat of making a computer duplicate of a human brain that could operate synchronously is presented as nothing more than a fancy bit of technology. "Minds, Brains, and Programs" invites us to imagine a person hand simulating a language-processing program which, if it were realistic, would be so huge that no person could perform the steps for a single interchange in less than a lifetime, but we are cajoled into imagining the system engaging in Chinese conversations occurring in a normal time scale. The problem of scale is faced directly in "A Conversation with Einstein's Brain," where we are asked to tolerate a book with a hundred billion pages we can flip through fast enough to extract a few conversational gems from the posthumous Prof. Einstein.

Each setting of the dials on our intuition pump yields a slightly different narrative, with different problems receding into the background and different morals drawn. Which version or versions should be trusted is a matter to settle by examining them carefully, to see which features of the narrative are doing the work. If the oversimplifications are the *source* of the intuitions, rather than just devices for suppressing irrelevant complications, we should mistrust the conclusions we are invited to draw. These are matters of delicate judgment, so it is no wonder that a generalized and quite justified suspicion surrounds such exercises of imagination and speculation.

In the end we must turn to the rigorous methods of hard science—the experiments, deductions, and mathematical analyses—to keep the speculations honest. These methods provide raw materials for suggesting and testing hypotheses, and even serve often as powerful engines of discovery in their own right. Still, the storytelling side of science is not just peripheral, and not just pedagogy, but the very point of it all. Science properly done is one of the humanities, as a fine physics teacher once said. The point of science is to help us understand what we are and how we got here, and for this we need the great stories: the tale of how, once upon a time, there was a Big Bang; the Darwinian epic of the evolution of life on Earth; and now the story we are just beginning to learn how to tell: the amazing adventure of the primate autobiographers who finally taught themselves how to tell the story of the amazing adventure of the primate autobiographers.

D.C.D.

27

ROBERT NOZICK

Fiction

I am a fictional character. However, you would be in error to smile smugly, feeling ontologically superior. For you are a fictional character too. All my readers are except one who is, properly, not reader but author.

I am a fictional character; this is *not*, however, a work of fiction, no more so than any other work you've ever read. It is not a modernist work that self-consciously *says* it's a work of fiction, nor one even more tricky that denies its fictional status. We all are familiar with such works and know how to deal with them, how to frame them so that *nothing* the author says—nothing the first person voices even in an afterword or in something headed "author's note"—can convince us that anyone is speaking seriously, *non*-fictionally in his own first person.

All the more severe is my own problem of informing you that this very piece you are reading is a work of non-fiction, yet we are fictional characters, nevertheless. *Within* this world of fiction we inhabit, this writing is non-fictional, although in a wider sense, encased as it is in a work of fiction, it too can only be a fiction.

Think of our world as a novel in which you yourself are a character. Is there any way to tell what our author is like? Perhaps. *If* this is a work in which the author *expresses* himself, we can draw inferences about his facets, while noting that each such inference we draw will be written by

"Fiction" by Robert Nozick appeared in *Ploughshares*, vol. 6, no. 3, Fall 1980. Copyright © 1980 by *Ploughshares*.

him. And if he writes that we find a particular inference plausible or valid, who are we to argue?

One sacred scripture in the novel we inhabit says that the author of our universe created things merely by speaking, by saying "Let there be . . ." The only thing mere speaking can create, we know, is a story, a play, an epic poem, a fiction. Where we live is created by and in words: a uni-verse.

Recall what is known as the problem of evil: why does a good creator allow evil in the world, evil he knows of and can prevent? However, when an author includes monstrous deeds—pain and suffering—in his work, does this cast any special doubt upon his goodness? Is an author callous who puts his characters through hardships? Not if the characters do not suffer them *really*. But don't they? Wasn't Hamlet's father really killed? (Or was he merely hiding to see how Hamlet would respond?) Lear really was cast adrift—he didn't just dream this. Macbeth, on the other hand, did *not* see a real dagger. But these characters aren't real and never were, so there was no suffering outside of the world of the work, no *real* suffering in the author's *own* world, and so in his creating, the author was not cruel. (Yet why is it cruel only when he creates suffering in his *own* world? Would it be perfectly all right for Iago to create misery in *our* world?)

"What!" you say, "we don't really undergo suffering? Why it's as real to us as Oedipus' is to him." Precisely as real. "But can't you *prove* that you *really* exist?" If Shakespeare had Hamlet say "I think, therefore I am," would that prove to us that Hamlet exists? Should it prove that to Hamlet, and if so what is such a proof worth? Could not *any* proof be written into a work of fiction and be presented by one of the characters, perhaps one named "Descartes"? (Such a character should worry less that he's dreaming, more that he's dreamed.)

Often, people discover anomalies in the world, facts that just don't jibe. The deeper dug, the more puzzles found—far-fetched coincidences, dangling facts—on these feed conspiracy and assassination buffs. That number of hours spent probing into *anything* might produce anomalies, however, if reality is not as coherent as we thought, if it is not *real.* Are we simply discovering the limits of the details the author worked out? But *who* is discovering this? The author who writes our discoveries knows them himself. Perhaps he now is preparing to correct them. Do we live in galley proofs in the process of being corrected? Are we living in a *first draft*?

My tendency, I admit, is to want to revolt, to conspire along with the rest of you to overthrow our author or to make our positions more equal, at least, to hide some portion of our lives from him—to gain a little breathing space. Yet these words I write he reads, my secret thoughts and modulations of feeling he knows and records, my Jamesian author.

But does he *control* it all? Or does our author, through writing, learn about his characters and from them? Is he surprised by what he finds us doing and thinking? When we feel we freely think or act on our own, is this merely a description he has written in for us, or does he *find* it to be true of us, his characters, and therefore write it? Does our leeway and privacy reside in this, that there are some implications of his work that he hasn't yet worked out, some things he has not thought of which nevertheless are true in the world he has created, so that there are actions and thoughts of ours that elude his ken? (Must we therefore speak *in code?*) Or is he only ignorant of what we *would* do or say in some *other* circumstances, so that our independence lies only in the *subjunctive* realm?

Does this way madness lie? Or enlightenment?

Our author, we know, is outside our realm, yet he may not be free of our problems. Does he wonder too whether *he* is a character in a work of fiction, whether his writing our universe is a play within a play? Does he have me write this work and especially this very paragraph in order to express his own concerns?

It would be nice for us if our author too is a fictional character and this fictional world he made describes (that being no coincidence) the actual world inhabited by *his* author, the one who created him. We then would be fictional characters who, unbeknownst to our own author although not to his, correspond to real people. (Is that why we are so true to life?)

Must there be a top-floor somewhere, a world that itself is not created in someone else's fiction? Or can the hierarchy go on infinitely? Are circles excluded, even quite narrow ones where a character of one world creates another fictional world wherein a character creates the first world? Might the circle get narrower, still?

Various theories have described our world as less real than another, even as an illusion. The idea of our having this inferior ontological status takes some getting used to, however. It may help if we approach our situation as literary critics and ask the genre of our universe, whether tragedy, farce, or theater-of-the-absurd? What is the plot line, and which act are we in?

Still, our status may bring some compensations, as, for example, that we live on even after we die, preserved permanently in the work of fiction. Or if not permanently, at least for as long as our book lasts. May we hope to inhabit an enduring masterpiece rather than a quickly remaindered book?

Moreover, though in some sense it might be false, in another wouldn't it be true for Hamlet to say, "I am Shakespeare"? What do Macbeth, Banquo, Desdemona, and Prospero have in common? The consciousness of the one author, Shakespeare, which underlies and infuses each of them. (So too, there is the brotherhood of man.) Playing on the intricacy both of our ontological status and of the first person reflexive pronoun, each of us too may truly say, "I am the author."

Note From the Author

Suppose I now tell you that the preceding *was* a work of fiction and the "I" didn't refer to me, the author, but to a first person character. Or suppose I tell you that it was *not* a work of fiction but a playful, and so of course serious, philosophical essay by me, Robert Nozick, (*Not* the Robert Nozick named as author at the beginning of this work—he may be, for all we know, another literary persona—but the one who attended P.S. 165.) How would your response to this whole work differ depending on which I say, supposing you were willing, as you won't be, simply to accept my statement?

May I decide *which* to say, fiction or philosophical essay, only now, as I finish writing this, and how will that decision affect the character of what already was set down previously? May I postpone the decision further, perhaps until after you have read this, fixing its status and genre only then?

Perhaps God has not decided *yet* whether he has created, in this world, a fictional world or a real one. Is the Day of Judgment the day he will decide? Yet what additional thing depends upon which way he decides—what would either decision add to our situation or subtract from it?

And which decision do you hope for?

Further Reading

Almost every topic that arises in *The Mind's I* has been explored in greater detail in the explosively growing literature of "cognitive science"—philosophy of mind, psychology, artificial intelligence, and the neurosciences, to mention the central fields. There has also been a mountain of science fiction on these themes, of course, but we will not attempt to survey that literature in this catalogue of the best and most readable recent books and articles, ranging from clinical studies of strange cases through experimental work to theoretical and speculative explorations. The catalogue is organized by topics in the order in which they arise in the preceding selections. Each piece we list will in turn lead to additional relevant literature through its citations. Those who pursue these leads will discover a huge tree of intricately intertwined branches of discovery, speculation, and argument. That tree will not include everything that has been written on these topics, certainly, but whatever it neglects will have escaped the attention of most of the experts as well.

Introduction

The idea of **body-switching** has fascinated philosophers for centuries. John Locke, in his *Essay Concerning Human Understanding* (1690), asked himself what would happen if "the soul of a prince" were to "enter and inform the body of a cobbler"—taking the prince's memories along with it. The theme has had dozens of variations since then. Two fine anthologies, full of imagined cases of brain transplants, person splitting, person fusing (two or more people merging into one person with several sets of memories and tastes), and person duplicating are *Personal Identity* (1975), edited by John Perry, and *The Identities of Persons* (1976), edited by Amelie O. Rorty, both in paperback from the University of California Press at Berkeley. Another good book is Bernard Williams's *Problems of the Self* (New York: Cambridge University Press, 1973).

Do minds or selves really exist—over and above the atoms and molecules? Such ontological questions (questions concerning the types of things that can be said to exist and the ways in which things can exist) have been a major preoccupation of philosophers since Plato's day. Probably the most influential of today's hard-nosed, tough-minded scientific ontologists is Willard V. O. Quine, of Harvard University. His classic paper "On What There Is" first appeared in 1948 in the *Review of Metaphysics*. It is reprinted in his collection of essays, *From a Logical Point of View* (Cambridge, Mass.: Harvard University Press, 1953). Quine's *Word and Object* (Cambridge, Mass.: MIT Press, 1960) and *Ontological Relativity and Other Essays* (New York: Columbia University Press, 1969) contain later elaborations of his uncompromising ontological stand. An amusing dialogue in which a tough-minded materialist gets tied in knots is "Holes" by David and Stephanie Lewis, in the *Australasian Journal of Philosophy* (vol. 48, 1970, pp. 206–212). If holes are things that exist, what about voices? What are they? This question is discussed in the first chapter of Daniel Dennett's *Content and Consciousness* (London: Routledge & Kegan Paul; Atlantic Highlands, N.J.: Humanities Press, 1969), where the claim is advanced that minds enjoy the same sort of existence as voices—not problematic (like ghosts or goblins) but not just a matter of matter, either.

The literature on **consciousness** will be introduced by subtopics later in this chapter. The discussion of consciousness in the Introduction is drawn from an entry on that topic by Dennett forthcoming in the *Oxford Companion to the Mind* (New York: Oxford University Press), an encyclopedia of current understanding of the mind, edited by R. L. Gregory. The quotation of E. R. John's definition of consciousness is from R. W. Thatcher and E. R. John, *Foundations of Cognitive Processes* (Hillsdale, N.J.: Erlbaum, 1977, p. 294), and the dichotic listening experiment discussed is reported in J.R. Lackner and M. Garrett, "Resolving Ambiguity: Effects of Biasing Context in the Unattended Ear," *Cognition* (1973, pp. 359–372).

Part I. A Sense of Self

Borges draws our attention to different **ways of thinking about oneself.** A good entry to the recent work in philosophy mentioned in the Reflections is "Who, Me?" by Steven Boër and William Lycan, in *The Philosophical Review* (vol. 89, 1980, pp. 427–466). It has an extensive bibliography that includes the pioneering work of Hector-Neri Castañeda and Peter Geach, and the fine recent work by John Perry and David Lewis.

Harding's strange ruminations **on having no head** find an echo in the psychological theories of the late James J. Gibson, whose last book, *The Ecological Approach to Visual Perception* (Boston: Houghton Mifflin, 1979), contains many striking observations—and results of experiments—about the information one gets about oneself (one's location, the orientation of one's head, even the important role of that blurry bit of nose one can see out of the corner of one's eye) from visual perception. See especially chapter 7, "The Optical Information for Self-Perception." For a recent criticism of Gibson's ideas, see Shimon Ullman, "Against Direct Perception," in *The Behavioral and Brain Sciences* (September, 1980, pp. 373–415). An excellent introduction to the Taoistic and Zen theory of mind and existence is Raymond Smullyan's *The Tao is Silent* (New York: Harper & Row, 1975). See also Paul Reps' *Zen Flesh, Zen Bones* (New York: Doubleday Anchor).

The physical background for the **quantum-mechanical ideas** presented in Morowitz's article and the accompanying Reflection is available at several levels of difficulty. A stimulating elementary presentation is that by Adolph Baker in *Modern Physics and Anti-physics* (Reading, Mass.: Addison-Wesley, 1970). And there is Richard Feynman's *The Character of Physical Law* (Cambridge, Mass.: MIT Press, 1967). At an intermediate level, using a bit of mathematics, are J. Jauch's elegant dialogues *Are Quanta Real?* (Bloomington: Indiana University Press, 1973) and *The Feynman Lectures in Physics,* vol. III, by Richard Feynman, Robert Leighton, and Matthew Sands (Reading, Mass.: Addison-Wesley, 1963). An advanced treatise is the monograph *The Conceptual Development of Quantum Mechanics* by Max Jammer (New York: McGraw-Hill, 1966). There is also a further-out book, edited by Ted Bastin, called *Quantum Theory and Beyond: Essays and Discussions Arising from a Colloquium* (Cambridge, Eng.: Cambridge Univ. Press, 1971) containing many speculative selections. Eugene Wigner, one of the major figures in physics this century, has devoted an entire selection, in his book of essays entitled *Symmetries and Reflections* (Cambridge, Mass.: MIT press, 1970), to the subject of "Epistemology and Quantum Mechanics."

Hugh Everett's original paper is found, together with discussions by other physicists, in *The Many-Worlds Interpretation of Quantum Mechanics* (Princeton, N.J.: Princeton University Press, 1973), edited by B. S. Dewitt and N. Graham. A recent and much easier book on these puzzling splitting worlds is Paul Davies' *Other Worlds* (New York: Simon & Schuster, 1981).

The strange problem of **personal identity** under such conditions of branching has been explored, indirectly, in a high-powered but lively debate among philosophers over the claims made by the philosopher and logician Saul Kripke in his classic monograph "Naming and Necessity," which first appeared in 1972 in D. Davidson and G. Harman, eds., *The Semantics of Natural Language* (Hingham, Mass.: Reidel, 1972), and has just been reprinted, with additional material, as a book by Kripke, *Naming and Necessity* (Cambridge, Mass.: Harvard University Press, 1980). In the Reflections, an issue is raised that must have occurred to you before: If my parents hadn't met, I'd never have existed—or could *I* have been the child of some other parents? Kripke argues (with surprising persuasiveness) that although someone exactly like you might have been born at a different time to different parents—or even to your own parents—that person could not have *been* you. Where, when, and to whom you were born is part of your *essence.* Douglas Hofstadter, Gray Clossman, and Marsha Meredith explore this strange terrain in "Shakespeare's Plays Weren't Written by Him, but by Someone Else of the Same Name" (Indiana University Computer Science Dept. Technical Report 96) and Daniel Dennett casts some doubt on the enterprise in "Beyond Belief," forthcoming in Andrew Woodfield, ed., *Thought and Object* (New York: Oxford University Press, 1981). *Meaning, Reference and Necessity* (New York: Cambridge University Press, 1975), edited by Simon Blackburn, is a good anthology of work on the issue, and the topic continues to be analyzed in current and forthcoming articles in major philosophy journals.

Morowitz cites recent speculation about the **sudden emergence of a special sort of self-consciousness in evolution**—a discontinuity in the development of our remote ancestors. Certainly the boldest and most ingeniously argued case for such a development is Julian Jaynes's *The Origins of Consciousness in the Breakdown of the Bicameral Mind* (Boston: Houghton Mifflin, 1976), in which he argues that consciousness of the familiar, typically human sort is a very recent phenomenon, whose onset is datable in historical times, not biological eons. The human beings told of in Homer's *Iliad,* Jaynes insists, were not conscious! That is not to say they were asleep, or unperceiving, of course, but that they had nothing like what we think of as our inner lives. Even if Jaynes has overstated his case (as most commentators think), he has posed fascinating questions and drawn attention to important facts and problems hitherto unconsidered by thinkers on these topics. Incidently, Friedrich Nietzsche expressed a similar view of the relation of consciousness and social and linguistic practices in *Die fröhliche Wissenschaft* (1882), translated by Walter Kaufmann as *The Gay Science* (New York: Random House, 1974).

Part II. Soul Searching

The Turing test has been the focus of many articles in philosophy and artificial intelligence. A good recent discussion of the problems it raises is "Psychologism and Behaviorism" by Ned Block, in *The Philosophical Review* (January 1981, pp. 5–43). Joseph Weizenbaum's famous ELIZA program, which simulates a psychotherapist with whom one can hold an intimate and therapeutic conversation (typing on a computer terminal), is often discussed as the most dramatic real-life example of a computer "passing" the Turing test. Weizenbaum himself is appalled by the idea, and in *Computer Power and Human Reason* (San Francisco: Freeman, 1976), he offers trenchant criticism of those who—in his opinion—misuse the Turing test. Kenneth M. Colby's program PARRY, the simulation of a paranoid patient that "passed" two versions of the Turing test, is described in his "Simulation of Belief Systems," in Roger C. Schank and Kenneth M. Colby, eds., *Computer Models of Thought and Language* (San Francisco: Freeman, 1973). The first test, which involved showing transcripts of PARRY's conversations to experts, was amusingly attacked by Weizenbaum in a letter published in the *Communications of the Association for Computing Machinery* (vol. 17, no. 9, September 1974, p. 543). Weizenbaum claimed that by Colby's reasoning, any electric typewriter is a good scientific model of infantile autism: type in a question and it just sits there and hums. No experts on autism could tell transcripts of genuine attempts to communicate with autistic children from such futile typing exercises! The second Turing test experiment responded to that criticism, and is reported in J. F. Heiser, K. M. Colby, W. S. Faught, and K. C. Parkinson, "Can Psychiatrists Distinguish a Computer Simulation of Paranoia from the Real Thing?" in the *Journal of Psychiatric Research* (vol. 15, 1980, pp. 149–62).

Turing's "Mathematical Objection" has produced a flurry of literature on the relation between **metamathematical limitative theorems and the possibility of mechanical minds**. For the appropriate background in logic, see Howard De Long's *A Profile of Mathematical Logic* (Reading, Mass.: Addison-Wesley, 1970). For an expansion of Turing's objection, see J. R. Lucas's notorious article "Minds, Machines, and Gödel," reprinted in the stimulating collection *Minds and Machines,* edited by Alan Ross Anderson (Engelwood Cliffs, N.J.: Prentice-Hall, 1964). De Long's excellent annotated bibliography provides pointers to the furor created by Lucas's paper. See also *Gödel, Escher, Bach: an Eternal Golden Braid* by Douglas R. Hofstadter (New York: Basic Books, 1979) and *Mechanism, Mentalism, and Metamathematics* by Judson Webb (Hingham, Mass.: D. Reidel, 1980).

The continuing debate on **extrasensory perception** and other paranormal phenomena is now followable on a regular basis in the lively quarterly journal *The Skeptical Enquirer.*

The prospects of **ape language** have been the focus of intensive research and debate in recent years. Jane von Lawick Goodall's observations in the wild, *In the Shadow of Man* (Boston: Houghton Mifflin, 1971) and early apparent breakthroughs in training laboratory animals to use sign language or other artificial languages by Allen and Beatrice Gardner, David Premack, Roger Fouts, and others led to hundreds of articles and books by scores of researchers and their critics. The experiment with high school students is reported in E. H. Lenneberg, "A Neuropsychological Comparison between Man, Chimpanzee and Monkey," *Neuropsychologia* (vol. 13, 1975, p. 125). Recently Herbert Terrace, in *Nim: A Chimpanzee Who Learned Sign Language* (New York: Knopf, 1979), managed to throw a decidedly wet blanket on this enthusiasm with his detailed analysis of the failures of most of this research, including his own efforts with his chimpanzee, Nim Chimpsky, but the other side will surely fight back in forthcoming articles and books. *The Behavioral and Brain Sciences (BBS)* of December 1978 is devoted to these issues and contains major articles by Donald Griffin, author of *The Question of Animal Awareness* (New York: Rockefeller Press, 1976), by David Premack and Guy Woodruff, and by Duane Rumbaugh, Sue Savage-Rumbaugh, and Sally Boysen. Accompanying these articles are a host of critical commentaries by leading researchers in linguistics, animal behavior, psychology and philosophy, and replies by the authors. In *BBS,* a new interdisciplinary journal, every article is followed by dozens of commentaries by other experts and a reply by the author. In a field as yeasty and controversial as cognitive science, this is proving to be a valuable format for introducing the disciplines to each other. Many other *BBS* articles in addition to those mentioned here provide excellent entry points into current research.

Although there is clearly a link of great importance between **consciousness and the capacity to use language,** it is important to keep these issues separate. Self-consciousness in animals has been studied experimentally. In an interesting series of experiments, Gordon Gallup established that chimpanzees can come to recognize themselves in mirrors—and they recognize themselves *as* themselves too, as he demonstrated by putting dabs of paint on their foreheads while they slept. When they saw themselves in the mirrors, they immediately reached up to touch their foreheads and then examined their fingers. See Gordon G. Gallup, Jr., "Self-recognition in Primates: A Comparative Approach to the Bidirection Properties of Consciousness," *American Psychologist* (vol. 32, (5), 1977, pp. 329–338). For a recent exchange of views on the role of language in human consciousness and the study of human thinking, see Richard Nisbett and Timothy De Camp Wilson, "Telling More Than We Know: Verbal Reports on Mental Processes," *Psychological Review* (vol. 84, (3), 1977, pp. 321–359) and K. Anders Ericsson and Herbert Simon, "Verbal Reports as Data," *Psychological Review* (vol. 87, (3), May 1980, pp. 215–250).

Many robots like the Mark III Beast have been built over the years. One at Johns Hopkins University was in fact called the Hopkins Beast. For a brief illustrated review of the history of robots and an introduction to current work on **robots and artificial intelligence,** see Bertram Raphael, *The Thinking Computer: Mind Inside Matter* (San Francisco: Freeman, 1976). Other recent introductions to the field of AI are Patrick Winston's *Artificial Intelligence* (Reading, Mass.: Addison-Wesley, 1977), Philip C. Jackson's *Introduction to Artificial Intelligence* (Princeton, N.J.: Petrocelli Books, 1975), and Nils Nilsson's *Principles of Artificial Intelligence* (Menlo Park, Ca.: Tioga, 1980). Margaret Boden's *Artificial Intelligence and Natural Man* (New York: Basic Books, 1979) is a fine introduction to AI from a philosopher's point of view. A new anthology on the conceptual issues confronted by artificial intelligence is John Haugeland, ed., *Mind Design: Philosophy, Psychology, Artificial Intelligence* (Montgomery, Vt.: Bradford, 1981), and an earlier collection is Martin Ringle, ed., *Philosophical Perspectives on Artificial Intelligence* (Atlantic Highlands, N.J.: Humanities Press, 1979). Other good collections on these issues are C. Wade Savage, ed., *Perception and Cognition: Issues in the Foundations of Psychology* (Minneapolis: University of Minnesota Press, 1978) and Donald E. Norman, ed., *Perspectives on Cognitive Science* (Norwood, N.J.: Ablex, 1980).

One shouldn't ignore the **critics of AI**. In addition to Weizenbaum, who devotes several chapters of *Computer Power and Human Reason* to an attack on AI, there is the philosopher Hubert Dreyfus, whose *What Computers Can't Do* (New York: Harper & Row, 2nd ed., 1979) is the most sustained and detailed criticism of the methods and presuppositions of the field. An entertaining and informative history of the birth of the field is Pamela McCorduck's *Machines Who Think: A Personal Inquiry into the History and Prospects of Artificial Intelligence* (San Francisco: Freeman, 1979).

Part III. From Hardware to Software

Dawkins's provocative views on **genes** as the units of selection have received considerable attention from biologists and philosophers of biology. Two good and relatively accessible discussions are William Wimsatt's "Reductionistic Research Strategies and Their Biases in the Units of Selection Controversy," in Thomas Nickles, ed., *Scientific Discovery*, vol. 2, Case Studies (Hingham, Mass.: Reidel, 1980, pp. 213–59), and Elliott Sober's "Holism, Individualism, and the Units of Selection," in *Proceedings of the Philosophy of Science Association* (vol. 2, 1980).

There have been many attempts to establish different **levels of description of the brain** and to describe the relations between them. Some pioneering attempts by neuroscientists are Karl Pribram's *The Languages of the Brain* (Engelwood Cliffs, N.J.: Prentice-Hall, 1971), Michael Arbib's *The Metaphorical Brain* (New York: Wiley Interscience, 1972), and R. W. Sperry's "A Modified Concept of Consciousness" in *Psychological Review* (vol. 76, (6), 1969, pp. 532–536). *Consciousness and Brain: A Scientific and Philosophical Inquiry* (New York: Plenum, 1976), edited by G. Globus, G. Maxwell, and I. Savodnick, includes several discussions of the problems faced by anyone who tries to relate brain-talk to mind-talk. An earlier work, yet still full of fresh insight, is Dean Wooldridge's *Mechanical Man: The Physical Basis of Intelligent Life* (New York: McGraw-Hill, 1968).

The general problem of **levels of explanation** in discussing mind and brain is one of the central themes of Hofstadter's *Gödel, Escher, Bach*. It is also the topic of the books *The Sciences of the Artificial* by Herbert Simon (Cambridge, Mass.: MIT Press, 2nd ed., 1981) and *Hierarchy Theory*, edited by Howard H. Pattee (New York: George Braziller, 1973).

Reduction and holism in biological systems such as ant colonies have been under debate for many decades. Back in 1911, William Morton Wheeler wrote an influential article entitled "The Ant-Colony as an Organism" in the *Journal of Morphology* (vol. 22, no. 2, 1911, pp. 307–325). More recently, Edward O. Wilson has written a remarkably thorough treatise on social insects, called *The Insect Societies* (Cambridge, Mass.: Harvard Univ. Press, Belknap Press, 1971). We are not aware of any literature exploring the *intelligence* of societies; for example, can an ant colony learn new tricks?

The explicitly **antireductionistic sentiment** has been put forward vehemently by an international group whose most outspoken member is the novelist and philosopher Arthur Koestler. Together with J.R. Smythies, he has edited a volume called *Beyond Reductionism* (Boston: Beacon Press, 1969) and has stated his own position eloquently in *Janus: A Summing Up* (New York: Vintage, 1979), particularly the chapter entitled "Free Will in a Hierarchic Context."

The quotations in the Reflections on "Prelude, Ant Fugue" are from Richard D. Mattuck, *A Guide to Feynman Diagrams in the Many-Body Problem* (New York: McGraw-Hill, 1976), and *Inside the Brain* (New York: Mentor, 1980), by William H. Calvin and George A. Ojemann. Aaron Sloman, who was probably the first person trained as a philosopher to join the field of artificial intelligence, is the author of *The Computer Revolution in Philosophy* (Brighton, England: Harvester, 1979). Like many revolutionary manifestos, Sloman's book vacillates between declaring victory, declaring that victory is inevitable, and exhorting the reader to join a difficult and uncertain campaign. Sloman's vision of the accomplishments and prospects of the movement is rose-tinted, but insightful. Other landmark work on **systems of knowledge representation** can be found in Lee W. Gregg, ed., *Knowledge and Cognition* (New York: Academic Press, 1974); Daniel G. Bobrow and Allan Collins, eds., *Representation and Understanding* (New York: Academic Press, 1975); Roger C. Schank and Robert P. Abelson, *Scripts, Plans, Goals and Understanding* (Hillsdale, N.J.: Erlbaum, 1977); Nicholas V. Findler, ed., *Foundations of Semantic Networks* (New York: Academic Press); Donald A. Norman and David Rumelhart, eds. *Explorations in Cognition* (San Francisco: W. H. Freeman, 1975); Patrick Henry Winston, *The Psychology of Computer Vision* (New York: McGraw-Hill, 1975); and the other books and articles on artificial intelligence mentioned in this chapter.

The strategy of speaking figuratively of **homunculi**, little people in the brain whose joint activity composes the activity of a single mind, is explored in detail in Daniel C. Dennett's *Brainstorms* (Montgomery, Vt.: Bradford Books, 1978). An early article in this vein was F. Attneave's "In Defense of Homunculi," in W. Rosenblith, ed., *Sensory Communication,* (Cambridge, Mass.: MIT Press, 1960, pp. 777–782). William Lycan advances the cause of homunculi in "Form, Function, and Feel," in the *Journal of Philosophy* (vol. 78, (1), 1981, pp. 24–50). See also Ronald de Sousa's "Rational Homunculi" in Rorty's *The Identities of Persons.*

Disembodied brains have long been a favorite philosophical fantasy. In his *Meditations* (1641), Descartes presents the famous thought experiment of the evil demon or evil genius. "How do I know," he asks himself in effect, "that I am not being tricked by an infinitely powerful evil demon who wants to deceive me into believing in the existence of the external world (and my own body)?" Perhaps, Descartes supposes, the only thing that exists aside from the demon is his own immaterial mind—the *minimal victim* of the demon's deceit. In these more materialistic times the same question is often updated: How do I know that evil scientists haven't removed my brain from my head while I slept and put it in a life-support vat, where they are tricking it—me—with phony stimulation? Literally hundreds of articles and books have been written about Descartes's thought experiment with the evil demon. Two good recent books are Anthony Kenny's *Descartes: A Study of his Philosophy* (Random House, 1968), and Harry Frankfurt's *Demons, Dreamers, and Madmen: The Defense of Reason in Descartes' Meditations* (Indianapolis: Bobbs-Merrill, 1970). A fine anthology is Willis Doney, ed., *Descartes: a Collection of Critical Essays* (New York: Macmillan, 1968). A particularly memorable and amusing discussion is O. K. Bouwsma's "Descartes' Evil Genius," in the *Philosophical Review* (vol. 58, 1949, pp. 141–151).

The "brain in the vat" literature, of which Zuboff's strange tale is a previously unpublished instance, has recently been rejuvenated with some new critical slants. See Lawrence Davis's "Disembodied Brains," in the *Australasian Journal of Philosophy* (vol. 52, 1974, pp. 121–132), and Sydney Shoemaker's "Embodiment and Behavior," in Rorty's *The Identities of Persons.* Hilary Putnam discusses the case at length in his new book, *Reason, Truth and History* (New York: Cambridge University Press, 1981), and argues that the supposition is not just technically outrageous but deeply, conceptually incoherent.

Part IV. Mind as Program

The theme of **duplicate people**—atom-for-atom replicas—has been picked up from fiction by philosophers, most notably by Hilary Putnam, who imagines a planet he calls Twin Earth, where each of us has an exact duplicate or *Doppelgänger,* to use the German term Putnam favors. Putnam first presented this literally outlandish thought experiment in "The Meaning of 'Meaning'," in Keith Gunderson, ed., *Language, Mind and Knowledge* (Minneapolis: University of Minnesota Press, 1975, pp. 131–193), where he uses it to establish a surprising new theory of meaning. It is reprinted in the second volume of Putnam's collected papers, *Mind, Language and Reality* (New York: Cambridge University Press, 1975). While it seems that almost no philosopher takes Putnam's argument seriously—that's what they all say—few can resist trying to say, at length, just where he has gone wrong. A provocative and influential article that exploits Putnam's fantasy is Jerry Fodor's intimidatingly entitled "Methodological Solipsism Considered as a Research Strategy in Cognitive Psychology," published, along with much furious commentary and rebuttal, in *The Behavioral and Brain Sciences* (vol. 3, no. 1, 1980, pp. 63–73). His comment on Winograd's SHRDLU, quoted in the Reflections on "Non Serviam," comes from this article, which is reprinted in Haugeland's *Mind Design.*

Prosthetic vision devices for the blind, mentioned in the Reflections on both "Where Am I?" and "What is it Like to be a Bat?", have been under development for many years, but the best systems currently available are still crude. Most of the research and development has been done in Europe. A brief survey can be found in Gunnar Jansson's "Human Locomotion Guided by a Matrix of Tactile Point Stimuli," in G. Gordon, ed., *Active Touch* (Elmsford, N.Y.: Pergamon Press, 1978, pp. 263–271). The topic has been subjected to philosophical scrutiny by David Lewis in "Veridical Hallucination and Prosthetic Vision," in the *Australasian Journal of Philosophy* (vol. 58, no. 3, 1980, pp. 239–249).

Marvin Minsky's article on **telepresence** appeared in *Omni* in May 1980, pp. 45–52, and contains references to further reading.

When Sanford speaks of the classic experiment with **inverting lenses**, he is referring to a long history of experiments that began before the turn of the century when G. M. Stratton wore a device for several days that blocked vision in one eye and inverted it in the other. This and more recent experiments are surveyed in R. L. Gregory's fascinating and beautifully illustrated book, *Eye and Brain* (London: Weidenfeld and Nicolson, 3rd ed., 1977). Also see Ivo Kohler's "Experiments with Goggles," in *Scientific American* (vol. 206, 1962, pp. 62–72). An up-to-date and very readable book on vision is John R. Frisby's *Seeing: Illusion, Brain, and Mind* (Oxford: Oxford Univ. Press, 1980).

Gödel sentences, self-referential constructions, "strange loops," and their implications for the theory of the mind are explored in great detail in Hofstadter's *Gödel, Escher, Bach,* and with some different twists in Dennett's "The Abilities of Men and Machines," in *Brainstorms.* That Gödel's Theorem is a bulwark of materialism rather than of mentalism is a thesis forcefully propounded in Judson Webb's *Mechanism, Mentalism, and Metamathematics.* A lighter but no less enlightening exploration of such ideas is Patrick Hughes's and George Brecht's *Vicious Circles and Paradoxes* (New York: Doubleday, 1975). C. H. Whitely's refutation of Lucas's thesis is found in his article "Minds, Machines and Gödel: A Reply to Mr. Lucas," published in *Philosophy* (vol. 37, 1962, p. 61).

Fictional objects have recently been the focus of considerable attention from philosophers of logic straying into aesthetics. See Terence Parsons, *Nonexistent Objects* (New Haven, Conn.: Yale University Press, 1980); David Lewis, "Truth in Fiction," in *American Philosophical Quarterly* (vol. 15, 1978, pp. 37–46); Peter van Inwagen, "Creatures of Fiction," also in *American Philosophical Quarterly* (vol. 14, 1977, pp. 299–308); Robert Howell, "Fictional Objects," in D. F. Gustafson and B. L. Tapscott, eds., *Body, Mind, and Method: Essays in Honor of Virgil C. Aldrich* (Hingham, Mass.: Reidel, 1979); Kendall Walton, "How Remote are Fictional Worlds from the Real World?" in *The Journal of Aesthetics and Art Criticism* (vol. 37, 1978, pp. 11–23); and the other articles cited in them. **Literary dualism**, the view that fictions are real, has had hundreds of explorations in fiction. One of the most ingenious and elegant is Borges's "Tlön, Uqbar, Orbis Tertius," in *Labyrinths* (New York: New Directions, 1964), from which the selections by Borges in *The Mind's I* are all drawn.

Part V. Created Selves and Free Will

All of the books on artificial intelligence mentioned earlier have detailed discussions of **simulated worlds** rather like the world described in "Non Serviam," except the worlds are much smaller (hard reality has a way of cramping one's style). See especially the discussion in Raphael's book, pp. 266–269. The vicissitudes of such "toy worlds" are also discussed by Jerry Fodor in "Tom Swift and his Procedural Grandmother," in his new collection of essays, *RePresentations* (Cambridge, Mass.: Bradford Books/MIT Press, 1981), and by Daniel Dennett in "Beyond Belief." The game of Life and its ramifications are discussed with verve by Martin Gardner in the "Mathematical Games" column of the October, 1970 issue of *Scientific American* (vol. 223, no.4, pp. 120–123).

Free will has of course been debated endlessly in philosophy. An anthology of recent work that provides a good entry into the literature is Ted Honderich, ed., *Essays on Freedom of Action* (London: Routledge & Kegan Paul, 1973). Two more recent articles that stand out appear together in the *Journal of Philosophy* (March 1980): Michael Slote's "Understanding Free Will," (vol. 77, pp. 136–151) and Susan Wolf's "Asymmetrical Freedom," (vol. 77, pp. 151–166). Even philosophers are often prone to lapse into the pessimistic view that no one can ever get anywhere in debates about free will—the issues are interminable and insoluble. This recent work makes that pessimism hard to sustain; perhaps one can begin to see the foundations of a sophisticated new way of conceiving of ourselves both as free and rational agents, choosing and deciding our courses of action, and as entirely physical denizens of a physical environment, as much subject to the "laws of nature" as any plant or inanimate object.

For more commentary on Searle's **"Minds, Brains and Programs,"** see the September 1980 issue of *The Behavioral and Brain Sciences* in which it appeared. Searle's references are to the books and articles by Weizenbaum, Winograd, Fodor, and Schank and Abelson already mentioned in this chapter, and to Allen Newell and Herbert Simon, "GPS: A Program that Simulates Human Thought," in E. Feigenbaum and J. Feldman, eds., *Computers and Thought* (New York: McGraw Hill, 1963); John McCarthy, "Ascribing Mental Qualities to Machines," in Ringle's *Philosophical Perspectives in Artificial Intelligence;* and Searle's own papers, "Intentionality and the Use of Language," in A. Margolit, ed., *Meaning and Use* (Hingham, Mass.: Reidel, 1979), and "What is an Intentional State?" in *Mind* (vol. 88, 1979, pp. 74–92).

What it means **to think in a language** (or in several) is explored from a literary perspective in George Steiner's *After Babel* (New York: Oxford Univ. Press, 1975) and from a scientific perspective in *The Bilingual Brain,* by Martin L. Albert and Loraine K. Obler (New York: Academic Press, 1978). **Simulation and emulation** in computer science are lucidly explained in Andrew Tanenbaum's excellent text, *Structured Computer Organization* (Englewood Cliffs, N.J.: Prentice-Hall, 1976).

Bennett and Chaitin's mathematical theory of the **limits on the speed of evolution** of complex systems is sketched in G. J. Chaitin, "Algorithmic Information Theory," *IBM Journal of Research and Development* (vol. 21, no. 4, 1977, pp. 350–359).

For recent versions of **dualism,** see Karl Popper and John Eccles, *The Self and Its Brain* (New York: Springer-Verlag, 1977), and Dennett's (caustic) review, in the *Journal of Philosophy* (vol. 76, (2), 1979, pp. 91–98). A keystone of Eccles's dualistic theory is Benjamin Libet's experimental work on the timing of the perception of stimuli (*Science,* vol. 158, 1967, pp. 1597–1600). This work has been vigorously criticized by Patricia Churchland in "On the Alleged Backwards Referral of Experiences and its Relevance to the Mind-Body Problem," in *Philosophy of Science* (vol. 48, no. 1, 1981). See Libet's response to Churchland: "The Experimental Evidence for a Subject Referral of a Sensory Experience, Backwards in Time: Reply to P. S. Churchland" (vol. 48, (2), 1981) and Churchland's Response to Libet (vol. 48, (3), 1981). Libet's work is also critically discussed by Chris Mortensen in "Neurophysiology and Experiences" in the *Australasian Journal of Philosophy* (1980, pp. 250–264).

Two other recent attempts to provide empirical grounds for dualism have appeared in *The Behavioral and Brain Sciences* (with the usual barrage of expert counterattack and rejoinder): Roland Puccetti and Robert Dykes's "Sensory Cortex and the Mind-Brain Problem," *BBS* (vol. 3, 1978, pp. 337–376), and Roland Puccetti, "The Case for Mental Duality: Evidence from Split-Brain Data and other Considerations," *BBS* (1981).

Part VI. The Inner Eye

Nagel addresses his musings on **what it is like to be a bat** against a "recent wave of reductionist euphoria," and cites as examples: J. J. C. Smart, *Philosophy and Scientific Realism* (London: Routledge & Kegan Paul, 1963); David Lewis, "An Argument for the Identity Theory," in *Journal of Philosophy* (vol. 63, 1966); Hilary Putnam, "Psychological Predicates," in *Art, Mind, and Religion,* edited by W. H. Capitan and D. D. Merrill (Pittsburgh: University of Pittsburgh Press, 1967), and reprinted in Putnam's *Mind, Language and Reality*; D. M. Armstrong, *A Materialist Theory of the Mind* (London: Routledge & Kegan Paul, 1968); and Daniel Dennett, *Content and Consciousness.* On the opposing side of the issue he cites Kripke's "Naming and Necessity," M. T. Thornton, "Ostensive Terms and Materialism," *The Monist* (vol. 56, 1972, pp. 193–214), and his own earlier reviews of Armstrong, in *Philosophical Review* (vol. 79, 1970, pp. 394–403), and Dennett, in *Journal of Philosophy* (vol. 69, 1972). Three other important papers in the philosophy of mind are cited by him: Donald Davidson, "Mental Events," in L. Foster and J. W. Swanson, eds., *Experience and Theory* (Amherst: University of Massachusetts Press, 1970), Richard Rorty, "Mind-Body, Identity, Privacy, and Categories," in *Review of Metaphysics* (vol. 19, 1965, pp. 37–38); and Nagel's own "Physicalism," in *Philosophical Review* (vol. 74, 1965, pp. 339–356).

Nagel has extended his imaginative work on **subjectivity** in "The Limits of Objectivity," three lectures published in *The Tanner Lectures on Human Values* (New York: Cambridge University Press, and Salt Lake City: University of Utah Press, 1980), edited by Sterling McMurrin. Other imaginative work on the topic includes Adam Morton's *Frames of Mind* (New York: Oxford University Press, 1980) and Zeno Vendler's "Thinking of Individuals," in *Nous* (1976, pp. 35–46).

The questions raised by Nagel have been explored in many recent works. Some of the best discussion is reprinted in Ned Block's two-volume anthology, *Readings in Philosophy of Psychology* (Cambridge, Mass.:

Harvard University Press, 1980, 1981), along with many other articles and chapters on the topics encountered in *The Mind's I*. For some fascinating thought experiments about how a different understanding of science might change what it is like to be us, see Paul Churchland's *Scientific Realism and the Plasticity of Mind* (New York: Cambridge University Press, 1979).

A careful discussion of **the mirror problem** is Ned Block's "Why Do Mirrors Reverse Right/Left and Not Up/Down?," in the *Journal of Philosophy* (1974, pp. 259–277).

The **perception of color**, which Smullyan exploits in "An Epistemological Nightmare," has often been discussed by philosophers in the guise of the **inverted spectrum** thought experiment, which is at least as old as John Locke's *Essay Concerning Human Understanding* (1690, book 2, chap. 32, par. 15). How do I know that I see what you see (in the way of color) when we both look at a clear "blue" sky? We both learned the word "blue" by being shown things like clear skies, so our color-term use will be the same, even if *what we see* is different! For recent work on this ancient conundrum, see Block's anthology, and Paul and Patricia Churchland's "Functionalism, Qualia, and Intentionality," in *Philosophical Topics* (vol. 12, no.1, spring 1981).

Stranger than Fiction

The fantasies and thought experiments in this book are designed to make one think about the hard-to-reach corners of our concepts, but sometimes perfectly real phenomena are strange enough to shock us into a new perspective on ourselves. The facts about some of these strange cases are still hotly disputed, so one should read these apparently straightforward factual accounts with a healthy helping of skepticism.

Cases of **multiple personalities**—two or more persons "inhabiting" one body for alternating periods of time—have been made famous in two popular books, *The Three Faces of Eve* (New York: McGraw-Hill, 1957), by Corbett H. Thigpen and Hervey M. Cleckley, and *Sybil* (Warner paperbacks, 1973), by Flora Rheta Schreiber. Both books have been made into motion pictures. It should be apparent that nothing in the theories sketched or implied by the fantasies and reflections in this book would rule out multiple personality as impossible. Still, it may be that the recorded cases, however scrupulously described in the literature, have been too much the products of their observers' theoretical expectations, rather than phenomena that had a crisp and well-defined existence before being studied.

Every experimentalist knows the insidious dangers of the inherent and inescapable bias with which a curious scientist faces the phenomena to be studied. We usually know what we hope to discover (for we usually know what our pet theory predicts), and unless we take great pains to prevent it, that hope may fool our eyes and ears, or lead us to lay down a subtle trail of hints to our subjects about what we expect from them—without us or our subjects realizing it. Laundering these "demand characteristics" out of experiments and using "double-blind" techniques of experimentation (where neither the subject nor the experimenter knows, at the time, which condition—test or control—is in effect) takes care and effort, and requires a highly artificial and constrained environment. Clinicians—psychoanalysts and doctors—exploring the strange and often tragic afflictions of their patients simply cannot and must not try to conduct their dealings with their patients under such strict laboratory conditions. Thus it is very likely that much of what has been honestly and conscientiously reported by clinicians is due not just to wishful thinking, but to wishful seeing and hearing, and to the Clever Hans effect. Clever Hans was a horse who astonished people in turn-of-the-century Berlin with his apparent ability to do arithmetic. Asked for the sum of four and seven, for instance, Hans would stamp a hoof eleven times and stop—with no apparent coaching from his master, and with success over a wide variety of problems. After exhaustive testing, skeptical observers determined that Hans was being cued to stop stamping by a virtually imperceptible (and quite possibly entirely innocent and unintended) intake of breath by his trainer when Hans arrived at the correct number. The Clever Hans effect has been proven to occur in many psychological experiments with human beings (a faint smile on the experimenter's face tells the subjects they're on the right track, for instance, though they don't realize *why* they think so, and the experimenter doesn't realize he's smiling).

Clinical marvels such as Eve and Sybil, then, ought to be studied under laboratory conditions before we embark on serious efforts to accommodate our theories to them, but in general that has not proven to be in the best interests of the patients. There was, however, at least one striking study of Eve's dissociated personality, a *partially* "blind" study of her—their?—verbal associations, by a method that revealed three very different "semantic differentials" for Eve White, Eve Black, and Jane (the apparently fused person at the close of therapy). This is reported in C. E. Osgood, G. J. Suci, and P. H. Tannenbaum's *The Measurement of Meaning* (Champaign: University of Illinois Press, 1957). A recent report of a newly discovered apparent case of multiple personality is Deborah Winer's "Anger and Dissociation: A Case Study of Multiple Personality," in the *Journal of Abnormal Psychology* (vol. 87, (3), 1978, pp. 368–372).

The famous **split-brain subjects** are another matter, for they have been investigated intensively and rigorously in laboratory settings for years. In certain forms of epilepsy a suggested treatment is a commissurotomy, an operation that *almost* cuts the brain in half—producing a left brain and a right brain that are almost independent. Amazing phenomena result—often strongly suggestive of the interpretation that commissurotomy splits the *person* or *self* in two. The huge literature that has sprung up in recent years about the split-brain subjects and the implications of their cases is lucidly and carefully discussed in Michael Gazzaniga's *The Bisected Brain* (New York: Appleton-Century-Crofts, 1970); in Michael Gazzaniga and Joseph Ledoux's *The Integrated Mind* (New York: Plenum, 1978); and by a well-informed philosopher, Charles Marks, in *Commissurotomy, Consciousness and the Unity of Mind* (Montgomery, Vt.: Bradford Books, 1979). Thomas Nagel has written one of the most provocative articles on the topic, "Brain Bisection and the Unity of Consciousness," which first appeared in *Synthese* (1971) and is reprinted in his *Mortal Questions* (New York: Cambridge University Press, 1979) along with "What Is It Like to Be a Bat?" and many other compelling essays, including several on topics raised by *The Mind's I.*

Another well-documented case that has recently interested philosophers and psychologists is that of a man who, due to brain damage, is blind in a portion of his visual field. He claims (not surprisingly) that he cannot see or experience anything in that portion of his visual field but (surprisingly) he can "guess" with excellent reliability the shape and orientation of certain symbols placed in his (rather large) "blind" area. This has come to be called "**blind sight**," and it is reported in L. Weiskrantz, E. K. Warrington, M. D. Saunders, and J. Marshall, "Visual Capacity in the Hemianopic Field Following a Restricted Occipital Ablation," in *Brain* (vol. 97, 1974, pp. 709–728).

Howard Gardner's *The Shattered Mind: The Patient After Brain Damage,* (New York: Knopf, 1974) is a highly readable and carefully researched survey of other remarkable phenomena, and contains an excellent bibliography.

Classical accounts of particular individuals who should be familiar to anyone seriously embarking on an attempt to theorize about consciousness and the self are to be found in two books by the great Soviet psychologist A. R. Luria: *The Mind of a Mnemonist* (New York: Basic Books, 1968), the story of a man with an abnormally vivid and compendious memory, and *The Man with a Shattered World* (New York: Basic Books,

1972), a harrowing and fascinating account of a man who suffered extensive brain damage in World War II, but who struggled heroically for years to put his mind back together and even managed to write an autobiographical account of what it was like to be him—probably as strange as anything a literate bat could tell us.

Helen Keller, who lost her sight and hearing when she was less than two years old, wrote several books that not only are moving documents but are full of fascinating observations for the theorist. *The Story of My Life* (New York: Doubleday, 1903, reprinted in 1954 with an introductory essay by Ralph Barton Perry) and *The World I Live In* (Century, 1908) give her version of what it was like to be her.

In *Awakenings* (New York: Doubleday, 1974) Oliver Sacks describes the histories of some real twentieth-century Rip Van Winkles or Sleeping Beauties, who in 1919 fell into profound sleeplike states as a result of an encephalitis epidemic and who in the mid-1960s were "awakened" by the administration of the new drug L-Dopa—with both wonderful and terrible results.

Another strange case is to be found in *The Three Christs of Ypsilanti* (New York: Knopf, 1964) by Milton Rokeach, which tells the true story of three inmates in a mental institution in Ypsilanti, Michigan, each of whom proclaimed himself to be Jesus Christ. They were introduced to each other, with interesting results.

This list of books and articles would be obsolete before anyone could read them all, and following up all the citations would soon turn into a life of scholarship in cognitive science and related fields. This is then a gateway into a garden of forking paths where you are free, happily, to choose your own trajectory, looping back when necessary, and even forward in time into the literature on these topics that is still to be written.

D.C.D.
D.R.H.

ACKNOWLEDGMENTS

Cover: Magritte, René. *The False Mirror*. (1928). Oil on canvas, 21 x 31⅞". Collection, The Museum of Modern Art, New York. Purchase. Pages 35, 37, and 40 illustrations by Victor Juhasz. Page 45 illustration reprinted from *The Many-Worlds of Interpretation of Quantum Mechanics*, edited by Bryce S. DeWitt and Neill Graham (Princeton: Princeton University Press, 1973), p. 156. Page 48 illustration by Rick Granger. Pages 148, 157, and 175 lithographs and woodcuts of M. C. Escher are reproduced by permission of the Escher Foundation, Haags Gemeentemuseum, The Hague; copyright © the Escher Foundation, 1981; reproduction rights arranged courtesy of the Vorpal Galleries: New York, Chicago, San Francisco, and Laguna Beach. Page 189 illustration courtesy of C. W. Rettenmeyer. Pages 278 and 279 illustrations from *Vicious Circles and Infinity: A Panoply of Paradoxes*, by Patrick Hughes and George Brecht (New York: Doubleday, 1975). Page 349 illustration by John Tenniel from *Alice in Wonderland* and *Through the Looking Glass* (New York: Grosset & Dunlap, 1946), copyright © by Grosset & Dunlap. Page 405 illustration by Jim Hull.

In addition to the credit line appearing on the first page of each selection, the following publishers are also acknowledged for having given permission to reprint selections in Britain and the British Commonwealth countries: selections 6, 18, and 19 are reprinted courtesy of Martin Secker & Warburg Limited; selections 7 and 8 are reprinted courtesy of the author and the author's agents, Scott Meredith Literary Agency, Inc., 845 Third Avenue, New York, New York 10022.

Excerpt from "Why Can't He Be You" by Hank Cochran is reprinted courtesy of Tree Publishers, Inc.

Index

ABOUT THE AUTHORS

DOUGLAS R. HOFSTADTER is Associate Professor of Computer Science at Indiana University and writes the "Metamagical Themas" column in *Scientific American*.

DANIEL C. DENNETT is Professor of Philosophy at Tufts University. He has recently served as President of the Society for Philosophy and Psychology.